WITNESSED

Also by Budd Hopkins

Missing Time
Intruders

WITNESSED

The True Story
of the Brooklyn Bridge
UFO Abductions

BUDD HOPKINS

POCKET BOOKS
New York   London   Toronto   Sydney   Tokyo   Singapore

POCKET BOOKS, a division of Simon & Schuster Inc.
1230 Avenue of the Americas, New York, NY 10020

ISBN: 0-671-56915-5

First Pocket Books hardcover printing September 1996

10 9 8 7 6 5 4 3 2 1

Printed in the U.S.A.

To Carol,
whose judgment has been this book's foundation,
and whose love has saved my life

ACKNOWLEDGMENTS

Linda Cortile is, of course, the heroine of this piece, and her determination to make the truth known puts all of us deeply in her debt. She, her husband, Steve, and their two sons, Steven and John, have shown uncommon bravery throughout an extraordinarily trying time. But there are so many others whose openness of heart has allowed this story to be told (though many are pseudonyms): Janet Kimball, who sent me her drawings along with her vivid recollections of the events of November 30, 1989; Erica, who generously shared with me her experiences of that evening; and Cathy Turner, whose warm presence and feisty account lent so much credibility to these incredible events. And there is Marilyn, who attended—involuntarily—one of the most unusual conferences one can imagine, and Dr. Lisa Bayer, who persuaded Linda to be x-rayed. There are so many whose testimony added to the weight of evidence: Carmela, Francesca, Joseph, Peter, and Brian and his family, among others.

Special thanks are also due to Robert Bigelow, John Mack, Gibbs Williams, Charles Strozier, Christine Morciglio, Sal Amendola, and Lou Anne Columbo for their unique contributions, as well as to those patient friends who gave my manuscript attentive readings. First among them is David Jacobs, my compatriot and research colleague for many years, to whom I owe so much. Peter Robbins, Jerome Clark, Richard Hall, and Jean-Luc Rivera have given insightful criticism at various stages of this project, as have Frank Turner, Martin Jackson, and Sideo Fromboluti.

My agent Phyllis Wender's faith in my work in this strange field has sustained me through a decade and a half, and for this I owe her a great debt. Dona Chernoff, my editor, has endured my missed deadlines with tolerance and good humor, while offering invaluable editorial assistance.

A very unique kind of thanks must be offered, finally, to the anonymous "Richard" whose letters, drawings, and desire to make these events public have from the beginning fueled the engine that drove the investigation. I also extend my gratitude to "the third man" for his decision to enlist me in bringing to light the events of November 30, 1989. It is my profound hope that he will now come forward and use his voice to help make the truth of that night known to the world.

—Budd Hopkins
New York City
May 14, 1996

CONTENTS

INTRODUCTION   *xiii*

PART ONE

November 30, 1989

1 Underneath the FDR Drive   *3*

2 Confrontation   *22*

3 The Tape Recording   *33*

4 The Third Man   *43*

5 Seizure and Interrogation   *53*

6 The April Abduction and the Third Man   *65*

7 The Search for Richard and Dan   *71*

8 The Downtown Chase   *80*

PART TWO

The Lady of the Sands

9 "Look and See What You Have Done"   *93*

10 Linda Hears Dan's Letter   *114*

11 The Long Island Kidnapping   *122*

12 "The Public Had a Right to Know"   *132*

13 The X ray   *143*

14 The Woman on the Bridge   *150*

15 A Letter from the Third Man   *165*

PART THREE

Mickey and Baby Ann

16 "She Wore Her Hair in Short Pigtails"   *173*

17 "A Sunny Place, No Horizon"   *188*

18 More Mickeys, Other Baby Anns   *207*

PART FOUR

Dan on the Loose

19 "Pack Your Toothbrush"   *217*

20 Showdown at the South Street Seaport   *222*

21 And Then There Were Two   *238*

PART FIVE

Physical Evidence

22 Drawings and Sand Samples   251

23 Richard Answers More Questions   261

24 Blood and Mystery   268

PART SIX

Johnny

25 Another Generation   275

26 The Helmet   288

27 Around the Conference Table   303

28 The Man in the Striped Pajamas   319

29 "That's My Little Boy on the Table"   332

PART SEVEN

Closing the Circle

30 "It Looked like a Giant Christmas Tree Ball"   341

31 Expressways and Blind Alleys   359

32 The Meeting at O'Hare   367

33 Final Thoughts   376

APPENDIX I
Addressing the Attacks on the Credibility
of the Linda Cortile Case   *385*

APPENDIX II
A Comparative Study of the Third Man's
December 23, 1991, Letter   *391*

APPENDIX III
Beta and Anna   *393*

ENDNOTES   *395*

INTRODUCTION

The story you are about to read, though true, is virtually unthinkable. In our familiar, everyday world it cannot have happened. Yet it did.

Over the past five years I have interviewed and communicated with nearly a score of individuals involved in this New York City UFO abduction case. After conducting many hypnotic regressions and studying the various types of physical evidence, I have come to a firm conclusion: This abduction event so drastically alters our knowledge of the alien incursion in our world that it is easily the most important in recorded history. No previous case has had such a profound effect on so many lives, and none has ever been observed by so many independent witnesses. Heretofore, UFO abductions have been conducted covertly, witnessed only by the participants. And yet in this one historical exception, Linda Cortile was floated out of her twelfth-floor window at roughly three A.M. in full view of anyone awake and near her lower Manhattan apartment. Among the many stunned observers was a political figure of international significance, whose presence was the likely reason for this demonstration of alien capability.

Opinion polls have consistently shown that a majority of the population accepts the physical reality of UFOs—there are too many photographs, eyewitness accounts, and radar returns to deny it—yet no one seems ready to face the implications of such a fact. Typically we say, "I believe intelligent life exists out there, but I'm not sure they've made contact with us." This ambivalent attitude has become less supportable in the past three decades as reports of the systematic abduction of humans by UFO occupants have appeared more frequently in the mainstream media. Supported by a range of compelling physical evidence, many highly credible people have presented similarly detailed accounts of being paralyzed and floated aboard hovering UFOs for extensive physical procedures in an austere laboratory environment. An all-too-human response I hear virtually every day underscores the problem: "I know there's plenty of reason to accept these accounts, but the subject is so unsettling that I really don't want to think about it."

Nor do I. Nor do the thousands of people who have undergone such experiences. No one wants these things to be true, most especially Linda Cortile and the others involved to one extent or another in the events of November 30, 1989.

Investigation of her case has led to many disturbing new insights about the depth of alien involvement in human life. In one of these, we have learned that specific pairs of children have been repeatedly abducted over the years and brought together periodically in the same strange environment. The purpose, apparently, is to allow the UFO occupants to study systematically the way human beings form friendships and, eventually, sexual relationships.

None of the skeptics' psychological "explanations" and reassuring dismissals of the abduction phenomenon is relevant to this case—not in the face of so many independent eyewitnesses. Instead, we are left here with only two options: either the events of November 30, 1989, took place as the many participants contend, or this is an intricate, cold-blooded hoax perpetrated by a large group of individuals—a conspiracy theory for which there is not a shred of evidence. In the following pages one will find the information necessary to decide the issue. The final judgment is yours to make.

PART ONE

November 30, 1989

Underneath the FDR Drive

Outwardly the envelope was unremarkable, but the letter inside drove a spike straight through the heart of reason. It was postmarked February 1, 1991, and addressed to my home. The envelope had been marked "Personal and Important," though inscriptions such as this are not at all unusual in my daily mail; as an investigator of reports concerning unidentified flying objects, I have received literally thousands of "personal and important" letters from witnesses and participants in these encounters. But, as I soon realized, none had ever conveyed news like this:

> *Dear Mr. Hopkins:*
>
> *My partner and I are police officers. We have been in a serious dilemma because of our strict profession and our lack of knowledge on this subject.*
>
> *We didn't know what to do or who to turn to and hadn't done so until recently. We searched the bookstores over and came up with you. There was an address in your book* Intruders *but it was through your publishers. In turn, we let our fingers do the walking through the white pages. Much to our surprise, there you were. We're hoping that you are the correct Budd Hopkins.*
>
> *So here it goes—*

One early morning, about three to three-thirty A.M. in late November, 1989, we sat in our patrol car underneath the elevated FDR Drive on South Street and Catherine Slip, observing the surroundings ahead. Sitting on the passenger side of our vehicle, I reached into my shirt pocket for a stick of gum. As I opened it, I looked down at the silver wrapping that was left in my hand and saw it reflecting a firelight type of reddish glow. I looked up through the windshield to see where it was coming from, and there it was—a strange oval hovering over the top of an apartment building two to three blocks up from where we were sitting. We don't know where it came from.

Its lights turned from a bright reddish orange to a very bright whitish blue, coming out from the bottom of it. It moved out away from the building and lowered itself to an apartment window just below. I yelled for my partner who was sitting beside me, behind the wheel of the patrol car, and he was just as excited as I was. I had to be sure of what I was seeing so I went into the glove compartment to get a pair of binoculars. We grabbed hold of each other and were going to get out of the car, but what could we do for that poor little girl or woman wearing a full white nightgown? She was floating in midair in a bright beam of whitish blue light, looking like an angel. She was then brought up into the bottom of that very large oval (about three-quarters the size of the building across).

This poor person was escorted out of her window. I don't know if she was willing or not. I don't think so, because it seemed as though she was being escorted up into this thing by three ugly but smaller humanlike creatures, one above her and two below. They seemed to be in charge. On top of our fear of getting involved we were also carrying a load of guilt because we didn't help her and we don't know what's become of her.

After she was escorted up and in, the oval turned reddish orange again and whisked away, coming in our direction, above us. It must have flown over the FDR Drive while we were sitting underneath it. It then plunged into the river behind us, not far from Pier 17, behind the Brooklyn Bridge. Someone else had to see what happened that morning. I know what we saw, and we'll never forget it.

Mr. Hopkins, the oval never came up from under the river. It's possible that it could have, after we drove away about 45 minutes later. We would have stayed longer but we couldn't ignore our radio call any longer. The guilt is brutal, more so than the fear we felt when we witnessed this terrible encounter.

The guilt has lingered into today and we find it difficult living with ourselves.

My partner and I have been debating for fourteen or fifteen months if we should seek her out. We know the building and we know which window she came out of. Perhaps she was just a figment of our imagination. If she isn't, is she alive and well? We have to know.

We're feeling much better now that we've had the chance to tell someone else other than ourselves. We wish to stay anonymous for the time being on account of our profession. If we should decide to seek this person out (and she may very well value her privacy as we do, and we respect that), we'll contact you again with further information if we do find her, and I hope we do.

Many thanks,
Police Officers Dan and Richard

My astonishment at reading this letter was all the more profound because I was almost certain that I knew the woman in the long white gown whom the officers had seen "floating in midair in a whitish blue beam of light." The name I shall give her here is "Linda Cortile." We had become acquainted in the spring of 1989 as the result of a letter she had written in response to my book *Intruders*. Our first meetings had to do with UFO abduction experiences she recalled from her youth and childhood, but on November 30, 1989, she telephoned me about an incident the night before. A little after 3:00 A.M., as she was about to fall asleep, she noticed a feeling of numbness creeping up her legs and sensed a strange presence in the room. With a sudden pang of fear she saw a diminutive, large-headed figure with enormous black eyes moving toward her. Her memories after that point become cloudy and fragmentary, but she felt she had been floated out of her living room window and then lifted up into a hovering UFO. The Cortile family lives on the twelfth floor of an apartment building in downtown Manhattan, near Catherine Street and only two blocks from the FDR Drive and the East River.

At the time of Linda's November call, I had been investigating similar UFO abduction accounts for fourteen years. Her report in no way deviated from patterns that I had encountered in hundreds of other cases. Not one of these many reports, however, included this kind of vivid, eyewitness description by an unrelated passerby. Within a few days of Linda's experience I was able to interview her at length about what had happened, and to use hypnotic regression to aid her in recalling more details. She had been seized in her bedroom by three short, nonhuman UFO occupants and floated out of a window. She vividly recalled the fear she felt as she levitated gently upward in the brilliant, bluish white beam of light that radiated from the bottom of the craft. Once inside, she was subjected to a series of quasi-medical procedures and was returned to her bedroom about two hours later. Like so many other reports, hers was recorded and filed away.

It was nearly forgotten in the torrent of subsequent cases that routinely come my way—forgotten, that is, until the letter from "Police Officers Dan and Richard" some fifteen months later. When I checked into my file on Linda's 1989 experience, I realized that their account corroborated, among other things, the time and the approximate date of her abduction, the location of her building, the color and style of her nightgown, and the hue of the beam of light that lifted her up into the UFO. In view of all this it was difficult to avoid the thought that the event they were describing was the event Linda Cortile had reported fifteen months earlier.

Astonishing as their letter was to me, it would prove to be only the beginning of an extraordinarily complex saga. In less than a year, I would receive six more letters and a tape-recorded account from Richard and Dan; Linda would suffer two hours-long forced confinements and interrogations at the hands of these confused and frightened "law-enforcement" officers; she would be struck by a car during a chase through the streets of lower Manhattan; and one of the two officers would suffer a serious psychological collapse. There would be a great deal of persuasive testimony and even more witnesses to support the fact that Linda Cortile was, in fact, literally abducted from her Manhattan apartment by the occupants of a hovering UFO.

Reading Richard and Dan's first letter, I had no way of knowing how powerful the evidence in this case would finally become, nor how crucially important to our understanding of the purpose and methods of the UFO occupants. Nor could I have imagined that the events of November 30, 1989, would eventually reach into the highest ranks of government.

My connection with Linda Cortile did not start with her November 30, 1989, phone call. It began that May when I received the following letter, forwarded to me by my publisher:

April 26, 1989

Dear Mr. Hopkins:
  First off, I want to say that I have never seen a UFO of any kind. I am a 41-year-old wife and mother. I came across your

book Intruders *sometime last year on a shopping trip. I read only a portion of it and then I had to put it down. I felt overwhelmed with fear because the pieces of a 22-year-old puzzle may have come together. I don't know . . . I hope I'm wrong.*

In the course of a year I have tried to construct a letter to you, and failed many times because I am feeling so confused and unsure of myself. So, at the risk of seeming like a raging lunatic, I'll start at the beginning.

All of what I have to say is based solely on feelings. Whatever has taken place took place in my room for the first time 22 years ago, and I kept my eyes tightly shut because I thought I would never survive the fear I felt.

When I was single and living at home with my parents here in NYC, at night, in my bed, my body became numb and too heavy to move. It slowly started from my toes and went up to my shoulders and head. I just couldn't move and didn't know why. I kept my eyes shut because I had the strange feeling that someone was there and I just didn't want to see it. Although my eyes were shut, a mental image of a shrouded or hooded person appeared in my mind, whether I liked it or not. Although my body was asleep and I couldn't move, my mind put up a struggle I'll never forget. Unfortunately, it didn't do much good, but several times I did manage to get my lips apart wide enough to scream for my parents who were sleeping in the next room. I screamed loud enough to be heard in China!

After a while the numbing sensation slowly went away, from the head down to my toes. I buried my head in the pillow and waited for morning to come. At breakfast I told my parents what happened and how loud I screamed for them, and why didn't they answer me? They said it must have been a bad dream. I told them that I wasn't asleep yet, because I had just kicked off my slippers and laid down when it happened. They insisted it was a dream. I never believed it was a dream, and felt quite insulted when they suggested it. So I just chalked it up to poor circulation.

Two nights later it happened again. Only this time there was no mental image—just the strong presence of someone or many of them. I don't know. I just kept my eyes shut.

This happened off and on for 5 years. I just let it go. (What a weak person I must have been.) After the third time it happened I didn't discuss it with anyone but a doctor, and it turned out that my blood circulation was fine. The experiences contin-

ued to happen, unchanged. When I found out I was healthy, the numbness scared me even more. I thought that although I have a good heart I would die from heart failure one of those evenings.

At the age of 25 I was married. The experiences grew less. Though I was sleeping beside my husband, he never heard me scream, either. Afterwards he tried to comfort me but that was all he could do. It must have upset him because I used to see the worried look on his face.

Sometimes I doubted my sanity. There just weren't any answers for me. I thought that if there were such things as ghosts, then perhaps that was what was happening.

Three years after we were married I gave birth to my first child. Shortly after he was born I noticed that in some of the photos we'd taken of the baby and me, that my nose looked crooked. I never had a crooked nose. It was noticeable to me in the photographs, but nobody else seemed to be able to see it but me. They thought I was imagining it because I had just had a baby, and attributed it to "after baby blues." I looked in a mirror and touched that area of my nose, the right side of it, and there was a small bump. (Till this day, it's still there.) Well, I panicked and all sorts of negative things went through my mind. I said to myself: Linda, you're so very happy now, you have such a wonderful husband and a beautiful son. How can anything go wrong? My life is so complete. Now I have a tumor, and it's on my nose! I started to picture myself without a nose, as if it were malignant. I immediately made an appointment with a nose doctor, a specialist.

When I arrived at the doctor's office, he took me into the examining room right away. He examined the inside and outside of my nose, which was quite embarrassing to me. He looked and looked, and then said that I had nothing to worry about, which was just fine with me. It was just cartilage. However, he said he was concerned about a scar I had inside my nose where the built-up cartilage was. He wanted to know why I had had surgery. I told him that I had never had surgery in my nose or on any other part of my body, outside of an impacted wisdom tooth. He looked at me real funny, which made me feel like a fool, and said that I definitely had had surgery. I asked him if it were possible that maybe at one time or another I may have picked my nose too hard, and that that might have been the reason for the scar? The doctor looked at me with a half *smile on his face—which made me feel like a complete idiot—and said very clearly, "Mrs. Cortile, this scar was not made with a fingernail, it was made with a scalpel."*

I was at a loss for words. We could have gone on debating the matter all day; he knew what he was talking about and so did I! This was so strange and shocking to me that I didn't know what to say. When I arrived home I called my mom and then my sister (as if I couldn't take my mother's word for it), and asked them if I had ever had surgery in my nose as a small child. They both said no. Mr. Hopkins, I have never had surgery. Surely I would remember. I remember when I had a large water blister on my foot at the age of 3.

I don't know if I lost any time during my experiences at night with the numbness. To tell you the truth I don't remember much of anything. I made sure I kept my eyes tightly shut. I've had a strong feeling for many years that there is much more there than meets the eye. I feel as if, secretly, there is something on the tip of my tongue and I just can't remember it, no matter what I do.

I haven't discussed any of this with anyone for at least 10 years. I have the feeling that it will come back again if I do. I haven't had this experience for about 8 years or more. I've been avoiding sleeping nights. I've been sleeping days for a long time.

The one thought that's been haunting me for 14 years is: WHO OPERATED ON MY NOSE? AND WHY DON'T I RE-MEMBER?

All of this seems so unreasonable to me. I don't know the answer, and I don't know if I want to know. Which is worse, knowing and trying to come to terms with it, or not knowing and feeling withdrawn the rest of my life? I would like to stop being afraid, confused, withdrawn, with bottled-up feelings inside of me. Most of all, I would like very much to start sleeping at night again.

Please forgive me for sending you this very long letter. I hope I haven't wasted your time. Whatever happened to me, I wouldn't wish it on a cockroach. I was just fine before these things started to happen. Thanks so much for your concern. And maybe someday I'll get to finish your book.

This four-page, neatly typed letter was signed "Linda Cortile," in a precise, flowing, legible hand. In its expression of deep personal disquiet, self-doubt, and fear, it was very like literally thousands of letters I have received before and since in response to my books about the UFO abduction phenomenon. In addition to Linda's natural eloquence, two features caught my eye immediately: First, she was easily accessible, since she lived only a few miles away from my home in New York City, and, second, there might be some kind of tangible medical evidence to be discovered in her case.

Virtually every detail Linda recounted in her twenty-two-year saga of mysterious, disturbing events was familiar to me from other UFO abduction cases. The nighttime paralysis, the sense of a strange presence in the bedroom—a hooded figure or group of figures—and the inability to rouse other members of her family: These are basic components of the UFO abduction scenario. Over and over again, abductees have reported that long, thin needles with small, metallic objects on their tips were inserted into their nostrils (usually the right nostril, but sometimes through the ear or the eye socket) while they lay paralyzed and motionless on examination tables inside UFOs. When the needles are removed, the small objects that had apparently been impaled on their tips are no longer visible. Investigators have theorized that these tiny objects are implants of a sort—perhaps locators (transmitters) or monitoring devices. Linda later told me that she had become too frightened to continue reading when, on page 36 of *Intruders,* she came upon the following passage: "... there is evidence that both Kathie and her son Tommy have had implants inserted near their brains, one through the nasal cavity and the other through the ear.... The object most often described is a tiny ball, only two or three millimeters in diameter, that is put in place by means of a long needle." She told me later that that was as far as she ever progressed in reading my book; she was so disturbed that she put it away, and to this day she has not finished reading it.

It was clear from her letter that she found the almost invisible "bump" on the side of her nose and the tiny scar inside extremely disturbing; her emotional reactions were out of proportion to any physical problems these tiny imperfections might cause. When we finally met a few days later, Linda brought along the receipt she had been given by the ear, nose, and throat specialist after her visit fourteen years earlier. Obviously, her examination by the doctor had been so significant to her that she had carefully preserved for over a decade this otherwise useless piece of paper. Psychologists tell us that an individual may not consciously recall the meaning of certain objects or bits of memory even though the unconscious mind continues to attach great significance to these fragmented and puzzling artifacts. UFO investigators, wrestling with the partial amnesia that is an all too common aspect of most abduction experiences, see this psychological phenomenon in operation in virtually every case. The profound concern about her "forgotten" surgery that Linda's letter demonstrated, her description of paralysis and the sense of mysterious figures in her room, and her emotional reaction to the implant passage in my book led me to one conclusion: Her case was potentially significant. The next step was a phone call.

Linda Cortile is a slender, attractive woman in her late forties, with wavy, dark brown hair and high, prominent cheekbones. The stylishness of her clothes contrasts nicely with her natural informality. Though she is very ladylike and proper most of the time, she can be very frank and amusing in conversation, and when she's angry she can be surprisingly earthy. During our first interview, for example, we were discussing several possible UFO-related memories that dated from her early twenties, before she met her husband-to-be. "Were you living in your own apartment at the time?" I asked. "Oh, no," she answered quickly, "I was still living at home with my parents. With my people, the only way an Italian daughter leaves home is in a wedding dress or a pine box."

In my initial interviews with people like Linda who contact me because they suspect UFO abduction experiences, I try to create a relaxed atmosphere. Very often these conversations mark the first time my invariably nervous guests have ever told anyone about their bizarre recollections. Their anxiety, as they later describe it, has several levels: "Will he think I'm crazy? (Maybe I *am* crazy!) Maybe I'm just wasting his time—and my time as well. Should I be telling this to anyone? (I feel like I'm not supposed to talk about it.)" And so on, on a roller coaster of fear, denial, and hope.

In order to reduce this natural anxiety I often conduct initial interviews in the living room of my apartment. If I sense that the subject is unusually nervous, I will not even take notes, preferring to suggest a friendly, social context rather than a formal interrogation with a written record. Only when an atmosphere of calm and trust has been established—on either this or a subsequent occasion—do I take up pen and paper and begin a more thorough interview. Ultimately I use a tape recorder and ask more probing questions, but not until the subject is relaxed and comfortable and willing to speak freely.

These interviews eventually cover basic issues of family, employment, health, childhood dreams, and memories, and finally focus on specific experiences that seem to the subject to be connected with the

UFO abduction phenomenon. Linda came for her initial interview in early May 1989, and our first hypnotic regression session took place on the tenth of that month. We began by examining an odd childhood experience that had bothered her for years. She was eight years old at the time of the incident, when she recalled seeing through her bedroom window a strange figure or object on the roof of the adjoining building. It was bedecked with colored lights, and was moving. To her surprise, when it reached the edge of the roof it slid over, falling, she assumed, to the courtyard five stories below. The next morning she told her mother about this strange sight, and asked her to inquire as to whether any of their neighbors had seen something dropping from the roof; apparently no one had.

The conscious memory of this peculiar experience was still vivid over thirty years later, but during hypnosis, the image and its meaning shifted. In a note Linda made a few days after the session, she described it this way:

> What I saw at the age of eight, looking out of the bedroom window, was perceived through a child's eyes. To me, at the time, it was something like Casper the Ghost in Christmas lights, or a large toy top. Seeing it again during hypnosis as an adult, I saw a different picture. It was a cone-shaped object approximately 9' × 13' that glided across and over the rooftops of a multiple dwelling complex. This wasn't a dream, and I wonder what all the other people thought when they saw it. I'm sure I wasn't the only one.

While the details of this and subsequent hypnotic sessions are fascinating, what concerns us here are the events of a particular night—the early hours of November 30, 1989. When Linda telephoned me from work later that morning she was emotionally distraught. Until then she had thought that her UFO abduction experiences were behind her, events of her childhood and younger years; now she knew this was not so. What was even more disturbing to her was the *conscious* memory of having seen a small, gray-skinned alien approaching her bed. Just before it came close to her, she felt a familiar numbness flowing upward from her toes toward her torso and upper body. Her husband, sleeping beside her, could not be roused, so, thinking quickly, Linda seized a heavy decorative pillow near her bed and threw it at the intruder. The instant it left her hands, she told me, her body became totally paralyzed and she was filled with the fear and remorse of one who has just done something terribly wrong. Here her recollections ended, except for an odd memory of seeing a white cloth come up toward her face and then recede, and the fragmentary sensation of sitting on a table while someone pounded lightly and systematically down the vertebrae of her back.

On December 2 Linda came for a hypnotic regression session about the events three days before. I led her through the various steps of the induction. Then I set the stage by describing her bedroom, her sleeping family, the late hour, and so on. In the transcript that follows Linda describes her experience:

L: My toes. My toes are numb. Ooh, it's familiar. What time is it? Now I get from my side, onto my back to the other side of me. It's 3:15 in the morning. By the time I turn my head back and I can't move from my toes up to my neck. And I can't move my body. Oh! I know what this is. I know what this is! "Steve. [Linda's husband] Wake up! Wake up, Steve! Wake up, Steve!" He's not hearing me. I want this feeling to go away. I know what it means. I haven't forgotten. [Crying] I can move my arms. Oh, look at that! Behind the drapes. There's something there. [Frightened voice] I know what I'll do. I'll take my pillow and I'll throw it. [Crying] If only my legs could move . . . "Wake up, Steve! Wake up! Wake up! There's someone in the room!" There! [Throwing the pillow] "I hope you got it good with my pillow." Ooh. I can't move my arms anymore. Now one, two, three, there's four and five. I wanna shut my eyes. I wanna shut my eyes. I don't wanna see 'em. They're taking me outta bed. I won't let them. I won't let them take me outta bed. "Steve! Why don't you wake up?" My children. What's happening to my children? [Crying]

B: You said there were four or five. I don't know what you mean. . . . Four or five what?

L: Four or five of those things . . . people.

B: What do they look like?

L: They're short. They're white and dark.

B: Are their clothes white? Is that what you mean?

L: They look like a lighter color than the picture screen on my TV set.

B: What else do you notice about them?

L: [In a quavering voice] Their eyes. Very intense eyes.

B: What color are their eyes?

L: [Whispering] Black. They shine. I can see a reflection in them.

B: Do they speak to you, these people, when they come in?

L: [Barely audible whisper] No. They don't.

B: In what direction did you throw the pillow?

L: Straight ahead. But then I can't move my arms and they lift me up and they bring me into the living room.

B: How do they do that? Is it hard for them to move you?

L: Yes. But they get me in there. They do whatever they please.

B: When they get you to the living room where do they leave you?

L: They took me to the window. They took me to the window. And there was a bright light. Blue-white. Not like a flashlight. [Inaudible] right outside. I'm outside. [Frightened voice]

B: Down on the ground?

L: Nooo. I'm outside my window. It's weird.

B: Did they open the window?

L: Yup. [Voice distorted by fear] I went through the fence. Right through the fence. [The regulation child guard]

B: So, you're outside.

L: I'm outside. It's weird. I can see my nightgown above my head. "Put my nightgown down."

B: How come your nightgown's above your head?

L: I'm standing up on nothing. My nightgown is above my head. I can see it. And I wish they'd put it down. And they take me out all the way up, way above the building. Ooh, I hope I don't fall. It [the UFO above her] opened, almost like a clam. And then, I'm inside. And I see benches, similar to regular benches. Up against the walls. And they're bringing me down a hallway. And doors open like sliding doors. And inside are all these lights and buttons and a big, long table. I don't want to get up on that table. [Tearful voice] And they get me on the table anyway. They start saying things to me, and I'm yelling. I can still yell. And one of them says to me: "NOBBYEGG. [Loudly] NOBBY-EGG." "NO KAVE. KAVE." "NOBBYEGG" "NO. KAVE." He puts his hand over my mouth, and then I can't talk anymore. I can't yell anymore. [Sniffing, still crying] And then the one behind me pushes me up and starts pounding on my back. What do they want? "What do you want from me? What are you doing to me? What do you want? I wanna go home." [Crying]

B: Now, you said that he said "NOBBYEGG" to you. Do you know what that means? Do you have any idea?

L: He said "NOBBYEGG" and my eyes were shut. And I can see the word. I can see the word in my mind. It didn't look like it sounded. The word was different from the way it sounded. It was *N A* with a line over the *A*, horizontal line. Then it was *B, BI* with a line over the *I* and then a *Z*.

B: And then a *Z* instead of "EGG"?

L: And I think that they were trying to tell me to be quiet because he put his hand over my mouth. I don't know what I said to him.

B: You might've said something rather impolite to him, I might just guess. You were plenty mad, and you had every right to be.

L: I didn't answer them in my language, and I don't know where that came from.

B: When you answered them, what was that phrase you used?

L: KAVE-me or KAVE-y.

B: That's what you said back to them?

L: I get the feeling that I told them to shut up. But I don't know if that's what it means.

B: Okay. Now let's just move on. He pounded you on the back. Was it hard? A doctor will touch your back, you know.

L: Harder than that. It didn't hurt. I just felt the vibration of it. And he just kept doing that.

B: All in the same spot?

L: No. All over my back. All over. And I want them to just bring me back home. I don't want to stay up there.

At this point, having dealt with the strange business of Linda's apparent familiarity with what seemed to be an alien language, I decided to take another tack. I began what I call the "body inventory," a system of inquiry designed to elicit any remembered physical sensations. (When I begin the body inventory, I ask the subject to close her eyes, *not to look at anything.* In a hypnotic trance state, the eyes are literally closed, but this command temporarily frees the subject from the often frightening prospect of having to look (in recollection) at the aliens standing nearby. If particular sensations are described in this process, I retain the option of asking the subject to "open your eyes for a moment and look down" to see what's causing these particular feelings.)

B: What else do they do while you're there? We'll start with your feet.

L: They're fine. But my legs can't move.

B: Any other sensation besides being paralyzed?

L: [Jumping ahead] They're looking at my nose. I can feel it. They're looking at my nose.

B: And what are they doing to your nose?

L: They're feeling the contour of my nose and they're looking in my nose on the left side. And then they go to the right side and they're looking inside of there. And I'm just saying to myself, "I hope I sneeze. And I hope they get it right in the face." They're spending a lot of time on the right side of my nostril.

B: You say they're looking in. How do they do that? Do they bend their heads down and look up?

L: I have my eyes shut. They make me open my eyes. They opened my eyes and they look in my eyes with a light like a doctor would. And then the one that's doing the examining turns around and looks at two others. Almost approvingly. And then he looks in my ears and then he starts examining my scalp and going to the back of my head and looking at my head, my temples.

B: So he's kind of looking you all over. Let's go back to the body inventory, and we'll do this methodically. We'll get up to your head in a minute. How about your thighs?

L: I can't feel them, but I can feel my feet. I can feel my nose and that part of my face and head, but I can't feel my mouth. My arms are numb

B: Let's move up from your thighs then to your female parts, your sexual parts. Is there anything there?

L: Numb.

B: How about your abdomen, from your navel down to your groin? Does that part feel normal?

L: Numb.

B: Your chest. You said your arms and hands were numb and your mouth—

L: Yes. Just my nose and eyes have feeling. I was able to yell and speak until one of them put his hand over my mouth and then I couldn't yell and speak anymore.

B: And you lost sensation in there too?

L: But I still had control of my toes and my eyes.

B: What are you wearing when you're on the table there?

L: I wasn't wearing anything.

B: Do you remember taking your nightgown off?

L: No, I don't remember that. Gee, that's embarrassing.

B: How do you feel about the fact, I mean before I mentioned this, that you weren't wearing anything? Did you have any feelings about that?

L: I didn't even think about it because I was too afraid.

B: Let's go on now to your head. Does anything else happen to your body?

L: They check my neck, and my head, my shoulders.

B: How did they do that? Do they have instruments or do they use their hands?

L: Oh. They have instruments. There was one particular instrument that was maroon and thin and silver, with a square, no, not square, rectangular tip. And they went on my arms and my shoulders with that thing. And then they put that down and they picked up another instrument.

B: Now was this first instrument something they held in their hands or was it something attached to an apparatus? You know, dental equipment is attached—

L: It looked like dental equipment only a little bigger.

B: So they put that down . . .

L: They put that down and picked up another long thing, an instrument, and it had a ball at the end of it, and that's what they examined my nose with.

B: Now when you say examined the nose, they just ran it down the side of your nose?

L: Down the side and up inside the nose.

B: Can you see that thing when it goes in your nose?

L: Yes.

B: Does it go in very far?

L: Yes.

B: Is there any pain connected, or sensation, or does it just feel odd?

L: No pain.

B: Can you see it coming out?

L: I open my eyes a slit. I don't wanna open my eyes all the way. And I can see what they're using on me, and they took this long instrument with a ball at the end of it and put it on the side of each nostril, but they were more concerned about the right side of my nose. They put this instrument all the way up there in my nostril on the right side of my nose. I don't think they went that far, though.

B: When they take it out can you see it? Is it just exactly the way it was when it went in? Or does it look different in some way?

L: No. It was the same. And they were pleased. They seemed very pleased. I don't remember seeing an instrument used on my back. I think they were just pounding on my back.

B: You mean with their hands?

L: Yeah. Fists. Felt warm.

B: Do you say anything else to them during all of this?

L: No. It didn't matter. It just didn't matter what I said. They do what-ever they want. I couldn't speak anyway, but, I had an awful lot of mental words in my mind. I could see words. And I had gotten the impression they're trying to teach me their language, but I won't learn. I don't want to.

B: What happens next?

L: After they finish examining my nose, they keep me sitting up. And they're examining my fingers and looking at each finger, one at a time. They turn my hand and look at the palm and examine that. Only by sight. No instruments. They look at my toes and I can wiggle the toes. The toes can move. And they watch them wiggling. And the three of them stand in front of me and just stare at me.

B: How close are they when they stare into your eyes?

L: [Whispers] Very close. Very, very close. They almost have their faces on my face.

B: What do you feel like when they look at you that close?

L: I feel like I can drown in their eyes. They're blank. They're so big. I find them very frightening.

B: Three of them looked in your eyes?

L: Three of them. One takes his hand and puts it through my hair. Takes his hand and gently places it on the left side on my cheek. And just stares and then he moves back, just moves back. That was the one that was examining me. He moves back and he must be speaking with the other two. The other two leave. He, he wasn't as cold as the other two. And I'm thinking to myself, "I don't want any more children. Just don't want any more children."

B: Why do you think about children at this moment?

L: I don't know. He's looking at me as if he has some ideas. I just don't like it. . . . He asks about my family.

B: Did he know their names or did he just talk about them in general?

L: He wanted to know how everybody was and I said they were fine, and I asked, "Why am I here?" and he said, "Just for a visit." He knew I was angry. I wanted to go home. So I got up off the table and I don't know how I got dressed. I don't remember being dressed. And he took my hand and walked me to the door and then those other two schmoes showed up and down I went and then out of the door. Down, and then out of the door. There was a big bang and I was in my bed sitting up, trying to wake Steve up. He wouldn't get up. He looked like he was dead. And then I got out of bed and ran in the boys' room, and they were sleeping, but I didn't see any breathing. [Crying] I tried to wake them up! I'm gonna call the police. My family is dead!

At this point I intervened to calm Linda. I reminded her that her family was well and behaving normally and that their "switched-off" state was only temporary. She was extraordinarily upset, nevertheless.

L: [Crying] And then I shook John [her younger son]. I shook John. He wouldn't wake up. I shook him. I pulled him up in a sitting position. He just wouldn't wake up. So I ran and got my compact, my powder compact and I put the mirror under his nose and ran out of the door to look in the light and he was breathing. And I did the same with Steven.

B: To see their breath on the mirror?

L: Yes. And he was breathing. And then I went back into my room and Steve was snoring and I got back into bed and I saw that the time was 4:45, quarter to five. So it started at 3:15. That's a long time to be awake. And then I went back to sleep, but it really wasn't a sleep because I hadda get up at six to make the boys their breakfast. Steve is on jury duty now, so he was able to sleep a little longer.

At this point, several details of this November encounter triggered Linda's recall of a childhood experience we had explored at an earlier session and she began to redescribe that abduction. This is a common occurrence in the trance state; a hypnotized subject can glide effortlessly from an event being explored to a chronologically different but internally similar event. The segue in Linda's case led to an extended digression in which she informed me that the UFO occupants who carried out the earlier abduction were the same individuals involved in the later, November 1989, encounter.

Shortly afterward I brought Linda out of the trance state. I gave her several positive posthypnotic suggestions, reminding her, for example, of the great reserves of inner strength that had helped her survive these disturbing experiences and that could be relied upon in the future. The session had been harrowing but extremely valuable to both of us. The episode in which she apparently spoke in an "alien tongue" was something I had never encountered before, as was one particular detail from her daytime childhood abduction. (In this years-earlier incident, the UFO in which she was being held came to rest, apparently, *underwater*. Through a large window she could see the murky bottom of what she took to be the East River; garbage and even a soft-drink bottle were visible in the UFO's lights.) These recollections would have special relevance fifteen months later, after I received the first letter from Richard and Dan and began to reinvestigate the astonishing events of that November night.

Confrontation

When UFO abductees come upon evidence that, for them, confirms the physical reality of their encounters, their reactions are invariably shock and depression. No one I have ever worked with has indicated pleasure or relief at any kind of confirming news. Treating their UFO memories as earthly, explainable dreams or fantasies is for abductees a necessary hope, a bulwark of denial against the unthinkable. But when that protective dam bursts and the abductees' tightly held systems of defense are swept away, they are left with a frightening and intolerable truth.

But in February 1991, after I received the letter from Richard and Dan, I had no choice; I had to call Linda Cortile and inform her of my strong suspicion that two police officers had witnessed her 1989 abduction. She had to know that if she was the woman they had seen, they intended to visit her. If I didn't warn her and they arrived unannounced at her apartment, her shock would be infinitely greater. This was one of the strangest and most difficult phone calls I had ever had to make. I decided to contact her at work, a more emotionally neutral environment, away from her children and the sight of the window she had floated out of in 1989.

Linda was employed at the time as a secretary and receptionist at a printing company near Canal Street. When she answered the phone I asked if she was sitting down. "I have something important to read to you," I explained. I tried to soften the letter's impact in advance by telling her a little of what it contained, but her shock was all too clear; shock and denial. "Maybe it wasn't me that they saw," she said. "Maybe it was somebody else who lives near me." I told her that was possible, but that she should nevertheless prepare herself for a possible visit from two policemen in the near future.

In this and several subsequent conversations we planned our strategy. Linda was not to tell Richard and Dan anything about her recollections of that night. It was extraordinarily important that I receive their account firsthand, untainted by what Linda might tell them. She was to say that she was too frightened to remember and that her recollections were still very unclear. I impressed upon her again the need to keep her account separate from theirs, and instructed her to urge Richard and Dan to contact me directly, by phone or otherwise. If they were hesitant to do so, as I was afraid they might be considering the cautious tone of their letter, I told Linda to ask them for an audiocassette recording of their recollections. I was determined to have *something* from their visit if they did decide to contact her.

Though Linda was naturally uneasy about meeting them, she was also determined to talk to both men and find out if, in fact, they had witnessed her abduction. Initially I was somewhat apprehensive that she might tell more than she should about her recollections, thereby reducing the value of separate accounts. These men were, after all, professionals, and Linda has demonstrated from time to time an overly trusting nature. But as it turned out, I need not have worried; she acted coolly and intelligently when the meeting finally took place.

At 10:45 P.M. on February 19, more than two weeks after I received the letter from the police officers, Linda called me, and in an agitated voice she told me that the men had just left. A few moments into our conversation I pressed the memo button on my answering machine, and with Linda's permission recorded her call. The following is a somewhat shortened transcript of our conversation:

L: [Agitated] I can't believe this.

B: Did they tell you their names?

L: Oh, "Richard and Dan," and I don't believe it. I could have taken my life in my hands . . . I let them in. They're detectives. [Not uniformed officers as she had expected.]

B: When did this happen?

L: They came in about ten minutes ago . . . my hands are shaking . . . they came about a quarter after ten. [Linda's agitation led her to underestimate the duration of their nearly half-hour visit.] They knocked on my door. I said, "Who is it?" They said, "Police." I said, "How do I know you're police?" so they showed me identification through the door . . . the peephole.

B: Did they have a badge?

L: Yes, and it looked gold . . . so I put the chain on and opened the door, and said, "Yes, can I help you?" [As she later explained, since these men were in civilian clothes she thought they were detectives on another mission.] I'm saying to myself, you know these guys, detectives, they do knock on my door every now and then when there's a crime on the street that I'm facing. So I said, "Can I help you?" and they said to me, "Are you Mrs. Cortile?" I said, "Yes, I am," and they said, "It's okay, you can open the door," and I opened the door and they introduced themselves. One said, "My name is Richard and this is my partner, Dan." Well, I almost died. You could see that they were very shy. I said, "I know why you're here. In fact, Budd Hopkins and I are working on a few experiences I've had—he works with many, many people." So the other one—Dan—says to me, "You know, we feel rather silly, but we just want to know, how did you do that?" Budd, they asked me, how did *I* do that? [Voice very unsteady] I said, "How did I do what?" And he said, "How did you manage to get outside of the building the way you did?" And I said, "Well, I didn't do it." Budd, you know, that's strange. That's almost as if . . . as if . . . someone is raped and you say, why did you make him do that? So I said, "I didn't do that." . . . That was Dan who asked. Dan isn't very friendly, but Richard is. So Richard said, "We wanted to stop that [the abduction], and we felt very bad that we couldn't." I didn't know what to say. I felt like a real idiot. He seemed relieved, though, but when I told him that I knew you, they were shocked.

Richard . . . he was much, much nicer. I think the other one was really freaked, to tell you the truth, Budd, he didn't look right. So Richard said to me, "You know, we've been feeling pretty bad about what's happened. Is there anything that we can do for you? So I said, "As a matter of fact there is . . . but first I want you to know that what you did was the right thing, because there was nothing that you could've done. What you can do now is call Budd Hopkins. I'll give you his phone number and you can call him from here, you can call him from wherever you want to call him, but call him, because it's very important. You can help a lot of people like me." He hestitated and didn't say anything. Then he said, "You know, I don't want to be identified." So I said, "Well, that's understandable, I don't want to be identified either. I've had many an opportunity to show my face, and I didn't because I'd feel silly . . . I'd feel as silly as you do." So he said, "You want me to call?" And I said, "That's what you can do for me, and that's what you can do for a lot of other people like me." I said, "It's very important; Budd would like to see you and talk to you. You don't have to worry about your identity, Budd would never . . . if you don't want to be seen and you want to stay anonymous, Budd'll keep it that way." I explained to them about you and how helpful you've been . . . he didn't look too happy about [contacting you], so I practically pleaded with him. He didn't want to make a phone call.

I said, "I don't know how much this will help, but if you would even send Budd an audiotape about what you saw, be technical about it, it would be something. You have no idea how important it would be." Richard looked like he was going to break down and cry.

B: You really think he was moved emotionally?

L: Richard was. Dan, I don't know. He was freaked. I don't want to say he wasn't nice. . . . He was very nervous. He just looked frightened to me.

B: Did anybody else see them come into your place?

L: Not that I know of. [Linda's husband was at work.]

B: The kids were asleep?

L: Yes, they were sleeping. But I hope nobody did see them.

B: Well, I want some way to establish that they were actually there. You see, a skeptic would say you made it all up.

L: Oh, I don't really give a damn. I'm still skeptical myself. Well, it ended up that Richard is going to make an audiotape and he's going to send it to you, and that was all I could get out of him. I told him, I have Budd's number here and you can call him right now. I'll leave the room. I'll walk in another room and you can say what you want to.

B: Was there any actual conversation about what happened that night? [November 30, 1989]

L: I told them I didn't want to talk about it.

B: That's good, because, you see, we have to have their version of it first.

L: I really *didn't* want to talk about it, I felt like such an idiot. But I was more shocked to see that they weren't police officers in uniform. They're detectives.

B: Did you notice what the badge said on it?

L: No, I saw it through the peephole. It was gold. . . . I don't understand why Richard didn't want to call. What's he afraid of?

B: Well, I've written a couple of books. I'm an author.

L: I'll tell you one thing about Dan. After he stopped talking he put his hands over his face and he said, "That's her. That's her." I almost fell over.

B: Did he say that when he first came in?

L: No, he came in, he sat down, they introduced themselves and what-not, and then he said, "How did you do that?" [Float out the window] Like he was holding me responsible. I said, "I didn't do that." And then he put his hands over his face and said, "That's her."

B: Did anybody say "aliens" or "UFO" or anything?

L: No, he didn't say that, he just wanted to know how the hell I got outside the building. He said I came out of the window in a sitting position. I don't know if I did that. I sure know I was vertical when I was outside.

   You know, Budd, I was hoping it wasn't going to be me, but I had a funny feeling it was. Do you know what this means? I can't be as skeptical as I was, and that's scary. See what this means to me . . . it's not so much about me . . . it probably means they've been taking my children. That scares me more than anything.

I knew immediately why Linda was so concerned about her two sons. Several months before, I had interviewed both boys about certain disturbing memories each had. These memories strongly suggested that both had undergone abduction experiences. Even more to the point, in 1990 I had conducted a hypnotic regression with Linda to explore her recollections of an earlier abduction in which John, her younger son, had also been taken. I knew she was worried about the two boys, so I decided to change the subject and ask for descriptions of the two policemen, beginning with Richard.

Linda is very careful about her own appearance, and, being interested in clothes, she is equally attentive to the appearance of others. I've been surprised more than once after a support group meeting by

the accuracy of her memory as to who had been wearing what. I knew
that she would have observed the policemen carefully.

L: Richard's a redhead and graying. He's tall . . . about your height. He's
in his fifties . . . between the early and middle fifties. They both look
like they've been in the police force for quite some time. He was
wearing a tweed overcoat.

B: Did he take his coat off?

L: Yes, he was wearing a sports jacket, a pink shirt opened at the neck,
and no tie. His slacks were brown. The tweed overcoat . . . I don't
know if it was brown or gray, I don't remember that. His sports jacket
was a plaid . . . brown, different shades of brown. He was clean
shaven. A little balding in the back. But you could see he was a redhead. He had light eyes. He did have a ruddy complexion, though,
redlike. He's tall, too. Over six feet. A big bruiser.

 Dan was olive complected, with dark hair. Richard could be Irish
or German, but Dan looked Italian to me. His hair was graying, too,
and he was losing some in the back. He had a bald spot. He was
thinner, lankier, but he was tall, too. He was wearing a black leather
jacket, a blue shirt underneath, dark slacks. He was clean shaven.

B: Did they go to the window and look out or anything?

L: Yes, they did. See, I have different windows now than I did [in 1989],
with safety gates because John is under ten. It was hard for Richard
to get his head out there . . . he pulled up the window and the blinds
and he squeezed his head through there, and looked to his right and
to his left and he saw, I guess, the distance from where they were
sitting [in their car] from my window.

 Dan wanted to know how the hell I did that. I can't believe he
asked me that, Budd. You know how I felt? I felt like a spy or something, that saw something they don't know about. I wouldn't be living
in this apartment building on the lower East Side if I knew how to do
something like that. I'd be in some think tank, and I would have liked
to tell them that. I felt offended.

B: Which one looked out the window?

L: They both looked, one at a time.

B: Did they try to get you to tell them anything about that night?

L: Well, they started to talk about it, and I just told them I didn't want
to talk about it . . . it was too personal and too frightening to talk

about, and I was there by myself with my children and I just didn't
want to talk about it.

B: Did you tell them I've worked with other police officers in similar
cases?

L: I didn't know you did. I wish I would have known that. Maybe it
would've made them feel a lot more comfortable.

During our conversation, Linda kept returning to her initial impressions of the two men and the sharp contrast between Richard's
warmth and Dan's distance and state of shock. She could not forget
that Dan accused her of being somehow responsible for her own abduction; it was a theme that would surface again and again in the
ensuing months. The image of this tall and very shaken law-enforcement officer sitting on the couch, shielding his eyes from the sight of
her, was impossible for her to forget, and she described it to me once
again:

L: He put his hands over his face . . . he covered his face and said, "It's
her, oh no, it's her." He sounded like he was in pain. And that's when
I said, "How do you know it's me?" He just got up and went over
and looked out the window. Right here in my living room, my living-
room window.
    Richard . . . I felt sorry for him, 'cause in a way I could relate to
how he was feeling. He had tears in his eyes. He was very shy about
it, he hesitated a lot, he couldn't explain himself very well, 'cause it
was so bizarre. These guys looked like, especially Richard, since he
was such a big bruiser, truly red, white, and blue, patriotic type of
macho . . . machoism. A big guy like that, almost crying like a baby,
trying to hold it in . . . I felt bad.
    I felt sorry for Dan, too, but after a while I felt offended because
he wanted to know what I had done, how did I [float out the win-
dow]. [Agitated] How in the world, how could anybody do that?
You'd have to be a real superscientist.

Our conversation ended with a final discussion about the audiocassette tape Richard had promised to send to me. I explained to
Linda that I would do nothing until I received it, and asked again if
she had underlined its importance.

L: I did. Richard thought that he ought to do something and you could
see that he felt guilty. He felt relieved, but he still felt terrible and he

wanted to make amends for what he hadn't done. This is the impression I got. He wanted to know what he should say on the tape, and I said, "You should just tell Budd about your encounter, what you saw. What he needs is details." He wanted to get details from what *I* remembered, but I didn't want to tell him that you asked me not to talk to them about it, because then I don't know how they would feel about you. That's important, how they feel about you. So I just said, "I'm alone here, my husband works nights, and if I talk to you about it, it's going to frighten me, because I'm all by myself with my children. It's just not the right time to talk about it."

B: Good. That's good thinking.

L: My heart is pounding.

B: Linda, take a deep breath, calm down, and I want you to feel some relief.

L: [Speaking very softly] You know, out of all my thoughts . . . I can't believe this . . . I can't believe this happened. It's just unbelievable. I remember Rosemary [a friend of Linda's] once told me there was a lawyer, a woman, who saw a UFO in this area in the 1970s, and it frightened me. But that's nothing compared to the way I feel now. Now, I'm thinking about the kids . . . if they saw this happen to me, then it might have happened to my children.

I tried to reassure Linda that despite her fears, her children at that moment were healthy and safe. And yet nothing I could say would diminish the helplessness she was feeling. We ended the call, but within ten minutes the phone rang; it was Linda calling me back, and this time she was in tears, evidently finally experiencing the full emotional shock of Richard and Dan's visit. The control she had shown throughout our earlier conversation had crumbled and now it was my turn to do the talking, to try to calm her and to put as optimistic a face as possible on the fact that her abduction had been confirmed by the two law-enforcement officers. But there was another detail she wanted to tell me about the end of their visit. As she was closing and locking the door behind them, she looked through the peephole. Dan stood a few feet from her door, facing Richard. He had seized the lapels of his partner's tweed overcoat and seemed to be almost shaking him. He kept repeating two words, over and over: "Jesus Christ, Jesus Christ, Jesus Christ . . ."

* * *

On Thursday afternoon, two days after the detectives' visit, Linda returned from work and found Richard waiting for her at the bus stop. His sudden reappearance was a jolting reminder of the event that had brought them together. She felt no desire to linger and talk, but Richard explained that he had come to apologize for his partner's behavior. He said that for Dan the experience of actually meeting the woman they had seen floating out of the window so many months before had been emotionally devastating—so devastating, in fact, that Dan had put in for a leave of absence from work. Richard again asked Linda what he should include in the tape he was preparing for me, and she repeated her earlier request that he simply provide as many specific details of the 1989 sighting as he could recall. Their conversation lasted only a minute or two because Linda had no desire to prolong the meeting.

As soon as she was inside her apartment she called to tell me what had happened. We both assumed that she had probably not seen the last of the two detectives. I decided to prepare a message for Richard and Dan that Linda could carry with her whenever she went outside. In this short, handwritten note I insisted again that they contact me directly, and assured them that I would respect their desire for anonymity. I mentioned the fact that over the years I had worked with a number of police officers, some of whom had had dramatic, low-level sightings and some of whom were themselves abductees. I included the name and phone number of an undercover detective in the police force of a large southern city, and suggested that they contact him if they had any questions or doubts about my trustworthiness. By the next day Linda was carrying my note in her purse so that whenever she left her building she would be prepared for another encounter. To her surprise she did not have long to wait.

Shortly before noon, three days after seeing Richard at the bus stop, Linda and her husband Steve left their apartment building and walked north on Catherine Street on the way to twelve o'clock mass at St. Joseph's, a few blocks away. As they approached the church, Richard stepped forward from a cluster of people and called to Linda. Apparently he had been at the church, awaiting their arrival. She stopped, surprised to see him for the third time in less than a week, and introduced him to her husband. (From the beginning Steve had been told about her dealings with the two men.) After pausing briefly to exchange a few polite words, Steve proceeded into the church to give them a chance to talk. However, not knowing what to expect and feeling uneasy, he remained just inside the glass-paneled door so that he could observe the detective and, if necessary, protect his wife.

Linda handed Richard my note, which he put in his pocket to read later. The reason he had come to see her again, he explained, was for further guidance on the tape he was preparing for me. "Would it be all right," he asked, "if I write everything down first, and then just read it?" Linda assured him that that would be fine. Again, Richard apologized for the coldness of Dan's behavior and said that his partner was off on a trip to try and sort through his feelings about actually meeting the woman he had seen that night back in November 1989. Their conversation was quite short, and Linda joined her husband a few minutes later, her thoughts and emotions once again in something of a turmoil.

When she reported this latest incident to me, it became obvious that Richard knew quite a bit about Linda's day-to-day movements. In answer to my question on this point, she told me that she and Steve attended church at least every other week, usually twelve o'clock mass. It would therefore have been an easy matter for Richard to know where and when to wait for her on Sundays. On weekdays, Linda took her younger son to the school bus every morning at the same time and place, and the hours of her traveling to and from work were also quite regular. But obviously, if Richard knew where to wait for Linda on a Sunday morning only five days after his visit to her apartment, he would necessarily have been carrying out surveillance of her movements *prior* to their initial meeting. He would have had to observe her on at least one other Sunday morning, and therefore his visit to her apartment was undoubtedly not the first time he had seen her up close. Since Richard also knew at what time of day and at which bus stop to intercept her on her way home from work, he would also have had to maintain surveillance during the week.

While Linda's description of the detectives' initial visit to her apartment included a vivid account of *Dan's* shock upon first seeing her, she reported no comparable sense of shock in Richard. His reaction, as Linda described it, was one of warmth and relief. Richard's emotions, I felt, were appropriate to a first-time conversation with a woman whose appearance was familiar. It seemed likely to me that his reaction would have been more like Dan's if the apartment visit had been Richard's first close-up look at a woman he had seen only once before, nearly a year and a half earlier, floating in midair beneath a hovering UFO.

Everything that had happened so far suggested that Dan's and Richard's prior knowledge of Linda, and their attitudes toward her, were extremely different. Later events were to illustrate these differences with graphic clarity.

During those months before either Linda or I knew that her November abduction had been witnessed, I had asked her, as I ask anyone I'm working with, to report any dreams or incidents that seemed disturbing or unusual in any way. Some time in December 1990 or January 1991, a month or two before Richard and Dan's original letter, Linda casually mentioned an odd experience she had while shopping in her neighborhood. She had just bought some fruit and vegetables and was heading out the door onto the sidewalk when a man approached, staring just past her, but coming directly into her path. At the last moment he walked straight into her, nearly knocking her down. He immediately apologized, and as he knelt to help her pick up the scattered produce, he stared directly into her face. She was flustered and angry. The man's behavior seemed so odd that she deliberately avoided making any kind of eye contact. She told me, however, that as she stood up, she saw an older man across the street, staring at her. He was wearing a Russian-style Persian lamb hat and a very expensive-looking chesterfield overcoat, and he seemed quite out of place in that working-class neighborhood. Still angry and believing that the collision had been, for some reason, deliberate, Linda turned away and walked back to her apartment. She said that she hoped her account didn't make her seem "too paranoid."

I recalled this earlier incident and asked Linda if the man who bumped into her on the street could have been either Richard or Dan. She thought a moment and said that she wasn't sure but that it certainly seemed possible. But, she insisted, the older man in the expensive clothes was definitely not Dan or Richard. In retrospect, she really did not know if he had been staring at her because of some covert connection with the person who bumped into her or if he had been staring just because he happened to notice a collision between two pedestrians.

For me, it was distinctly possible that there was a connection between this odd incident and the evidence of Richard's subsequent surveillance a month or so later. But if there was a connection, and the older man in the fur hat was neither Dan nor Richard, who was he? I was soon to learn that each new development in this complex story would solve certain problems that had seemed to have no answer— and at the same time leave us with a new set of problems, more profoundly baffling than before. It would be many weeks, however, before I learned the probable identity of the man in the Russian hat, and why he was watching Linda.

The Tape Recording

On Saturday, March 9, 1991, I received a small padded mailer containing the cassette tape Richard had promised to make for me and a short typewritten note:

Dear Budd—
We're hoping that this audiotape is satisfactory. We don't know how it will help, but use it as you wish. Will keep in touch. Thanks,

Dan and Richard

P.S. Linda is a darling little lady.

The recording was of Richard alone. He was clearly anxious as he spoke, for the dramatic events he was narrating were as unsettling as anything one could imagine. His speaking voice was generally steady and uninflected, with a slightly nasal overtone and the accent of a working-class New Yorker. Overall, his delivery had the quality of a typical police report, calm, objective, and deliberately unexcited. However, careful listening revealed several pauses filled with deep, barely controlled emotion. This is most obvious when he first describes Linda: "We have met people in all walks of life . . ." The sentence is interrupted by a short pause and a deep intake of breath that strongly suggests a struggle with his emotions. He continues, ". . . and can judge a person's character pretty well. Linda's of good character, and you can bring that to the bank." In the context of his cool delivery, this subtle break is surprisingly poignant.

The tape begins in midsentence:

. . . your feelings on this whole matter I understand, because your work is very much like mine. As far as this tape is concerned, I've written everything down so that it will be easier to express on tape. Please excuse my reading voice. There can't be much feeling in reading, however, but if I'm going to do this I want to do it right, even if I do feel like a jerk. I suppose Linda has already spoken to you of our unexpected visit to her apartment one evening about a couple of weeks ago. Indeed it was very uncomfortable, to say the least. The subject matter was the strangest ever in my line of work.

Linda is a nice person. We saw it through all the discomfort she felt. She didn't want to talk about it. Linda offered us something to eat and drink but we didn't have the stomach for it. I guess I'm afraid that Linda is the one we saw that November 1989. My partner is very disoriented and embarrassed. This is what he said to me: "You know, I feel as though I've been chasing a thief for months and couldn't catch him because he was always too fast for me. The idea of catching him and getting shot seriously is a rude awakening. Rich, I feel like I've been shot." I can't blame him.

Linda expressed the deep importance of our reaching you. After actually seeing her and speaking with her we could see just how frightened and sincere she was. We have met people in all walks of life and can . . . judge a person's character pretty well. Linda's of good character, and you can bring that to the bank.

I am making this tape for you because of the importance that was expressed. Yes, I do want to help others; however I don't want to risk all the years of hard work and the wounds I received in the line of duty and the good name that I made for myself. For all the years of sweat and blood, I just can't do that.

What we saw actually happened and I hope that it doesn't drive me nuts. I won't dwell on it anymore because it won't change anything. What happened in late November of '89 is real and left us all victims of circumstance. There is only one difference for us. There is no law or prison that could convict or hold those thieves that have stolen this woman in the middle of the night. This is what happened.

In the early morning, somewhere between 3:00 and 3:30 A.M., late November 1989, my partner and I sat in our car, undercover, underneath the underpass of the FDR Drive on South Street near Catherine Slip observing the surroundings. I was sitting on the passenger side of the vehicle when I reached into my shirt pocket for a stick of gum. As I looked ahead and unwrapped the top layer of paper, I looked down at the silver wrapping that was left to unwrap it and I saw what looked like fire, a reddish glow. I looked up through the windshield of the car to see where the glow was coming from.

There was an oval-shaped object hovering over the top of the apartment building two or three blocks up from where we were sitting. We don't know where it came from, it happened too fast. Its lights turned from a bright reddish orange to a whitish blue coming out of the bottom of it. There on the side of the craft near the top of it, just above the protruding saucer ledge, I could see horizontal, rectangular-shaped windows around the object. At the very edge of the object, on the edge of the protruding saucer ledge, were green rotating lights rotating round and round while the craft stood still, just hovering off of the building. It moved out away from the building and lowered itself to the apartment window below, about two windows down. I yelled for my partner sitting behind the wheel of the car. He was astonished as I was. Yes, it was like science fiction objects that we used to laugh at many years ago on TV.

Now, I said to myself that I had to be sure of what I was seeing, so I quickly went into the glove compartment to get a pair of binoculars. We were seeing what we were seeing. We grabbed one another. We wanted to get out of the car to see what we could do. What were we going to do? Shoot at it? We stayed in the car and the worst happened. A little girl or woman wearing a full white gown sailed out of the window in a fetal position. Linda was there now in a standing position in midair in this beam of light. She looked like an angel or a Christmas-tree doll. Then the lights underneath the object dimmed a little and we directed ourselves towards Linda.

With my binoculars I could see three of the ugliest creatures I ever saw. I don't know what they were. They weren't human. Their heads were all out of proportion. Very large heads with no hair. The eyes were very large, very large eyes. I don't know what color they were, maybe white. Very thin, too thin, smaller than Linda in height. One of them was standing above her in midair and two were beneath her. Those buggers were escorting her into the craft. They were in charge, all right. Something was moving them. They weren't moving of their own accord.

They slowly moved up higher in the light. My partner screamed. I felt as though I lost my breath. He screamed, "We have to get 'em, we have to get 'em!" We tried to get out of the car again but we didn't. She was whisked up quickly. She was gone, they took her. The whitish blue light turned into a reddish orange glow. It lifted itself up and above the building. It darted up towards us and above us. It must have flown over the FDR Drive where we were sitting underneath it. We turned and saw it plunge into the river, behind us, behind the Brooklyn Bridge, not far from Pier 17.

My partner grabbed hold of the steering wheel of the car and shook it. I thought he was going to pull it off. I remember saying, "We let it happen." We waited and looked over the river for about forty-five minutes. It never came up again. It stayed under there. As far as we were concerned Linda was a goner. We'll never forget the look on her face, pure white with no expression, a white marble doll hanging in the air like a Christmas-tree doll.

Well, we found our Christmas-tree doll fifteen months later, thank God! Thank you, Budd, for keeping her in good hands. I don't know what you're gonna do with this tape but I do know this is all I can do for you, Budd, for Linda and all the other people like her. Please respect the importance of our credibility at work. We just can't be identified. We'd be laughed at. We'll be fine. It's just a matter of time, I guess. Thank you, Budd.

I replayed the tape several times, listening to the subtle undercurrents of emotion in Richard's generally controlled reading. The last few paragraphs were particularly moving. I was struck by the personal sense of responsibility for Linda's safety that Richard and Dan exhibited, and their profound feelings of guilt when they could not help her: "We let it happen." My respect for these two men was genuine, as was my gratitude that Richard had provided me with this remarkable recording.

His account supported Linda's in most details, but one discrepancy between their versions was immediately apparent. Under hypnosis, Linda recalled that right after she went out through the window she saw the white fabric of her long nightgown "above her." She was also certain that she had been naked when she was on the examining table inside the UFO. So, in light of these two recollections, it was not illogical for her to assume as she did that her nightgown had been removed *before* she entered the UFO. And yet there was nothing in Richard's taped account or letter to suggest that he and Dan saw her standing *naked* in midair. To the contrary, they described her as standing in the light "wearing a full white gown."

Another seeming discrepancy appeared in Richard's statement that she "sailed out of the window in a fetal position." When I called Linda to tell her that I had received the tape, I asked her about this detail. She insisted that she did not remember ever having been in that curled-up position. I recalled that during her original 1989 hypnosis session, when she described passing through the window gate to the outside, her perceptions seemed definitely unclear, as if she were indeed in an altered state. After that session she told me that she had not been able to look around at her surroundings, and that before she went up into the ship her eyes were fixed straight ahead.

In addition to this apparent discrepancy, Richard mentioned another very important detail that Linda had not recalled: the presence of two small alien figures floating below her and another above. She remembered seeing the aliens in her apartment and, later, inside the UFO, but not hovering in midair outside her window.

It took me a day or so to unravel what seemed at first to be interconnected problems, and to see that, rather than damaging either Richard's or Linda's credibility, the differing recollections of subject and witnesses *supported* the truthfulness of all. I called Linda to explain my discovery. "Imagine you're lying on your living-room floor and wearing your long white nightgown," I began, "and you're in some kind of groggy mental state. Next, lift your head as much as you can and bring your knees up, and back toward your face. You are now in what might be called a fetal position, curled up as much as your body permits. If your eyes are open, what part of your nightgown would you see while this is taking place?" Linda gave the obvious answer: "I would see the fabric across my knees moving up toward my face." I asked what would happen if she were then "unrolled" into a standing position. "I'd see my nightgown moving away," she replied.

As Linda passed through the window she evidently never sensed that she was in a fetal position, and thus could easily have mistaken the maneuvers of her head and knees for the *literal removal* of her gown. The apparent discrepancy dissolved. But I continued my hypothesis. "If you are now standing upright in this intense light and your vision is frozen so you're looking straight ahead, what would you see above and below you?" Linda answered my rhetorical question the only way it could be answered. "If I can't move my head I'd probably not see anything much above or below me. Just what's straight ahead of me and in my peripheral vision, I guess." It was obvious to both of us that the strict physical and perceptual limitations of Linda's situation had created such false problems as her failure to report seeing the single figure hovering above her and the two below. However, her peripheral vision was apparently high and wide enough to take in at least the front part of the very large spaceship hanging above her as she levitated toward it.

When analyzed carefully, the differing perceptions of the same scene by the subject and the witnesses made perfect sense. In fact, given the circumstances, these divergences were absolutely necessary. This would not be the only time in Linda's case in which details that seemed, at first glance, to be discrepancies turned out after examination to be powerful evidence in support of the integrity of all concerned.

It was only after I had listened to the recording several times, taking notes as I did so, that I telephoned Linda to tell her of its arrival. She was eager to hear the tape, so we made arrangements to meet that evening for dinner at her apartment. My wife April and I arrived about six o'clock, bearing the cassette and a bottle of wine to go with the classic Italian meal Linda proudly told us to expect. She was determined to keep her sons uninformed about the UFO phenomenon and its effect on their household; she wanted them to be, in her words, "as normal as possible," so she avoided any discussion of her abduction in their presence. After dinner, when both Steven and John were out of earshot, Linda, her husband, Steve, and my wife and I were ready to listen to the recording. I knew that it would have a strong effect on the Cortiles, but I was not prepared for its effect on myself, even after a number of hearings.

At one point during Richard's reading, I looked over at Linda and saw tears sliding down her cheeks. Steve was holding her hand, and his eyes, too, were clouded. My own vision blurred with sudden tears for Linda, for Steve and their sons, for all of us for whom the boundaries of the familiar world were slowly eroding. Together we listened to a clear and honest description of the unimaginable—an eyewitness account of the interference of unknown alien life-forms in our own everyday lives. For all of us in that room—as for Richard—the abduction represented a shocking and absolute intrusion upon innocence. It signaled an end to any bedrock illusion of human control and empowerment. The timbres of Richard's voice conveyed our own bereavement for the end of so many safe and reassuring boundaries.

When I considered this moving audiocassette recording along with Richard's behavior toward Linda during their meetings, I felt I had a fairly accurate idea of his attitude about his experience. However, any knowledge of its effect on Dan was a matter of inference and secondhand testimony. Within a few weeks, however, I had direct and disturbing evidence. On the fourth of April I received a four-page typewritten letter from Dan that vividly illustrated the despair he was feeling:

Dear Mr. Hopkins:

My name is Danny. You are acquainted with my partner, Richard. He wrote to you about what had happened to us in late November of 1989, early in the morning.

I decided to get in touch with you after a long fishing trip in Nova Scotia. I had plenty of time to think things out and relax at the same time. Relaxing didn't come easy, either.

Do you have any idea of how I'm feeling? This whole situation flies in the face of everything I have ever learned and believed in over a period of a lifetime. I'm not confused because I know what I saw. I'm not depressed anymore, because Linda is alive. Seeing Linda for the first time in her apartment one evening, about a month ago, pushed all my depression and guilt away. However, anger, fear and embarrassment set in.

Richard is dealing with these very same feelings in his own way. He remedies it by secretly watching Linda (I don't think she would like to know that), whenever he starts questioning the reality of the whole incident. Seeing Linda reinforces the reality of it all, and then he doesn't feel crazy anymore. I tried this remedy once. It doesn't work for me. When I see Linda I tremble because she's real and the whole damned situation is real, and I don't want it to be fact. I don't need reminders. I'll never forget what happened for the rest of my life.

That November incident was the worst time of my life. It wasn't interesting or exciting. It terrified me. It was completely out of my control. I don't like not being in control. It's damned dangerous in my line of work.

When I thought I was seeing the sunrise above that apartment building, I realized that it wasn't late enough in the morning for that to happen. My second thought was that it wasn't rising in the right direction either. For God's sake, it was a UFO! A damned stupid UFO! Why did it have to be something as dumb as that? As luck has it, it had to happen to Richie and me.

Seeing a UFO wasn't enough. As luck had it, we had to see some young woman being taken. It was the manner in which they took her that drove us nuts. Strange thoughts entered my mind, but they weren't stranger than what we had seen. What if those bums decide to perform an autopsy on that poor young woman or child? What were they going to do to her aboard that craft? What could I do to help her? These thoughts were more than I could take.

I still keep asking myself, "Who is she? Is she one of

them?'' She doesn't look like them. Richie has to remind me that he, myself and Linda are victims.

Did Richard tell you about our nightmares? One of mine is that I am able to reach Linda in the process of an abduction. In the dream I am able to arrest them, but one of those SOBs shoots me with a ray gun and it's all over for me. If you think that's a nightmare, here is one of Richie's: Richie is shielding Linda, and reading those bums their rights. They get annoyed with him, and levitate him high above a building. Then they drop him.

Mr. Hopkins, I sleep with a sledgehammer by my side instead of a woman. My pistol is beside my bed. Logically, if they can take Linda, they can find me and take me. I wonder if they know that we saw them. We saw what they did. Richie has the same fear. He bought a blowup dummy of a man, and puts him in his bed every night, and sleeps in the spare room. Is this normal for two grown men? I wouldn't think so. If the department knew this, we would be out on our asses.

I'll never forget the combination of a low humming-whistling sound we heard while sitting in the car and watching this thing. But as soon as the blue-white light beamed on, there wasn't a sound. The lights weren't like anything I have ever seen in some of the greatest light shows. This thing really put on a show.

When it flew over us, I could feel the hair on my head, arms, legs, etc., stand straight up, and it wasn't from fear. The static cling was incredible. The electricity was tremendous. I wasn't amused at all.

As it splashed into the river behind us, way back behind the Brooklyn Bridge, with Linda in it, I never felt so angry and helpless as I did at that time. We waited around for a while, but the object didn't come up. Don't know where in the river it went after it landed in there. It could have gone anywhere under there.

I let myself go, Mr. Hopkins. I shower, but I just don't care about my appearance. I haven't shaven in a long time. My nights are sleepless. I have just about had it with this stuff. My fellow workers are whispering behind my back, I can feel it. They must have noticed the change in me. Richie says the lost motivation will come back again, and I'll start being my old self again. Richie keeps busy. Too busy for that matter.

For all of these months we have been completely out of

*our minds with worry about this young lady. Although I'm
sounding like a basket case, I must say I'm feeling a lot better
than I have been feeling in the past. Linda is alive and that has
helped a tremendous amount.*

*Can you imagine what would happen if we told anyone
what I am writing you about? They would laugh us right out of
town. It was a risk finding Linda. She can identify us. But we
had to find her. It was worth the risk. Dealing with this incident
is problem enough, without having to worry about our careers
and what others are thinking about us.*

*I just wanted you to know that I'm going to keep trying to
live with this. Tell your people to try hard, too. I'm sure that is
what you are trying to help them with. It is good that they have
each other. Richie and I know that we are welcomed in your
circle. However, this isn't possible for us, even though Linda has
mentioned other police officers involved.*

*Richie was glad that I was going to write to you. He asked
me to tell you that he received your note when Linda and her
husband went to church one Sunday morning. He said that it
was good that Linda still keeps her faith, as we do too.*

*We understand that you need us to come forward because
these people of yours are considered crazy. We know that they
aren't crazy. But, to be honest with you, you're going to need
more than two detectives to figure out what the hell has been
happening to a lot of people, and I do believe that a lot of
people are affected.*

*Good luck in your investigations. If you ever stumble upon
good tangible evidence, be careful whom you give it to. There's
an obvious cover-up going on.*

*I think I'll go and give myself a shave. I'm feeling better
tonight. Thanks for taking the time to read this very long letter.*

Sincerely,
Danny

These simple but eloquent paragraphs were filled with disturbing
new information. I knew now that Dan had been suffering as much
as anyone touched by this bizarre event. I also understood that Richard had been drastically understating the anxiety and confusion he
was still feeling. Because they witnessed Linda's "impossible" abduction, two self-proclaimed law-enforcement officers, obviously trained
to handle whatever danger came their way, had been existing for
many months under a self-imposed state of siege. Dan's description

of their nighttime dread was unforgettable: two normally self-reliant armed men sleeping fitfully, a sledgehammer at the ready and a decoy figure set up in a bedroom. Equally vivid was my impression that they passed their daylight hours in constant fear of being abducted themselves: "If they can take Linda, they can find me and take me. We saw what they did."

Dan's state of depression seemed almost crippling. His burgeoning paranoia obviously nourished his dread that Linda might be "one of them"—an alien creature and therefore someone to be feared. I remembered Linda's anger during Dan's visit weeks before when he demanded to know how she had passed through the window and remained suspended in midair. To me, it seemed that he was treating her not as a victim but more as someone possessing the strange powers of the UFO occupants.

I had no idea at the time that Dan's suspicions would eventually threaten the safety of Linda and her family. I could never have foreseen that his fear of her would ultimately put her life in danger. But after reading his letter and listening to Richard's tape I was certain of one thing: I needed to find these men and talk with them face-to-face.

| C | H | A | P | T | E | R |

4

The Third Man

The search for Richard and Dan began on an optimistic note. I assured Linda that they would be very easy to locate because we not only had excellent descriptions of both but also knew their real first names. I had two reasons for believing that "Richard" and "Dan" were not aliases adopted just to mislead us. On the tape recording, Richard quoted Dan as saying, "I feel I've been chasing a thief for months and couldn't catch him . . . the idea of catching him and getting shot seriously is a rude awakening. Rich, I feel like I've been shot." In his reading, Richard pronounces the name "Rich" and the next six words *very* quickly and naturally, without a trace of the hesitation one might expect if he were remembering to use a made-up name.

My second reason has to do with the fact that he is variously referred to in the letters and tape as Rich, Richard, and Richie, and his partner as Dan and Danny. These different usages suggest the easy informality of longtime friends and colleagues. If the names had been invented, I felt, the formal versions, "Richard" and "Dan," would have been used with careful consistency. Finally, since "Richard" and "Dan" are such common names, the detectives may have assumed that there would be no need for aliases; using their real first names would involve little risk of discovery.

My hopes of finding them easily were soon dampened when I

realized that I had made two erroneous assumptions about the New York Police Department. First, I assumed that on the night of the incident the two detectives had been doing undercover work within their own precinct. Naturally, I thought that by going to that precinct station house with their first names and Linda's descriptions I could easily find them. It was a major disappointment when I finally realized what I should have known at the outset: Jurisdiction depends upon the location of the crime, not the current home address of the criminal. Thus, two detectives investigating a crime committed in their precinct on the upper West Side might very well have driven that night to a different precinct on the lower East Side in search of a suspect. Or, for that matter, two detectives stationed in Brooklyn could easily have been involved in a stakeout near the FDR Drive, across the river in Manhattan.

My second false assumption had to do with police partnerships. I had always thought of pairings among New York's thousands of detectives as being akin to professional marriages: fixed, solid, and immutable. In my mind I had established a long-term, well-known partnership in which the linked names "Richard and Dan" would instantly be familiar to their colleagues. The actual situation is far more fluid.

So I began what I naively assumed would be an almost effortless search for the two. My initial phone call to the police department for information brought an uncertain answer as to which precinct had jurisdiction over the area where the car had been parked. "It's probably the First," I was told, "but maybe it's the Fifth." (The Fifth, I discovered later, was the correct jurisdiction.) I decided to begin with the First Precinct, and prepared a notice to post in the squad room. It was addressed to "Officers Richard and Dan," and went on to mention "an event of importance that took place in November of 1989 near the Brooklyn Bridge." I stated that I had "new information about this case" and that it was extremely important that the officers "call Mr. Hopkins." I listed my home telephone number but not my first name, lest someone recognize me and associate Richard and Dan with the UFO phenomenon.

At the station house, I found an obstacle I had not expected. The Rodney King beating had taken place in Los Angeles on March 3, and as a result security in New York City's precinct stations was very tight, since it was assumed that a police brutality case with racial overtones in faraway Los Angeles could easily set off antipolice violence on the East Coast.

A patrolman guarding the entrance to the building barred my

way. He asked me what I wanted, and I naturally had some difficulty in describing my notice and its contents. I muttered something about "a personal matter" that involved two police officers, and said that it would take just a moment to post a sign in the squad room. After further questions and vague but evidently disarming answers from me, I was finally escorted inside. There, accompanied by another watchful officer, I was able to tack my notice to the crowded bulletin board.

In the days that followed, the sign elicited no response. I assumed that though Richard and Dan might have seen it, they still refused to contact me. About a week later I returned to the station house, this time with Linda, to see if there were any detectives attached to the precinct who resembled the men she had seen. I also hoped for a miracle—that by accident we might encounter either Dan or Richard while we were there and that she could instantly identify them.

This visit was even more strained than the first. Again we had to talk our way into the building, and when we approached the desk sergeant we could feel his suspicion deepening second by second. We inquired if there were two detectives named Richard and Dan attached to the precinct, and Linda described them. "Why do you want to know?" he asked, his eyes narrowing alarmingly. "What is this about?" I explained that there had been "an incident" involving these men and my companion Mrs. Cortile. "What kind of incident?" he wanted to know. "Did you file a complaint?" I again explained that it was a personal matter, which only seemed to make things worse. "File a complaint or shut up," was the gist, if not the precise wording, of his response. He glared at us as two other officers took up defensive positions at his left and right. Whether or not they thought Linda and I were there to charge two of their colleagues with police brutality, their behavior was distinctly suspicious and unfriendly.

We waited uneasily while the desk sergeant picked up the phone and dialed a number. After a moment in which he continued to stare at us, he spoke into the receiver. "Do you have two detectives up there named Richard and Dan?" It seemed odd to me that a desk sergeant who worked regularly at this station would have had to ask, but I also realized that he might be going through the motions just to satisfy two questionable visitors. After a short colloquy, he hung up and stated flatly that no detectives with those names were assigned to the First Precinct.

The next attempt to find Richard and Dan was made a few days later by Linda and April (my wife), when they visited the Fifth Precinct. I hoped that two women might be treated with less suspicion than a woman and a man. At this station house there actually was a detective named Richard, and though Linda and my wife declined to say why they wanted to see him, they were sent upstairs to his office. Unfortunately, it was the wrong Richard, but he, too, wanted to know why the women had come, what they wanted, what had happened, and so on. Both women felt they were being scrutinized and challenged rather than helped, and made their exit as quickly as they could.

Soon after these forays into distrustful officialdom I realized that Richard and Dan were going to be much more difficult to find than I had thought. I also now understood that they could be attached to *any* precinct—or even to different precincts—in any of New York's five boroughs, making them virtually impossible to trace. Equally depressing was the fact that since the city's four thousand police detectives do not work in fixed partnerships, the linkage of Richard and Dan on the night of November 30, 1989, might have been purely coincidental.

My search for the two men had ground to a temporary halt when I remembered that an abductee with whom I had worked is a highly placed civilian employee of the New York Police Department. I decided to contact him to discuss my dilemma. I told him the reason for my call and played Richard's tape over the telephone. After listening carefully, he made an interesting observation: "Budd, I think Richard and Dan may not be New York City cops." The reason he gave was a subtle one. He pointed out that when Richard described Linda's building, he said that it was "two or three blocks up" from the location of their car under the FDR Drive. My friend went on to explain that "police are trained to always report things specifically by direction and location. A cop would have said 'two or three blocks *north* or *west*' or whatever, but never 'two or three blocks *up*.'" As to Richard's delivery and the tone and wording of the report, my friend said that, except for the one discordant note, everything seemed quite typical and believable. He was particularly struck by the way Richard described his reluctance to go public with his UFO account: "I don't want to risk all the years of hard work and the wounds I received in the line of duty and the good name that I made for myself. For all the years of sweat and blood, I just can't do that." Specific phrases such as "in the line of duty," in addition to the sense of contained emotion and the persuasive reasons Richard gave for his hesitancy, all seemed convincing to my friend. "Richard may not be a cop," he said, "but he sounds like a guy with some kind of military background."

I thanked him, feeling even more at sea than before about Richard and Dan's identities. If they weren't New York City police officers, who were they? I had had a tiny tinge of doubt myself after their visit to Linda's apartment when they described themselves as plainclothes detectives rather than uniformed officers. In his original letter, Richard had said they were parked "undercover" in their "patrol car." To my knowledge, plainclothes detectives drove unmarked cars—not *patrol cars*. It would not be easy to remain "undercover" in an attention-getting police car bearing a siren, lights, and identifying markings.

I had not told Linda about this and I continued to keep my uncertainty to myself. Consequently I did not inform her about the conversation with my police informant friend. Telling her would have had no clear-cut purpose, and for the moment I saw no course of action but to simply sit tight and await new developments. I was not prepared, however, for the breakthrough letter that arrived in my mail on Friday, April 12. This communication was written by Dan but had three typed signatures. In somewhat shortened form it appears below:

April 10, 1991
Wednesday

Dear Mr. Hopkins—
We are writing to you once again because of the utmost importance of what has to be said. When you have completed this letter we hope you will try and understand the seriousness and the extent of our situation. The extenuating circumstances involved led us to reveal to you only partial justification for our feelings and behavior. There is much more involved.

We were given permission to reveal more facts from a third party also involved in the November 1989 Incident. This third party is a very important person . . . and often speaks to many corners of the globe. Early on, before we contacted you, we advised the third party that we were going to do so, and wanted to know what his thoughts were on that. He thought that if we felt this was a good measure to take for our own sanity, then it was fine with him, so long as we didn't mention his name or the extenuating circumstances involved.

So, here is the other portion of our experience. [Dan proceeds to describe certain political affairs that I have deleted along with certain other passages in order to protect the anonymity of the third man.]

That day in November of 1989, after a very late meeting . . . which lasted through the night, we followed our instruc-

tions. Our orders were to bring this third party safely to the meeting and then safely to the heliport, way downtown afterwards. From there, the three of us were to board a helicopter out of Manhattan Island.

We drove downtown on the FDR Drive . . . and exited on South Street. . . . We continued to drive south, down on South Street for a few blocks, when all of a sudden our car started to die for no apparent reason. I pumped the gas pedal all the way across the street before the car would completely die, with Richard pushing the car from behind. We needed to park under the underpass of the FDR Drive because it was out of the way. We were on South Street and Catherine, facing the street so we could observe the area ahead of us.

It seemed that at that point, a simple instruction had become somewhat complicated. Richard had to ask the third party sitting in the backseat of the car to lay down, so as not to be seen, at least not until we could get the car started again. The third party certainly had a good sense of humor about it. . . . I tried the first time to start the car, but it wouldn't start. It was dead! Our radio call system didn't work either. The car telephone was dead too! Asking a passing car for help was completely out of the question, considering who we had sitting in the backseat of the car. So we waited awhile with the hope that the car would start on a second try. If it didn't, then one of us was going to have to leave the other alone with this very important person, to get to a pay telephone in a very unfamiliar area.

We were going to wait about 10 or 15 minutes before trying to start the car a second time, and in the process of waiting and observing the surrounding area ahead, we joked about demoting ourselves to undercover POs. Can you imagine how the third party felt playing peekaboo in the backseat? We all laughed some more.

About 3 to 5 minutes into our waiting time, all hell broke loose. The rest is history. The third party saw everything we saw. He saw the UFO, the creatures and Linda surrounded by the bright beam of light.

Seeing Linda suspended in midair without support from below was more than he could face. But when she was taken away, this very bad situation had bcome holy terror for us all. After the incident occurred and the object with Linda in it was nowhere to be found, the third party became hysterical. . . . You can't imagine the condition we were all in after such a bizarre experience.

However, afterwards he did say to us, "Fellows, forget that I was here, is that understood?" Mr. Hopkins, we understood. But others must have seen what happened. Someone out there must have seen it all too.

We have been in contact with the third party ever since the November 1989 Incident. Consequently, position and power have nothing to do with the human side of people. His guilt, like ours, has plagued him like a disease throughout these months. He has suffered no less than us. Recently, when we contacted him with the good news of finding Linda, he was very happy that she is alive. He wanted to know everything about her. We had to check her out so we could have something to tell him, and in the process we found out that Linda and her family are in good standing. . . . He was pleased with all the information given to him in our report. So much so that he had a bit of a change of heart, and gave us permission to reveal the extenuating circumstances.

When I returned from my long fishing trip, I learned that he, too, had seen Linda twice, without Linda seeing him, of course. He has seen her from afar, kissing her little boy good-bye before putting him on the school bus in the morning. Mr. Hopkins, we hope that you can understand why we won't be coming forward. This whole situation goes too high in the ranks to do so. However, whatever information we have given to you also gives you a free hand to do as you wish, so long as WE ARE NOT IDENTIFIED. . . . As he [the third party] said— Considering the toll this whole incident has taken on [the three of us and Linda], and possibly on thousands of other people in the past and in the present, "This incident may be the perfect opportunity to develop a cushion, so as to soften the hard blow society will feel in the future when certain information comes out."

We realize that there isn't much fact for you to go on because you can only say what we have told you, as far as our situation is concerned. There is no other information we can give you, other than our feelings on this matter (the third party included), and our mental progress.

We will be telling Linda what we have told you (no more and no less), as soon as we can break away from our work. We haven't seen her lately, has she been in good health? We believe that she should know what the extenuating circumstances were at the time of her horrible ordeal.

It seems to us that together, you, Linda and your families
have hope enough for the whole world. Perhaps someday soon
the whole world will be full again [sic] and we'll understand the
unnatural goings-on of today.
　　Mr. Hopkins, remember it all, and write it down.
　　　　　　　　　　　　　Sincerely,
　　　　　　　　　　　　　Richard, Danny and Him

I was astonished. A thousand disparate thoughts, suspicions, questions, hopes, and feelings swept through me as I tried to sort things out. It would take weeks of investigation, a major new incident to come on April 29, and many more letters and other pieces of evidence before I came to fully believe in the existence of the third man. But the details I have deleted from Dan's letter left no doubt that he wanted me to know, without directly stating his name, the identity of the third man. Whether I could believe him, of course, was another matter.

At each step of the way in this unusual case I have tried to weigh every possible interpretation of the evidence at hand. But Richard and Dan's new claim—"admission" is perhaps the more precise word—to be security agents, made sense on several levels. First, it explained why Richard *sounded* like a police or military officer even though he used an unpolicelike term. He would be, in a sense, a law-enforcement officer without being a cop carrying the geography of New York City in his head. Second, I could more easily understand the freedom the men felt, both to use their real first names and to run the risk of being identified by Linda. If they were not police officers traveling around the city, they would be much less traceable; in fact, they might not even be stationed in New York City. Third, if they were indeed guarding the third man that night, their hesitancy to come forward was much more understandable.

A very different issue began to make more sense in light of these new revelations. Two remarks from Richard's tape had intrigued me because of the many reports I have received of alien control in abduction situations. People describe being paralyzed or denied any movement or normal activity while abductions are taking place. Parents, in particular, suffer immense guilt because they have been frozen and prevented from trying to help their children. And sometimes in that position they have no choice but to watch helplessly while their sons and daughters are floated off into hovering UFOs.

It was in this context that I thought of Richard's words as he saw the UFO above the apartment building: "We wanted to get out of the car to see what we could do. What were we going to do? Shoot at it? We stayed in the car and the worst happened. . . ." And a few moments later, as Linda is floated up into the UFO: "[My partner] screamed, 'We have to get 'em! We have to get 'em!' We tried to get out of the car again but we didn't. . . ." Richard's phrasing had been immediately suggestive to me: "We *tried* to get out of the car *again* but we *didn't.*" Does "didn't" mean "couldn't"? Had they actually tried to get out of the car when they first saw the UFO? Did the doors not open? Were they at that moment under some kind of external control, and although they couldn't *act* they could still observe and *react* emotionally? Why did this particular abduction, unlike thousands of others, have witnesses with normal recollections? Was Linda's abduction witnessed by accident, or does the presence of the third man, an important political figure, mean that it was a deliberate performance? Was it possible that the entire event was staged for the benefit of a major player in the arena of national affairs?

However intriguing these possibilities, the doubter in me was, as usual, far from silent. Perhaps there never was an important third man. Perhaps he had been invented by Richard and Dan to conceal someone else they felt guilty about. Were they parked under the FDR Drive in some kind of tryst? Was someone's girlfriend in the car with them? Or a prostitute or drug dealer or underworld character? Yet if they had something to conceal, why would Dan and Richard have bothered to mention another person in the first place? And there was even less reason for them to have written me such a detailed letter about this invented person. There were, after all, certain details in the letter that I could check, such as the whereabouts of the third man at 3:00 A.M. on November 30, 1989.

The doubter in me returned: If this particular political figure *had* witnessed an abduction, it seemed too good to be true. And yet I reminded myself that the history of the UFO phenomenon is full of authenticated reports that were doubted at first because they seemed too good to be true. This "accidental" good fortune includes visual sightings of UFOs that were simultaneously recorded on radar, lucky daylight UFO photographs such as the famous 1950 Trent pictures, and the Trans-en-Provence treasure trove of physical evidence after a UFO landing.[1]

The revelations in Dan's letter made sense of still other unresolved issues connected with the events of November 1989. The surveillance of Linda seemed more reasonable than before, and I now had a clue to the identity of the older man in the Russian hat, the man who coolly witnessed Linda's collision in front of a grocery store a few months earlier. As this case unfolded, each new event or communication or fresh detail simultaneously did three things: It raised new questions, advanced the level of present understanding, and lent logic and meaning to puzzling details and past events that had previously made no sense.

Seizure and Interrogation

The message from an agitated Linda on Monday, April 29, 1991, was alarming.

"Budd, Richard and Dan abducted me . . . they forced me into their car and drove me around for about three hours just asking me questions." The abduction had begun about 7:30 in the morning, immediately after she put little Johnny on the school bus. Having recently resigned from her job at the printing company, she had the day to herself. Near the corner of Cherry and Pike Streets, on her way to Pathmark to do some grocery shopping, she heard someone call her name. She turned and saw Richard. He was smiling as he approached her, and though she felt as uneasy as she had during their earlier meetings, she greeted him in a friendly way. Richard asked her where she was going, and she replied that she was on her way to the store to buy some apples to make a strudel. "I bet you're a good cook," Linda remembers him saying as he glanced off toward a black Mercedes-Benz parked nearby, its rear door open to the street. He asked her if she would come for a ride with him. "We can talk while we're driving around." She refused, citing a series of errands she had to do that morning. The errand excuse, she told me, was essentially to spare Richard's feelings. "There was no way I was going to get into a car with him," she said. Not only was he almost a complete stranger, but his presence was an unpleasant reminder of the events of November 1989.

When we were able to talk about her experience, I asked Linda to write down as soon as possible *everything*, no matter how trivial, she could remember about the morning's episode: what Richard and Dan said to her, which questions they asked, how she answered them, what the car looked like inside, and anything else that took place while the men held her captive. That night she began to honor my request, and about two weeks later handed me a forty-four-page, double-spaced, typewritten memoir. With as much accuracy as she could muster considering the traumatic nature of her experience, Linda reconstructed the conversation that transpired. Much of the following account is taken from her extensive notes.

After Linda refused to get into Richard's car, he urged her to reconsider. She said that she had too many errands to do that morning and invited him instead to come to her apartment that evening if he wanted to talk. "You can have some coffee and strudel with Steve and me, and I can call Budd Hopkins and ask him to come over." She wrote that Richard "had a troubled look on his face . . . his eyes said that he was feeling hopeless." He said that he couldn't go to her apartment, "although the invite sounds nice." Again he asked her to come with him now, and again she declined.

Linda said good-bye and they shook hands. She turned around, and as the traffic light changed she stepped off the curb. Suddenly a strong hand gripped her upper arm. It was Richard, telling her she had to come with him. She began to struggle. "You have to come with me—now. Are you going to walk with me in a civilized manner, or not?" She twisted and fought, and at one point managed to get an arm free. She was angry, frightened, and in a state close to panic. Using a left hook her father had taught her, she caught Richard on the side of the neck. She described the action: "I missed his nose . . . he was so much taller than me and he was holding my upper right arm so I couldn't swing as far as I wanted to. But I did manage to hit him and it made matters worse. It made him angry.

"Richard sort of twirled me around with my back facing him. He slipped his right arm under both my arms and tried to carry me off. I couldn't believe this was happening."

As he hauled her toward the car, he pleaded, "Don't make me take you this way!" She continued to kick and squirm. "He was hurting me because my shoulder-bag strap was around my neck and across my chest, and he was pressing it with his arms. A few people walking with their shopping carts just stared and kept on walking."

When they reached the open back door of the Mercedes the struggle became even more fierce. Linda put her hands on the roof of the car and tried to force herself back, away from captivity. "I stiffened my body because he was trying to bend me in half by pushing my waist in and pressing down on my back. I kept my body as stiff as I could while holding on to the roof of the car." I could easily picture in my mind the irony of the situation: a tough, trained security man struggling with a small, light, determined woman, angered by her resistance and having an extremely difficult time getting her inside without harming her. "Linda," he begged, "I don't want to hurt you. Get in the car!"

Realizing that she was tiring, she started to cry. From the driver's side she heard Dan's voice, asking his partner if he needed help. "Yeah," Richard replied, "but I don't want to hurt her. Linda! *Get in the car!*" Dan then told Richard to tickle her. Linda's arms were up, bracing herself on the roof of the car as Richard held her from behind with one arm. With his other hand he began tickling her. She was desperate, yet she knew they were trying to take her without causing injury. The situation was both frightening and absurd. Dan called out tauntingly, "Come on, cutie. He's got you." The closer she came to being forced into the car the more she struggled. Finally, Dan came to Richard's aid.

Both the men were finally able to pry Linda's fingers away from the roof of the car. They doubled her over and wrestled her onto the rear seat. Once inside she fought with even more frenzy. Richard tried to hold her. "Don't worry," he said as they struggled, "everything will be all right." Dan hurried around to the driver's side, preparing to start the car. The doors locked automatically and Linda realized she was trapped.

She had begun crying and opened her purse for a tissue. There she saw something she had forgotten about—the stun gun her husband had given her for protection in their crime-ridden neighborhood. She pulled it out and touched it to Richard's shoulder. He cried out and tried to grab it away from her, but before he could do so she turned around and pressed the weapon to the back of Dan's neck. Evidently the gun's batteries were low so that its effect served more to anger than to stun. As Richard wrestled the gun out of her hand, Dan scolded her. "There's a dark side to you, Linda. . . . If you don't put that thing away *I'll* put it away and you'll never see it again. What you have there is illegal."

A few minutes later, after she had calmed down a bit, Richard handed her the stun gun and she put it back into her purse. Linda's sense of helplessness was fueled by anger and she railed at Dan. "Illegal? You're crazy. You've taken me against my will, kicking and screaming. . . . You haven't even shown me any identification. My stun gun is illegal? You're both crazy and you're trying to drive me crazy, too!"

She recounted her thoughts at that moment. "I kept thinking of my husband and children. Who was going to pick up Johnny at the school-bus stop this afternoon? What will Steve think when he gets home and I'm not there? There isn't even a note. These thoughts disturbed me to the point of outrage and desperation. I became hysterical! These guys have interfered in my life in a bad way. I can't allow this to happen."

She turned around, and, with her back against Richard, attempted to kick the window out. This action provoked an even more intense struggle as Richard tried to restrain her. She screamed for help, and from the front seat Dan voiced his exasperation: "I can't start the car until this shit stops."

But now Richard made the threat that finally broke her will to resist: "If you don't stop, Linda, I'm going to have to knock you out." She knew that he probably meant it. There seemed to be no escape, so she calmed down; Dan started the car, and they drove off.

Linda recorded her recollection of the conversation: "Where are you taking me?" she asked. "Why are you doing this?"

"We just want to talk to you," Richard replied, but her anger did not abate.

"I don't think so, Richard. There's something else you want besides conversation. You went too far for conversation's sake. What do you want from me?"

"Don't worry, you'll be all right," he said to reassure her, but her response was not what he hoped for.

"I'm not all right! Do you understand, I have a family?"

Perhaps to soothe her, Richard moved closer, but she backed away from him, once again overwhelmed by fear. Because now an extraordinary metamorphosis suddenly took place, a process that has occasionally been reported by other abductees. No one knows whether such a terrifying transformation is an artifact of human mental processes or the result of the UFO occupants' paranormal powers, but for a split second the eyes of her human captor were transformed into the black, bottomless eyes of an alien. She screamed in sudden panic. Even as it faded away, this all-too-vivid image—perhaps a flashback from an earlier abduction—left her trembling and crying. Not understanding what had happened, Richard tried to calm her, while Dan responded in his cooler, less sympathetic way: "Wow! You flipped out . . . Rich, she really flipped out." For the next few minutes Richard did what he could to reassure her. And for Linda, after the sudden, jolting image of alien eyes, Richard's kind, familiar, human face was now enormously comforting.

As they drove up the West Side of Manhattan, Linda began to relax somewhat and accept the unwelcome reality of her situation. As he had said at the outset, Richard had forced her into their car in order to question her, so finally, with everyone somewhat more composed, he began his interrogation. Linda recorded for me as carefully as she could both the wording of the agents' inquiries and their sequential order.

Richard began by asking her what must have been a pro forma question: "Linda, who are you working for? You know, which government agency?" She responded with mocking disbelief. Richard persisted. "If you're working for a government agency, tell me now and we'll let you go."

"You're serious, aren't you?" Linda asked, and Richard responded affirmatively. "So, if I'm *not* working for a government agency you won't let me go. And if I am, you will let me go? Okay, I *am* working for a government agency. Now let me out of the car."

Dan's reply from the front seat was in character. "No, cutie. Not so fast. Be completely honest with us. We have to know."

Linda stated what must have been obvious to them, that she was a wife and mother, living with her family in a small apartment on the lower East Side, and that was that. She was not some kind of government agent. The next question was, if anything, more absurd than the first: Richard wanted to know if somehow the incident had been a *hoax.* Had Linda staged some kind of illusion? Her answer was a short and decisive rejection of that idea. The next series of questions came closer to the agents' true concerns. What was in the beam that caused her to float in the air? What kind of creatures were they? Where do they come from? Did Linda see any other "normal" people up there? And so on. Linda pleaded ignorance to some questions and said that since she had been in the "altered state" typical of abductions, she hadn't been conscious enough to answer some others accurately.

One question she did answer caused the men some consternation. Dan asked her the color of the light in which she floated up to the UFO. "I'm not sure," she answered. "Maybe a whitish blue." As Linda described it later, "They both went silent for a minute or so, and I saw Dan's hands clutch the steering wheel and the car swerved slightly. This reaction told me something. I'd better not say too much.

I don't need two guys twice my size going crazy in the car. I just couldn't handle that."

After this very noticeable pause, Richard returned to the point. "Whitish blue, huh?" Linda, trying to lessen the tension, replied that she wasn't sure.

"She's not sure," Dan said, a bit relieved.

"I think she's sure," Richard responded. "You're sure, aren't you?" She shrugged her shoulders in an attempt to duck the issue.

As they drove up West Street and onto the Henry Hudson Parkway the questioning continued. Trying to avoid answering their queries, Linda said she thought she was put to sleep inside the craft. "Did they use drugs?" Richard asked, and again Linda claimed she didn't remember. The men asked about the craft's means of propulsion, what its interior looked like, and so forth.

Since Linda had to say that she couldn't possibly answer their questions, she turned the tables and asked one of her own. "Richard, what happened to you? This whole thing must have been a shock. I'm sorry you had to see it." He admitted that it "shocked my whole system, and on top of that I felt helpless not being able to help you."

Dan seconded his partner's words. "We were powerless. There you were, many stories up in the air, this enormous object towering over you. We could have left our car to shoot at it, but it wouldn't have done any good."

Richard described one of the plans they thought of in those moments of panic and confusion: "We should have somehow gone up to the roof, to jump down to the balcony below. But we couldn't leave the car because of the third party, and we didn't know how long that craft was going to hang around. It might have left while we were on our way up."

Dan picked up on their concerns: "If we went up there and jumped down on the balcony we would have been face-to-face with that thing. . . ." Richard added that "we would have had a good shot at it, but what if we frightened it away and they dropped you?"

Apparently eager to describe their dilemma, Dan continued. "What if afterward, no matter how it turned out, the third party was gone or something happened to him? What explanation would we have? Could we say that we were away from the car to save a girl from a UFO?"

"Linda, it was a terrible situation," Richard added. "You have to understand our position. The man in the back was completely freaked out. So were we. We'd never seen anything like that before. . . . We were there to keep this man safe. It wasn't safe leaving him there. He was hysterical. We were all out of control."

Linda assured Richard and Dan that she understood their position. "I'm glad you didn't leave the car. It might have been dangerous for you, too."

"Under the circumstances, how were we supposed to behave?" Richard asked. "The weirdness of it was too much to handle. Seeing you up there in a comalike state made things a lot worse. Do you realize you didn't move? Nothing moved. Nothing in the light moved including those misfits. Something in that beam of light moved them and you. You weren't moving on your own. Can you understand that?"

"The leaves of the trees moved in the wind," Dan added, "but nothing in the light moved. Nothing. We weren't even sure if you were alive. Imagine trying to rescue a dead person."

For a time Richard continued his discussion of the events of November 30, almost ignoring Linda's presence. "You know, Dan, I still feel that when they moved up into the light something moved them. They didn't move on their own."

"I know what you mean," Dan replied. "It looked at one point as if they and you, Linda, were waiting for a cue before you all raised up into the light, closer to the bottom of the craft."

"I don't understand most of it," Richard said, turning back to Linda. "One thing bothers me. How did you get out of that window? When I looked out your window when we were in your apartment, there was a window fence. How did you get through that?"

Linda admitted that she had no idea. She told them that "there are different windows there now. New windows were put in the entire complex last year." Richard mentioned that he hadn't seen if the window was open or not.

"Surely," Dan said, "the window must have been open. How else could she get out?"

When I read that statement in Linda's notes, I realized that neither man knew of a particularly bizarre aspect of an already bizarre phenomenon: Over and over again, abductees report having been effortlessly transported through *closed* windows and doors; even, for that matter, through brick walls.

At this point in their discussion, Richard announced that he now wanted to review the sequence of events of November 30. Obviously, this debriefing was one of the reasons they had abducted Linda in the first place, but though it was their goal, it was surely not hers. As she wrote in her memoir, "I didn't want them to go over it. It was difficult for me to sit there and listen to them. I didn't want to know any more. It scared me. I thought I would have a nervous breakdown if I heard any more. And yet I thought that if they didn't speak about it in my presence they would go on bothering me for some time to come. I realized I was the only person they felt they could talk to about this stuff without being made fun of. I know what it's like, not being able to talk to anyone. I could see the difference in them as we all spoke. They loosened up and just kept discussing it."

As they drove along, Linda listened quietly as the two men described what they had seen. "Here you come," Richard said, "sailing out of the window after one of those creatures. First, this ugly little squirt comes out of your window in a squatting position. His head is up and he's holding his knees. He moved up into the light, above your window. Then you came out. You were in a fetal position. I couldn't see your face but I knew you were human. You moved up into the light underneath the first little fellow. At this point I went totally wild."

Dan picked up the story. "I took the binoculars away from Richard. Two more little guys came sailing out of the window, one at a time. Both were in the same position as the first one. They parked themselves directly under you, only side by side. All of you resembled a Christmas tree in position."

Richard continued their account. "I took the binoculars from Dan. He was trying to handle the third party in the back. All four of you moved further up into the light. Like soldiers, you all straightened out exactly at the same time. Bodies straight, arms at your sides. They were looking straight up at the craft and you were looking straight ahead."

Dan asked Linda what she was seeing at the time. "Only light," she replied, "bright light."

"We saw your face clearly," Richard added. "It was you we saw. It seemed you were waiting for a sign or something. You waited a moment and then, suddenly, all of you moved up into the light quickly and disappeared into the craft."

The vividness of their description was too much for Linda and again she began to cry. "Letting them speak hurt me," she wrote. "I had enough to deal with just being there in the car with them. I couldn't stand it anymore."

But Dan chose this emotional low point to reveal his anger and suspicion: "Oh, shut your face! Stop crying! You were in complete agreement with them. You did exactly what they did."

Richard immediately chided his partner. "Don't say that . . . you don't know what was happening. How can you say that to her?" Linda, more angry now than hurt, told Dan that he deserved everything he was feeling.

But Dan replied with another, even more wounding accusation: "You're one of *them*, aren't you?" When she shouted her denial, he said, "Don't hand me that shit! You *are* one of them." Nothing could possibly have infuriated Linda more than being called an alien, an ally or relative of those who had abducted her and, she had reason to believe, had at some point also taken her children against their wills.[1] She lunged for Dan, trying to pull his hair, and another struggle ensued until Richard, shouting at both of them, was able to restrain her.

A period of relative calm ensued as the car continued north, away from Manhattan. My later conversations with Linda were not particularly helpful as to the specific route they took. Since she does not have a driver's license and rarely travels outside of New York City, she lacks the seasoned driver's habit of consciously observing landmarks and road signs. Besides, the events taking place inside the car were emotionally draining enough to occupy her full attention. Largely because of Richard's attitude, her fears subsided; the threat of deliberate physical injury or permanent kidnapping no longer consumed her and she assumed that eventually she would be taken home. She remembered that they crossed a toll bridge (probably the one joining Manhattan and Riverdale) and passed through at least one more tollgate farther along the road. At some point they pulled into a rest area and stopped, and after a rambling discussion about such issues as their religious beliefs and the pros and cons of contacting me, the inquisition continued.

Dan's suspicions had not for an instant been allayed. "I still think you're one of them," he said, staring at her over the back of the front seat.

"I'm not," Linda replied furiously. "I'm me!"

"No, you're not you . . . you have their blood," he insisted. "You're one of them." This continuing exchange of accusations and denials led to a peculiar request from Dan. "Richard, pull her shoes off. I want to see her feet." Linda refused, calling his request "weird," suddenly fearing that this might be only the first of several disrobings they might demand. Another argument followed until Richard assured Linda that this was all they would ask of her, and that she should comply just to satisfy Dan. Finally, reluctantly, she took off one sneaker. Dan ordered her to take off her sock, too, and she did so.

"I thought I would die of humiliation," Linda wrote. "There was my big toe standing out like one of Dumbo's ears. It looked like a thumb in a cartoon." Richard lifted her foot and began to examine it. He looked at her ankle, the heel and the underside of her foot, and all five toes. Then he asked to see her other foot.

Linda could not resist a joke, telling him that "when you've seen one, you've seen 'em all." The mood in the car lightened for a moment, but she made no motion to comply with what she regarded as an absurd request.

"Come on, cutie," Dan said, and when she expressed irritation at being called "cutie," he found another way to anger her:

"Okay, sweetheart."

"Stop calling me names," she insisted. "I'm not a sweetheart. Right now I have a bitter heart."

Richard's kinder rejoinder was also repulsed. "You're a sweet kid," he said.

"Stop treating me like a kid!" she retorted. "I'm a grown woman."

Richard's tender response to her anger both shocked and surprised her: "I wish you were mine," he said quietly.

In this tense context Linda took off her other sneaker and sock so that Richard could examine her other foot as he had the first. "I felt so ridiculous," she said, "sitting there with one leg crossed over the other while he looked at my toes."

The conversation and behavior of the two men during the baring of Linda's feet only added to the mystery. Richard spoke to Dan with an air of triumph, telling him to look for himself.

"You're right," Dan responded, peering over the back of the seat. "I can see it."

To Linda, they both seemed very happy at their findings, though she had no idea what it was they had discovered. But Richard's next remark was disconcerting; he asked Linda for a hug, and Dan echoed the request. She wanted to know why they wanted hugs, and Richard answered that he just needed one. Once more, feelings of danger and confusion and helplessness welled up inside her. She wrote about her predicament: "I didn't want to give this man a hug, but if I didn't, was he going to take it anyway? As far as Dan was concerned, he could forget it." She protested that she was not in a hugging mood, but Richard moved closer. She was becoming frightened. He begged her once more, and she saw that he had tears in his eyes.

His emotion failed to soften her fear and anger. "I didn't care," she said later. "I didn't want to give him a hug, and I didn't want him to take one. But finally I thought it best to hug *him* so that I would be in control of it. I reached up and put my arms around his neck. Then I put my head on his shoulder facing Dan to avoid anything else he may have planned for my face. Afterward I let go and sort of pushed Richard away, but he didn't go anywhere. He took control of that hug."

What he did next was even more perplexing. Pressing Linda's cheeks between his two hands, he kissed her lightly on the nose, saying, "I wish you were my little girl." She pushed him away and moved back toward the door. Though she whispered diplomatically that she was flattered, inwardly she wanted no more of it. "He knew I had a family. I wondered if he wanted to be my father? Or even my husband?" The confusion and fear left her trembling.

Dan started the engine, and as they drove off, the detailed questioning about Linda's UFO abduction resumed. Clearly the events of November 30, 1989, had consumed the men's thoughts. Richard wanted to know where the UFO had taken her, and Linda replied that, after all, *they* had watched it from the street; she had no idea where it had gone. Richard said that they had seen it go into the river, and he wondered if there was a door down there, an entrance in the river bottom. Dan asked if there had been a window in the craft that she could have looked out of, and again Linda, disturbed by the continuing interrogation, said she didn't remember.

One of the interesting bits of information that emerged as a result of these questions had to do with the sequence of time of the November events. Apparently after their automobile engine died but just before the beginning of their sighting, Dan's watch stopped at 3:17 and Richard's at 3:18. In our hypnotic regression session of December 1989, Linda had recalled glancing at her clock just as the paralysis was beginning; it was 3:15, only seconds before she saw the small figure approach her bed. Even assuming that the men's watches and Linda's clock were not absolutely accurate, the initial events both inside and outside her apartment seem to have occurred within a very narrow time frame.

Richard and Dan asked Linda more questions about the creatures they had seen: What did they look like up close? How did they function? Where do they come from? Is their intelligence greater than ours? And so on. Linda, following my original request, avoided giving the men any specific information. She answered again and again that she did not remember since she had been only half-conscious during the abduction.

However, all through Richard and Dan's interrogation she had noticed an edge of nervousness, a personal uneasiness that now deepened as the conversation focused on the alien beings. It was Dan who made the crucially revealing inquiry. "Linda," he asked, "do you think they saw us?" It was as if most of their questioning had been leading up to this, their single most important query. In light of Dan's letter and his description of the extreme protective measures they took at home—the sledgehammer and pistols at the ready and the blowup dummy in Richard's bed—his question came as no surprise.

Linda insisted that as she hovered in midair outside her building she saw nothing down on the ground. Her vision was fixed straight ahead, and she did not remember even seeing the FDR Drive. Richard and Dan were neither pleased nor relieved by her answer, but they apparently accepted it as the truth. Richard informed Linda that they were on their way back now, and she would be delivered to her apartment. "I know what we did wasn't nice," he told her, "but we had to do it for other reasons."

Linda responded in her own direct way. "You know, I never felt right about the two of you. Now I can honestly say that I'll never trust you." Richard asked if she was going to report them. "Report you?" she responded incredulously. "Report you to who? The police?" She began to laugh and then to cry, relieved that she had lived through it all. She knew for sure, now, that she would see her family and friends again.

The drive home took a long time and they rode mostly in silence. When they finally arrived at the place she had been picked up, the car stopped and the doors unlocked. It was a marvelously welcome sound. She wanted to scream, "I'm alive, I'm alive!"

Richard said, "I'll see you, okay?"

"No, you won't," she replied. "Not if I can help it." She opened the door and stepped out onto the sidewalk, not looking back. It was 11:05 A.M. She had been gone three hours and thirty-five minutes.

C H A P T E R

6

The April Abduction and the Third Man

From the moment Linda and I first talked about her coerced interrogation by Richard and Dan we knew that things had shifted to a new and more ominous level. The two agents were more desperate than we had thought, more emotionally distraught, and therefore more unpredictable. Though Linda dreaded further visits from the UFO occupants, until now the prospect of a visit by Richard and Dan had only made her uneasy, not fearful. They were, after all, fellow human beings, government employees presumably on the side of law and order, and they claimed they were only trying to help her. But suddenly everything had changed. She was no longer safe anywhere. She had been abducted and mistreated by humans as well as by aliens.

As she later wrote about her encounter with the two men, "When I arrived home I felt like a wreck. As it was, I couldn't accept what happened in 1989, let alone having to cope with this. I was glad that the children were still in school and that Steve was out on a temporary side job he'd acquired the week before. He worked day and night. How was I going to tell him what happened? How long was I going to be able to keep this a secret from the children? Why was I in so much trouble? How did it get this way? It was going from bad to worse."

My own reaction was one of profound anger. These two men had become involved with Linda, so they claimed, in order to see that she was safe and well. They said they were only trying to help, but now they had terrified her by forcibly seizing her in what one could legitimately characterize as a kidnapping. I insisted that she immediately call the police and report the incident. Though we had no idea of Richard's and Dan's last names or what agency they worked for, perhaps the New York City police could find them. After all, we did have excellent descriptions of Richard from both Linda and her husband, a tape recording of his voice, and Linda's description of Dan.

I hadn't reckoned on Linda's compelling reasons for *not* reporting the incident. As we talked it became obvious that there was no way she could describe the two men and how she met them without mentioning the November 1989 UFO abduction. To file a complaint she would have to explain that the agents first came to her because they had seen her floating in the air twelve stories up in the company of three aliens. I knew that Linda was a hopelessly inept dissembler and that she would only arouse suspicion if she tried to present some complicated story concocted to avoid telling the truth about the UFO. The police would want to know why two government agents had become so involved that they had eventually seized her for interrogation. She would be closely questioned about what her kidnappers said to her during the time they held her, and what reason they gave for her capture. Reluctantly I came to the conclusion that the very essence of the incident could not be told to the authorities without Linda's losing all credibility. It was a classic catch-22.

Her deeper fears lay in yet another area. She was concerned that Dan and Richard might seek some kind of revenge if she brought felony charges against them; Dan in particular had seemed coldly menacing. And on an even more paranoid level she wondered about the issue of government security and what might happen to her if she went to the police with criminal charges against two security/ intelligence agents. Though I tried to calm her anxiety I could easily understand it. "What if the rumors *are* true," she wrote, "about how people are kept quiet? Is it worth the risk? Who would help my husband raise the children? If rumors aren't true, what helpful information could I give the police to enable them to find Richard and Dan? None! I only knew their first names. After I told them about this crazy situation would they believe me? It was hopeless. Unless God himself asked me, I wasn't about to go head-to-head with any government agency." Though on some level I still wanted her to report the incident to the police, I knew she was right. It would be senseless. To bring charges would mean that she would only suffer more humiliation from yet another official source.

Linda knew that sooner or later she would have to tell her husband what had happened to her and that he wouldn't take it well. Though he's quiet and easygoing, Steve is also a proud man, a traditional son of Italy. It took days before she felt courageous enough to tell him. She planned the moment carefully. "I sent the children off to my sister's house for the weekend and started preparing his favorite meal. I worked from Friday night into Saturday afternoon. I gave myself a much needed beauty treatment. Steve wanted to know what the occasion was, and this logical question made me nervous so I told him it was a surprise. That made him happy. He thought he'd forgotten an important day.

"That evening we sat down at the beautiful table I had prepared. Candlelight shone on our faces in a special way. Steve's face was calm and he seemed pleased in the anticipation of what lay ahead. We smiled at each other lovingly, and he gave a toast, to good health and happiness. I needed self-assurance. If he would only say those three words 'I love you.' I wanted to get this over with. Nervously and too quickly I blurted out the story of my seizure and interrogation.

"He responded with three little words all right. *'They did what?'* He karate-chopped the table. Before I knew it the linguine clung to the wall and my veal scallopini fell to the carpet. The Italian cheesecake I'd baked from scratch—it was all mushed together. The candle fell and set the tablecloth on fire. I tried to put it out with a glass of wine—not a good move. With the fire out, Steve threw his jacket on and left, saying 'I'm going to find my brothers.' He has six brothers, all hotheads. I didn't want to see them that evening.

"That was the night that my life with my family changed. Steve was never the same. He was not the same man I married. Tension was thick and the children sensed something was wrong at home. Their behavior changed. Their grades fell."

After her seizure by Richard and Dan, I had begun to see changes in Linda herself. Many UFO abductees exhibit a certain wariness in their everyday demeanor, something that was certainly true of Linda. Since our first meeting she had complained of trouble sleeping at night and was always, I thought, unnaturally protective of her children. But now she was afraid even to leave her apartment. The dark circles under her eyes showed that she was getting less rest at night than before and her normally slender figure seemed even thinner. I realized that Linda's health was at stake and that I must redouble my efforts to reach Richard and Dan. They should be made to realize what harm their own frightened behavior was causing an innocent and already tormented woman.

The first step was to conduct a hypnosis session with Linda about the events of that April morning. I hoped to recover details about the car the men had used—even, if we were really lucky, its license plate number. I remembered a case from 1976—the infamous Chowchilla, California, kidnapping of twenty-six schoolchildren, during which the school-bus driver was forced at gunpoint to lift the children one by one into the back of the kidnappers' van. He was quite naturally terrified and did not recall glancing down at the van's license plate. However, under hypnosis he later remembered enough of the number to identify the vehicle and ultimately to solve the crime. I hardly dared to hope for such a dramatic outcome.

Linda was willing to try hypnosis, but like the Chowchilla bus driver, she didn't think she had had a clear look at the plate in the midst of her ordeal. I asked if she had looked at the agents' car—a Mercedes-Benz—after she had been returned to her apartment building. She had not. She was so frightened and so relieved to be home that she just ran away from the car as fast as she could, never once looking back.

She had seen something interesting, however, at the outset of her experience. There was a second conspicuous automobile parked about ten feet in front of the black Mercedes Dan was driving—an immaculate and distinctively colored Rolls-Royce, an unusual sight in her working-class neighborhood.[1] Though the streets near Linda's building are used as a parking area by a limousine company and she is quite familiar with stretch limos and other luxury cars, she had never seen a Rolls-Royce there before. It was this car rather than the Mercedes that had immediately caught her attention.

As we prepared for the hypnosis session I made a mental note to ask about the British car, on the assumption that it might have played some role in Linda's kidnapping. I proceeded with my usual induction and began the session with Linda's setting out for the supermarket. She described Richard's calling to her and their ensuing conversation. Before she told of the struggle and of being pulled into the agents' car, I asked her to try to make out its license plate. Still thinking that Richard was about to force her into the Rolls-Royce, she had paid more attention to it than to the black Mercedes parked behind it with one of its rear doors open on the street side. "I thought he was going to put me into the first car," she said, speaking carefully, as if she were studying the image in her mind's eye. "Don't see anybody in it. The license plate . . . I don't know what that would be. It's red, white, and blue. Blue on the bottom, a blue strip, and then it's all white and a red strip on top. . . . I didn't notice the state."

Searching for letters that would spell out the name of a state, she slowly began to count off a row of characters: a *D* followed by some she couldn't at first make out, and then an *O*. She went back to the beginning and started again: "In the red strip . . . a *D* and an *I* and a *P*. There's no state. *D, I, P* . . . can't make it out . . . *M A* . . . I don't know what that is." As the process continued I realized that what Linda was seeing on the Rolls-Royce was a United States diplomatic license plate.

At my suggestion she began to study its central numbers and letters. Gradually she came up with a few she was sure of and a few about which she had some doubt, but she was clear about their order from left to right. I had to restrain my hope that we might have retrieved enough information to identify the automobile's owner.

We moved on and I directed Linda's attention to the black Mercedes. She had evidently glanced at its license plate, too; it had the same kind of red, white, and blue diplomatic tag as the Rolls. Slowly, carefully, she described a few numbers and letters in left-to-right order, though she was unsure of several. While in the past I had always found Linda an accurate observer, we were both amazed that she had been able to see and remember anything clearly under the circumstances.

If her recollections were correct it was safe to assume that the two cars were part of the same operation. The fact that two well-kept vehicles with diplomatic plates would be parked, one behind the other, on a street in Linda's neighborhood was too unusual simply to be a coincidence. A wild thought crossed my mind: Could the third man possibly have been in the Rolls-Royce that morning, observing the scene or even planning to join Richard, Dan, and Linda for the interrogation? Had that been the case he would surely have decided not to participate once Linda began struggling and calling for help.

The hypnosis session provided a few more details, such as the presence of a blue United Nations window decal that tied the black Mercedes to that organization. And since both automobiles bore diplomatic plates, I felt it was safe to assume that they might be official vehicles owned by one or perhaps two different national missions to the UN. After I brought Linda out of the trance state, I immediately set about to find out what I could about the two diplomatic plates.

Over the years I have worked with a number of people in law enforcement and I knew that some of them would be willing to help me check these license numbers. The first law-enforcement officer I called was eventually able to provide definitive information about the Rolls-Royce. Because of its distinctive color and the characters that

Linda had seen on the license plate, he was able to identify the Rolls-Royce with certainty as belonging to a particular nation's delegation to the UN.[2] He explained that diplomatic license plates are issued with a fixed number of characters and in a certain order; thus, since Linda had not remembered the full sequence of those on the much more common black Mercedes-Benz, he was only able to narrow the range of possible owners. Both cars, he assured me, belonged to national missions to the UN. Linda's hypnosis had scored one bull's-eye—the Rolls-Royce—but the Mercedes must be called a very near miss.

Though I was extremely pleased that our session had worked so well and that we had received such immediate and helpful confirmation, a number of mysteries remained. How had two intelligence/security agents of the United States secured the use of an automobile owned by a foreign government? Was this foreign mission somehow involved in the November 1989 incident? Had the third man been in the Rolls-Royce that morning even though Linda hadn't noticed him? And if this were the case, what was his connection to the UN mission of the country that owned the Rolls? Why had he taken the risk to be there that morning? What had he hoped to accomplish?

Months would pass and a number of increasingly forthcoming letters and tapes would be exchanged between Richard and me before I learned the answers to a few of these questions. Richard eventually informed me that the third man had indeed been in the Rolls-Royce. He explained that the Rolls had followed immediately behind their car and had remained in constant radio contact; thus the third man had been able to hear all of Linda's interrogation. He had originally intended to join her in the black Mercedes but, as I suspected, decided against it once he saw that she had had to be taken forcibly.

And yet at the time, before I received Richard's corroboration, I had had to wrestle with the problem of the third man's possible involvement with Linda's interrogation. Why would he risk being present during an operation that could easily result—as, in fact, it did—in a struggle and the forced seizure of an American citizen? And why would he show up in such a conspicuous car? Why hadn't he simply stayed away and asked Richard and Dan for a transcript or even a tape recording of the interview? It seemed obvious to me that he must have been extremely eager to meet Linda face-to-face, or at least to see her again close up. Clearly the third man's interest was deeper and more complex than I had thought. I was soon to learn just how involved he was.

C | H | A | P | T | E | R

7

The Search for Richard and Dan

One of the advantages of having worked with so many different abductees and investigators over the years is that they provide me with a pool of potential consultants in various fields: law enforcement, medicine, entertainment, science, mental health, and so on. I have often taken advantage of their wide range of knowledge and expertise when I needed help in a case I was investigating. And so one night, after I shared some of the details of what I had come to call the Linda case at a meeting of my abductee support group, a young man, "Peter," spoke up and volunteered to help me with the problem of locating Richard and Dan. He said that if the agents were in any way officially associated with the United Nations, then perhaps he could be of service. For quite a few years he had been deeply interested in the UN, Peter informed me, because his job in law enforcement often involved that organization. And as an electronics hobbyist who made extensive use of his VCR, he'd recorded over the years a number of TV specials and news programs dealing with the Security Council and with the various summit meetings held under its auspices. If Richard and Dan were security/intelligence agents attached to the UN, Peter felt that Linda might actually be able to spot them on one of his video-tapes. It was a kind offer and one that presented us with an interesting opportunity, albeit a long shot.

And so on a Sunday afternoon in May Linda went to Peter's home to view what turned out to be nearly six hours of videotapes. About five o'clock she called me in great consternation. "Budd, I saw Dan on a tape . . . it's really him . . . I saw him in close-up, and he may be a Russian, a KGB agent or something." I tried to calm her down but she was very upset. After dealing with the aliens and with Richard and Dan, to think that the KGB might be involved was almost too much for her. The program on which Dan had appeared was an ABC news special on Gorbachev's December 1988 visit to the UN and his subsequent summit meeting with Reagan and Bush on Governors Island in New York Harbor.

At one point, Linda explained, Dan was seen standing close to Gorbachev and acting as if he were a bodyguard; it was this that made her think he might be Russian. She was so afraid of Dan by this time that her instinct was to expect the worst of him. I asked to speak to Peter, our mutual friend, and he assured me that Linda had indeed been terribly shaken when she first saw Dan on the tape. He appeared several times, and in each segment was behaving as if he were a security agent, possibly, Peter thought, for the UN or the U.S. Secret Service. He said that Dan was in extremely sharp focus and was more than once quite close to the camera. I asked Linda how certain she was that she had identified the right man—90 percent sure? "A hundred and fifty percent sure," she answered. "I'd recognize that scary face anywhere."

Richard, she assumed, had not been present at this summit meeting because she hadn't seen him anywhere on the tape. But the positive identification of Dan was an enormous coup for us. When I later viewed the program it seemed clear to me that Dan was just a member of the enormous security detail that had been assembled for the occasion. His sporadic proximity to Gorbachev did not suggest to me that he was a Russian agent, and when I quizzed Linda about Dan's voice and inflection, she assured me that he hadn't a trace of a foreign accent. She had no reason to suppose that he wasn't what he said he was—an American security/intelligence agent. But her fear of him was such that it was easier for her to think of him as a cold-war enemy than as a fellow American citizen.

Peter made a copy of the ABC program for me so that I could study Dan's face. Linda's description of him was right on target. He looked cold, sullen, tense, humorless, and forbidding, with an edge of cruelty in his eyes and in the set of his mouth. I sent the tape to a video duplicating firm, which produced a set of excellent still photographs from the occasional close-ups. We were ready, now, to launch a serious investigation. Understandably, Linda was even more anxious than I to locate Dan in order to hand him an ultimatum: If he didn't stop harassing her we would have him arrested. Though she was still afraid to swear out a warrant, we both felt that once he realized that we knew his name and where he worked, he could easily be forced to stop his interrogations. Identifying Dan gave us a great deal of potential leverage, and made possible a face-to-face interview about the events of November 30, 1989.

We discussed how to begin our investigation. Linda was eager to accompany me and I wanted her along on the chance that we might actually meet Dan, since she had dealt with him in person and I had only seen his photographs. We decided that our first target should be the United Nations Security and Safety Service because that was his most likely place of employment. I called Richard Ward, the chief of this small, independent police organization, to set up an appointment, but gave him very little information as to why I was seeking this particular individual. My hesitancy to explain exactly why we were trying to locate Dan was a problem that dogged us throughout our inquiry. Since we couldn't mention the UFO abduction experience that had brought Dan into Linda's life, we were inevitably forced to construct a series of semiplausible stories to use in order to gain access to various agencies.

When I told Chief Ward that I wanted him to look at photographs of someone who might work in his department, but was not free to explain why I was trying to identify this person, he was quite naturally suspicious. Instead of agreeing to a meeting with me, he asked me to photocopy the pictures of Dan and then to fax them to him. He then called back to say that the man in the pictures did not work at the UN and that he had no idea who he was. He claimed he had never seen him before.

Under the circumstances I couldn't be sure if he was telling the truth, though he sounded quite believable. The ABC tape clearly showed the man moving through the UN building as part of a security detail, yet the chief of UN security claimed not to recognize his picture. Though Ward had been hired *after* Gorbachev's 1988 visit and had not been at the UN when Dan was filmed, I assumed the chief had shown the photo to men who had been present in 1988 and that they, too, had failed to identify Dan.

To check further, Linda and I decided to go up to the UN and pretend to be a married couple who had met Dan during a summer vacation in Nova Scotia—a place I knew he had visited. According to our story we had all become good friends, Dan had told us he worked at the United Nations in New York, and he had given us his phone number. "Call me whenever you're in the city," he'd said, but in the meantime we had lost his number and so had come up to the UN with his photograph to try to find him. On top of everything we couldn't remember his last name, so the photograph was our only recourse. It was a threadbare story, but we hoped it would work.

We tried our story with a number of UN employees and security personnel. We questioned the guards at every place we could find where UN employees would have to show identification to enter, yet no one recognized the man in the photograph. One young woman told us that the picture looked vaguely familiar to her; she thought she had seen the man before but didn't know if he worked for the UN. After three days of searching, her extremely tentative recollection was the closest we came to connecting Dan with the United Nations. I reluctantly decided that he was probably not a member of UN security.

So who did he work for? The videotape established for me the fact that Dan was a security agent, prowling about like a watchful and suspicious guard at an international summit meeting. I began to make a list of other possible organizations: the U.S. Secret Service, the State Department's diplomatic security section, New York City's police intelligence unit, the FBI, the CIA, the NSA, or possibly the security service of some nation's mission to the United Nations. In the interest of thoroughness I decided to investigate them all, so far as I was able, though checking on Dan's possible employment by a secret intelligence agency was clearly beyond my capacity.

We began with the State Department because its diplomatic security service seemed a likely place to look for information; even if Dan didn't work there, someone who did might at least recognize him as belonging to another agency doing similar work. And so on a warm spring afternoon, Linda and I went to the Federal Building in downtown Manhattan to visit the State Department office. Once more we rehearsed our story, essentially the same account we had given before, except that now we claimed that Dan said he worked for the *government* "in security" rather than the UN. In the lobby we passed through the metal detector and took the elevator to the department's rather modest New York office. A friendly clerk heard our request—we mentioned both Dan and Richard this time—and she explained that in fact there was a Dan who worked there in security. He was temporarily out of the office, she said, but would be back shortly. Thrilled and hopeful, we left to have lunch.

When we finally met the State Department's Dan we saw immediately that he wasn't our Dan. In fact, he had begun working in the

New York office after the 1988 Gorbachev summit and so could not have been on the tape. Another strikeout. I continued the search, crossing off the possibilities on my list. At one point I made a solitary visit to the Soviet mission to the United Nations simply to check out the chance that Dan was an employee of the Russians, or might be known to them. Security was even more stringent there than at the State Department. I rang an outside buzzer while standing on the sidewalk under a surveillance camera, and then tried to explain through an intercom why I wanted to talk to a mission official. I used a variant on my basic story and ultimately was admitted to a fairly shabby waiting room. There, amid some worn and ancient furniture, a few hapless nationals were filling out papers of some kind beneath yet more surveillance cameras. With no discernible expression on his face the official who received me studied Dan's photograph and then wandered off to show it to someone "in security." (I had said that I thought Dan might be in that department.) Again I drew a blank. No one at the Soviet mission had ever seen this man, I was informed, and what was worse, only a few officials working there now had been in New York in December 1988. Power changes in Moscow, I was told, had meant drastic personnel changes in New York.

I felt I must cross another possibility off my list and move on. Through a series of conversations with a confidential source in the police department I had been told that no plainclothes New York City officers would have been on duty inside the General Assembly Building during the summit conference. Since the NYPD's jurisdiction only began outside the United Nations' neutral grounds, the agent seen marching down the hall in the videotape could not have been a police officer. That left the Secret Service, the CIA, the FBI, or the NSA, each of which seemed plausible as Dan's department, but none of which, I was certain, would ever confirm or deny that the man in the photographs was in their employ. Though I felt stymied in my search, Linda, living in an ongoing state of fear, was even more discouraged than I.

The next step was to try a professional detective agency. A well-to-do friend and supporter of my research answered my request and informed me that he would pay the expenses of a private investigation agency to look for the elusive Dan and Richard. The head of the firm I chose assured me that his operatives had contacts in the various intelligence communities, and he said that with the photographs I gave him, Dan would be easy to find. Promising though it seemed, unfortunately it also turned out to be a blind alley.

After a flurry of phone calls, meetings, false trails, and further questions from private operatives, I received a call from one of the investigators. At last he had a "positive ID" of Dan! His excitement and assurance almost carried me along with him, but after all I had been through I couldn't allow myself to think that locating Dan would ever be this simple. The operative informed me that the man in the photographs was a Secret Service agent attached to the New York office, and he went on to give me his name, which I shall change here to "Robeson." The detective explained that "Robeson" had been positively identified as the "Dan" in my pictures by a confidential informant with ties to the Secret Service.

When I telephoned their New York office I was told that an agent named Robeson had worked there for a number of years but had recently retired. He still lived in the New York area, however. When the agent I was speaking to asked me why I wanted to locate Mr. Robeson, I decided to tell at least part of the truth. A woman friend of mine, I explained, had been forcibly detained, questioned, and mistreated by two men representing themselves as government security agents. I said that I possessed photographs of one of these rogue agents, a man she knew as "Dan," and that a confidential informant had identified Dan as Secret Service Agent Robeson. However, I emphasized that Dan and Mr. Robeson might not be the same person; this could easily be a case of mistaken identity.

The main reason I decided to tell the agent this much of the actual story was that it ensured my entrée to their office. Since the Secret Service would obviously be interested in maintaining its good reputation by policing its agents, the New York supervisor would have to cooperate with my inquiry by checking Dan's photographs to see if he really was Agent Robeson. And even if this was a case of mistaken identity, someone in the New York office might still be able to identify Dan.

I said that it was very important to settle the matter once and for all, so arrangements were made for me to bring my photos to the Service's office in the World Trade Center. On the day of the appointment, as I waited in the reception area, two men came into the room, one almost visibly seething. When introductions were made I learned that the angry man was retired Agent Robeson. Unfortunately, he bore only the most superficial resemblance to Dan's photograph. I privately cursed our detective agency for its mistake, but I was still eager to show the two men the photographs. I informed Mr. Robeson that he was obviously not the man I was looking for and apologized for any inconvenience I might have caused him. I had not, after all, expected him to travel from his home to the New York office for this appointment. When he finally calmed down and examined the pictures, neither he nor the other agent could identify the man they depicted. Considering Dan's sensitive position near Presidents Reagan and Gorbachev at this summit meeting, one can infer that he should have been known to these two senior Secret Service officials at the New York office—if, in fact, he belonged to their organization. I was forced to abandon the idea that Dan and Richard were Secret Service agents.

Linda was even more discouraged than I when I told her about this latest failure. With no identification of Dan—neither his name nor his place of employment—she was as vulnerable as ever. And even worse, it now seemed virtually certain that Dan and Richard worked at one of our country's secret intelligence agencies and so would be nearly impossible to locate.

One tactic did occur to me, however. I told Linda that she must at all times carry a photograph of Dan in her purse or wallet. Thus, if he or Richard ever tried to seize her again she could show them the photograph and let them know that I also had copies. She could then tell them that if anything happened to her I would immediately go to the police with Dan's picture, the audiotape of Richard's voice, and whatever other information I had about them. She should tell the two agents that she would press charges this time for sure. In reality it was still an empty threat because there was no way for Linda to report another kidnapping or harassment to the police without having to tell how she first met Richard and Dan and why they were interested in her. Their shared (and for the police, probably unbelievable) UFO experience was the only factor that made Dan and Richard's subsequent behavior toward Linda believable.

I had one other solid lead still to explore—the issue of the Rolls-Royce. I was operating on the assumption that the third man had been in the Rolls that morning, but since I knew with certainty which nation owned the car, I phoned the chief of security for that country's UN mission. Here I felt I had struck pay dirt for the first time. I began by asking the chief if he knew a pair of American security agents named Richard and Dan, and if they might have been involved in using the Rolls-Royce on the morning of April 29. There was a short hesitation before he replied, stating that he didn't think he knew anyone named Richard and Dan, but he immediately asked why I wanted to know. I explained, using our standard story, but when I tried to ask more questions the situation became subtly reversed. The security chief was now grilling me—and rather uneasily, at that. None of the other people I had interviewed in my search for Richard and Dan had ever gone beyond a perfunctory denial, with one or two questions about the reasons for my inquiry. Most seemed to regard me as an overly inquisitive and not very forthcoming annoyance. All seemed eager to get off the telephone and back to work, subtly implying that I was wasting their time as well as my own. But this man was different. He answered none of my questions simply and directly, and in fact I sensed an evasiveness in the way he phrased his replies. More significantly, he continued to quiz me in detail about my reason for calling, asking what I knew about Richard and Dan, why I thought they were connected with his nation's UN mission, and so on. Fishing for information, he was in no hurry to terminate the phone call. An uninvolved person, I thought, would probably have behaved quite differently. So, when at last I was able to ring off, I felt that he not only was acquainted with Richard and Dan but also knew where the Rolls-Royce was on the morning of April 29 and who had used it.

In the weeks since Dan had first informed me by letter of the existence of the third man, I had come to feel certain of his identity. (His position, however, meant that it would be virtually impossible for me to meet with him.) I also had reason to believe that when the three men were together on the night of November 30, 1989, Richard and Dan's job of escorting him was probably a temporary arrangement involving an off-the-record political meeting the three had attended earlier. Dan provided enough clues in his letter as to the third man's leadership position to enable me to check his activities on November 30. Microfilm copies of the *New York Times* for that week were particularly helpful. But since it is my fervent hope that this internationally known political figure will come forward voluntarily to give his account of what he saw that night, I am honoring his desire for anonymity, a request he has communicated to me and that I shall discuss later.

After I received Dan's original letter about the third man, I began to do some research on his career. From available biographical material I learned a significant fact: He had had an ongoing relationship with the diplomatic corps of the country that owned the Rolls-Royce! Apparently it would not have been a problem for him to borrow this official car, and if necessary a chauffeur or security agent to do the driving. Had he been hesitant either to use his own official vehicle or to involve his regular security detail in the questioning of Linda, a car owned by the UN mission of an unrelated country would seem a reliable cover.

One other piece of this particular puzzle was to come to light later, in September, when Linda underwent another hypnosis session.

I was curious to see if she could recall any more details from Richard and Dan's original meeting with her on February 19, the night they came to her apartment for the first time. When they knocked on the door and identified themselves as police officers, Linda had said that Dan showed her a small gold badge as a credential. Under hypnosis she recalled what the badge looked like and some of the letters on its surface. It was not an American badge—it was, in fact, the badge of an agency of the same nation that owned the Rolls-Royce, the country whose mission security director had seemed so interested in my inquiries about Richard and Dan. Clearly, Dan also had some sort of connection with that country.

Despite all the time and effort Linda and I had spent in our futile search for the two men, we had learned some things. First, I had come to the conclusion that the two men were not employed by the UN, nor were they Secret Service agents or police detectives. My best guess was that they were agents of the FBI, the CIA, the NSA, or some other supersecret agency. Second, my theory as to the identity of the third man had been supported by his apparent use of a car owned by a country with which he had had extensive prior contact. Third, alone of all the security agencies I had talked to, the chief for that nation's UN mission had behaved most suspiciously. So, despite the many continuing mysteries and uncertainties, what we did know was beginning to form a consistent and coherent pattern.

The Downtown Chase

All of us, I suppose, have some sort of compulsive but personally reassuring habit we fall into when we're anxious or unhappy. Sometimes this stress-induced behavior is self-destructive—the temporary oblivion of alcohol and drugs, for example, or the momentary escape into compulsive gambling or overeating. But for Linda Cortile—a woman suffering from stress if there ever was one—her solution was benign but expensive: When she felt low and fearful she simply went shopping.

Early on the afternoon of May 17, 1991, she left her apartment for a bit of shopping at a store on Cortlandt Street in lower Manhattan. Since less than three weeks had passed since her forced automobile ride and interrogation by Richard and Dan, she was somewhat uneasy to be out without a companion. Even though the sidewalks were crowded with lunch-hour shoppers, she still didn't feel safe. There was, however, a particular lure. A few days earlier she had seen a very pretty blue blouse, and the more she thought about it the more she wanted it. An hour or so of shopping would cheer her up, she decided.

As she paused at the northeast corner of Broadway and Cortlandt Street, waiting for the light to change, she heard her name called. There are lots of women with my name, she told herself, so it's probably not for me. But she heard it again, more insistent now. With every muscle and nerve on alert, she turned around to see who might be calling her. About a half-block north on Broadway she spotted Richard, calling and waving to her. A black car was parked at the curb behind him. This was all she needed to see. Like a frightened deer she bolted out into the traffic, heading west across Broadway. She hadn't had time to look—she just turned and ran. Brakes squealed and people yelled as a car tried to avoid her. She felt a heavy bump and found herself sprawled on the pavement on her hands and knees. People were rushing over to her and she could hear Richard shouting. Panic-stricken, she jumped up and began to run, across Broadway and down Cortlandt Street.

Not until a few minutes later was she able to assess the damage, which luckily had been slight. The car had stopped in time, hitting her only hard enough to knock her down and cause some bad scrapes and bruises on her knees and elbows. She had been very, very lucky.

But now she had to run away, away from Richard, away from the black car, away from Dan, who she knew must be at the wheel. If they grabbed her it would be another kidnapping or perhaps something even worse. She raced down the sidewalk, weaving in and out of the lunchtime crowds. She saw Richard coming after her, calling her name, though he was still a half-block away. She darted into a store and headed for the uptown exit out onto Dey Street. Her legs and elbows hurt and her scraped knees were bleeding slightly, but she ran on, turning west on Dey Street.

Though when she looked back she couldn't see Richard, she refused to slacken her pace. She headed for the World Trade Center and from there took the elevated pedestrian walkway across West Street to Battery Park City. If she was up above the street, she thought, she would be able to look down to see if Richard was still on her trail. Even though he was nowhere in sight, her panic hadn't lessened.

At Battery Park City and the World Financial Center Linda wandered through the outdoor cafés and park areas, nervously looking for Richard and Dan but growing increasingly sure she had eluded them. She had been wearing a pair of her best jeans that day but now the fabric at both knees was ripped open. The few remaining threads stretched raggedly across the rents were embedded in the shallow wounds of her skinned knees.

After a few hours she slowly made her way home by walking downtown, past the Staten Island Ferry Terminal and up South Street toward her apartment. The closer she was to home the more wary she became, but neither Dan nor Richard nor the black car was anywhere in sight. So much time had elapsed that they must have given up their pursuit, she decided as she hurried into her building and took the elevator to her apartment. Finally, now, she was able to dress her wounds. For the time being she was safe.

When she called to tell me about her experience on Cortlandt Street, I realized that something had to be done. Linda could not continue to live in a state of fear so acute that she could get killed trying to escape Richard and Dan. But as I mulled over various ways of helping her, I was also thinking about this day's kidnapping attempt—if indeed that was what it was. One peculiar feature of Richard's approach called attention to itself: Knowing how fearful and distrustful Linda was, it seemed odd to me that he would call to her from a half-block away rather than approach silently from behind in order to take her by surprise. And why, less than three weeks after their hours-long interrogation, did Richard and Dan seem to want her again?

In the ensuing weeks yet another problem began to surface, causing Linda even more uneasiness. Often, when she left in the morning to take her son to his school bus, she had noticed an unmarked gray van parked near the Cherry Street entrance to her apartment building. The driver, usually clad in a white dress shirt, seemed to be watching her. The absence of any lettering on the vehicle's sides and the sense she had, day after day, of being under surveillance only confirmed her already debilitating fears. Did Richard and Dan have associates working with them? Could she possibly be imagining the whole thing? More and more she was afraid to leave her apartment.

When she first reported the suspicious gray van to me, I attributed her nervousness to the paranoia that her experiences with Richard and Dan would naturally cause. The presence of the van and its well-dressed driver probably had a simple and innocent explanation. And yet I couldn't be sure. I knew that I must get some help for Linda, some regular protection. Perhaps I could arrange for someone to accompany her on her trips to the supermarket and on her increasingly rare shopping sprees.

Already she had learned to be careful in the mornings when she took little Johnny to the school bus. When she left the building she always made sure that other mothers walked with her to and from the bus stop, but after her return she was a prisoner in her own small apartment. As her uneasiness deepened, normal family life became more difficult; the emotional well-being of her husband and sons was obviously being affected. Things simply could not continue as they had. My solution was, again, to call my friend Robert Bigelow, a concerned businessman and philanthropist, whom I had kept informed about the progress of the case. When I explained Linda's situation he generously offered to pay for an off-duty law-enforcement officer to act as her part-time bodyguard.

I knew immediately who would be a perfect candidate for the job: "Joseph," the man I had called weeks before to ask about the diplomatic license plates on the Rolls-Royce and the Mercedes-Benz. Joseph worked in the area of law enforcement and was well versed in various surveillance techniques.

When I called to offer him the job, I described Linda's case in great detail: her initial 1989 abduction, her subsequent visit from Richard and Dan, the existence of the third man, Linda's seizure and forced questioning, and all the rest. At first he seemed rather dubious; the story was so complex and so many people were involved in it that it was difficult for him to accept its validity. I understood his reaction. The Linda case was, in certain respects, different from virtually all other UFO abduction accounts I had heard of, a fact that I would be the first to acknowledge. Nevertheless, Joseph was intrigued by my offer and accepted this part-time position. Privately I regarded his hesitancy as an advantage because it would help ensure an objective evaluation of Linda's still uncertain surveillance experiences. Was she really being watched—a distinct possibility—or were her suspicions merely the natural result of her frightening encounters with Richard and Dan? I trusted Joseph—a law-enforcement professional with a skeptical disposition—to help solve the problem for me, one way or the other.

Meanwhile things were about to take yet another surprising turn. During the time I had spent searching for Richard and Dan, I continued my usual work with other abductees. I interviewed new people, conducted a number of hypnotic regression sessions, and led abductee support groups. And yet, without knowing it, all the while I apparently had been in contact with a distant witness to the first stage of Linda's November 1989 abduction.

In the winter of 1990, a young woman reported a consciously remembered UFO abduction experience to a local UFO organization. After a preliminary investigation, that group passed her account on to me. Since the incident had occurred in Manhattan and concerned an abduction, it was not only my kind of case but one convenient for me to look into. The general outline of the young woman's encounter had been presented to me before I met her, so I had been told that her experience occurred in late 1989—most likely in the month of November. At the time I failed to notice the proximity of dates between her experience and Linda's.

In early 1991 I met and interviewed the young woman, whom I

shall refer to as Erica. She is an articulate and very observant witness, a resident of Manhattan's Murray Hill section on the East Side. As a result of our initial conversation I gradually became aware of several intriguing parallels between her experience and Linda's: Erica consciously remembered having been floated to a UFO at the edge of the East River somewhere near Thirty-eighth Street. And looking down the river in the general direction of the Brooklyn Bridge, she had seen, in the sky, a glowing, fast-moving, *bright red* UFO. She could not remember the exact date of the late-November–early-December incident, but it seemed possible that she had seen the same bright red craft that had taken Linda.

April 29, 1991, was the day Linda had been forcibly abducted and questioned by Richard and Dan. Eight days before that disturbing encounter I conducted my first hypnotic regression session with Erica. At that time the only information that I had about the craft's external appearance had come from the letters and the tape I'd received from the two agents, so I was eager to hear what Erica might remember. Was she, potentially, an important corroborating witness in this complex case?

Her experience had begun sometime after 2:00 A.M. She had been up late and was preparing to go to bed when she noticed several bright flashes of light in her living room. This display was perplexing, but eventually Erica went into her bedroom and lay down beside her sleeping husband. Almost immediately after dozing off, she awoke to find three small bald figures standing beside her bed. She was told that she should go with them, but that her husband would not be taken. He would be maintained "in a very deep sleep."

After putting on her blue jeans and a ski jacket, Erica was taken outside where she found herself gliding involuntarily down the street. Though she resisted in her mind—"I don't want to be doing this"— she floated along toward the East River in a standing position, about a foot or two above the pavement. There is no need here to discuss the components of what seemed to be a mass abduction—she saw about twenty other people being similarly taken—except to recount those few specific details that parallel Linda's experience. Erica described the parking-lot-like character of her final location, the huge craft hovering above her, and the appearance of her fellow abductees.[1] She continued her hypnotically induced recollections: "There's other things flying in the air. They're moving very quickly. They're coming from Long Island and they're heading to the east coast of Manhattan, but south of me. I'm looking south of me. I see something blue, something bright blue, and something bright red moving very quickly. I have the understanding that . . . maybe they're doing this [taking other people just like herself]."

I asked her how far the other craft were flying above the water, and she answered, "They're very high above the water, very high. They're about the size of a quarter. And the other one is further away, and it's smaller." "Which one is further away," I asked, "the blue one or the red one?" "The red one is further," she replied. I told her to watch the red one and see what it does. "It's moving very quickly," she answered. "It's going way downtown."

The general area where Erica was apparently standing is a little less than three miles from Linda's apartment building. Because of the irregular shape of Manhattan Island, the Brooklyn Bridge is not visible from an East River location near Thirty-fourth Street. But if the UFO had been flying above lower Manhattan and as high as Erica claimed—higher than the intervening buildings—she could easily have seen it at some point during its travels. Since Linda had not observed the *outside* of the craft, the only descriptions I had of the UFO's bright red color had come from Richard and Dan. But now, if the dates exactly coincided, Erica would make a third independently corroborating witness to several important details: the time of night of Linda's abduction, the location of the object, and its color. It is crucially important that each of these three details was consciously recalled by Erica *months* before she met me or had heard of Linda's encounter.

In this kind of difficult research, errors are unavoidable and can cause enormous difficulties. But every once in a while an error can be a blessing in disguise, and this is what had happened back in 1989 with regard to the date of Linda's original abduction. When she phoned me on November 30, 1989, to tell me about what had happened to her the previous night, I took notes, arranged a meeting, and wrote down the date of the night before as November 29. Obviously, I thought, if today is the 30th, the night before must be the 29th, right? Wrong, if the incident occurred at 3:15 A.M. of the night that had just ended, as happened in the Linda case. And so, a year and a half later, my file on the incident still carried the wrong date.

Richard and Dan had been no help. In their letters and cassette tape they consistently described the event as having taken place "in late November, between 3:00 and 3:30 A.M." Therefore, as recently as April 1991, I had assumed that the proper date for Linda's abduction was November 29, 1989.

At the end of my April hypnotic regression session with Erica I asked her to try and find the correct date of *her* experience. Naturally,

I did not tell her why I needed to know the specific night of her abduction, nor did I discuss with her which night Linda had been taken. It took nearly two weeks, but Erica finally came up with the exact date of her encounter: November 30, 1989. Her assurance was based on the fact that she had consciously remembered so much about her abduction. When she awoke the morning of the incident she told her husband "Paul" about her recollections—the aliens, the craft, the other abductees, and the bright red object she saw in the sky downtown.

Paul has his own small business and recalled hearing his wife's account over breakfast before going off to do his banking. He always visits the bank on *Thursday mornings* to avoid the Friday crush. In addition, Erica's sister remembered that she had dropped in that morning to tell her about her Thanksgiving Day visit to their parents the previous week. She, too, recalled hearing Erica's odd experience on Thursday morning. To confirm this information, I spoke both to Erica's sister and to her husband. Each was certain that it was around breakfast time on *Thursday* morning, November 30, 1989, that Erica told them about the bizarre events of the night before.

For me, this was a very frustrating outcome. Erica had seen the red UFO sometime after 2:30 A.M. on the 30th instead of the 29th. It was the right neighborhood, the right hour, the right color, but the wrong day. So near, I thought, and yet so far. When I called Linda to tell her the disappointing news, she immediately set me straight. "But it did happen on the *30th*," she said. "Don't you remember, when I called you on Thursday I told you it happened *last night* about 3:15?" I realized my mistake, consulted my notes, and felt enormously relieved.

Now I had my first independent confirmation of *four* key details in Richard and Dan's account of the events of November 30, 1989: the correct date and hour of the night, as well as the color and location of what was, very possibly, the craft that carried Linda away down near the Brooklyn Bridge. Though Erica's testimony helped to buttress Linda's abduction account, there were to be more dramatic confirmations yet to come.

Meanwhile I was receiving intermittent reports from Joseph, Linda's part-time bodyguard, concerning the possibility of her being under some kind of irregular surveillance. Joseph's first news was of a more general sort. In a private conversation he told me that as he had spent time with Linda and had gotten to know her two sons and her husband, his initial skepticism about the case had begun to melt away. The Cortile family seemed to him to be exactly as it presented itself—a modest, hardworking, traditional Italian American family.

The two sons, Steven and Johnny, were the type of youngsters one characteristically referred to as "good boys," and Linda's husband, Steve, who had described meeting and talking with Richard, was transparently honest and believable. There was no sign of guile anywhere.

And as someone with experience in law enforcement, Joseph pointed out an interesting set of facts. Obviously, Linda's account was either true or a hoax; there was no middle ground. Richard and Dan were either real, or Linda had made them up. It seemed impossible to Joseph that the Linda and Steve he had come to know had the will, the motive, or the capacity to forge so much consistent evidence, hire and train accomplices, discover arcane facts about diplomatic license plates, and in Linda's case, convincingly act the part of a genuinely frightened woman.

But more important, there was the matter of Linda's positive identification of Dan on the videotape. "That's him, I'm 150 percent sure," she had told me. As Joseph pointed out, no hoaxer would ever run the risk of identifying someone in this way, arbitrarily picking someone who might easily be traceable and who might also have a perfect alibi for his whereabouts on the night of November 30, 1989. What if the man Linda had so positively identified as he came down the corridor in the UN building turned out to be an elevator operator? Using our photographs of the man, what if someone among the many people we interviewed identified him as, say, Secret Service Agent Smith who had been stationed in San Francisco on November 30? Or as Jones, a member of the State Department's diplomatic security service, who had spent 1989 in Turkey? Or a plainclothes member of the United Nation's police detail who had been a deputy sheriff in Rochester that winter? No, Joseph assured me, no hoaxer would ever have run this dire a risk. He or she would have backed off gracefully, refusing to identify anyone on the tapes lest the whole elaborate scam come crashing down in an instant. I couldn't fault his logic.

Throughout the summer Joseph had been accompanying Linda on various trips out of her apartment, though there were many occasions when he was not available and she had had to venture out on her own. He often picked her up at her apartment building, but sometimes met her at the nearby South Street Seaport, a trendy combination museum and shopping mall that is usually crowded with tourists and native New Yorkers. Joseph would stay with her while she shopped and then escort her safely back to her apartment.

On September 3, he was scheduled to meet Linda at the Seaport at 4:00 P.M. But that day a disturbing incident occurred, about which he later gave me a written report:

"When I arrived at the Seaport I saw Linda waiting for me at the corner," he wrote. "As I neared her I noticed that she looked like she'd seen a ghost. Her face was devoid of color and her features were unnaturally contorted . . . something was terribly wrong." He continued walking toward her, trying to figure out what was the matter, and when he reached her, "She told me to look to my immediate left, that a man had been following her. As I glanced over in the direction she stated I noticed a man approximately 5' 9", black suit, and with a complexion that immediately brought to mind 'Middle Eastern.'

"I didn't want him to know I was aware of him, so my glances were quick and seemingly nonchalant, just long enough to mentally photograph and observe this individual. At this point in time all I could think of was getting Linda out of there as fast as possible. . . . I turned towards her and said, 'Let's move, now!' Linda seemed terribly frightened and also quite stiff. As I grabbed her by the arm and started to pull, I again looked back at the individual. . . . He had turned sideways and was talking into what looked like a tiny transmitter or walkie-talkie. That's it, I said to myself, and looking back at Linda I said, 'Let's go!'

"The walk across Pearl Street seemed to take forever, not knowing if the people he was speaking to were right in front of us, next to us, or wherever. As we reached the other side of the street I again looked back and he was still talking into the transmitter or whatever it was. Linda still wasn't speaking, but she was breathing as hard as if she'd just run a marathon. . . .

"We went up a flight of stairs to a platform that held some tables and chairs. No one else was up there, so I thought it was perfect. . . . When we stepped onto the platform we both turned around to see what was happening. . . . A gray van with no back windows or any identifying signs on it sped to a halt next to the man with the transmitter. He immediately jumped in and within seconds the van disappeared up Pearl Street. . . . I didn't know what to think except that the reason for his quick departure was because of something he hadn't counted on: me showing up.

"I believe that had I not met Linda at the Seaport this particular day she would have been kidnapped again, taken against her will for something she had no control over. As we watched the van pull away, all I could see of the driver was his long arm holding on to the steering wheel. He was wearing a solid white dress shirt."

Joseph explained that though he could tell by its color that it was a New York State plate, he could not read its numbers. He went on to write that there was a possibility the incident may have been only a series of unrelated coincidences, though that was not his opinion. "I can honestly say that something very bizarre is going on and Linda seems to be right in the middle of it. After this event I cautioned her about waiting for me or anyone else for that matter on a street corner. It's just too easy to be grabbed and thrown into a car or van."

And so we had a major new factor to consider: Dan and Richard might have at least two associates working with them. But if these two men had had Linda under surveillance, were there even more? Were these men working under the direction of Richard and Dan, or were they associated with some other intelligence faction? What, exactly, was going on? The bad news was that everything we knew came together to make Linda's life and safety seem ever more precarious.

PART TWO

The Lady of the Sands

"Look and See What You Have Done"

Normally when summer comes I leave New York and head for Wellfleet, Massachusetts, where I spend the hours painting, making sculpture, enjoying the ocean beaches and reimmersing myself in the Cape Cod art world where I regularly exhibit at a Provincetown gallery. But as one might guess, the subject of UFOs is never totally absent from my life during these summer months. I continue interviewing possible abductees, conducting hypnotic regressions, and leading a Cape support group, though the volume of such work is far less demanding than it is in New York.

However, those months in 1991 were spent more under the shadow of the UFO phenomenon than any previous summer. The problem was, of course, the Linda Cortile case. Unlike the other New York area people who might continue to undergo abduction experiences, for Linda there were the unsettling—and truly unknown— extra problems presented by Richard and Dan and their presumed associates. In a few short months the two agents had questioned Linda in her apartment, had forcibly taken her into their car for hours of interrogation and discussion, and had yet again tried to seize her, apparently for more questioning. And then there was evidence that she was under fairly regular surveillance. How far would they go? Why were they behaving toward her this way?

For these reasons I tried to keep in touch with Linda while I was away to make sure she was all right. It was reassuring to know that her sons were home for summer vacations, since their presence afforded her a bit of protection. And Joseph would be there much of the time when Linda had to venture out alone.

Though I had learned a great deal about Richard, Dan, and the third man, I was still frustrated by my lack of understanding of their motivations and general behavior. The precise nature of their roles in the events before, during, and after November 30, 1989, was as much a mystery to me as was the cause of their relentless interest in Linda.

On my return to New York in the fall, I assumed that I would soon be working again on the Linda case in my usual one-foot-in-front-of-the-other manner, methodically following up leads, digging away slowly at the mass of information that still lay buried tantalizingly out of reach. But within two weeks of my return to New York things took a sudden and extraordinary turn. A new letter from Dan vastly expanded my understanding of the case. This letter is the single most important document of all those I've received from the many witnesses and security personnel involved in this case:

Sept. 17, 1991

Dear Budd—

I hope this letter finds you in good health and happy spirits. My work has been taking most of my time and I have been unable to write. However, much has happened since I've last contacted you.

We have read your book Intruders, *and consider ourselves modestly informed enough to understand what has happened to Linda and possibly to us.*

We behaved in a bullish manner, as some uninformed persons I'll assume behave. Please extend our apologies to Linda, to yourself and to all the others in your group. The three of us have been under tremendous pressure. Still, there is no excuse for our actions.

The third party, Richard and myself remembered a similar memory having to do with the November 1989 Incident. This memory was of a single word, "sand," which triggered other memories. During a time, not long past, we remembered another particular event which occurred immediately following Linda's 1989 abduction. However, we agreed not to disclose this memory to one another until we could see each other in person. The third party insisted that all of us write down our memories and bring them to light when we meet, in order to test for imagination or reality.

When we met at the designated place, we put all three papers with our written recollections down on the center of a table. Together, we read all three notes to ourselves, and surprisingly came up with reality. There were three separate memories of one exact sentence reading "Lady of the Sands." Needless to say, we had our minds set on imagination and not on the totality of real events. Thereafter, a separate incident began to unfold for all of us.

The following details are of what we uncovered in its final stage (not knowing there were going to be stages) on May 13, 1991, pertaining to the November '89 Incident. These details had to be considered separate, which foolishly led to an unsuccessful but frenzied pursuit of Linda through the downtown Financial District on May 17th.

This is what we uncovered—
After the object splashed into the river with Linda in it, the third party wanted to swim out to find her. We stopped him and walked with him to the car. Instantaneously, we found ourselves sitting on the seashore somewhere, approximately 25' away from the sea. We didn't know how we arrived there, which was mind-boggling in itself. We looked straight ahead of us, and there we saw the girl we had seen in the light of the UFO earlier on. She was bending down by the sea alongside of those creatures. They were digging in the sand, using what looked like scooped shovels. They put their findings in square or rectangular metallic boxes or pails. Each pail and/or box, had a bright white light attached to it. They carried their boxes around with them by their handles.

The three beings didn't appear to speak. But we could hear a voice coming from the girl's direction (Linda) through the sounds of the surf. She spoke in a peculiar foreign tongue. Perhaps the sound of the ocean distorted what we were hearing. The others appeared to be listening, and then they continued to dig once again. We didn't know what they were digging up. We didn't even know how or why we were there sitting on the sand somewhere in the first place.

At one point in this event, which for us is the climax, all of them walked up to us as we sat there. The girl (Linda) held up what

*appeared to be a lifeless fish and said to us in a bold voice—
"LOOK AND SEE WHAT YOU HAVE DONE." Our first impulse
was to escape, but instead I asked her who she was. She didn't
answer. One of the beings replied, "Lady of the Sands." I can't
be sure which of them spoke because I didn't see lip movement,
but I could hear the direction it came from and it came from
one of those creatures.*

*Linda stood there bold as brass in her bare feet, with tears in
her eyes. She was angry. The lights from their boxes reflected
tiny silver particles that seemed to be stuck on Linda's hands
and feet. It was all very peculiar.*

*Soon after they turned on their heels (no toes, except for Lin-
da's) and they walked away towards the sea. It appeared as if
they were waiting for someone or something as they faced the
ocean.*

*Next, Richard and I were back by our car trying to pull the third
party off the roof of it. We didn't understand how he managed
to get up there without our knowledge. He didn't remember
climbing up there. After we helped him climb down from the
roof of the car we walked back to the riverfront and watched
over the river for about 45 minutes, to no avail. We walked
back to our car, entered it, started the engine, and drove off to
our original destination.*

What is your impression of Linda?

Can you understand what happened here?

*Up till now we have been hard at work questioning ourselves.
Why didn't we remember the seashore? These beings spoke to
us. How is it possible to forget that? Her sparkling hands and
feet were also memorable, but we didn't remember. We didn't
know how we arrived at that place. We couldn't all be dreaming
the same dream and remembering it at the same time. We can't
all be crazy with the same disorder, either. None of this makes
any logical sense, even after reading your book.*

Budd—something is wrong here!

*When we questioned Linda last April (we're sure you must be
aware of this) we had no memory of the seashore. However,
we had strange feelings about her at the time, and couldn't put*

our fingers on it. Perhaps these feelings stemmed from a memory we didn't remember at the time.

Consequently we now believe that Linda told an untruth when she stated that she wasn't one of them, when in fact we saw her working side by side with them on the beach that November 30th morning. We know she was withholding information from us and we didn't know why at the time. Perhaps she was frightened and didn't know what our intentions were if we found out that she was one of them. I'm determined to find out the truth, and I will.

The fact remains we still don't know who she is. We were led to believe that she is "The Lady of the Sands," whoever that is. Environmental, I suppose. On the other hand, it is possible that we're jumping the gun. We don't know if Linda remembers any of this herself. She may very well be telling the truth after all.

Whatever the case, we need to know who she is, to determine the questionable position we are presently in. If she proves to be who she appears to be, then we are safe. We will not allow her graceful appearance or supposed ancestral background to hamper our judgment anymore.

As for me, Linda is a pain in the rump. I dislike admitting that she has turned my emotions and part of my life into disorder. She can fly to the moon in her spacecraft and the distance wouldn't be far enough away as far as I'm concerned.

However, on occasion, without her knowledge I too have peered at her from a place of concealment. This foolish action stops the uncontrollable disbelief I feel. A bad day consists of overwhelming disbelief and denial. The thought of being taken hangs over my head. On a good day I think about having a heart-to-heart talk with Linda. I feel the need to keep her with me so that the bad days will seem half as bad.

But then I remember the fighting words we had with each other last April. This thought makes me come to realize that Linda would never consent to such a meeting, and such a planned meeting would be much too risky after all. However, we will meet, but we will meet spontaneously in the near future.

I can't understand what I'm feeling, Budd. Nor can I comprehend what we may have already experienced that November morning at the seashore. Our present fears of abduction may have happened. If so, it may very well happen again, won't it. You see, we read your book after we uncovered the seashore event.

The third party is left with a confused amazement. Apparently Linda brings a smile to his lips, especially after we questioned her last April. He couldn't get over the fact that she keeps her mischievous temperament so well hidden beneath her graceful self. She gives him a keen satisfaction. He said—"Yes, she is very much alive and thrashing about. She is absolutely and pleasantly real. We'll soon find out who she is."

He can't see Linda as often as he would like to. Richard seems to be the only one of us who believes that Linda is who she appears to be. He doesn't care if she worked alongside those creatures on the beach. He believes that there may have been unforeseen circumstances involved. He has concluded that we don't know enough about the UFO subject. Therefore we shouldn't make judgments. Richard has a good point, but he always has something good to say in Linda's behalf.

Linda says she isn't different. Budd, she is different, and I'm going to find out the difference. Please, if you can, prepare Linda for a visit from us. I don't want her running off again because I will catch her, and that will frighten her more. Linda won't let anyone near her and we are to blame.

We tried to talk with her a couple of times this summer, but we don't know if she was aware that it was us. She has the talent of disappearing in a crowd each time. She will not run too far if I have anything to do with it. However, I don't want her frightened. This is a situation we must complete for security reasons.

We feel the need to stay in contact with you because you are the only one who is able to get word to Linda. Also, your open-mindedness (although we have never met) gives us temporary relief in this hopeless situation.

Please stop trying to find us or else we will cut all contact with you. If you have a message for us, please give it to Linda. I'll be seeing her soon.

Linda told us to "LOOK AND SEE WHAT WE HAVE DONE" and so we have seen what we have done to her. We're sorry.

Please tell her, we honestly didn't kill that fish. Thank you,
Budd—

Danny

Sitting at the cluttered desk in my New York studio, I read Dan's amazing letter over and over. Had this bizarre series of events actually taken place? Had two security agents and a very important, internationally known political figure actually been abducted that night along with Linda? Had she somehow failed to recall, even under hypnosis, a central event of the November 30 scenario? Was it possible that she had somehow been temporarily "taken over" by the UFO occupants and used involuntarily as a symbol of alien ecological concern?

As I weighed the credibility of Dan's letter, I considered the possibility that Linda may indeed have been unable to remember this part of her experience at the time of her first hypnosis session. Like most of my colleagues, I've always felt that even with the careful, probing use of hypnotic regression, some details and incidents of any abduction account may elude recollection—especially the first time around. Many abductees also believe that at some time during their captivity they have received "instruction," and yet the nature of what the aliens taught them simply cannot be recalled. If that is true, then, selectively, some information or the memory of particular details can be effectively blocked—repressed—by the UFO occupants. In any case, it was imperative to put the issue to the test and to review with Linda the events of November 30. Perhaps with care and patience some more information might be shaken loose that would either confirm or contradict Dan's letter.

If his account can be trusted (and so far there was no evidence to suggest that it couldn't), it points to a startling possibility: On the morning of November 30, 1989, Linda Cortile was apparently a temporary and involuntary participant in an attempt to convey to a major political leader a benign alien concern with earth's ecology.

In this interpretation, one can deduce a two-pronged "message" from the UFO occupants' demonstration. First, because Richard, Dan, Linda, and the third man were so effortlessly abducted from New York City, they were made to see the omnipotence of alien technology. Second, through their use of Linda as the ecologically concerned "Lady of the Sands," these witnesses were left with the impression that the UFO occupants' purpose on earth is selfless and caring, focused, it would seem, on the health and well-being of our planet. If the first part of the "message" is hard to doubt, the second is obviously debatable. Granted the supposition that ecological concern is, indeed, what the Lady of the Sands was supposed to convey, is this concern the true alien motive or is its appearance yet another, and in this case a very major, deception? The precedents for each of these interpretations are extremely important, and I shall return to them later.

At the time, I decided that there were certain things I must do to test the accuracy of Dan's account. First, I would not tell Linda about the Lady of the Sands section of his letter, or say anything to suggest that the three men had also been abducted on November 30. Next, I would propose that we try another hypnosis session on the events of that night. I would explain to Linda that we should go over it one more time just to see if there was anything we missed before, some previously unremembered detail that could help us identify Richard and Dan. Perhaps, I hinted, she had actually seen their car as she floated in the bluish white light. Considering the success we had had in using hypnosis to aid her recollection of the license plate numbers on April 30, I knew she would try again.

For the moment, in order to analyze the meaning of Dan's letter as carefully as possible, I decided to break its contents down into discrete bits of data and see what kind of light each shed on the case. Taking these morsels of information in sequence, the first mystery the letter explained was the motive for the agents' pursuit of Linda on May 17, only eighteen days after her earlier forced interrogation. Their recently recovered memories of the beach scene, coupled with their assumption that Linda was at least partly alien, gave them reason enough to want to question her further. The central issues would undoubtedly have been what *she* remembered about that scene, and whether she was or was not a "half-breed."

The next thing to emerge was an important cluster of corroborative detail about the tools Linda and the aliens used to dig sand on the beach—the scooped shovels and the illuminated rectangular boxes or pails. I was familiar with just such devices from cases I had investigated earlier: the North Hudson Park landing in New Jersey and the 1973 Michael Bershad abduction in Maryland.[1] In both instances, small, spoonlike shovels and boxes with handles were described. Similarly, other odd work lights had turned up in several as yet unpublicized "digging" cases.

One of the most eerie correspondences between Dan's letter and information known only to Linda and me was the fact that she spoke in what seemed to be the aliens' language. I thought back to the hypnotic session I had conducted in early December 1989, only a few days after the original incident. At that time Linda recalled speaking to the aliens in phrases that sounded, phonetically, like NOBBYEGG and NO KAVE. After the session ended she had been very upset by the idea that she apparently knew at least a few words of the UFO occupants' language. She worried that she knew even more, and that hypnosis might be the only way she could remember. It did not please her to think that her unconscious mind might have been systematically—and involuntarily—coached and instructed by the aliens throughout the many years of their encroachment upon her life.

One of the aspects of any UFO report that investigators have long been concerned with is the appearance—of lack of it—of what has come to be known as "the soda pop factor." This homely term applies to the kind of simple, precise, quotidian detail that anchors an otherwise bizarre and unbelievable account into the weave of everyday reality. It is the kind of vivid yet gratuitous observation that neither advances the story nor contains seductive or threatening overtones. Instead, because of their emotional neutrality, "soda pop" details suggest that the experience was tangible and observed rather than an exotic fantasy or invention. In this case I was struck by Dan's description of the effect of the alien lights on Linda's obviously wet and sand-spotted hands and feet. He referred to the look of "tiny silver particles" (mica?) clinging to her, and later he mentioned her "sparkling hands and feet." These graphic visual details are exactly what one would expect from someone watching a barefoot woman digging at night in moist sand, illuminated by a collection of cold, white lights.

Another extremely telling detail has to do with Dan's description of the aliens' feet; apparently they have no toes. I immediately thought of the agents' earlier questioning of Linda in their car and their peculiar order that she remove her shoes and socks so that they could study her feet. At the time it made no sense, but now, considering their suspicions about her possible alien identity, the demand seemed plausible. Their distinct ambivalence could be explained by the fact that back in April, neither Dan nor Richard *consciously* remembered the beach scene. "We had strange feelings about her at the time," Dan wrote, "and couldn't put our fingers on it. Perhaps these feelings [as well as their need to examine Linda's feet] stemmed from a memory we didn't remember at the time." In other words, an intuitive prompting, a "feeling," the source of which they did not consciously understand.

Two of the most bizarre details in Dan's letter had to do with the third man. The first—before any of the men had recalled the episode on the beach—was his desire to swim out into the East River to rescue Linda, an utterly useless and extremely dangerous undertaking. What could he have been thinking? The UFO had plunged into the river and disappeared into the unbearably cold water. How did he imagine he could possibly rescue her? The only plausible explanation for his irrational behavior came from Dan's previous letter, the one in which he first told me about the existence of the third man. When the three saw the UFO go into the East River, he wrote, the third man had become "hysterical," in this context, quite an understatement.

The other bizarre detail involving the third man had to do with the fact that when he, Richard, and Dan were brought back after their unremembered abduction that night, the third man found himself sitting on the roof of the car! Was this just an alien mistake or was it deliberate? Did the UFO occupants understand that he was in a truly irrational state and so made it more difficult for him to rush the fifty feet or so from the car to the water's edge? Since Richard and Dan had to help him down, they obviously had both the time and the physical proximity to prevent him from risking his life. That much, at least, is certain, but it is hard to know whether the aliens were being subtly protective or merely careless.

One of the most significant and ominous details in Dan's letter is his stated suspicion that Linda is "one of them"—alien or part alien, and therefore a potential enemy. "If she proves to be who she appears to be [human], then we are safe," he wrote, the unstated corollary being that if she is even part alien, then she is dangerous: "The thought of being taken hangs over my head."

Dan's very first letter to me spelled out the extent of his fear of the UFO occupants. "I sleep with a sledgehammer by my side . . . my pistol is beside my bed . . . if they can take Linda, they can find me and take me." Even then he was suspicious of Linda: "I keep asking myself, 'Who is she? Is she one of them?' " What was even worse, that early letter revealed a deepening and potentially dangerous paranoia: "I let myself go, Mr. Hopkins. I shower, but I just don't care about my appearance. I haven't shaven in a long time. My nights are sleepless . . . my fellow workers are whispering behind my back, I can feel it."

In this current letter Dan implies that he can prove Linda is a liar because "when she stated that she wasn't one of them . . . we saw her working side by side with them . . . she was withholding information from us . . . perhaps she was frightened and didn't know what our intentions were if we found out that she was one of them." I found the threat implied by that last sentence to be distinctly unsettling. What were Dan's intentions? What would he do if he decided that she was "one of them"?

The volatility of his emotions was clear from these contradictory statements about Linda: "[She] is a pain in the rump . . . she can fly to the moon in her spacecraft and the distance wouldn't be far enough away," and then, a moment later, "I feel the need to keep her with me so that the bad days will seem half as bad." Though all of his comments were ominous, I was most disturbed by this last remark. Was he actually thinking of seizing Linda and taking her away permanently, "so that the bad days will seem half as bad"?

Dan's underlying anger is revealed in what can only be seen as a literal, unambiguous threat: ". . . Prepare Linda for a visit from us," he warned me. "*I* will catch her . . . she will not run far if I have anything to do with it . . . she *is* different and I'm going to find out the difference" [his emphasis].

By contrast, Dan's depiction of his partner's attitude toward Linda is distinctly benign. This very different opinion coincides with Linda's own reaction from the moment she first met Richard. She sensed that he was more caring, more gentle, and definitely less menacing than Dan.

Equally interesting is Dan's version of the third man's viewpoint: "Linda brings a smile to his face, especially after we questioned her last April . . . she gives him a keen satisfaction . . . 'She is absolutely and pleasantly real.' " I took this to be a reference to Linda's spirited struggle against Richard and Dan during her forced interrogation. She had punched Richard in the neck, zapped him with her stun gun, and at one point she kicked Dan in the back of the head as he sat in the driver's seat. All of this from a small, slender woman the third man described as graceful. He regretted that "he can't see Linda as often as he would like to."

The three attitudes revealed in this letter are in fascinating contrast to one another. Whereas the third man is warmly avuncular and amused by Linda's vitality, Richard feels the need to defend her and even to make excuses for her cooperation with the aliens. His feelings are distinctly more personal and affectionate while, as we have seen, Dan harbors a disturbing amount of fear and hostility toward her. I realized with some relief that neither Richard nor the third man exhibited any of the paranoid tendencies that made Dan seem increasingly dangerous and unpredictable.

Perhaps the most enigmatic comment in the letter is Dan's remark that "this is a situation we must complete for security reasons." What, I thought, is the "this" he's referring to? In context it would seem to imply the question of Linda's possible half-alien identity, but that is far from certain. How could her identity constitute an official issue? Was the security national in scope or was Dan only referring to his own personal sense of safety? Was he simply using a scare phrase—national security—to intimidate me and, by extension, Linda? And what was it, exactly, that had to be "completed"? It would be many months before I was to discover the true meaning of this remark, but for now I had no opportunity to explore it.

A final detail in Dan's letter has to do with his warning to me: "Please stop trying to find us or else we will cut all contact with you." Someone (perhaps several) among the people I contacted during my search for the agents had passed the word that I was trying to locate them. Though I suspected the director of security for the mission that owned the Rolls-Royce, there could have been others, too. For some reason I felt better knowing that my efforts, and Linda's, had not been entirely in vain, and that our search had at least made Richard and Dan a little nervous. I was also pleased that Dan appreciated my "open-mindedness," as he put it, and that it gave him temporary relief from what he called "this hopeless situation." It was a phrase I cannot imagine either Richard or the third man using to describe their complex predicament.

We were all involved in a strange six-sided relationship. On one side were the UFO occupants with their as yet unknown agenda. Next were the four people whom they had apparently abducted: Linda, Richard, Dan, and the third man, each with a different take on the aliens and with a variety of attitudes toward one another. And last, there was I, the investigator, struggling to make sense of it all, working to protect Linda, hoping to defuse Dan's irrational wrath, and striving to gain the trust of Richard and the third man. I wanted nothing more than that they might finally contact me and describe publicly what they had seen, particularly the third man because of his worldwide prestige.

My next task was to contact Linda and set up a hypnosis session to review the events of November 30, 1989. I told her that I had received another letter from Dan containing an apology for the May 17 downtown chase. But I also read the few final sentences that dealt with Dan's threat to abduct her yet again for further questioning: "I will catch her . . . she will not run too far if I have anything to do with it." I knew that this kind of warning would hit home, making her even less likely to take unnecessary risks.

As I expected, Linda was quite willing to try hypnosis once again to explore her nearly two-year-old abduction. On Saturday, September 21, only three days after I received Dan's letter, she came to my studio. We had a relaxed, informal conversation about the process we were about to begin, which I described as a fishing expedition that could easily fail to yield a single new detail. With her expectations effectively lowered, she understood this session to be a casual but necessary experiment.

After I completed the induction we began at the moment Linda felt herself outside her apartment building, hovering twelve stories off the ground in the intense bluish white light.

L: I can't see anything but the light. I'm afraid I'm going to fall down. I can't see anything. I know that I'm outside but I can't see anything but the light. I know I'm outside my window . . . I feel stable . . . I feel as though I might be standing on something. . . .

Earlier I had deliberately planted the suggestion in Linda's mind that she might be able to see Dan and Richard's car and that she could possibly describe it. The idea was not taken up. Just as before, she can see nothing around her but the light, not even the three aliens who hovered above and below her. Her vision is fixed straight ahead. Linda, as I had come to know, was not in the least suggestible.

She goes on to describe being pulled up into the craft, then being stretched out on a table with no clothes on. Four small gray figures gather near her and begin the series of physical procedures she had described back in 1989. She repeats the same few alien words and expresses the same fear when she sees the huge syringe, "like a turkey baster." Then she moves ahead, to the part of the scenario I was most curious about.

L: . . . The one that examined my back pulled me up and helped me off the table. He gave me back my nightgown.

B: Where is your nightgown?

L: It could have been on the floor. Could have been resting on some-thing, but he bent down to pick it up. Then he gave it to me. I put it on. I felt cold and I was able to move, and I said to myself, is it possible that they can read my mind? I wanted to go home so bad, and did they take my husband and did they take my children? I just want to know if they're safe. I told 'em I want to go home. And he helped me down from the table, and he—we—walked a little ways, and it was an entrance. [Pause] And then there was like a small hall, and then there was a door. [Long pause] He's gonna take me home . . . I'm gonna go home now. That's what he's going to do. He must be able to read my mind. . . .

B: Let's go through the door, Linda. You may see almost anything. We don't know what you're going to see. We could see your room, we could see the apartment building, we could see a whole other scene. When I count to three you're going to pass through the door. [Counts slowly up to three]

L: [Very frightened] I'm not home! I thought I was going to go home!

B: We know you do go home eventually, Linda. Where are you now?

L: The one that escorted me to the door didn't go through the door with me. We walked to the entrance door and he stayed behind . . . and he was kinder than the others.

B: And where are you when you go through the door?

L: It's windy and *cold.* And I walk . . . it's a strange door. There's no door. The door, the door opened out and down [whispering], out and down.

B: Like steps? Like airplanes have? Or is it different than that?

L: A little different. There are no steps. They're lines . . . more like coming off a ship, only there are lines so you don't slide.

B: You said it's windy. Look around. Where are you?

L: I'm standing on this . . . door, and I see the three . . . they're back again [upset] . . . they're beckoning me to come down. So I walk down, but it's cold and it's windy . . . and they're holding something. They have lights. They have . . . I don't know what that is. I get down there and . . . it's noisy. It sounds like a [makes the sound: *shoosh . . . shoosh*]. I can't make that out. What can that possibly be? The surface under me, it's wet. It's very cold and wet. God, where am I? Then I walk out with them [pause] and I hurt my foot, the bottom of my foot. I feel as though I was cut . . . and I turn around—[quiet gasp] I know where I was . . . [frightened] I wasn't going home. What am I doing there?

B: Where are you?

L: I don't know where I am, but I'm at a beach. A beach. [Long pause] One of them hands me . . . [whispers] a box. He gives me the box and a light goes on. [With sudden recognition] Oh, I've done this before! I'm not feeling so bad. Oh, yes, yes, I see, now they're giving me the scoop. Yes, and know what that is? It's a pail. I've done this before. I remember. They're walking along the beach . . . I must have hurt my foot on a seashell, a broken seashell. Yes, it's very cold but I have to go with them. It's important. We have to dig. We have to find soil samples. We have to see if we can find a trace of basaltic lavas.

B: A what?

L: A mineral that's made from . . . [inaudible] rock formations. If we can find traces of that, then they'll know . . . why the sea creatures are dying. So we are going to try to find some samples of the minerals.

B: Could you describe this little scoop to me . . . what it looks like? Just a little thing you hold in your hand?

L: Yes, it's almost like a spoon . . . no . . . it's almost like a ladle [pause] but deeper, and longer . . . sort of a teardrop shape. Comes to a point at the very end. And we use it to dig. And we need to get, to find some traces of basaltic lavas, and the reef limestone, some gray-wackes and shales. The crustaceans . . .

B: Crustaceans?

L: Yes, but they don't call them that. They feed on the shales. There's something wrong with the minerals. They aren't as pure as they used to be and our sealife are dying and we've got to find out what's polluting the minerals, we're going to understand why our sea crea-tures are dying, and we've been doing this for a long time. You know that? I've done this many times. Why don't I remember that? So, soon as we get those soil samples they're going to test them and they're going to tell everyone why our sea creatures are dying. Then we're going to have to stop what we're doing.

So we begin, and one of them wasn't digging right. One of them couldn't get the shovel in the sand. He was using a side motion.

B: When you say shovel, was that different than the ladle?

L: No, it's like a scoop, like a spoon. I'm going to call it a shovel. And he isn't using it right, and I'm telling him how to use it. Use the tip of it, and dig in and out. And so we—

B: Do you use English? Regular English?

L: No. I'm thinking it. And he knows, and that's what he does. And we just keep on digging and putting everything in these pails that have lights so we can see what we're doing. It's so dark and noisy . . . the ocean . . .

B: Now Linda, while this is going on, I want you to look around the beach. I want you to see if you can see any landmarks or anything. I know it's dark, but think of the things you might be able to see . . . a house somewhere, or people living near there. . . .

L: I see rocks. Lots of rocks. And I told them, look at that. It's a dead little fish. How did that happen? So I picked it up and I looked at it and it made me feel so sad and angry. And one of the beings beckoned to me and said, "Let's sample the sand." So then we walk toward the shore with our pails, and I'm carrying this poor creature, and I'm so angry. And there are these, yeah, three people sitting on the sand. It's so cold. And they're watching us. And so we walk up to them, the four of us, and I look at them. I can see them, the lights on the pails, I can see them and they're all male. And I feel this overwhelming sense of sadness and anger. Then I pick up the bluefish and it's their fault, people like them that kill our sea creatures. And one of them wants to move away from me. And I looked at them and I said, "Look what you've done [sadly]. Look at this creature now." And one of them just backs off, just wants to back off. And one of them says to me, he asks a question. I can't remember the question. I think he wanted to know who I was. What's the point? Had I answered him he wouldn't have known who I was anyway. I've never seen him before. [Long pause] And then I heard something after that. One of the beings told him who I was. I felt it was pointless because—

B: Does he give your name? What does he say?

L: It wasn't a name, it had something to do with . . . sand. [Pause] Sand.

B: Does he say your name is "Sand"?

L: No. No, it was a sentence. It was a title . . . which is silly because I know who I am.

B: What's the title? Does he say Mrs. Sand?

L: No, I heard him, I heard him in my head . . . um . . . girl . . . woman. [Long pause] Woman? Lady? [Long pause] Lady? I don't understand it. Lady? And the next thing I heard was "sands" and then we turned around and walked away from those three people. They were pathetic.

B: Let's look back at these three people before you walk away. You have enough light to see them from the pails. . . . You said they're sitting on the sand?

L: Yes.

B: How are they dressed? Pajamas on?

L: No. I'd never dress that way if I were a man, to go to the beach. They're all dressed up. They're all wearing suits. Nice suits. They look very expensive.

B: Probably hard to tell the color at night . . .

L: Oh, those lights [on the pails] were very white—bright and white— and one—the older man—there was an older man—his suit looked as though it was a charcoal gray suit. He was older. He looks familiar to me but I don't know from where . . . where I would have known him from.

At this point I began to inquire about his appearance: the color of his hair, if he had a mustache, the shape of his face, whether he wore glasses, his approximate age, and so on. (In the interest of preserving his anonymity I will not repeat her answers; she was able, finally, to make a tentative identification.) Then I asked Linda to tell me what kind of expression he had on his face. Her answer was terse and predictable: "I think that he was upset."

I moved on to a series of questions about the other two men.

L: Okay . . . yeah . . . these men are . . . you can see they're big men . . . they're long . . . [extended pause, then a very frightened voice] . . . Oh! . . . I know who one of them is. Oh! I know who that is. [Very upset] I can tell from the light. I can see that . . . [whispering] he has red hair . . . but not carrot-top hair. He has small features [continuing fear in her voice] and the other one has dark hair. I know who they are. [Very upset] I don't know what they're doing there. I see Richard and I see Dan. Looking at them now . . . I know I'm here [in my studio in September 1991]. At the time I didn't know who they were. But I know where I am now . . . presently. I'm here, and I can recognize them.

B: You mean you know you're here in my studio with me?

L: Yes.

At this point I decided to end what had been a harrowing session for Linda, so after a few minutes of positive posthypnotic suggestions, I brought her out of the trance state. In accordance with my plan I gave her absolutely no hint that I was aware of the things she had remembered. I professed surprise and amazement, and began my usual posthypnotic debriefing. When I questioned her under hypnosis about the appearance of the older man on the beach, she had said that he resembled pictures she'd seen of a certain political figure. She told me his name. It was the same well-known individual who, months ago, I had come to believe was indeed the third man. Since I had discussed this hypothesis with Linda at that time, the surprise was not her identification but his presence on the beach.

But in other things Linda recalled and in the way she expressed her feelings and observations there were many dazzling surprises. First, of course, there was the extraordinary and highly detailed consonance between Dan's letter and Linda's recollection of her seaside experience. But equally fascinating to me was the way that the fear and hesitancy she felt when she first left the craft shifted to a new and enthusiastic role when she began to work side by side with the UFO occupants. It happened in the blink of an eye. Her querulous and uneasy "What am I doing here?" suddenly yields to a nearly triumphant "I've done this before! I remember!" One moment she is a cold and frightened abductee with an injured foot, and a second later, "I'm not feeling so bad . . . We need to dig!" It would seem that this nearly instantaneous change marked the end of normal human autonomy and the beginning of full-fledged alien subservience. In this thankfully short-lived period one can easily see why Dan became convinced that she was at least part alien.

In the conversation that followed, I tried to see what connections there might be between the Linda I knew and the alien-oriented automaton she seemed to have temporarily become. "Are you involved in the animal rights movement?" I asked her, thinking about her grief over the dead bluefish. "Do you identify with the plight of animals?"

"I care for animals," she said, "but I'm not a fanatic about it. I eat meat. I own a fur coat and I like to wear it. And I'm afraid of dogs."

I tried another tack. "When you buy fish to cook for dinner, do you feel easy about cleaning it and preparing it?"

"To tell the truth," she replied, "I always have the man at the fish store clean and fillet it. I really don't like to handle fish. I can't imagine picking up a dead fish on a beach."

I asked about her knowledge of minerals—basaltic lavas, reef limestone, and the other materials she had mentioned. "You know, Budd, I flunked science in high school. I don't know how I know about these things. But I know I've done it before. I've dug before." And so the tantalizing mystery remained unresolved. Though Linda repudiated the aliens and was angry at how they had treated her over the years, she still clung to the idea that sea creatures were dying because of what we humans were doing to the environment. Implicitly, she still defended her "alien" work.

And there was the troubling issue of Linda's use of an apparent alien language. It was almost as if the UFO occupants allow her to be herself most of the time: a typical, somewhat squeamish, meat-eating, fur-wearing New York woman who loves to shop and nurtures her children and fights any unwanted intrusions into their lives. And yet it seems that whenever they need her, the aliens can throw a mental switch, as it were, transforming her into a fire-breathing environmentalist, railing at her fellow human beings, waving dead fish and effortlessly speaking an alien language.

The UFO occupants' seeming ability to control the recall of their human abductees has long fascinated me. It appears at times to be absolutely precise, as if the aliens were expert anesthesiologists, able to erase any time period they choose and "spontaneously" to reinstate memories on command. In this case, recollection of the beach scene was blocked for Linda and the three men for many months, even though she had undergone hypnosis on the events of that night. Then, somehow, Dan, Richard, and the third man are allowed to "spontaneously" recall the Lady of the Sands. A letter is sent to me about their recollections, I bring Linda in for another hypnosis session, and she, too, recalls the scene. There is an unsettling—and unearthly—precision in all of this.

After Linda left my studio late that afternoon to go home, I sat quietly by myself with a warming, reassuring cup of coffee in my hand, trying to absorb the impact of the day's revelations. Until this moment I had not fully realized the international significance of the events of November 30, 1989. For the first time in my experience the UFO occupants were apparently trying to influence earthly politics at an extraordinarily high level. A political leader of international stature and importance had been abducted and shown a scene designed to demonstrate to him the aliens' selfless interest in the problems of pollution on earth. They had come, their behavior seemed to imply, not to take anything from us but rather to contribute to the well-being of the planet. And Linda Cortile, personally innocent of any conscious ecological concerns, had been used as their star in an eerie and utterly theatrical performance.

But there was another disturbing new detail in this case. Until Linda's hypnosis session I had never heard of an abductee being temporarily "taken over" by the UFO occupants and behaving as if he or she were in complete sympathy with the aliens, wholly accepting their goals and techniques. When, during her hypnosis, I became aware of Linda's full cooperation in the digging operation and her contempt for her three fellow humans, I was dismayed. However, one case does not a pattern make, so I decided to put this new detail on a mental back shelf and to wait to see if any similar cases would eventually turn up.

Sadly, they have. Linda Cortile's alien subservience was merely the first of what I now regard as a previously overlooked feature in at least some abduction cases. To date, four other people I have worked with have separately recalled being used by the UFO occupants within their ship to shepherd and control other abductees, as if they had no choice and were willingly acting as allies of their captors. Three of the abductees describe themselves during these moments as wearing smooth, blue, form-fitting, one-piece garments with no noticeable fasteners, garments they do not remember putting on or taking off.[2] All felt both a deep-seated anger and a sense of profound humiliation after their experiences, in which they realized their wills had somehow been overridden. All hated the fact that they had been used as a kind of involuntary fifth column to create a false impression in other frightened abductees.

The fact that Linda was the first to report this hitherto unknown facet of the abduction phenomenon, something that has since been replicated by others around the country, is yet another sign of her credibility and the importance of her case.

For my part, there were several immediate steps to be taken in this ever expanding investigation. First, I needed to contact a geologist to gather information about basaltic lavas, reef limestone, and the other minerals Linda had talked about.

Second, and more immediately important, I had to plan the way I would tell Linda about Dan's letter. My ace in the hole was the fact that she had no idea the three men also recalled the scene at the beach. For that reason it was essential to record the moment she first heard Dan's account. Her reactions, caught on videotape, would allow anyone—skeptic and informed investigator alike—to see and judge for themselves the authenticity of her emotion.

I decided to invite two neutral witnesses—a psychologist and a historian—to hear Linda's and my narration of the case from the very beginning, thereby creating a formal, visual record. All the early letters and tapes would be presented, the two witnesses could ask whatever they wished, and an objective atmosphere would be maintained. What neither Linda nor the witnesses would know, however, was that after she described *her* recollections of the beach scene, I would read

Dan's letter while the camera captured her reactions in a close-up. This seemed to me the best way to record for posterity a crucial moment in the case. It would provide a powerful visual vindication of Linda's authenticity.

Before I went to bed, Linda called me once more to tell me she had remembered the full title the alien used to describe her. "I knew it had 'sands' in it, and 'lady,' " she told me. "The whole name was 'Lady of the Sands.' I don't know what that means, but that's what the being said my name was." That phrase, of course, was the clue that brought Dan, Richard, and the third man together to share their recollections, the small leak that grew to a dramatic flood of memory.

Linda Hears Dan's Letter

At 7:00 P.M. on Tuesday evening, October 8, five of us gathered in my apartment for a review of the case thus far. Besides Linda, myself, and "Frank," a friend of mine who had volunteered to work the video camera, there were the two guest observers, historian Charles Strozier and psychotherapist Gibbs Williams. Chuck Strozier is a highly intelligent and perceptive writer and teacher, and though I didn't know him well, he had, in the past, expressed some mild curiosity about my work on the UFO phenomenon. I had never met psychotherapist Gibbs Williams before this October evening, though two friends of mine, psychologist Carol Beauvais and her husband David, a psychotherapist, had suggested several times that I call Mr. Williams, a colleague of theirs who they believed would be interested in hearing about the UFO phenomenon. When I finally spoke to him and explained who I was and what I wanted, he agreed—with perhaps a hint of wariness—to come to the meeting.

In describing the content of the proposed gathering, I informed the two men that I was working on an extremely important and unusual UFO encounter, a *witnessed* abduction that involved a major political figure. I explained that the main participant and I would go over the details of the report sequentially, and that the two observers would be encouraged to ask any questions they wished. The purpose of the meeting, I told them, was to create on videotape an accurate, chronological record of the case before fair-minded, objective witnesses. With a historian and a psychotherapist in attendance, I felt I had the relevant disciplines covered.

Of course, what neither they nor Linda knew was my arrangement with Frank, the cameraman—the hidden reason for the gathering. After I played the audiotape of Linda's "Lady of the Sands" hypnosis session, Frank was to keep her in a tight close-up as I read to her, for the first time, Dan's "Lady of the Sands" letter. Her spontaneous reactions would become part of the permanent record.

Frank arrived a bit before the appointed time to set up his tripod and camera, and Linda, Chuck Strozier, and Gibbs Williams came shortly after. After introductions were made, Linda and I sat side by side on the couch, while Chuck and Gibbs took chairs somewhat to our right. Frank reported that the camera angles and voice levels were fine, and so the meeting began. The first thing I asked of Linda was that she tell the two guests why she had originally decided to contact me in April 1989, after having read only a few pages of *Intruders*. Next, she recounted what she had recalled initially about the events of November 30, 1989. Chuck Strozier was the quieter of the two observers, making a few perceptive, clarifying comments, while Gibbs did not hesitate to ask probing questions. Linda spoke evenly and precisely, but when she described her fear on November 30 that the aliens might harm her children, her barely controlled emotion was obvious to us all.

The pattern of our presentation was as follows: I would read a letter I had received from Richard or Dan, Linda would explain her reactions or her involvement in the incident, and then I would try to put things into perspective. Certain important events, such as her seizure and forced interrogation by the two agents, were discussed at length. The camera, of course, was recording our testimony as well as Chuck's and Gibbs's questions and comments.

After nearly two hours we arrived at the recorded hypnosis session in which Linda recalled the beach scene. I placed the audiocassette in my tape machine and we all listened. It was, I believe, the first time I had played one of Linda's regression tapes in her presence, and as she heard herself describing, in the slow, calm voice of hypnosis, the search for the minerals and, moments later, the three men sitting on the sand, she shifted a bit uneasily and took out a cigarette. Clearly, she had not yet had time to digest these unsettling new memories.

We had arrived at the critical moment—the reading of Dan's corroborative "Lady of the Sands" letter. I thought back to the time eight months before when I first told Linda of Richard's original letter, the triggering factor in this unnerving series of events. I remembered her shock and stunned disbelief when she heard that two law-enforcement officers had apparently seen her floating in midair twelve stories above the ground. No abductee ever wants to have an abduction experience absolutely confirmed by independent evidence. It is too final, too upsetting to have that last bit of hopeful skepticism shredded beyond repair.

I was therefore concerned about Linda's reaction this time, particularly since she would be receiving this unwelcome confirmation in the presence of three men besides myself, two of them total strangers, and since her responses would be recorded on videotape. I felt a great deal of guilt about what I was about to do. It could be said with truth that I was misleading Linda, deliberately exposing her emotions to an audience, and yet I felt that I had to create a public record. Anyone in the future who showed an interest in the case would naturally want to see how Linda reacted when she heard that Richard, Dan, and the third man all remembered exactly what she had recalled about the bizarre beach scene. Her response to that news was too important not to record.

And so I began to read the letter from the beginning. Linda took out another cigarette without having finished the previous one and lit it, giving her nervous hands something to do. When I read Dan's apology about the downtown chase—"we behaved in a bullish manner"—Linda showed clear but subtle traces of anger, moving her head from side to side slightly, as if to say "You never should have done what you did." When I arrived at the first crucial passage—the three men's collective memory of a single word, "sand"—her eyes widened for a shocked split second and her facial muscles went rigid. She gave a helpless, sidelong glance toward Chuck and Gibbs, and continued listening intently to my words.

An even more decisive moment came when I read that "There were three separate memories of one exact sentence reading 'Lady of the Sands.'" Again her eyes widened in shock. Almost unconsciously she lifted herself up nervously and repositioned herself on the couch. As if she could not believe what she had heard, she asked me, in a whisper, "Could you run that by me again?" At this point Gibbs interjected his own question: "Where were Dan, Richard, and the third man when they came up with this memory?" I explained that I didn't know their actual location, only that they had met together somewhere to discuss their respective flashback recollections.

Responding to Linda's request, I repeated Dan's key sentence about "the Lady of the Sands." She stared at me in stunned and silent disbelief, her mouth open wide. "Are they *aware*," she asked, "of what happened?" I replied that it would be explained in the rest of the letter. She sat back tensely and looked over at Gibbs and Chuck with an expression of helpless incredulity.

Dan's letter went on, mentioning a "separate incident which began to unfold for all of us," leading to an explanation: "These details had to be considered . . . which foolishly led to an unsuccessful but frenzied pursuit of Linda through the downtown Financial District on May 17th." Again, she seemed about to speak but merely stared at me in amazement.

As I read Dan's account of the three men suddenly finding themselves on the seashore, close to the water, her mouth again flew open in shock. As if her entire body was undergoing an involuntary reaction, she again lifted herself up and then sat back down on the sofa. At the description of Linda and "those creatures . . . digging in the sand, using what looked like scooped shovels," she closed her eyes and lowered her head, shaking it, as if to say, "No, no."

The letter went on to describe Linda speaking "in a peculiar tongue," an aspect of the encounter that had upset her from the first. Now, her eyes began to fill with tears. I continued reading and a few moments later she began to dab at her eyes with a tissue. At the sentence, "LOOK AND SEE WHAT YOU HAVE DONE," she gasped, lowered her head, and like a grieving child, bit down gently on her lower lip. The muscles of her chin tensed and I thought she was about to begin sobbing.

Throughout this unsettling episode we could see that Linda was working to rein herself in, trying desperately to control her emotions, as if to break down in front of Gibbs and Chuck and Frank and me would be unbearably humiliating. Days later, when I watched the videotape and saw Linda's face in close-up, the force of her internal struggle was vividly clear. The emotional reactions registered on the screen were both subtle and devastating—perhaps more devastating *because of* their subtlety.

But the saddest moment of all occurred when I read the part of the letter in which Dan accused Linda of being an alien—"one of them"—and of "having told an untruth." Her eyes brimmed with tears and her lips moved as if she were silently mouthing words of denial and hurt.

When Dan wrote that for him, "Linda is a pain in the rump . . . she can fly to the moon in her spaceship and the distance wouldn't be far enough away," she parted her lips and pressed her teeth together, lifting her chin to one side in a gesture of deep anger and resentment.

This was the only moment in the reading of the letter in which she responded with what seemed to be bitter outrage. When I read the part of the letter dealing with Richard's more benevolent and support-ive view of her, she blew her nose, sniffed, and nodded gently, like a child who, in the middle of a scolding, finds herself soothed by an uncle's few loving words.

At Dan's final threat—"She *is* different and I'm going to find out the difference . . . *I* will catch her"—Linda rolled her eyes back and sighed. It was the expression of long-suffering weariness brought about by repeated contact with an impossibly trying individual. But throughout the reading, Linda's typical reactions had been shock, sad-ness, and helpless disbelief. When it was over, she closed her eyes and sighed. Her mood and posture were those of profound resignation.

I put down the letter and there was a moment or two of silence before Linda spoke slowly, her thoughts obviously in a jumble, her voice flat and barely audible. "So they're aware of everything . . . that . . . [pointing to herself] . . . When they were there on the beach . . . They're aware of what we just heard on the tape . . . my hypnosis tape." And then with sudden animation, as if the unwelcome truth were finally clear, she exclaimed, "No *wonder* they think that I'm in cahoots . . ."

My experiment, if that's what it can be called, had been success-ful. A permanent record of Linda's reaction to the shock of confirma-tion was now available. No one need ever have to take my testimony or the testimony of Gibbs Williams or Chuck Strozier on faith. Die-hard skeptic and open-minded researcher alike could see for them-selves. Though what I had done might be thought of as the deception of an already traumatized abductee, I feel that ultimately—historically—the gain was worth the temporary sorrow and pain I had caused her.

All of us in the room that night had been moved by the under-stated power of Linda's response. Yet days later, when I watched the videotape, the force and reality of her emotion struck me even more as vividly authentic. In the tight close-ups her smallest gestures were fraught with barely controlled agitation. Many months later I showed the tape to a documentary filmmaker who knew little of the case but whose opinion I greatly respected. As she studied her face, she re-marked with empathetic sadness that Linda's reactions reminded her of those she had once seen in the haunted eyes of a trapped and help-less animal.

During the final wrap-up conversation that ended our meeting, Gibbs Williams asked about an allusion in Dan's letter to Linda's "supposed ancestral background." I explained to him that the remark had to do with a curious earlier incident that—if my interpretation were true—demonstrated the depth of Richard's and Dan's interest in the Cortile family. I had been aware of what lay behind this "ancestral" reference issue ever since the evening back in March when Linda first called to tell me about it.

She explained that when her older son Steven came home from school that afternoon, he casually mentioned that he had met a "bum" on the bus who asked him a lot of questions about his family. Sixteen-year-old Steven had been waiting as he always did at the bus stop closest to his school when he noticed a shabbily dressed man smelling of alcohol nearby. As the bus pulled up and stopped, the man followed Steven aboard and took a seat next to him. When he started talking to Steven, the boy, a street-wise New Yorker, got up and moved. The man also moved and again sat near him, though a few seats away. Before Steven could respond or move again, the man asked him where he went to school and what grade he was in. Though he was naturally hesitant to reply, Steven, an innately polite young man, answered him. "That's a good school," the man replied. "Your parents must think a lot of you to send you there." He went on to tell Steven that it was important to study hard and to make good grades, but then he began to ask more personal questions: "Do you do well in school? How do you get along with your parents? Do they treat you well?" As Steven related these questions to his mother, she asked if the man had seemed drunk when he spoke, or if he slurred his speech. No, said Steven, he didn't appear to be drunk; he just smelled of alcohol, and in fact he didn't really act like a bum.

Linda wanted to know what he looked like. He was tall and well built, Stephen said, with graying red hair. He was probably in his forties, and he seemed friendly—not threatening or weird like a wino. Thinking, now, that this "derelict" seemed suspiciously like Richard in disguise, Linda asked another question. Beyond the reek of alcohol, she wanted to know, did the man have the all-too-familiar sour smell of someone who hasn't bathed or changed his clothes for a long time? No, her son replied, there was just the smell of alcohol. There wasn't any body odor.

Steven said that as the man continued to ask what he considered overly personal questions about his family life, he became both puzzled and annoyed. But one final query seemed the strangest of all: "Is there anything unusual about your family?" the man had asked. Steven told his mother that he had been completely taken aback by the question and didn't know how to respond. What did the man mean by "unusual"? In any case, Steven wanted to end this uncomfortable dialogue, so he decided to answer in a way that would be both startling and final. He remembered something that he hoped might shut the man up. "Well," he told his questioner, "there is something unusual about us. My mother's family is descended from Joan of Arc." Apparently it worked. The man seemed so astonished by this answer that when Steven turned away to read one of his schoolbooks, the questioning ended. A stop or two later the big, redheaded man left the bus.

I informed Gibbs that when Linda told me about this strange incident, she had explained, with a slight air of embarrassment, that what Steven said was, in a sense, true. Linda's mother's family claimed descent from Saint Joan. Linda was quick to point out that she took no particular stock in the authenticity of this claim, and in the two and a half years I had known her I had never once heard her refer to her grandfather's alleged illustrious forebear.

If the man on the bus was merely a wino, then his questions about Steven's family seemed very peculiar. But if, as Linda suspected, he was Richard in a rather ineffective disguise, we had a further demonstration of the agents' profound interest in the Cortile family. How many other people had Dan and Richard questioned about Linda, her husband, and her sons? How extensive was their surveillance and how thorough their background checks? And most important, what was it they were trying to find out?

Toward the end of my videotaped meeting with Gibbs Williams and Chuck Strozier, one final question also required an explanation. It was Gibbs who felt that the third man's remarks about Linda, as quoted by Dan in his letter, seemed rather stilted and artificial: She gave him "a keen satisfaction," was "very much alive and thrashing about," and was "absolutely and pleasantly real."

I explained first that my research into the third man's background had revealed his long-term connection with the United Kingdom, suggesting that along the way he might easily have picked up a British way of phrasing things. An American "thrashes *around*," while a Brit "thrashes *about*," for example. There is the distinct possibility that Dan was quoting from letters the third man had written to him, since three of the sentences Dan cited he deliberately set apart by the use of quotation marks. Thus they may have seemed a bit stilted because they bore the more self-conscious and formal stamp of the written, rather than the spoken, word.

In the months ahead I was to notice other distinctly English phrasings in remarks that Dan and Richard ascribed to the third man.

And when, as the reader will learn, I finally received a letter from him, I noticed that it was composed in a style more typically British or European than American. The third man employed a vocabulary richer and more eloquent than that which either Richard or Dan characteristically used, and his phrasings were a bit more florid.

In contrast, the two American agents usually expressed themselves in a kind of simple, direct, police-report style, though Dan was more given than Richard to moments of impassioned writing. And there were other, physical differences among the communications of the three men, having to do with their choices of stationery, typewriters or printers, and layout.

For me, it was inescapable that Richard, Dan, and the third man were three distinct personalities, with varying degrees of fear, insight, and self-control. Two were younger and more military in their approach while the third was older, more worldly, and more sophisticated. One—Dan—was sunk in what seemed to be an ever deepening spiral of paranoid suspicion, while Richard's response to his partner's distrust of Linda was to give his support to her ever more openly. It would be only a few days after our October 8 videotaping that Richard and Dan, close friends and longtime professional partners, came into a dramatic and ultimately ruinous confrontation over Linda in what would be the most terrifying experience of her life.

C H A P T E R

11

The Long Island Kidnapping

At approximately 2:30 on the afternoon of October 15, 1991, while I was out on an errand, my wife received a frantic telephone call from Linda. She had been seized and badly roughed up by Dan. As she tried to tell April what had happened, the words tumbled out almost incoherently. Dan had taken her to a beach house on Long Island where she had been "dragged through the sand." She was, she said, "a mess . . . and Steve will be home with the kids any minute, and I don't want them to see me this way." April told her to drop everything and come over as soon as possible.

I walked into the apartment moments later, heard the news, and immediately went to the phone. But before I dialed Linda's number I set up my tape machine to record the conversation.

"Oh, Budd," she said through tears, "he grabbed me by Pier 17. He dragged me all over the beach. . . . There's a house there. I don't know whose house it is. My picture was on their desk—a picture of me kissing Johnny. It was awful. . . ."

I asked if she had been able to show Dan the photo of him she had been carrying as a kind of insurance policy. "Yes, I did, and he went nuts. He grabbed me by my shoulders and started to shake me until I was dizzy. And Budd, I was wired and he found it."

"You had a tape recorder with you?" I was amazed.

"Yes. Joseph gave me this tiny little tape recorder and I've been wiring myself every day, just in case. And I have this son of a bitch on tape. I don't have much of it because he found it."

When Linda arrived, her eyes wide with remembered fear, she was carrying a plastic shopping bag, which she put on the floor next to the couch. I was furious that Dan had put her through yet another ordeal, and with my tape recorder running she began her fresh but fragmented account.

She had started off about 11:00 A.M. to do a little shopping for her sons at The Gap, a clothing store at Pier 17 (the South Street Seaport). As she walked down South Street she noticed Dan ahead of her, jogging in place, though he abruptly stopped when he saw her. "He stood still, and I stood still," she told me. "I'm saying to myself, 'If I run he's going to chase me. I'm going to end up wherever he wants me to end up.' I'm not that fast. I'm a smoker. I can't run that far without thinking I'm going to collapse. . . .

"So what I did is, I took one step, and then stood still. . . . And he took one step forward. Then I saw him motion to someone across the street. . . . And it was, I'm almost sure, the guy Joseph and I had seen weeks ago, when I saw the van. . . . So I started to run. And I turned around to look and [Dan] was coming. He started to chase me.

"So I kept running and running and then . . . my big mistake. I turned around to see where he was and he wasn't there. And I'm saying to myself, 'Where the hell did he go?' And as I'm looking behind and I see he isn't there, I ran right into him. He grabbed me, like that. Made me run along with him. You could hear his footsteps, like a giant. He made me run with him and then he threw me right in the car. I can't believe how fast this happened."

I asked if there was anyone nearby who might have seen Dan pursuing her. "People. Sure," Linda answered. "They don't care. They didn't care when they took me that time by the Pathmark and, boy, did I fight like hell. They don't care. They don't want to get involved."

I knew that it was important to try and get whatever details I could while they were fresh in Linda's mind—especially details that might help us locate Dan and Richard. I asked about Dan's car in which, I later realized, she had spent at least three hours. Dan had taken her on the long drive from Pier 17 to a house on eastern Long Island, and later that afternoon Richard had brought her back in the same vehicle.

"It was a sports car, that I can tell you. I don't know what kind of car it was. It was red. On the hood . . . in the front, was a cat. It could have been a lioness. It could have been a cougar. A jaguar . . .

He threw me in, and my mind is going a hundred miles an hour. And he gets in." She uttered her next sentence in a whisper: "Nasty bastard that he is. So I sat there and I said to him, 'You're never going to do this to me again. You've got to come forward. You've got to speak to Budd Hopkins or leave us alone.' You know, what the hell is the point in this? They're sending you [B.H.] letters and they don't want to come forward. They're chasing me around scaring the hell out of me. What's the point?"

The next thing that happened as Linda sat, a captive, in Dan's small car, was extremely unnerving: "All of a sudden he whispered. It was weird. It reminded me of that movie, 'Rosebud' [the final murmured name in *Citizen Kane*]. 'Come here, half-breed.' He called me a half-breed! Then he started to kiss me all over my face." Once more she became very upset and began to cry. "I started to yell and scream. I went for the door. I got it open, but he pulled it closed and he wouldn't let me go. . . . I told him, 'You know you really need help. You need a lot of help.' "

Her hand shaking, Linda took a sip of coffee before resuming her account. "Then he took out this contraption. I'd say it was about the size of my Mace, maybe a little longer. I asked him what it was, and he said it was a scanner, whatever the hell that is. At the time I didn't know. Now I do. . . . The thing beeped, and when it beeped he grabbed my purse, the green purse. He took out my Mace, my stun gun, and then he started to scan me. I had the tape recorder right here in the top pocket of my blazer. And he said to me, 'You're wired?' which scared the hell out of me. He was angry. And what am I going to say? I said, 'No, no.' And there he had this thing in his hand and I was holding the other end . . . the microphone."

Linda told me that she hadn't known whether her recorder was in fact switched on because she's so farsighted that she couldn't read the on/off button without her glasses. She begged Dan to give her back the tape machine, saying that it belonged to a friend and she had to return it. Apparently feeling agreeable for a moment, he removed the little cassette, put it into his jacket pocket, and handed back the empty recorder. As Linda recalled them, his words had nothing to do with what was happening in the car. "I know you're real," he said to her. "You're real, aren't you?"

When I had first equipped Linda with a photograph of Dan, hoping that it might function as a kind of insurance policy, I had also given her an audiocassette recording in which I addressed Richard, Dan, and the third man in my own voice. On the tape I explained a few things about the UFO phenomenon and told the men what, in my experience, the aliens did and did not do. My goal was to calm them, to assuage their fears as far as possible, and, above all, to try to persuade them to stop their harassment of Linda.

And now, as Dan seemed about to start the engine of his car, she reached into her purse and handed him the photograph and the audiocassette. He tossed the tape onto the seat, but his reaction to the picture was predictably extreme. Linda said that "he became nuts. He took me by the shoulders—I thought my head was going to fly right off—'cause he shook me by my shoulders and made me dizzy as hell. I thought I was going to pass out. 'Where'd you get this picture, half-breed?' he said. 'Tell me!' So I said, 'It's none of your business,' which provoked him. I said, 'We know who you all are. You're not going to do this any more. Either you come forward and you talk to Budd Hopkins or you leave us alone.' He said, 'Yeah, yeah, yeah,' and denied it was his picture! Then he started the engine and we drove away."

I made an effort to find out where Dan had taken her. I hoped that Linda might have memorized a few landmarks, but I was soon disappointed. In addition to being in a state of near panic, Linda did not drive and had virtually no firsthand knowledge of Brooklyn or Long Island. She remembered that Dan drove from South Street over the Brooklyn Bridge, and then that they were on "a highway that was high up," probably the Brooklyn-Queens Expressway. They passed the Verrazano Bridge on the Belt Parkway, heading farther east on Long Island, driving very fast. There was little conversation.

She paused a moment in the recollection of her harrowing experience and took a deep breath. "I'm all right now," she said, as if to reassure April and me.

"You're a tough one," I added, hoping by a compliment to bolster her shattered self-respect.

Her response promptly brought things back to reality: "Not as tough as I thought I was."

At intervals during the drive, she said that Dan would put his right hand on her knee, and she would have to use both of her hands to try to pry his away. Later, in answer to a question of mine, she realized that his maneuver usually happened when he was making a turn from one road to another. If it was his intention to momentarily distract her from noticing any road signs or memorable landmarks, it was effective.

"We kept going and going," she said. Aware of her perilous position and Dan's unpredictable mental state, she attempted some small talk to calm him down. She asked about his work, if he lived on Long

Island and commuted to New York, if he liked his job, and so on, but his answers were brief and noncommittal.

Eventually they turned down a driveway and stopped in front of a two-story contemporary beach house. Dan insisted that she get out of the car and come inside. On the drive out to Long Island, he had promised that they would soon meet Richard, but when they entered the house Linda was depressed to find that Richard hadn't yet arrived. The place was nicely furnished in a contemporary style, and was quite spacious. "It had an upstairs," she explained. "I know, because I asked to go to the bathroom, and it was upstairs."

Dan took off his jacket, dropped it onto the sectional couch, and "went into the kitchen to make some coffee for us." She thought about going through his coat pockets to retrieve her tiny cassette but decided that, with Dan standing in the open kitchen, it was far too risky. At this point, she said, he was "very cordial. He was very nice and I felt more relaxed, but I still had my mind back on what happened in the car: He kissed me, wet my whole face. Now he told me to make myself at home, but I was still very nervous." Hoping to learn Dan's full name or a way to identify the house, she walked over to a desk at one side of the room. "I didn't even see a damn telephone," she said, "but on his desk there were two picture frames. There was a picture of me bending down and kissing Johnny good-bye. This had to be before I put him on the school bus, because I don't stop in the middle of the street and bend down and kiss him. The other picture, on the other side of the desk, was me standing by the lighthouse." (This small, commemorative structure near the South Street Seaport is the place she sometimes met Joseph during her guarded outings.)

While the coffee was presumably perking, Dan returned to the living room and handed Linda a white, gift-wrapped box, a present for her, he explained. She opened it nervously. Inside was a sheer white nightgown and negligee set. "He told me, 'I have to prove something to myself. I want you to put this on because I want to be sure that it was you I saw that morning in the light, the light of the UFO.' I said, 'Well, I thought that you were pretty clear that it was me.' He says, 'I want to see and I want to take a picture to show the others.' I said, 'I'm not going to put that on. Don't you think this is inappropriate? You give someone, your wife, a gift like that. You don't . . .' I wouldn't even wear a thing like that in my own home because I have sons. I wouldn't wear it even if I had daughters.

"I was trying to talk my way out of putting that damn thing on. I said that the only way I'll put it on is if I put it on over my clothes. 'No,' he says, so I say, 'Well, you can forget about it, you can torture me, you can do whatever you want to me, but I'm not putting that on.' So then he agreed I could put it on over my clothes since I was wearing a white blouse. Thank God.

"I put it on and he asked me to stand by the window where the desk was. He told me to pick my head up and put my arms straight down. He wanted to watch and 'think' for a while. So I put my head up and my arms straight down and stared at the ceiling, and my neck started to ache me. And then he started to freak. 'Oh, my God,' he said. 'Why me? It was really you.' He started to cry and I had to listen to this while I was looking up at the ceiling. I put my head down to see, and he was on his knees with his arms up, like he was trying to get God's attention or something. And at that point I felt sorry for him. I really did, but I was afraid to go to him because I didn't know . . . I didn't understand his state. I was afraid. I wanted to go over to him and tell him I was sorry . . . that . . . you know, I really was sorry . . . but I was afraid he was going to grab me. So I started to walk toward the door, nightgown and all, and I left my purse, everything there. The hell with the jacket, and I ran out the door [to the beach]. I still had my blouse and jeans on. I could have gotten home. I didn't have my pocketbook, but I could have asked somebody for a quarter or something to call somebody.

"He started to yell at me, telling me to 'just get over here. Come back.' And I kept running, and then before I knew it he was behind me. I thought he was going to shoot me. . . . He had something in his hand. I was afraid. I thought it was a gun. Anyway, he caught me. I fell on my stomach. He had my arms behind me like I was a criminal and I felt something hard on the back of my head. I thought it was a gun. Scared the hell out of me. I said, 'Please don't hurt me. You're going to shoot me, aren't you?' He says, 'I'm not going to shoot you. I'm not going to hurt you.' I says, 'Well, get that away from my head.' He says, 'It's my fingers.' They were hard and flat. So I says, 'Well, get your fingers out of my head.' And he did.

"And then he flipped me over like a pancake, and then he started to get weird on me again. Not that this isn't all weird, but he started to get weirder. He held me and started to rock me and he said, 'Isn't this nice? Isn't this nice? You'll stay with me. You'll always make me feel better. You'll stay with me.' He started to kiss me all over my face, and I says, 'Damn it, I have a family.' You know what he said? He says, 'We'll go far, far away and we'll make a new family.' So I said, 'But I don't want a new family.' "

What happened next was another of Dan's violent mood swings. Perhaps angered by Linda's rejection of his strange proposal, he suddenly reached down into the damp sand and smeared a handful of it across her face. He laughed and said, "Look at you now. Lady of the Sands." He lifted himself up, and taking hold of Linda's hands, started to drag her across the beach on her stomach. "Dig holes," he ordered. "Come on, start digging. Let's see you dig some more holes."

In her panic, Linda realized that as far as she could see, the beach was deserted. Many of the large houses along the shore were closed for the winter, so there seemed to be no one to come to her aid. Worse, a moment later another idea apparently came into Dan's mind. He reached under Linda's nightgown and began to unbutton her jeans. She screamed and tried to turn over onto her stomach, but Dan put his leg across her knees and pinioned her. With one fast, hard pull, her jeans were down around her knees, and a moment later he yanked them off and threw them about ten feet, away from the water.

He pushed her down on her back and tried to kiss her. He tried to brush away the damp sand he had smeared on her face only moments before, scraping her skin and spreading the sand more widely. Annoyed, he picked her up and waded into the surf. Gathering whatever strength she still possessed, Linda began hitting him in the face and head, to no avail: "He didn't say a word and moved like he was made of steel."

"Let's clean your dirty face," he said, and, holding tightly to her hair, pushed her head down into the water. He repeated this several times, holding her under to the point that she thought he was going to drown her. "He pulled my head up out of the water and I started to choke and cough. I wanted to kill him. I would've killed him with my bare hands if I'd had the strength."

With the undertow and mild surf apparently aiding her struggle, Linda finally broke free and waded out onto the beach. Exhausted, she said that at this point she didn't care anymore what happened to her. She only wanted to rest, and sank down onto the damp sand. In seconds Dan was sitting behind her with his arms around her, cradling her nearly limp body against his chest. "Hold me," he asked, but she made no response. "Isn't this nice? Just you and me." Too frightened and too unsure of his volatile emotional state to venture any sort of reply, Linda remained silent.

"You're not legal," Dan said to her. "You're a half-breed." Though the statement enraged her, she showed no reaction. "Give me your hands," he said. He took her left hand, loosened her wedding ring, pulled it off, and threw it into the ocean behind him. Then he began to murmur softly that she belonged with him and that he would find a place for her.

At the very outset of her abduction at Pier 17, Dan had told Linda that they would eventually be meeting Richard. But after the long drive and the horrors and humiliations she had undergone during the past few hours, she had all but abandoned hope of rescue. She assumed now that she had been lied to and that Richard was probably unaware that Dan had taken her to the Long Island house. But then, she said, she suddenly looked toward the beach house and saw Richard standing in the doorway.

He quickly approached the bedraggled pair who were still sitting on the wet sand, with Dan holding Linda from behind. "What the hell are you doing?" he said to Dan. "What are you doing?" Linda told me, with profound relief in her voice, that "it was so good to hear someone who's normal." Dan still wouldn't release her, and after a few exchanges between the two men, Richard began to speak very calmly and gently to his partner, in Linda's words, "as if to a child."

"Okay, Dan. It's all right, now. It's okay. You can let go of her. We're going into the house, now." She said that Richard was looking at her "as if . . . 'let me do the talking,' 'cause at one point he put his finger on his lips. He didn't 'Shhh.' He didn't make any noise. He says, 'It's all right, Danny. Everything is fine. We're going to go in the house.' But Dan was saying, 'Yeah, well, you're going to take her away now, and she has to go away with me.' And Richard says, 'Yeah, that's right,' like he was agreeing with him. Humoring him."

Richard helped Linda up off the damp sand, and after retrieving her blue jeans from the place farther up the beach where Dan had thrown them, the three headed for the house. Once inside, Linda peeled off her soaking wet nightgown while Richard continued to speak softly and calmingly to the distraught man. "Dan, you know, you're a mess. Let me take you upstairs, and you can shower and change your clothes. I'll stay downstairs with Linda. Don't worry."

Dan allowed himself to be soothed and persuaded, and when Richard helped him upstairs, Linda remembered the microcassette tape in Dan's jacket, thrown casually across the back of the sectional couch. As soon as the two men were out of the room, she frantically searched Dan's pockets, and when she found the tape, she quickly hid it in her purse. Richard, she realized, would have had no knowledge that such an important piece of evidence even existed. Linda had a straight shot, and she took it.

Sitting in my living room, listening to her account of the tape's retrieval, my curiosity was at a peak. I insisted that we listen to it. No one—not even Linda—had yet had time to play it. I put the tiny cassette in the microrecorder and turned it on. Predictably accompanied by street noises, this is what we heard:

L: [Speaking into the microphone pinned into her coat pocket, her voice low, quick, panicky] He's here. Dan. He's standing across the street and he's watching. God! He's motioning to somebody. I see a van. It's the van I think Joseph and I saw. I'm scared shit. I think it's the same guy, too. It doesn't look right. I gotta get the hell out of here. I'm scared. [Gasping as she runs] Oh, God, he's coming! It's the smoking. Never gonna make it. [Panting] I don't see him anywhere. Where the hell is he?

[After a few heavy, running footfalls, Dan's voice is heard, deep, quick, authoritative]

D: Hey! You're not going anywhere. Get in the car.

L: [Panting and speaking in a whisper] Oh . . . Oh . . . Oh, God. Oh, God . . . he got me. [And then, after the sound of a car door closing a few moments later, she speaks louder, directly to Dan] You're never . . . you're never gonna do this to me again.

D: Yeah, yeah. [His tone cold and disdainful]

L: Either you come forward and speak to Budd Hopkins or you just leave us alone. [A few seconds pass] What?

D: [In a nasty, slow whisper] Come here, half-breed.

L: [Terrified] No, no. I'm gonna get out of here. [Smacking, kissing sounds] Ow! Stop it! Ahh. Ehh. [Screams] Stop. [More screams] No! [Half crying, shaky voice] Help. You really need help. [Hysterical yelling, sounds of struggle] I wanna go home! Why don't you let me out of the car! You . . .

[After a pause, a new set of sounds: a loud, sustained, metallic beep, followed by clicking noises]

D: [In a deep, almost bored voice] Stun gun. [Beep and more clicks. Then, his voice, amazed] A tape recorder? You're wired?

L: No, I'm not wired. . . . It's not on. [Voice very shaky with fear] It's not on. See?

Here the tape ended abruptly. "How could I claim I wasn't wired when he'd just found it?" Linda asked us. "It was just crazy, but I was so afraid of him." Her denial seemed understandable to me when I realized that a large, terrifying man was holding in his hand the incontrovertible evidence of her guilt. I suppose that any of us, if we had been caught like this by a dangerous authority figure, might have done the same.

As Linda frantically went through Dan's coat she had been sure that he would suddenly remember it and come back downstairs to threaten her once more. However, her tribulations that afternoon came to an end moments later when Richard, having talked his partner into taking a shower and changing his ruined clothes, came back downstairs alone. He escorted her outside and into the same red sports car Dan had used to bring her there. The long trip back was a relief, and Linda had been so frightened, tense, and exhausted that she fell asleep during the drive home. She was aware that she was on the Long Island Expressway, and she recalled at some point passing exit 14, but most of the return trip was hazy.

She remembered telling Richard about his partner's crazy behavior. "I told him Dan kissed me all around my face and that he tried to get me on the lips. And he did it twice. He did it in the car and he did it on the beach. That's really strange 'cause he can't stand me. He *doesn't* like me. I despise the man but I feel sorry for him. He wanted to go far away and start a new family. That's crazy. That doesn't make sense."

Linda recalled Richard's reply. "You're right," he agreed. "He's not well. He's really gone over the line. I didn't think it was this bad. I'm so sorry this happened."

Richard seemed genuinely choked up, Linda thought. "He really felt bad." It was, most likely, the end of a long friendship.

And now, after having told us in detail about her frightening experiences with Dan and her rescue by Richard, Linda gave me the rest of the evidence she had retrieved. When she handed me the plastic shopping bag she had brought with her I noticed that it was a bit heavy. Inside, wadded up at the bottom, was a white, sodden, sandy mass: the nightgown and negligee set that Dan had made her wear. As I lifted the soiled garments partly out of the bag to examine them more closely, Linda averted her eyes. The humiliation and fear she had so recently felt had not yet lost their force.

I noticed that there were still traces of sand in her hair and eyebrows, and though she had changed her blouse to a dry one, she was obviously wearing the same damp jeans.

Again, I told her how sorry I was that she had been so terribly manhandled. I vowed to locate Dan somehow, and if necessary to have him arrested. Or, if it seemed possible, to have him committed to a psychiatric hospital. But now Richard was the key figure, and his actions might very easily define the future for all of us.

C H A P T E R

12

"The Public Had a Right to Know"

A few days after the Long Island kidnapping I began to plan a search for the beach house where Linda had been held. I knew I should act as quickly as possible while her recollections were still fresh, though I wanted to give her whatever time she needed to regain her composure. She was still terrified of Dan, and far from eager—even with me by her side—to risk running into him again.

But in the meantime I received yet another surprise. On Wednesday, eight days after the incident at the beach, my afternoon mail included a letter from Richard, dated October 21. In seven pages he provided further details of the Long Island kidnapping and its aftermath, and to my astonishment, he enclosed a series of five color photos of Linda racing down the beach, obviously taken by Dan shortly after she escaped from the house. Linda was wearing the white nightgown and negligee over her jeans and blouse. The photos showed her running toward the water in what seemed like a confused, uncertain fashion.

But Richard's letter contained something even more important: his personal recollections of the November 1989 "Lady of the Sands" incident I had previously only heard about from Dan. Leaving unchanged Richard's somewhat idiosyncratic style of paragraphing, capitalizing, and punctuating, the following is his October letter:

Dear Mr. Hopkins

I'm typing this letter in a hurry as we always do. So please excuse whatever errors you may find. I was angered and saddened about the whole incident that took place on October 15, concerning Linda and Dan. Linda is very special to me and Dan is my closest friend. Budd, I want my friend back, but he just isn't the same.

I should have known better than to have Dan pick Linda up that day, without me. However, it couldn't be helped. I was unavailable at the time, and Dan was available. Although we never liked Dan's methods concerning Linda, it was important to speak with her that day.

In between our travels, we have spent half of springtime and all of the summer months trying to talk with Linda. But she never stayed in one place long enough, because she was afraid of us. The only thing left was to contact you, so you could prepare her for our meeting. I didn't think Dan would behave as he did, or I would have waited until I was available sometime in November.

After Dan sent his last letter to you, we didn't see Linda for about two weeks, which was a waste of precious time, considering our schedule. She may have been at home or on vacation, we didn't know.

We had to speak with her before our up and coming trip, knowing our mission was abroad somewhere in Europe, and soon. We'll be leaving for Madrid October 25th, in preparation for the Middle East Peace Talks. I won't be able to speak with Linda until I return. I couldn't really speak with her in the car while driving her home.

Dan will not *be present during our next talk. The third party may be there instead of Dan. We spoke about it, but a decision has not yet been made.*

I listened to your taped message and now it's in the hands of the third party. I saw Dan's photograph and I commend you on your investigations. Your sources must be well trained and very valuable to you. Your taped message and Dan's photograph is one of the reasons why I'm going to give you the following information, never mentioned before, for obvious reasons. This additional information will be the last information divulged, pertaining to the November 1989 Incident.

Secrecy, pertaining to all persons involved in the November 1989 Incident is necessary for National Security reasons . . . Lives will be ruined (mine included), if those involved are revealed. However, I will tell you, <u>others were involved</u>. Other major figures, and three of us (one of which is major), ended up on a beach somewhere that November '89 morning.

When we returned from the beach, back to our car, the other cars (two to be exact) were no longer there under the FDR Drive highway. They, too, saw what happened. These important figures, along with their security people, refused to discuss the matter by declining to appear at a <u>Special Meeting that was going to be held by the third party, shortly after the occurrence</u>. [His emphasis]

Budd, I'm torn between my life, the love for my country, and what turned out to be a tremendous international coverup. I won't be putting my head on a butcher's block.

We originally contacted you because we needed your help by way of comfort, knowing someone knew about this incident beside ourselves. At the same time, we couldn't come forward for obvious reasons. We thought the public had a right to know what was going on in their own town, and thought you were the one to do it. But instead, you're trying to track us down! These actions will cause an international incident if you go too far. Take our word for it.

Your message is very clear. We understand perfectly. There is no doubt that no one will get hurt. I'm sorry for whatever hurt we may have already caused.

Linda certainly is a tight-lipped lady. I know first hand. When I asked her if she knew who your sources were, in her ladylike manner, she told me that it wasn't my concern. She then tightened her lips and wrinkled her nose! I can't help it, Budd—I just couldn't get mad at her. Instead, I wanted to take a bite out of that face. I wish she were mine. But I understand that it isn't possible. Presently Dan doesn't understand this fact himself. Or shall I say he doesn't care. He's getting outside professional help and won't be around for sometime to come, after the Peace Talks have ended.

Dan is a lot better now than he was on October 15th, when I found him sitting on the water's edge at the beach with Linda cradled in his arms. I was so shocked that it even scared me. He just sat there rocking Linda to sleep and playing with a long curl of Linda's hair that had fallen down in front of her eyes.

After I talked Dan into letting her go, we walked on the beach to the house. I took Linda's hand and she held it so tight that by the time we reached the house my fingers were numb. She was trembling with fear and from the cold. The poor kid was a wreck. At the same time I had to continue to calm Dan, as he warned me to stay away from her—or else—and started to paw at her, trying to get her back again.

Dan showed no signs of his feelings for Linda, other than dislike and anger. I can't understand how infatuation could develop out of such negative emotions. The strangeness of it all is that he doesn't care what Linda is feeling. It doesn't mattter to him that she has a family. He wants what he wants, and he usually gets it. But not in this case. When he let go of Linda at the house he didn't realize that he has lost her forever.

He has mentioned to me his unrealistic plan of taking Linda far away somewhere, to keep her with him until his death. Of course this will never happen, we will see to it. At the present time Dan is stabilized and will continue to be. Provided he doesn't see Linda and he does expect to see her again. This will be an impossibility for him to achieve.

Dan needs, and will get, the very best of in-patient treatment when we return from Madrid. He hasn't handled the '89 incident very well from the beginning. The beach incident that we uncovered was what I think drove him over the edge, together with the after effects of a downright messy divorce 4 years ago. Apparently to him Linda is everything his ex-wife wasn't. I was divorced too, years ago. Both Dan and I are childless. I added this personal information so that you may have a better understanding of what may be involved, concerning Dan.

According to Dan, the whole idea of meeting with Linda alone was to prove if she was or wasn't a half-breed human. I don't know how he was going to prove or disprove this, but I can imagine. He knew that I wouldn't like the idea and that's why he tricked me by arriving at the house with Linda at an earlier time.

Dan wanted to get some photographs of Linda in night clothing to show us that it was really her that November morning. I don't know why he felt the need to do this. We were always convinced that Linda was the one we saw that morning. These photos were a very bad idea. The enclosed copies are the product of Dan's discussion with Linda that October 15th.

Incidentally, after I returned to the house from driving Linda home that day, Dan mentioned to me that Linda was wired with a little tape recorder. Considering his unstable condition at the time, I found this information to be non-sensible and uncharacteristic of Linda. Evidently he cannot produce the tape which leads me to believe there isn't one. I'm hoping this isn't true of Linda. I can't imagine anyone as sweet and lovely as her behaving like James Bond. She's just too fragile to take such a risk. Yes, she's a spitfire when it's called for. However, a deliberate deception just doesn't seem to belong to Linda's character.

Budd, is she a rose with harmful thorns? Or is she as Dan puts it—"Rich, perhaps she's an onion growing on an apple tree."

Strange things happened on the beach that morning of November 1989. It was so unreal. You have Dan's version of it, but you haven't heard mine. Has he told you everything? This is my version.

After the aircraft spun into the river we found ourselves on a beach, not knowing how, why or where. In the not too far distance, there was the girl we saw, that was taken up into the object earlier on. Along with her at the water's edge were those three critters.

All four seemed kind of cozy with one another. They walked back and forth with their strange-looking pails and shovels. These pails had white lights attached to them. Each one of the four had the same pail and shovel. These pails had handles and were carried around while they did their work. Budd, they dug holes everywhere! Every now and then they'd scoop up wet sand and drop it into their pails.

Suddenly their digging stopped when the girl (Linda) spoke to them. I couldn't hear exactly what she was saying because there was too much background noise. But what I heard wasn't spoken in the English language. In fact, I couldn't recognize the language. It was unusual.

They started to dig again. Linda wandered off toward the beach, to bend down and pick something up. She looked at it and then walked back to those critters. They turned around facing us. Budd, this is very hard for me to write. My pride is involved. I can't begin to describe what I felt when they all started to walk toward us.

When this beautiful girl and these three little monsters appeared in front of us, the girl (Linda) started to talk to me. She told me things in my head. I can't explain it any other way. Her voice was in my head, not in my ears. I started to feel all sorts of feelings. I felt anger, sadness, warmth, love. You name it, I felt it. I think I was feeling her emotions, because my own feelings started to develop and it wasn't until then that I realized how important she was to me. I had wondered if she knew what I was feeling, because I felt what she was feeling. At the same time I wanted to get up and run away. I'm well over 6 ft. tall and I wanted to run away.

Budd, she felt love for me, too.

Soon after that Linda held up a dead fish and said 'Look and See What You Have Done.' Dan asked her who she was, but she never answered him. Instead, one of those critters verbally identified her as the "Lady of the Sands." My first question at that moment was a silly question. I asked myself if she was a Mermaid. Her hands and feet glistened in the light of their strange-looking pails. I'll never forget her little hands and feet. They glittered like tiny diamonds.

They turned around and walked away. This is when Dan felt his deepest threat. He thought that they were going back to the water's edge to finish their work, only to return and take us with them. So, Dan reached for his pistol. The critters just kept on walking straight ahead without looking back. But Linda turned her head around and glared at him. The third party, Dan and myself heard what she said in our heads. It <u>was</u> her voice, we realize that now. She said "Stop! Keep your arms down." At that instant, Dan couldn't move his arms and we were forced to turn our heads away from Linda. She stopped Dan dead with just one casual look.

Now here is where our problem with Linda comes in. When we questioned Linda in the car last April, she stopped Dan again with one of her casual looks. Both of us heard her say in our heads, "Be Kind, Don't Hurt Me." Once again she forced me to turn my head away from her. Dan had stopped the car at a car rest to pull Linda bodily from the back seat, forward to the front seat with him. She made a comment that made him very angry and he pulled over to get Linda in the front seat with him. It took just one look and she stopped him dead. He couldn't move his arms. We didn't understand at the time what had happened. It was all too strange to comprehend. Whatever it was, it left a bad taste in our mouths. It wasn't until we uncovered the beach incident recently that we could understand what had happened. This is one of the reasons Dan believes Linda is a half-breed human, and I can't say I blame him. I have had my moments, too. But for me, Linda is what she is.

Continuing on—the three critters and Linda continued to walk toward the ocean and just stood there waiting for something. Maybe they were waiting for their aircraft to return. I don't know.

Next, we were back at the car, and somehow the third party was up on the roof of the vehicle, trying to slide down. We helped him down and then walked over to the riverfront to wait for the object to come out of the water, to return Linda. It never returned after a good 45 minute wait.

The other cars must have driven off sometime while we were gone. I often wondered if they wondered where we were, because our car was still there and we weren't. They were nowhere to be found, and they were not on the beach with us.

The third party and ourselves strongly suggest that Linda be tested by a para-normal professional, to prove or disprove her difference. Although I gather from some passing conversation with Linda that she isn't as open-minded about the para-normal as she is about Ufology. We weren't open-minded about anything strange until this whole crazy incident was born and we met Linda.

I don't know if Linda can be talked into a para-normal test, but we hope that you can try to talk her into it. Linda is different. There is no question about it. We know, because we have seen and heard it at the beach and in the car.

She is kind and giving. Does Linda have this effect on others? Or are we the unusual ones? I can tell you this,

if she were the ugliest woman around I would care for her just the same.

At any rate, when I return from my trip I'm going to speak to Linda. I mentioned this to her while I was driving her home on October 15th. But while I was driving she was falling in and out of sleep, so when I reached a traffic light I laid her down on the front seat and covered her with my coat. I don't know if she remembered what I had told her. Please remind her that I'll be seeing her sometime at the beginning of November.

If, by any chance, you have a message for me, please give it to Linda. We'd like to know (the third party and I) about the paranormal testing, and we have an interest in whatever you have to say.

Please tell Linda there is no reason to be afraid of our talk. Tell her if she runs away, I won't chase her. I'm so sorry for what has happened on October 15th. I would have given anything to prevent it.

Hope to be hearing from you soon, Budd.

> *Many Thanks and Kind Regards,*
> *Richard*

Richard's confessional letter affected me deeply, but I forced myself to draw back from its obvious emotional content to analyze what it really meant. Could I trust it? Was secrecy about the November 1989 incident really a matter of national security? (I noticed that Richard capitalized both words, as was his habit when dealing with important issues.) How could the 1989 event lead to, in his version, an International Incident? Was he being melodramatic, exaggerating his own importance to impress Linda and me? Was he trying to scare us into silence? Or was it all true?

I tried, first, to imagine what a skeptic might think, someone without access to the tape recordings, the other letters, or the various witnesses in this extraordinary case. The skeptic would necessarily have to assume at the outset that the letter was a hoax and that the Long Island kidnapping never occurred. The presumed culprit would have to be Linda. She would have had to invent the kidnapping, hire an actor to impersonate Dan and convincingly fake the tape recording, and at some point make a trip to Long Island to arrange for the set of photographs to be taken. She would have had to flawlessly simulate panic when she called me up, then prepare the soggy shopping bag, and before arriving at my house, put traces of sand in her hair and eyebrows. And then she would have continued to act—perform—convincingly for April and me for the next hour or so with the tape recorder taking it all down, registering fear, anger, and confusion. Why, I wondered, would anyone go to such trouble?

The skeptic would have to believe that, whatever her motivations, Linda was a sociopath so remarkably skillful that she could carry it all off—for example, hiring and training two male actors to speak on the two tape recordings (Dan's and Richard's voices are distinctly different). Her literary abilities would be such as to allow her to produce the Dan and Richard letters in different styles, registering authentic emotional reactions, maintaining two different sets of phrasing, punctuation, paragraphing, and idiosyncratic grammatical errors, and all the while referring to herself in unflattering terms. A hoaxer, I imagine, would generally wish to represent herself as someone strong and heroic rather than as a helpless "alien half-breed" dragged across a beach by an emotionally unstable middle-aged man.

Subtle locutions in his letter immediately suggested to me the way a somewhat conservative, even courtly man like Richard would tend to speak. The phrases he uses to describe Linda—"a tight-lipped lady" with a "lady-like manner" who attracted him enough to make him want "to take a bite out of her face"—imply more the sweet and clumsy musings of a polite but smitten middle-aged male than the kind of glamorous images a hoaxer might invent to dramatize herself. I have yet to meet a woman for whom the phrase "ladylike" is taken as the most desirable of compliments.

But beyond these subtleties of language is the uncanny way in which Linda, in her account to me, and Richard, in his letter, describe the psychotic breakdown of a troubled, macho man. Dan reveals over and over his hopelessly mixed and contradictory emotions. Linda is simultaneously the object of his obsession, his desire, his hatred, and his profound fear.

In this context I thought of Mark David Chapman, the young man who shot John Lennon outside the Dakota apartment building in New York City. A short time before the murder, Chapman had set up a veritable Lennon shrine in his hotel room, attesting to an obsession that verged on adoration. The afternoon of the fatal encounter he approached his idol on the street and asked for his autograph on a record album. Meanwhile he lingered outside the Dakota, and a few hours later, when Lennon appeared once more at the building's entrance, Chapman walked up and shot him. His hopelessly tangled emotions veered all the way from veneration to lethal hatred.

Though I had no reason to suspect that Dan was either schizophrenic or a potential killer, I couldn't be sure. Clearly, on October 15, he had suffered a profound breakdown. To protect Linda, it seemed essential to try as soon as possible to locate the beach house and then to take some kind of legal action against Dan.

Linda agreed to drive with me out to Long Island to retrace, if we could, the path that Dan had taken that afternoon. However, in order to let her recover, I put off the trip for several weeks. The delay, I realized, involved a trade-off. Postponing the search would offer Linda an increasing sense of safety and calm after the traumas she had suffered, but each day we waited would mean a decreasing freshness in her recollection.

Marty Jackson, a friend and neighbor who owned a roomy old Cadillac, offered to provide the transportation, so early on Veterans Day, November 11, he, Linda, April, and I began the drive to the scene of the crime. I knew from Dan's photographs that the beach Linda had been taken to lay beyond Fire Island, which otherwise would have been visible offshore, so our goal was the more easterly towns: Quogue, Hampton Bays, and the Hamptons.

At first Linda was helpful, identifying, among other sights, an unusual bridge she and Dan had driven across. But it soon became clear that her memories of various turnoffs from what I took to be the Belt Parkway were quite confused. When we came to one familiar landmark, she said that she thought they had driven past it twice, approaching it each time from a different direction. It struck me that Dan could easily have made a circle or two to conceal the route he was taking. This possibility, on top of his fondling Linda's knee at crucial moments and her total lack of familiarity with eastern Long Island, virtually doomed our project from the beginning. Our daylong search yielded nothing.

But there were other leads to follow. Richard's letter contained many intriguing suggestions and clues that demanded careful analysis and systematic investigation. Who were the other major figures involved in the November 1989 incident? What happened to the people in the other cars, and what had they seen that night? Exactly where were they headed? To the Wall Street Heliport, or to the heliport on Governors Island, the secure Coast Guard installation where Reagan, Bush, and Gorbachev met in their 1988 summit conference?

And what about Richard's statements concerning Linda's "paranormal powers," including her apparent ability to "talk to him in his head"? Dan's insistence that she was a "half-breed" had to be dealt with somehow. After all, Linda had remembered cooperating willingly with the aliens in the sand-sample taking, a very disturbing idea for her as well as for me.

Coincidentally, in the tape I had made for the three men and that Linda had given to Dan, I addressed this very issue. I cited the case of a Seattle man I had worked with who one day "felt a need" to ask his young nephew to get in the car for a short trip. The driver had then headed for the countryside without knowing where he was going or why. With his nephew asleep beside him in the front seat, he finally turned down a side road and stopped the car, somehow understanding that this was his destination. A UFO landed, and while he sat calmly watching, three small alien figures approached the car and took the inert boy back to the craft. Sometime later they emerged, still leading the apparently unconscious child, and placed him back in his uncle's car. The man started the engine and drove home, feeling that for the time being he had been acting in absolute but involuntary cooperation with the UFO occupants.

Back in late August, when I made the tape recording, I had hoped that this example might lessen Dan's anger. "Your suspicions about Linda are false," I had said. "There are times when the aliens control people and force them to do things they wouldn't ordinarily do." Then I cited the Seattle man's account, not knowing that dozens of such cases would surface in the next few years. I would eventually deal with a guilt-ridden father who recalled having handed his sleeping child to the aliens without hesitation; a remorseful mother who heard her eight-year-old son cry for help from his room, and calmly told him to "go back to sleep, everything is fine." She realized, an hour or so later, as her sobbing and terrified child described the aliens who had taken him away, that her unruffled behavior had been completely unlike her normally concerned, watchful, protective nature.

But before I could explore the issues raised by Richard's letter or proceed in my search for the elusive and dangerous Dan, there were three major developments in the case: an X ray, a letter from a new witness to the November 1989 incident, and yet another face-to-face meeting between Linda and Richard.

C | H | A | P | T | E | R

13

The X ray

Since her November 1989 abduction, Linda's most troubling encounters had been with Richard and Dan rather than with the occupants of UFOs. Even so, I had noticed that earthly confrontations,
albeit thoroughly unpleasant ones, were far easier for her to contemplate than the other sort. In the many months I had worked with her,
I observed that whenever she was faced with a truly peculiar incident
or memory, she chose to discount its possible connection with the
UFO phenomenon. Despite her history of alien encounters, she clung
to a basic skepticism, despite the claims of logic and experience.

And so it was with some hesitation that about a week after our
abortive drive through eastern Long Island, she called to tell me she
had had a serious and virtually unprecedented nosebleed some time
during the night. In the morning she had found extensive bloodstains
on her face, the blanket, and the top sheet of her bed. Elsewhere there
was yet more dried blood, which she traced to a small laceration on
the top of her head. "The pillow was stuck to my hair" was Linda's
way of describing how seriously she had bled.

Compounding the mystery was the fact that she hadn't recalled
waking up during the night. She couldn't imagine how she had slept
through such a heavy nosebleed, nor how she had received the wound
on the top of her head. Yet despite these puzzling circumstances, she

still didn't want to let herself think that any of this might be UFO-related.

When she called me, she neglected to mention another recent incident, which she regarded at the time as unimportant. On November 12, the week before her nosebleed, she had gone to see her niece Lisa at her office in Poughkeepsie, New York. This routine visit turned out to be extraordinarily important. Before it ended, Lisa Bayer, a doctor of podiatric medicine (and presently a podiatric surgeon), made an X ray of her aunt's head. The picture clearly shows the presence of a complex, radiopaque, metallic object in Linda's nasal cavity. When I finally saw the X ray—nearly two weeks after it was taken—I was astonished, for it provided solid evidence of an alien implant, a radiologic smoking gun.

Lisa knew some of the details of Linda's UFO experiences and her encounters with Richard and Dan, and she decided to pursue what she felt was a related subject. "Since I was about ten years old," Lisa later told me, "I remember my aunt talking about this bump on the side of her nose, and the scar the doctor found up inside. She didn't know what caused it, but it always bothered her. She was really paranoid about it." Then, in 1989, Linda had passed on to her niece what she had come to suspect about her scar, that it was the product of a UFO abduction experience. Lisa, as a young physician, had naturally been curious. Now, in November 1991, she decided to put at least that one mystery to rest. "Let me x-ray your head," she told her aunt, "so we can find out once and for all if there's something there."

As Linda described it, "The only X-ray machine she had in her office was the one she used to x-ray people's feet. There was a little low footstool people would put their foot on, and then she'd swing the X-ray machine over to take the picture. I had to get down on the floor on my hands and knees, with my butt up in the air, kind of like a baby when it's sleeping, and put my head sideways on the footstool. I felt so foolish. Lisa put the X-ray machine over me and then left the room and took the picture.

"Right afterwards I had to leave to take the train back to the city, so Lisa drove me to the station. She didn't call me for more than a week, so I assumed the picture didn't show anything."

But Lisa told me what happened next: "I dropped Linda off at the train and then came back and developed the X ray. I'd never x-rayed anything but feet before, so I wasn't exactly sure how much to raise the amperage and kilowatts. It's not a perfect picture. But when I developed it I was stunned when I saw the thing in the side of her nostril. It scared me. I was afraid even to use the phone to call her and tell her about it. After what she'd told me about Richard and Dan, I was afraid of the government. I didn't even like having that X ray in my house.

"I waited till the day I was due to come into New York to work in a kind of internship at a podiatrist's office, and then I called my aunt and asked her to come uptown and have lunch with me. That was when I gave her the X ray, and when she saw it I think it upset her more than it had upset me."

Apparently the UFO occupants were also aware of what Lisa had done. Unlikely—impossible—though it may seem, given our idea of technological capability, it appears that the aliens can somehow tell when an implant has been x-rayed and is likely to be removed, thereby allowing us a crucial piece of their technology. It is unlikely that they would ever let us capture such a prize if they could possibly prevent it.

And so before Linda or I had seen Lisa's X ray, the UFO occupants apparently abducted Linda from her apartment and removed the implant, thus causing her nosebleed and preventing us from recovering the artifact. That, at least, was my surmise. (A later X ray and an examination by a nose and throat specialist confirmed that the object was no longer present in her nostril, though a conspicuous ridge of built-up cartilage showed where it had once been embedded.)

From the beginning of our awareness of the UFO phenomenon, almost every aspect of alien technological capability has staggered our earthbound imaginations. From our perspective, we simply cannot begin to understand how UFOs seem able to accelerate to incredible speeds in mere seconds, nor how they can make right-angle turns without decelerating. We have no idea how abductees can be moved through solid surfaces, nor how individuals—even automobiles—can be lifted by beams of light. We have no idea how telepathic communication is effected, nor how the aliens are able to paralyze their captives and gain their apparently willing cooperation.

In the face of all this regularly observed "magical" behavior, the notion that the UFO occupants knew of the X ray and were able to remove Linda's implant before it could fall into our hands does not seem surprising. Other abduction cases have afforded examples of this pattern, and in fact, situations in which a detected implant is apparently recovered by the aliens are far from rare.[1]

On the X ray, the object in Linda's nostril consists of a cylindrical shaft at the side toward her cheek with two thinner, spiraling extensions—one at the top of the shaft and one at the bottom—that curl out away from her face. We can only guess at the purpose of this object.

Three possible functions come to mind, individually or in combination. The implant might be a locator device, a tiny transmitter similar to the electronic collars and tags zoologists use to keep track of animals in the wild. It could be some kind of monitoring device, relaying anything the aliens may be curious about: human thoughts, sensations, emotions, information of any and all kinds. Or such an object could be a controlling device, a way of affecting the individual's behavior or inputting information. Or none of the above.

The difficulty in speculating accurately about an advanced alien technology can be illustrated by a simple example. Imagine some very primitive tribesmen in, say, New Guinea, who come across the remains of an elderly westerner, a deceased anthropologist. When they examine his body they discover a pacemaker implant. What would they make of it? We might be—in fact we probably are—in just such a position of ignorance with regard to implants created and installed by UFO occupants.

The circumstances of what I assume to be the placement of Linda's nasal implant are worth relating. In the late summer of 1975, when she was pregnant with her first son, Linda and her husband vacationed at a Catskill Mountain resort that catered to Italian American families. The place was called Cedrini, and Linda recently mentioned—twenty years later—that though she and Steve enjoyed their stay, she had one reservation: "They put too much salt in the food." But there had been another, more serious problem at Cedrini, one that troubled her for some time afterward. It was there that Linda experienced a period of lost time, in which she found herself far from her cabin in the middle of night, extremely frightened and disoriented.

In July 1990 I undertook a hypnosis session to look into this incident. Without recounting the lengthy abduction experience that hypnosis revealed, the most important detail for our purposes here is Linda's recollection of a long needle with a small object on its tip being inserted into her right nostril. As she described it, this small, metallic object did not have anything like the protruding, curling spirals that showed up in the X ray.

This detail is important because of two earlier cases in which female abductees described objects being *removed* by the UFO occupants. The apparent implants were taken from the ear of one woman and from the navel of the other. In both hypnotically retrieved accounts the women were shown simple, shaftlike cylinders. When these narrow cylinders were touched by the aliens handling them, small, flangelike appendages popped out from their sides. These flanges functioned, one could surmise, like the barbs on a fishhook, making sure that the implants would be held firmly in place. I have never before published this information or a drawing of either flanged object, so I am certain that until Linda saw the X ray of her implant she was completely ignorant of this particular anchoring feature. Her 1990 hypnotic recollection of a smooth, *unflanged* object supports this assertion. The X ray therefore provides further evidence of Linda's reliability and the fact that her UFO experiences help buttress certain little-known patterns.

Because of other developments, I postponed any investigation into the events of the night in November 1991, just before Linda woke up bloodstained and, apparently, minus her nasal implant. However, on January 9, 1992, about eight weeks later, I conducted a hypnosis session to find out what had happened. After the induction, I set the scene, and Linda began describing her feelings. Her husband was at work, the boys were asleep, and she was feeling depressed.

L: I'm going to go to sleep. I get into bed. Shut the light. I'm thinking how depressed I am. I'm supposed to see Richard sometime this month and I haven't seen him yet. I don't know why I feel sorry for myself. Nothing good comes of it. I'm going to go to sleep. [Pause]

No. I'm hungry. Gonna get up and get a piece of fruit. I put my slippers on and go into the living room. There's a plate of fruit on the kitchen table . . . oranges, tangerines, apples. I take an orange, and get a knife. I put a paper towel down and start paring my orange. [Pause]

I don't feel right. I hear a noise in the living room. What's that? [In a frightened voice] Who's there? [Whispers] Who are you? Sometimes Johnny gets up. . . . Who's there? Johnny, did you get up?

I hear something. I walk out of the kitchen. I see a solid . . . but more light . . . Oh . . . no. [Sadly, with resignation]

Someone's in the house. Oh . . . not again. Oh, that man again. He's with two of those creatures. . . . I don't want to go again. . . .

The man Linda is referring to is a very tall, hairless figure with features more like humans than those of his small, gray, alien companions. She feels she's seen this hybrid creature before in a previous abduction experience. Retreating back into her kitchen, she tries without success to avoid looking at the three intruders. Glancing away, she sees their reflections in the wall mirror. At this point the tall man speaks to her in what seems to be an alien language, which she tries to pronounce.

L: He says [Repeating his "alien" words]. I don't understand. What did
you say? [Crying] He says, "Don't be afraid." What do you want?
You're driving me crazy.

"Go back to sleep." I can't go back to sleep if I have people in
my home. There are two of those creatures . . . wearing little blue
tight suits.

"Go back to your room," he says. No. He takes me to my room.
He's big . . . over six feet tall. He puts me in bed, on my side. I feel
numb. I can speak and I can hear, but I can't move. What does he
want?

"Don't be afraid." I *am* afraid. What are you doing here? I've
seen him before. He puts his finger on my nose. He looks at me. "I
have to take this out."

There's something there? I ask him. "Yes." I know . . . but I don't
know what it is. What is it? "A regulator." What's a regulator? Why
is it in my nose?

Whether or not the tall, hybridlike figure intends to answer
Linda's question literally or merely wants to conjure up an effective
smoke screen, he offers an explanation. It is short, enigmatic, and
steeped in a mix of quasi-scientific language. The regulator, he tells
her, is there to control her "chemicals." He describes what they are,
how they are released into her body, and how the regulator "keeps
them evenly balanced." He even employs the term "genetic engineering" in this confusing context.

The longer his "explanation" runs on, the more it frightens Linda.
Whether the strange man's intention is to mislead, to intimidate, or to
share the truth, the effect of his words is clear. Linda is made to feel
like a helpless pawn in someone's experiment. "You have no right to
do this to me," she says through tears. His terse, unequivocal reply is
one I have heard from other abductees: "We do have the right."

Next, the tall figure lifts Linda up to a sitting position, and she
feels "a hit in the face, like I've been smacked." She's carried down
the hall, into the living room, and over to the window. But now her
account suggests a break in continuity, the sequence of events imperfectly recalled. And since her memories end and apparently resume
at the same window through which she was floated in the November
1989 abduction, it's possible that she is taken into a ship for the removal of the implant. Her next conscious recollections suggest that.

L: I can't stand up anymore. He's carrying me too low, as if I'm too
heavy. I hurt myself. He made me hit myself, my head, against the

bureau [presumably causing the wound at the top of her head]. He put a blue light attached to a wire . . . a needlelike contraption, put it on my head. I don't know what he did, what happened.

And then Linda recalled waking up, noticing that her hair was stuck to the pillow, and discovering the blood. She climbed out of bed and looked at herself in the mirror. Since she had slept with her right hand under her chin, the blood from her bleeding nose had run down across her hand and wrist. She had no memory of what had caused any of this.

After I brought her out of the trance state, we talked about what it all might mean. I assured her that the strange man's explanation about "chemicals," "regulators," and, particularly, "genetic engineering" must be taken with many grains of salt. Anything that implied Linda was not a normal human being left her profoundly angry and depressed. It made no difference whether it came from Dan, a paranoid and violent security agent, or from a semihuman intruder in her home, or from Richard, a man for whom she felt a deepening fondness. Her humanity was the most important fact of her life, and she would permit no one to cast doubt upon it.

I wondered if the UFO occupants might not be conducting a subtle and subversive campaign—not unlike the methods used by radical religious cults—to convince Linda that she belonged to them rather than to the rest of us. I'm familiar with many abduction cases in which very small children are told by the aliens, "We're your real parents. You belong to us. You come from the stars." This pattern of misleading, deeply disorienting persuasion has been reported time and again.

During a panel discussion at a UFO conference, I recall how a woman named Karla Turner described her first abduction memory. As a frightened five-year-old she found herself standing in a field while "a tall, bug-eyed creature was trying to tell me it was my mother." More indicative of the sheer persistence of the aliens' strategy, however, is a case in which an abducted child was told, "We're your real parents." The child demurred. "No, you're not. My real mommy and daddy are sleeping down there in their bed." The resourceful alien then retreated to his backup position: "We're your parents' best friends," he replied, without missing a beat.

I was determined to defend Linda's firm conviction that she belonged to us rather than to those who asserted the right to treat her and her family as laboratory specimens whenever they wished. She was, I knew, a fighter, but she would be sorely tried in the coming weeks and months. In the meantime I had the X ray as evidence of what the aliens had done to her.

C | H | A | P | T | E | R

14

The Woman on the Bridge

Putting together what I knew or surmised about the events of November 30, 1989, from the sudden appearance of the hovering UFO, the suspension of Linda and the three aliens in the blue beam of light, and the abduction of Richard, Dan, and the third man—everything, including the craft's disappearance, took place almost certainly in less than two minutes. Despite that strict time limitation and the fact that these events occurred around 3:15 A.M., I had always assumed that other people must have witnessed this grandiose spectacle. Yet two years after the event, the only person other than the four central participants to have contacted me was Erica, the woman who saw the red UFO around 3:00 A.M. on November 30 above the East River. Although I had made no effort to locate additional witnesses (I wasn't sure how that could be done), I was certain that one way or another I would eventually hear from some.

At the end of November 1991, seven months after Erica had explored her recollections of the 1989 incident, I received a large manila envelope in the mail. It bore the name and return address of a woman from a small town in upstate New York. Typed onto a red-edged label attached to the lower left of the envelope were these words: CONFIDENTIAL RE: BROOKLYN BRIDGE.

Inside the envelope were a cover letter with photocopies of three hand-colored drawings and an earlier letter.

Dear Mr. Hopkins:
The enclosed letter and drawings dated July 17, 1991, are cop-
ies of the originals I have sent to you last July. I expected some
form of response from you by now because the sighting took
place in your own city. I've seriously considered the possibility
that the originals I've sent to you were lost somewhere in the
Post Office long ago. If I don't hear from you, then I'll assume
you are aware of the goings-on in New York City. Thank you.

Sincerely,
Janet

A later search through my box of unopened correspondence
turned up the July letter and the original crayon drawings. The earlier
letter reads as follows:

Dear Mr. Hopkins,
My name is Janet. I'm a middle-aged woman and retired.
Some time last May, CBS aired a one-hour show entitled "Visi-
tors from the Unknown." I watched the show because it just so
happened to be on my TV set at the time I walked into the
room. From that evening on I thought about what I saw in New
York City about 1½ years ago more than I have ever thought
about it before. It's disturbing to me. I was getting along just
fine until that show aired.
During the course of this year and a half I spoke of what I
saw only once and was made to feel ridiculous. I have never
spoken of it again. In fact, I have never traveled back to New
York City after what I saw and I never will again for any reason.
Although we don't know each other and probably never
will, I can't help but to feel silly writing about this. On the other
hand I'm feeling some relief. Please let me explain how I found
you. The day after the show aired I was determined to find
someone I could tell about what I saw, but I couldn't tell just
anyone. I have never read anything on the UFO subject (maybe
I should have). However, I knew that books were written on
the subject, so I went to the local bookstore. There I quickly
paged through many UFO books and liked the sound of your
name. I read a little of what you wrote in your book entitled
Intruders and it piqued my interest. I'm sorry I didn't buy your
book but I will in the future, as soon as I calm down.

Janet explained in her letter and in later conversations that she
had phoned my publisher for my address and was told that, though

my address could not be given out, the receptionist thought I lived in New York.

I called Manhattan Directory Assistance, asking if a Budd spelled with two D's Hopkins was listed somewhere in NYC, and she said yes! Had she said no I would have forgotten about this letter, rendering my situation with what I saw hopeless. I went out to find the Manhattan White Pages and found your address in there. I'll feel humiliated if this letter is received by the wrong Budd Hopkins. I'm sure you won't be contacting me, but if you do you'll find my phone number at the end of this letter. I do wish to remain anonymous. My family and friends do not take too kindly to the UFO subject. I have had firsthand experience and I refuse to be made into a fool.

It has taken me two months to build up the courage to write you this letter and draw the enclosed drawings. I don't want to be involved with these unnatural goings-on. However, I must know, if you know, what is going on in NYC and if it happens often?

One Wednesday evening, November 29, 1989, I attended a retirement party in Brooklyn for my sickly boss. The party lasted into the early hours of the next morning, Thursday, Nov. 30th, 1989, exactly one week from Thanksgiving Day. My boss invited me to stay at her house for the night, but I was anxious to get home. I drove to the Brooklyn Bridge with the intention of crossing over to the Manhattan side, to drive to the FDR Drive to go home from there. I drove more than halfway across the bridge when my car came to a slow but dead stop. I was so upset. It was about 3 in the morning and I wanted to get home. I saw my headlights dim and then go out. None of the car lights worked after that. I didn't know what went wrong.

I was afraid to get out of the car because it was so dark up there on the bridge. I didn't want to get hit by an oncoming car, nor did I want to get mugged if my car wasn't hit. I looked through the rearview mirror to see if other cars were coming, and they were. This scared me half to death because they had no way of seeing my car parked. But their headlights dimmed out, too, and their cars stopped right behind mine. I just couldn't understand the strange coincidence, and I still don't. How could anything get stranger than this?

From the corner of my right eye, on the passenger side of the front seat window, I thought I saw a building on fire in

Manhattan. The whole sky lit up. Mr. Hopkins, words can't express what I saw that morning up on the Brooklyn Bridge. I can't begin to explain it verbally. You would have had to of seen it yourself.

Enclosed please find three drawings, and one flap drawing taped to Drawing #2, explaining what I saw. You can have them. These pictures will always be in my mind. These drawings are of myself watching what was going on from the bridge as I sat in my car. After you finish looking through this little package I managed to send to you, you may think I'm crazy. If I am, so were all the other people sitting in their cars up there on the bridge with me that morning. If you don't think I'm crazy and you have questions, I can only say what I saw, and I know what I saw.

DRAWING #1—From the corner of my eye I thought a building was on fire. I was shocked to see what it really was. The lights were so bright I had to shield my eyes. I was frightened and found this aircraft very threatening.

DRAWING #2 (Flap Drawing)—They came out of a window, one right after another (second window from left). There were 6 windows on that side of the building. I purposely counted them. There was enough light for thousands of people to see what was happening. I'll bet you dollars to donuts that thousands did see what happened from other areas of the city. I didn't know what they were because they were all rolled up into little balls.

DRAWING #2 (Lift Flap)—I didn't want to look. I was petrified, but something made me look and I saw the balls unroll at the same time. It wasn't until then I realized that they were 4 children standing up in midair. Yes, in midair! While I watched I could hear the screams of the people parked in their cars behind me. Their screams were from horror. They sounded like I felt.

Please excuse the stick figures I drew in this drawing, but this is honestly how I saw three of the children. It was obvious that these children were rickets-stricken. Their heads were so large compared to the normal girl-child standing in the air with them. I don't know what gender the three sickly children were, but I could see that the normal child was a girl-child because she was wearing some sort of a white gown. I would imagine that it was a white nightgown she was wearing because of the early hour of the morning.

She was taller than the others. Perhaps she was a little bit older? Maybe she was a procelain manikin? I don't know because I didn't see her move except to change position. Remember, I was far away, but close enough to see what they were and what was going on. I may not have seen anything if it weren't for the bright lights.

Their next movement was when they all moved up closer to the craft. Then they quickly whisked straight up into the object (underneath it) and disappeared!

DRAWING #3—The aircraft quickly rose up above the building and flew away at a very fast speed. A speed I have never seen before. It flew behind the building drawn on the right. It passed over a highway or drive below and then proceeded to climb higher, over the center of the bridge. I was parked more towards the Manhattan side of the bridge. I watched in horror. I don't know where it went from there, because I had to look up to see. There was a bridge platform [pedestrian walkway] above and I couldn't see anymore. I do know that when this UFO passed over the bridge my clothing clung to me and my body hair stood up. The clinging sensation went away after the object went away, and my car started again.

Mr. Hopkins, I wanted to talk to the people parked behind me. I was very shaken up and could of used some calming down, but they were much too upset themselves, and I couldn't communicate with them. Some of them were running all around their cars with their hands on their heads, screaming from horror and disbelief. I was feeling bad enough without having to see these poor people in worse shape than I. So I took off and drove home.

I have often wondered what became of these poor children. It all happened so fast. It happened suddenly and finished suddenly.

It felt good sharing this with you, but I don't think I will ever share this with anyone again. It's just too unbelievable. Are you aware of what is going on in that dreadful city? Is anyone putting a stop to this? Mr. Hopkins, I thank you.

Sincerely,
Janet Kimball*

*Although the letter writer used her real name, home address, and telephone number, I have given her the pseudonym "Janet Kimball."

At the end of the letter, she added her phone number and this instruction: "Call any day (except Wednesdays) from 9AM to 4PM." To say that I was astonished by her report would be to underestimate my reaction. Everything—everything—about her account reinforced the description of Linda's abduction I had received from Richard and Dan. I could hardly believe my good fortune.

Janet's letter and drawings were *so* corroborative that the suspicious pessimist in me immediately began to search for flaws. The only odd note that I found was the formality of her terms "Manhattan Directory Assistance" (instead of "Information") and "Manhattan White Pages" (instead of "phone book"), understandable when, a few days later, I learned that she had worked for years as a telephone operator.

One of my first tasks was to compare Janet's letter with those of Richard and Dan. Perhaps because she is an older woman with no need to project a macho image, she used words like "dreadful" and the colloquial phrase "scared me half to death," usages entirely appropriate to her age, sex, and temperament, but ones that never occur in the two agents' correspondence. The word "horror" appears three times in her letter. In addition to these significant vocabulary differences, there were, among the three writers, consistent differences in paragraphing, indentation, and line justification. I also noticed that Janet's typewriter had a different typeface from those used by Linda or the two men. (And, I was to learn when I finally received a letter from him, different from the typeface on the machine used by the third man. All in all, at least six different typewriters or printers produced the letters and notes I've received from the five principals in this case.[1]

My immediate need, of course, was to speak with Janet, but it took two calls before I found her at home. On my second try her son answered. When she took the phone she spoke softly and cautiously because, she explained, other people were in the next room and she did not want them to overhear. The events of November 30 made her very uneasy, as her answers to my questions made clear: "It was very, very late at night and I was scared out of my wits." To make things even worse, she found it difficult to persuade others of the reality of the event. "When I came home and told my family," she added with a small, self-deprecating chuckle, "they thought I drank too much." Her initial reaction to the craft and the figures she had seen was understandable: "The huge bright lights made me think they were making a movie." When I told her that I had heard from other witnesses to this bizarre encounter, she was relieved but not at all surprised.

I explained that I needed any verifying details she could supply about the party she had attended that night. With no hesitation she gave me the hostess's name and the name of the company where the two had been employed for years. I was also curious to know if she had read much about the UFO phenomenon. "Not really," she replied, "because, I tell you, it scares the hell out of me." In addition, her family discouraged any further exploration of the subject. "My two children, my son and my daughter, both said, 'Stop dwelling on this, you're going to drive yourself crazy. You didn't see anything.' " Janet told me that when she first briefly described the sight from the bridge, "They started laughing at me. They thought it was a joke. When they realized I was serious they said, 'You've got to stop this. What are you having, a breakdown?' "

The only other people Janet spoke to about the incident were her sister and her brother-in-law, the town supervisor of her small New York community. As one might expect, he, too, was incredulous about her experience: "His version in the end was that they were probably filming a movie. He kind of put the whole thing down." I asked if she was sure she hadn't told anyone outside her family what she had seen. "I really didn't tell anybody but my two kids and my sister and brother-in-law. Like I said, they all laughed it off. It's not something you go around telling everybody. Right away, people look at you like you're crazy."

I asked if she had realized how extraordinary her experience really was. "Well, of course," she answered. "But if my car hadn't stopped dead and everybody else stopped, I would have thought, like my brother-in-law said, they were filming a movie. That it was kind of . . . trick photography or something. You know, in New York things like this happen. But I thought, 'Why are these other cars stopping?' "

I asked about the specific reactions of the other people on the bridge, and Janet replied that when they first saw the light and the figures they were very upset. "Then," she explained, "it was like they started rationalizing and they decided that somebody on that bridge had some kind of equipment that was doing something. Remember what Orson Welles did with *War of the Worlds?* I think they thought it was some kind of trick thing. First they were yelling at what they saw, but then they started to get angry that somebody was playing some kind of a joke, because this couldn't be real. At that point I got back in my car, 'cause I really got unnerved."

When I inquired about the time of the sighting, another interesting detail emerged. "My watch stopped," Janet explained. It was battery operated and she had to reset it the next day. Apparently, the watch stopped just as her car engine and headlights died, at 3:16 A.M. "What does it make you feel to realize that other people saw the same thing?" I asked. Her answer was something I had heard over the years from hundreds of witnesses in other bizarre UFO encounters: "It's a little comforting to know I'm not crazy," she said. "It's just one of those things you put in the back of your mind."

In the course of a number of phone conversations and one long face-to-face interview, she answered every question I asked with complete openness, accuracy, and appropriate emotion. We met for the first time on December 9, 1991, at a restaurant near her home, and when I drove up she was waiting for me outside. Janet Kimball is a widow of about sixty, a mother, and was at that time a new grandmother. She is a tall woman whose deep voice is strongly tinged with the accent of native New Yorkers. When we entered the restaurant we took a table as far away from other customers as we could; otherwise eavesdroppers might hear a great deal more than they bargained for. After we ordered our food, I asked if I could tape our conversation, and Janet immediately assented. So, in the midst of coffee cups, cheesecake, notepads, and the cassette recorder, we talked for about two hours.

The entire November 1989 UFO experience, as we tried to reconstruct it in real time, might have lasted for as long as two or three minutes, but was more likely to have taken place in considerably less time—perhaps a minute or a minute and a half. As Janet had written in her original letter, "It all happened so fast. It happened suddenly and finished suddenly."

The time that passed between the moment Janet's car engine and lights died and the sudden appearance of the lighted UFO above Linda's building was at the most a minute or two. More crucial was the length of time it took for the four "balls" to come tumbling out of the window, to stand vertically, and then to be lifted up into the UFO. As we sat together, I asked Janet to close her eyes and picture in her mind's eye the UFO's sudden appearance, the four "balls" sailing out the window, unrolling into standing positions and then levitating into the craft. I counted out the seconds as she did so. This, the most dramatic part of the encounter, probably lasted only about twelve seconds. The UFO's subsequent flight behind an intervening building and then up over the bridge could not, I believe, have lasted longer than a minute, but probably much less. "It happened suddenly and finished suddenly."

After her engine died and the car began to coast to a stop, her headlights *and the bridge lights illuminating the roadway* began to dim, reminding her of "when we had the famous [1967 northeast] black-out." Alarmed, Janet immediately tried to find out what time it was by taking her cigarette lighter out of her purse and lighting it so she could see her watch. It was, as she had told me earlier, 3:16 A.M. She realized this could not be a citywide blackout since her car lights had also dimmed out. "But then [whispering nervously] when I saw [the floating figures], my first impression was 'They're making a movie. What are they, crazy? What did they do to the bridge? What happened to all these cars? . . .' It didn't look real." She said that she thought the film they were making might be *Snow White and the Seven Dwarfs*. She thought also of the TV commercials for the Jolly Green Giant "because he stands so tall against these little people, and they look funny. They don't look like real people. I'm telling you, it was so weird. I thought it was a movie, but, you know, there were no lights, the car died. I thought they're using some kind of equipment for this movie that's knocked everything out. And then I thought I must be crazy. . . . I have to be . . . you know, this isn't real."

I commented on the accuracy of her drawings. "Yes, because I kept staring, and look, I was watching a movie being filmed in New York." I asked if she remembered deliberately counting the windows in the interest of accuracy. "I was saying to myself, if I tell somebody this they'll never believe me. It's a terrible thing to be alone. There's nobody to say, 'Oh, my God, look at this!' Or 'What could it be?' or something. I'm saying to myself, 'How could I tell somebody this?' I just kept kind of concentrating on there. I remember saying to myself, 'There's only one window in the corner there, and they're not coming out of that window. They're coming out of the next. It looks like there's four more windows there.' I was so directed on that spot that I really couldn't tell you what was happening beneath that. There's that particular row of windows and that little cap on top that you told me was a water tower. . . ."

I decided to test Janet's visual memory to make absolutely certain she had made the drawings as she claimed. I took out a pad of paper and a pen and asked her if she would redraw the facade of Linda's building. Without hesitation she sketched the side of the building with its six windows, the smaller penthouse floor above it, and, crowning the structure, the square housing of the water tower. Her memory was obviously accurate and her drawing style the same as the drawings she had originally sent me.

We returned to her memories of the event. "First [the UFO] looked like an explosion almost. Because it was *so* red and white . . . that's what caught me, and then the red subdued and it got white . . .

[Whispering] 'What the heck is this?' And the light from underneath, it was, like, sharp, where the rays were coming down, but then it got like a haze as it went down. . . .

"Then I saw these balls . . . they all just tumbled out. And from a distance I thought it was a little girl . . . but you know, I'm glad you told me that this was seen by other people, so it definitely wasn't a movie, or some kind of flimflam thing. And it looked like they all tumbled out, and they all unrolled . . . unraveled."

I deliberately tried to lead Janet, or rather to *mis*lead her. I asked, "Did one unravel and then the next one unravel and then the next one?"

"No," she replied, and became thoughtful, searching for the right image. "It kinda looked like . . . let's see . . . like those commercials when they sprinkle water on flower buds and all of a sudden the flowers open? That's what it looked like. To be honest with you, it's silly looking . . . it couldn't have been real. I'm telling you what I'm thinking at the moment, while I'm looking. This is so silly looking . . . and then . . . I was thinking of Peter Pan. I expected everybody was going to go like this any minute [Moves her hands in flitting, flying motions]. And then all of a sudden they were moving up under the bottom. . . . It started moving up. It was red . . . a big ball of fire. . . ."

Next, we discussed the UFO's apparent size, and Janet stated that it was wider than the side of the building. I then explored issues of time, her drive home, and so on. But in a moment she brought up the television program which had finally caused her to write to me. The CBS documentary was entitled "Visitors from the Unknown" and dealt with three separate UFO abduction accounts. In the first and most important case, seven young workmen, riding in a truck near Snowflake, Arizona, came upon a UFO hovering only a few feet above the ground. The driver stopped the vehicle, and as he did so one of the men, Travis Walton, jumped out and ran toward the craft. His friends yelled for him to return to the truck, but a blue beam of light suddenly shot out of the UFO, hitting Walton and lifting him off the ground before knocking him down. The terrified men in the truck drove off in panic, and only after a few minutes passed and they over-came their fear did they return to the site. When they arrived at the place of their encounter, both the UFO and Travis Walton had disap-peared. The six witnesses later reported the incident to a doubting police department, and an investigation was undertaken. It would be another five days before Walton would be deposited alongside a high-way with only partial memories of his long abduction experience.

The other two cases were less relevant to Janet's own experience.

She had *observed*, rather than been the object of, a UFO abduction, and the Walton case was the only one of the three in which independent witnesses were a factor. The similarities as well as the differences fascinated her. "Both of those people [Mike Rogers in the Travis Walton case and college teacher John Salter in the third TV case] were driving pickup trucks . . . the gentleman that's a professor and the lumberjacks. They both had pickup trucks. The policeman [in the second TV case] had a car. And I noticed, 'cause I was looking for it . . . how come *their* lights were on and their motors were going? And the policeman's flashlight was on? He was, you know, dazzled, but those lumberjacks turned their pickup truck around and went back. And, like, I felt the same thing they felt. Fear. It's normal to be afraid of the unknown. That professor said everybody [the group of aliens] was very friendly. Well let me tell you something, if any strange creatures start punching needles in me, no, they're not friendly. How could you say unknown is friendly? And he is a learned man!

"And the thing that puzzled me was how come this [the Brooklyn Bridge incident] happened? Those three incidents were in rural areas and this was in the city! I'm saying to myself, 'Other people *had* to see it.' New York never sleeps."

Janet went on to describe the reactions of those on the bridge when their cars stopped. "It occurred to everybody, 'What the hell is going on? Move that car!' And then it was, 'Oh, my God! What the hell is that? There are people in the air!' When somebody yelled it—and I can't even tell you if it was a man or a woman—I thought, all right, I'm not seeing things. These other people are seeing the same thing."

Janet had a few questions she wanted to ask me, one of which brought up something extremely interesting I had never even considered. She wanted to know how the strange creatures found their way *into* Linda's apartment building, since she had not seen them going in—only coming out as little rolled-up balls. I could not answer her question; it had never crossed my mind. It is an interesting question, indeed. It suggests once more that the latter part of the abduction was deliberately made visible, staged, as it were, for Janet and the three men in the car below, while the beginning, the entrance of the aliens into Linda's apartment building, was like that of so many other bedroom visitations—technically "unseeable."

There is another matching element in the various accounts that supports the idea that Linda's abduction was a deliberately visible performance. It concerns the interesting correspondence among Janet's, Dan's, and Richard's descriptions of their first awareness of the UFO. When each of the three first noticed the craft, it was absolutely stationary. Despite the fact that all of the witnesses had been sitting in their stopped automobiles for a minute or so, none saw the fiery UFO *arrive*. It was suddenly just there. Richard noticed the reflection of its orange-red "firelight" color in the silver foil of his chewing gum wrapper, but said that he didn't "know where it came from." When Dan glanced up and saw the UFO, he described it as looking like the rising sun; in other words, it was just there, and not visibly moving. And from her immobilized car, Janet described the UFO as "an explosion," a sudden, stationary burst of fiery color above a nearby apartment complex. To use a theatrical simile, it was as if the stage had been deliberately set behind a curtain of invisibility. Unlit and silent, hovering in the darkness above the building, the UFO waited as several of its occupants slipped unseen into Linda's apartment. Meanwhile, one by one, the targeted cars were stopped. A few moments later, the puzzled people in those cars—we may think of them as a carefully selected audience—had adjusted to the initial confusion of their vehicles' malfunctioning and had calmed down. Then, when all was ready, the brilliant, attention-getting lights of the UFO were suddenly switched on and the show was allowed to begin.

In support of this thesis it is important to remember that all of the witnesses specifically referred to the theatrical nature of the abduction drama. Janet thought immediately of a movie being made, while down below Dan described the sight as "the greatest light show" he had ever seen. I've investigated many abductions that took place in New York City, some of which occurred during daylight hours, yet they were all apparently (and magically) unseen. In one nighttime case, the UFO hovered above a rooftop with all of its lights off; the abductee reported being floated up into a dark, circular mass that would have been virtually impossible to make out against the night sky by anyone on the street below. And yet the Linda Cortile abduction was as visible as one can imagine, with the witnesses feeling that hundreds or even thousands of people, even at 3:15 A.M., should have seen this spectacular sight. For me, one inference is inescapable: With the third man as the most important member of the captive audience, this initial part of the event was a deliberate display of UFO power. It serves as a provisional answer to the skeptics' hoary old taunt, If they are really here, why don't they land on the White House lawn? Before the eyes and ears and conscious minds of all the witnesses, the aliens were coolly demonstrating their authority: "See what we can do? We're real, we're here, and we can do this anytime we wish."

Yet another cluster of details adds to the credibility of Janet's account. In most car-stopping UFO cases, witnesses report that the automobile engine simply dies and then suddenly starts up again spontaneously after the incident is over, either seconds or hours later. Expecting that she would answer affirmatively, I asked Janet if, once the UFO passed over her and disappeared from sight, her car engine started up spontaneously. "No," she replied, "I had it turned off. Thinking it was mechanical [when it first happened], I immediately shut everything off. I shut the headlights off." She explained that after the UFO incident, the first thing to let her know that her car was functioning normally was this: "The inside light went on. . . . It went on because I had first opened the door and I guess I didn't really close it all the way, 'cause the [dome] light went on."

To an experienced investigator, these are just the kinds of subtle details that provide the ring of truth. As I spoke with Janet, I became aware that each detail she recounted, each recollection and emotional reaction, was appropriate and consistent with her personality and background.

Another revealing discussion had to do with Janet's drive home. I was curious where she went after the incident was over and she was able to start her car. If, as she said, she had been heading for the West Side of Manhattan, the most direct route would have been to exit from the Brooklyn Bridge onto the FDR Drive. This path would have taken her south to the Battery and, with a minimum of traffic lights, to an uptown merge with West Street. I asked if this is the route she had taken.

"No, it wasn't," she replied. "I was going to get off onto the FDR, but frankly I was so upset that I felt I needed to see some other people. I remembered that the Fulton Fish Market is always open and busy at that hour, so I took the local road off the bridge. I drove down on South Street, past the market." This decision, as Janet explained it, seemed completely in character and, under the circumstances, eminently sensible.

One of the first things I did after I received her letter was to drive across the Brooklyn Bridge at about 3:00 A.M. to see what she could have seen. The traffic was very light—perhaps two or three other cars were on the bridge at the time—and Linda's building was clearly visible some distance away. In the daytime I was able to see and count the individual windows, and even the air conditioners in some of them. Since I could easily make out the windows, I had them measured to give myself a comparative unit. They are fifty-five inches high, but Linda is sixty-five inches tall and therefore would have been even easier to see. She would have been ten inches taller than the windows and, because of the fullness of her floor-length nightgown, perhaps even wider. With the intensely bright light the witnesses reported streaming from the UFO, visibility would have been no problem.

I carried out the following experiment with Linda. In the daylight I stood on the pedestrian walkway of the Brooklyn Bridge while I watched Linda, more than a thousand feet north of me, hang a large and very visible towel out of her living-room window. But at 3:00 A.M. on November 30, under a glowing UFO and an extremely bright beam of bluish white light, she and the three aliens would have been even more dramatically focused and illuminated. From Janet's position on the bridge and against a night sky the scene would have been almost impossible to miss.

As she watched this astonishing scene unfold, Janet said that she couldn't tell if the central figure was a child, a woman, or a manikin, though she thought the three others, once they unrolled, must be "sickly children." There is an interesting similarity between the words Richard used to describe Linda hanging in midair in the brilliant light and the image Janet chose. To Richard, from his closer location and with his vision aided by binoculars, Linda looked like "an angel or a Christmas-tree doll," her face "pure white, with no expression, a white marble doll." She was "Snow White" in one of Janet's descriptions, but so still she resembled a porcelain "manikin." All of these images amply describe the pale, inert female figure the witnesses saw standing in the air more than one hundred feet above the ground. Their subtle consonance provides further evidence for the objective reality of this "unbelievable" event.

Janet's letter made me realize that three of the four people who reported seeing Linda Cortile floating in midair attest to the presence that night of other witnesses who had not yet contacted me. I wondered if these people presently remembered what they saw, or if their memories were being blocked in a pattern UFO researchers have found to be extremely common. Were they afraid to come forward, self-doubting, unaware of who to contact, or were they literally unable to remember?

A partial answer may be found in something else that Janet told me about the evening of November 30, 1989, some fifteen hours after the incident on the bridge. It was suppertime, and she and her children turned on the television to see if there were any news reports about the strange object and figures she had seen, or about any sci-fi film being made in Manhattan at 3:15 that morning, or about several cars whose engines simultaneously died for a few minutes on the Brooklyn Bridge. They switched across channels, but found nothing about the bizarre incident. They also checked newspapers, and again found nothing. Janet said that these negative results both confirmed her children's doubts and strengthened her resolve not to talk about what she had seen. I asked her if she had ever thought about reporting what she had seen to the press, TV newsmen, or the police. She answered without hesitation: "No, I never even considered it. They would have thought I was crazy." It is likely that other witnesses may have had exactly the same reaction.

When I first contacted Janet and arranged the interview, I asked Linda if she would like to go along with me. I was surprised when she firmly declined the invitation until she explained why: "Richard and Dan have caused me so much trouble and fear that I don't want to run the risk of somebody else knowing who I am." I assured her that Janet seemed to be a kindly woman and that meeting her would involve no risk that I could imagine. Nevertheless she refused to go with me, and even asked me not to give Janet her name, address, or telephone number. It was one of the strongest signs I had yet seen of the terror Linda faced every day of her life. Clearly, these extraordinary events had exacted a severe emotional toll. I began to worry about how long she could bear up under what seemed to be ever increasing pressure. And when yet another eyewitness surfaced months later, a *seventh* corroborating participant in the bizarre events of November 30, 1989, Linda was still too traumatized to meet her.

| C | H | A | P | T | E | R |

15

A Letter from the Third Man

It was in Dan's April 10 letter that I first learned that a third person was in Richard and Dan's car on the morning of November 30, 1989. And from the way he phrased this information, I sensed that, without naming him, Dan wanted me to know the identity of their fellow witness. He's "a very important person," Dan wrote, a leader who "speaks to many corners of the globe." He then went on to mention certain details, which I have deleted in order to protect the third man's identity.

Still, in anything they had said or written, neither Richard nor Dan had ever directly named the third man. They let me understand that they were determined to maintain his anonymity for what were apparently personal, professional, and, possibly, security reasons. The situation was—and is—a subtle one. My relationship with the agents was such that they could safely assume I would keep their secret. Even if their information led me to guess the identity of the third man, they knew that I had a compelling reason to keep his name confidential: It was essential that he come forward *voluntarily* to tell the world what he had witnessed on November 30, 1989.

To my surprise, on the day after Christmas 1991, I finally received a letter from this important political figure. The envelope bore a United Nations postmark, and it had been typed on notepaper with an embossed image of the UN building in the upper left-hand corner, the sort of stationery one buys as a souvenir in the UN gift shop. I read this, perhaps wrongly, as being a deliberate message—unofficial but precise. The letter ended with a typed signature: "The Third and Last Man."

In the copy that follows, I have maintained its author's style of paragraphing, spacing, and punctuating. Unlike any of the letters I had received previously from Dan, Richard, Linda, and Janet, the third man's note followed the conventional business-letter format and included my name and address above the greeting. (I omit details here, in the interest of my own privacy.) The writer's imagery, his curious syntax and vocabulary, all seem florid and unnatural by comparison to the others, and his range of reference is obviously wider. Although his tone is gracious and courtly, I found it at the same time oddly cautious and distant.

As I read and reread the third man's letter, I decided that its true purpose lay in the last sentence of the penultimate paragraph. After two pages of diplomatic gentility, this stark sentence came as a clear-cut warning and a profound disappointment, for the point of his letter was that under no conditions would he ever acknowledge his involvement in the UFO phenomenon.

23 December 1991

Dear Mr. Hopkins:

I'm aware that I should have established some form of significant communication with you before now. However understandable the cause may be, the lack of effort on my part has been unjust. Please pardon me.

I am thankful to have lived to see the most astounding event of my life. It was something awesomely mysterious and new to one's eyes. The appreciation I have felt is not solely based on the beauty of the aircraft. The fact that Linda is alive and in motion, after being sprung out from her window like a springbok, then fixed in a beacon of bluish white light (that may have been radiological), and driven beneath the sea, is miraculous. Her survival of this contemptuous treatment is nothing short of a miracle. I am thankful.

At the time this event occurred, it caused us grave distress. This happening could not be explained away. My good fellow, the 30 November 1989 episode was substantially real. Occasionally, I shudder at the thought of this dreadful sight and how it materialized, as we observed vigilantly.

As it was once said, "wonders never cease to be." Linda is wondrous. The excitement of having our very own "Lady of the Sands" is heartwarming, to say the least. It is my regret that she has endured many hardships throughout this whole affair. Linda appears to be withdrawn and isolated. This Lady shan't be forgotten. Her words (possibly related to the Celtic language) shall ring in my head forever more. Not to mention the phrases that were meant for me and I understood perfectly that I must adhere to them. Her special, but natural gifts shall remain in my eyes for as long as there is breath in me. This delightful and lovely being has put a spring back into my step. Perhaps someday, this kind and gentle heart will complete her work and be content. The possibility of others similar to Linda (wherever and whatever her origin), may exist. If so, I pray they find one another so as to cure the feeling of isolation.

What I have seen, heard and felt on the seashore that November morning in 1989, hastened a dream that has been in a talking stage for the past four decades or so. This dream has been "World Peace." I can only say, it was time to make it happen. Please tell her, "Look and see what we have done in such a short time. Thank you, Dear Heart."

Your amazing work is difficult. Surely, your knowledge has told you "only good shall come of your work." Allow your mission to intermingle with the visual process of "World Peace" as it presently unfolds. Won't it be amusing to sit back in an old arm chair and watch all the nations of the world pull together. It shan't be long before the Earth becomes whole again.

This spectacular, but real saga has come to an end, just as my work has come to a close. I will rest and enjoy the twilight years of my life. I shan't dwell on the mysteriousness of this experience any longer, because the mystery has been solved. When I reminisce, I will concentrate on the lovely being I have come to know as "Lady of the Sands." However, my position stands firm. I cannot and shall not give a hint concerning my involvement.

Thank you Mr. Hopkins for your remarkable patience. I hold you in the utmost respect.
Farewell and Good Luck!
The Third and Last Man

My first impression of the third man's letter had to do with his literary style, which seemed positively Victorian. In my earlier discussion of Dan's "Lady of the Sands" letter, I called attention to the third man's typical Briticisms, but here, in his own letter, they were present in virtually every sentence. In fact, the author's locutions were so odd that the letter seemed like a translation from the French by a genteel Cambridge don.

I had no way to tell whether this style was the author's normal one, an attempt to match the "cosmic" level of his subject, or an act of concealment. I suspected the second. But whatever the reason, it was a far cry from the direct, vernacular style of Richard, Dan, Janet, and, for that matter, Linda, in the material she had written for me.

Certain of his usages were particularly striking, such as his description of Linda's having been "sprung out from her window like a springbok." (According to *Webster's New Collegiate Dictionary*, a springbok is "A South African gazelle . . . noted for its grace and for its habit of springing suddenly into the air.") Janet Kimball, watching the same scene from a greater distance, described Linda and the three aliens as looking like "little balls," which, she said, just "tumbled out." There is a marked difference between Janet Kimball's simple description and the third man's esoteric simile.

His next observation is phrased with a mix of poetic elegance and scientific precision. He refers to the beam of light in which Linda floated as a "beacon," and goes on to speculate that it "may have been radiological." Then, instead of the UFO "plunging into the East River," as Dan and Richard had said, Linda is "driven beneath the sea." Janet Kimball wrote that witnessing these events left her "scared half to death," but for the third man, it "caused us great distress."

I also noticed that he used the European style of writing a date: "30 November 1989," rather than the American: "November 30, 1989," used by Richard and Dan. From my knowledge of the third man's biography I was aware that he had spent a great deal of time in England, Europe, and South America, where this way of writing dates is customary.

Most important, however, is the third man's account of Linda as the Lady of the Sands and her lasting effect upon him. Apparently she spoke to him on the beach in the alien language that Richard had previously described. "Her words (possibly related to the Celtic language) shall ring in my head forever more," he wrote.[1] ". . . The phrases . . . were meant for me and I understood perfectly that I must adhere to them." This description of words "ringing in my head" echoes certain statements I had read in the letters I had received—or would eventually receive—from both Richard and Dan. Linda, in her Lady of the Sands persona, apparently communicated telepathically with each of the three men as they sat side by side on the beach that night, frightened and somehow constrained. Her telepathic conversations had evidently been private, in the sense that none of the three men seemed aware of the precise content of her communication with the other two. How any of this is possible, with the three men sitting side by side, is anybody's guess.

Linda, of course, did not remember these telepathic conversations. She recalled speaking only in English, when, fish in hand, she demanded that the three men "look and see what you have done." In light of all this, it seems at least plausible that the UFO occupants, like flawless, cosmic ventriloquists, were able to speak *through* Linda, using her human appearance to add weight to their alien wishes. This thesis appears less implausible when one considers it against the long history of widespread and varied alien deception: enforced amnesia, screen memories in which UFO occupants appear as hairless cats, as four-foot-tall owls, as members of one's own family, and so on. In a recent case a terrified little girl told her mother that in the middle of the night "Daddy came into my room, and as I was kissing him, he just shrunk down to a scary little gray man with a big head and huge black eyes."

But on November 30, 1989, whether it was Linda or the aliens speaking through her, the third man felt that he was receiving orders. Though he didn't spell out exactly what he had been told, he said that these commands "hastened a dream that has been in a talking stage for the past four decades or so. This dream has been 'World Peace.' . . . It was time to make it happen. . . . See what we have done in such a short time."

The third man wrote these words at the end of 1991, in the midst of extraordinary world changes: the crumbling of the Soviet Union and the breakup of the Eastern bloc of Communist nations. After four decades of tension and fear the cold war was finally coming to an end. That the third man has had at least a marginal role in these global events seems likely; that the aliens played any part in easing the threat of nuclear war is another matter.

However, it would seem that, using Linda as a conduit, the aliens were determined to make the third man view the dawn of a more peaceful world as *their* accomplishment to some extent. The goal, apparently, was to extend the illusion of their benign power over human affairs. This grandiose vision of their easing the threat of war while working to save our environment served as a convenient mask for their profound, covert, and ultimately damaging interference in the daily lives of Richard, Dan, Linda, the third man, and many other individuals in this case. What I did not understand at the time I received the third man's letter was the degree of the aliens' involvement. It took yet another letter from Richard to alert me to its extraordinary depth.

(For a discussion of the issue of the authenticity of the third man's letter, please see Appendix II.)

PART THREE

Mickey and Baby Ann

C H A P T E R

16

"She Wore Her Hair in Short Pigtails"

On Thursday, November 21, 1991, Linda called to tell me that she had had another unplanned but this time very agreeable meeting with Richard. Early that morning she was on her way to the neighborhood post office to buy some stamps when he suddenly walked up and took her by the hand. He smiled and asked if she was up for a talk. She immediately agreed. The morning's errands could easily be postponed for a meeting she had been looking forward to for more than a month.

Ever since Richard rescued her from Dan at the beach house and told her he would be seeing her again soon, she had felt more trusting of him. There was, of course, a remaining tinge of suspicion. So she made it very clear that she would spend time with him only in very public places and that she would not get into his car under any circumstances. He was happy to accept her conditions, and in a moment they were off, by cab, to the midtown area of Manhattan.

Linda's choice of destination, Saint Patrick's Cathedral, was a safe, neutral zone. "If he had anything in his mind that wasn't Christian, he'd change his mind after being in church for a while," she explained to me. She was pleased when he mentioned that like her, he, too, was a Catholic. After establishing a properly serious and truthful tone, the pair eventually wandered across Fifth Avenue to Rockefeller Center, and sometime later up to Central Park.

At the very beginning of their meeting Linda had asked Richard if she could call and invite me to join them, but he said that would be impossible. "You're not in my shoes, Linda," she recalled his remarking. "You just don't know what's going on with me on my side of the fence." She took this to be a reference to his government work and decided to let the matter drop.

Their conversation was somewhat stiff and uncomfortable at first, as if neither knew exactly what to say to the other. But as they left the cathedral, Linda made a conversational stab in the dark that surprised both of them. "What are some of the things you like to do?" she asked. "Do you still like to collect baseball cards?" She told me later that she had no idea why she assumed he collected baseball cards, except that "he looks as though he did. He looks very athletic."

Richard's response was just as surprising. He admitted that it had been a childhood hobby of his, and then asked with the same degree of certainty, "You collect them, too, don't you, Linda? Lots of them, right?" She conceded that she did, with her boys, and that they sometimes went to baseball card shows. It was an odd exchange.

The drift of the conversation that followed made her even more uncomfortable. Richard told Linda that now he collected stamps, an expensive hobby that gave him pleasure. "But," he added, "the UFO stuff doesn't give me pleasure, though I have an interest in it. I have an interest in you, and I find no pleasure in that, either, because I know you're not interested in me."

Linda disagreed, saying she did care about him because they had so much in common: "I had a strange experience and you saw it."

Richard's rejoinder was absolutely to the point. "Linda, your interest in me doesn't go beyond what I saw happen in November 1989. My interest in you does."

This remark was the beginning of what was apparently a prolonged attempt to let Linda know just how deeply he felt about her. She protested that she was a married woman with a family and that what he had seen back in 1989 must have something to do with his current feelings. "You just don't know me long enough to feel what you're feeling."

"I feel like I've known you all my life," Richard replied.

As Linda recounted what she recalled of their conversation, she made no attempt to conceal the uneasiness these remarks caused. Richard spoke about his failed marriage and the fact that he had been in love with someone else at the time "without realizing it." Linda asked how that was possible, but he seemed deliberately vague, even evasive, in trying to explain it.

He was very curious about Linda's two sons and her disclosure that, before they were born, she had had a miscarriage. At this point he steered the conversation into an even more problematic direction. He informed Linda that he believed he'd once fathered a son. When she asked if he had spent any time with the boy, he replied that he'd just "seen him from time to time." Linda wanted to know if he was certain the child was his, and he answered, "95 percent sure." More enigmatically, he said that he had wanted to marry the boy's mother but "she didn't know me. She didn't even know I existed."

Linda's reaction was to back away from this kind of talk, which she connected with Richard's confusion—the odd remarks and behavior that she had noticed before and associated with his unsettling UFO experience. After all, she reasoned, look what these incidents had done to poor Dan. He had lost his mind. "I didn't know what to say to Richard," she told me. "I just didn't understand what he was trying to say."

He continued talking about the woman he had loved for years who hadn't known he existed, about her son who he believed was his, and about the fact that this magical woman was already married to another man.

Although I didn't let her see my suspicion about his remarks, I was increasingly certain that it was Linda herself and her son Johnny that Richard was referring to. And as Linda and I talked, going over her recollections of Richard's conversation, I came to feel that despite her confusion, this was Linda's interpretation as well.

Richard wanted to talk about Johnny, she said, asking about his schoolwork, his interest in sports, his friendships, and so on. In October, when he had driven her back from Long Island after the harrowing episode with Dan, he had mentioned that he thought Johnny looked like him. "I remembered he'd said that, and I didn't like it," she told me. But as they talked he repeated this claim. Linda became angry and accused him of acting as if Johnny were his son. He seemed pleased that she had finally understood the drift of his remarks.

They left Rockefeller Center, and though the weather was somewhat threatening, they walked uptown toward Central Park. There they settled on a park bench, and in a short time things became even more difficult. Richard asked for a kiss, which Linda refused. "He began to get strange on me," she explained. "I was beginning to feel I should go home." And yet it was clear to me that even while she was repelling his advances, his flattering attention was not being rejected. She had often told me how handsome she thought he was and how nice he had been to her at certain times. I could see that within her ambivalent heart a proper married lady was at war with a yearning romantic, and increasingly the romantic was gaining the edge.

At one point their conversation took a different and ultimately significant turn. Linda mentioned that she had an older sister, and Richard replied that, as an only child, he thought it must be nice to have a brother or sister. When he was little, he recalled, he had had an imaginary friend, "like a little sister. I always wanted a little sister. Did you ever have an imaginary friend?"

Linda said that she did. Most children have imaginary friends, she thought. She told Richard that her playmate "used to take the blame for everything. I remember when I ate the last cookie in the cookie jar and I said that he ate it." Richard asked if she could recall her imaginary friend's name, but she had forgotten it. "I made him older than me," she said. "You know, a big brother. Believe it or not, I miss him!"

Sitting on a bench in Central Park, dodging occasional rain showers, Richard spoke to her ever more intimately, searching out her feelings for him and openly declaring his affection for her. As she described their conversation I could sense that it had become increasingly difficult for her to resist his sad, relentless ardor. She dutifully reminded him of all the reasons why there could be nothing between them, while he stubbornly countered with all the positive grounds for beginning a relationship. At one point she reacted with a sudden flash of anger and attacked, not Richard, but his open umbrella. Fortunately, her sense of humor soon returned and she apologized as Richard assessed the damage to his umbrella's ribs.

As they argued, Linda mentioned that whenever she was faced with a dilemma she made lists to help her sort out the various pros and cons. Richard playfully suggested they do that, make lists of the reasons for and against the deepening of their relationship. He took out a pad of paper and tore off two sheets. Linda explained to me that she thought of the process as "a game which was certainly not going to resolve his problems," but she went ahead anyway.

She showed me the two lists, wonderfully innocent and touching souvenirs of their struggle. Richard's is written in a firm, blocky mix of lower-case printing and cursive script, while Linda uses a flowing, delicate, schoolgirl's calligraphy. His is titled "Richard's Good Reasons" [for beginning a relationship] and there are eighteen points:

1. A lot in common (baseball, etc.)
2. Physical attraction
3. Spiritual attraction

4. Good companionship
5. Smells sweet
6. Loves children
7. Affectionate (with words)
8. Intelligent
9. Good sense of humor
10. Richard in love
11. Nice mannerisms
12. She likes to travel
13. She likes to cook
14. She's understanding
15. Generous
16. She's kind
17. Healthy
18. Loyal

Although Richard undoubtedly made up his rankings rather quickly, it's a sign of his shyness and hesitation that he doesn't declare his love as a reason for a relationship until he's more than halfway through the list. His first reason, "A lot in common (baseball, etc.)," has a hearty, aboveboard ring to it, as if he feels he must be friendly before he can let himself admit to any physical attraction or say that she "smells sweet." When he describes her as affectionate, he immediately qualifies the adjective, lest she object, by adding "with words." The last four qualities, "Generous, Kind, Healthy, Loyal," have a semper fidelis or Boy Scout ring to them, and seem proper afterthoughts, a way of praising her objectively without emphasizing his (perhaps unwelcome) desire for her.

Linda's list is shorter, only fourteen items, four of which Richard supplied in his own handwriting. While his lines march straight across the page with military correctness, Linda's lines droop sadly downhill. For the most part they are terse and self-denigrating. Their title is "Linda's Bad Reasons" [for beginning a relationship].

1. Married
2. Not in love w/Richard
3. Bad temper
4. [In Richard's handwriting] Breaks umbrellas
5. Violent tendencies (toward Richard)
6. Complains a lot
7. A cold streak
8. Isn't physically strong
9. Smokes cigarettes

10. [In Richard's handwriting] Linda is impatient
11. Doesn't sleep much
12. Drinks too much coffee
13. [In Richard's handwriting] Won't hug Richard
14. [In Richard's handwriting] Says "I told you so"

The defensive and self-denigrating tone of Linda's list surely reflects both her low self-esteem and her wish to discourage Richard's attention. It is also interesting that he, with characteristic modesty, makes no reference whatsoever to his personal strengths and qualities. For Richard, everything is focused on the object of his affection. I found myself touched by the old-fashioned caution and chivalry of his plea for Linda's consideration.

Sitting together, holding their lists and sparring gently with one another in the cool November weather, Richard and Linda experienced an unexpected amorous epiphany. "If I should die before you," he suddenly said to her, "there's something I want to take with me."

Linda described what happened next. "He took me in his arms and gave me a kiss I'll not soon forget. I couldn't believe it. I haven't been kissed like that in about twenty-four years. I fought it off for about the first two seconds into the kiss. My honor was involved here and so was Steve's, but I'm human even if Richard doesn't think I am. I enjoyed it and found myself kissing him back.

"What was I feeling? I was feeling great. And very curious . . . curious because he ended the kiss with a gentle tug on my bottom lip with his lips. I had a big lump in my throat, and it must have been my heart that was stuck there. It was a good thing that he didn't leave it up to me because I would've kissed him again. Just one more kiss, I said to myself, just one more and then I'll know.

"But Richard pulled away and looked at me with a helpless expression on his face. I looked into his eyes and then I looked back down at his lips. I couldn't believe what I'd let him do. Why did he pull on my bottom lip and snap it back against my bottom teeth? Why did he do that? Why does he look so sad?

"I asked him why he kissed me. I told him he shouldn't have done it, and then I began to cry. I could see his eyes filling with tears, too. He said, 'Thank you, Linda.' He said he'd keep it with him always, that now we have something of each other. And then he apologized. 'I know you're feeling disloyal and I'm sorry. But it was just a kiss. I know you're feeling that I made you do something wrong.'

"I told him that he didn't make me do something wrong—I did it myself. He asked why I let him kiss me, and what I was feeling

Top of Linda Cortile's building, showing three-windowed structure

Janet's sketch of UFO above Linda's building, depicting the same three-windowed structure

Janet's sketch of Linda, accompanied by aliens, being taken into the UFO. Another version of this sketch showed Linda and the aliens in a rolled, or fetal, position.

"A ball of fire before Linda was taken on 11/30/89"
(Richard's rendering of the UFO with a bright red surface,
as sent to the author)

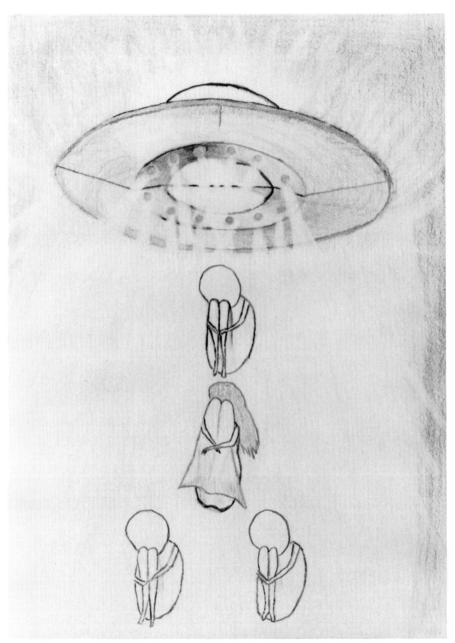

"Sprung out from her window one by one. Each in a fetal
position. They straightened out in the next drawing."
(Richard's drawing and description)

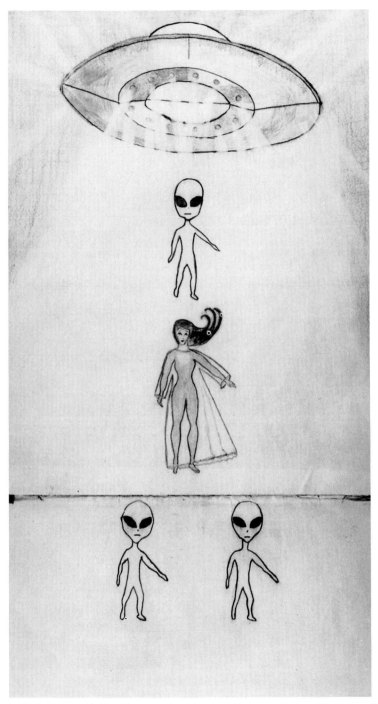

"The lights and shadows were so strong, I could actually see the silhouette of Linda's body. We even felt the static cling as the object passed over us."
(Richard's drawing and description)

Photographs of Linda running from Dan, after he kidnapped her and brought her to the eastern end of Long Island

Artist's rendering of black-haired alien, as recalled by both Marilyn and Linda *(Sal Amendola)*

Artist's rendering of alien hands, as described by Marilyn and Linda *(Sal Amendola)*

Artist's rendering of "conference scene" featuring Johnny on the table, as described by Marilyn and Linda *(Sal Amendola)*

Dear Poppii,

Thank you very much for the divers helmet. When I look at it, I think of you.

Did you know, my grandfather in Italy died before I was born. This means there has been room in my life for a grandfather. Someone like you!! I hope you feel the same way.

I would like to give you a hug, but I can't because you are not here with me. I hope I can see you again.

Love,
John
XXXX

Johnny's thank-you note for the Third Man, with sketch of diver's helmet

Diver's helmet given to Johnny and currently in his possession *(Linda Cortile)*

Johnny's happy sketch of himself, Linda, Richard, and Melody, along with two hybrids/aliens

Johnny's sad sketch of same group after Melody is taken away

Electron microscope photo of raw sand sample

Electron microscope photo of altered sand sample

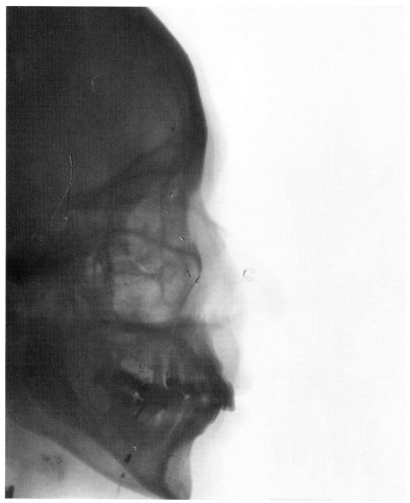

X-ray of Linda's nasal implant

now. 'Are you kidding?' I said. 'What am I feeling? I'm feeling that I want another kiss. I hope you're satisfied!' He smiled at me and said he really meant that kiss, 'and if it's another you want, you're welcome to it. I could sit here and kiss you all day long.'

"But I could have sat there and kissed *him* all day long. I've always wanted my first kiss again. This was like my very first kiss, only I can't remember who gave it to me!

"Of course, I wasn't about to let him kiss me again, though I would've liked to. I'm a fool. I should be ashamed of myself."

I told Linda that I could easily understand why she had responded as she did, and reminded her that whatever had happened, ultimately she had shown her loyalty to her husband. I wasn't sure whether my words were comforting or not. Obviously, being with Richard had been both a stirring and an unsettling experience for her.

Shortly after their kiss she told Richard that it was time to go home. When he threw his arms around her for a final hug, she warned him, no more kisses. He agreed with a smile, happy to settle for the one she had allowed him.

But Richard had one more piece of business to take care of. He handed Linda a little box and told her that it was a gift she should take to me for having been so supportive of him, of Dan, and of the third man. She gave it to me a few days later. The box contained a gold friendship ring with my name, Budd, engraved beneath a row of four small diamonds. Etched on the inside of the ring was the name "Richard" and two dates: "11-30-89" and "11-30-91." Though the date I received his gift was November 23, 1991, it was only seven days shy of the second anniversary of the original abduction incident, which had brought us all together. Like so much about Richard, the gift of the ring was gracious, thoughtful, and affectionate. I was touched to know that someone I had never met, but with whom I'd had complex, emotional, and often bizarre exchanges, would regard me as a friend.

But if the events of November 21, 1991, involving Richard, Linda, and, indirectly, myself, were surprising, nothing could have prepared me for the letter I received from Richard a few days later. Not only did it mark another major breakthrough in the case, but more importantly, it was the first in what has become a series of similar accounts that together comprise a dramatic new pattern within the UFO abduction phenomenon.

Dear Mr. Hopkins—

The meeting yesterday, between Linda and I went very well. She was very relaxed and comfortable.

I gave Linda the choice of where we should spend our day. She preferred to stay on Manhattan Island.

We went sightseeing and saw St. Patrick's Cathedral, Rockefeller Center, and we walked through Central Park. I wanted to hug and kiss her, but knowing Linda, "she would have run away."

Linda is a very interesting person. Theres no wondering why, considering what she may be. Yes Budd, I believe that Linda is from another place, but raised here. I know she doesn't agree and becomes angry when this opinion is expressed.

There is nothing more we need to know about her. We're convinced that she isn't working for anyone. However, if we possessed her talent of protecting ourselves, it would make our work a lot easier. It would stop the perpetrator in his tracks. At the same time, no one would get hurt in the process. What better way to protect our world leaders and each other? Only Linda knows what she possesses. But, she refuses to admit it, by saying that she doesn't remember. At any rate, I won't say a word to anyone. The third party decided it was best not to attend our little meeting. He had many other commitments to tend to.

He is an unhealthy man, who needs to slow down. Naturally, he refuses to admit this, and continues to race around anyway. However difficult this is for him, his interests regarding World Peace, art and French cuisine remain intact. Ironically, his interest in the physical condition of the earth, has heightened to a great level. He will most likely spend the last years of his life, dedicated to this cause.

The November 1989 Incident has taken its toll on him. We're worried about his health.

As for Dan, he has suffered another set back, at the tail end of our trip. Shortly after we returned to the States, we checked him into a hospital for observation. It was concluded that Dan be placed into a rest home for a while. At least, until he can get his head on straight. He checked himself into one of the best rest homes in the country.

He will remain there under treatment, for an indefinite period of time.

Dan has had problems long before this incident occurred. The incident itself brought him to the breaking point.

As for the others involved (those in the other cars), I'll assume that they haven't discussed it since the incident happened.

As for me, I'm still hanging on, but by a hair.

Budd, there's a need for me to tell you something that no one knows except for myself. I have to share this with you, because if I don't, Dan will have my company at the rest home, where he is now staying.

However personal, and embarrassed I am about this, I have to get it off my chest. You are the only person I know of, where there will be the possibility that you may understand. For the life of me, I don't understand and maybe its better that I don't. In fact, I find this particular situation harder to accept than the November 1989, Incident itself.

Please don't think that I too, have gone over the edge. If I have, then I must of been crazy for most of my life.

Throughout the years of my life, from the age of 10, to the age of 25, I've been dreaming of a girl from time to time. I never knew whom she was, or where she came from. She seemed to be a figment of my imagination. As strange as it seems, we grew up together in my dreams. The older I became, the more I dreamt of her.

As far as I can remember, my first dream occurred when I was 10 years old. In the dream, I didn't know where I was. But, it was a very bright white environment. I spent most of my time shading my eyes from the bright sunlight.

Two tall, fair, emotionless male adults walked towards me, holding the hand of a tiny little girl. I thought she was about 3 or 4 years old. She wore her hair in short curled pig tails, jeans, and a baseball cap placed the wrong way on her head.

She smiled at me, and asked if I wanted to play. I said no, because she was so much smaller than me. The two strange adults left her with me anyway, which gave me the feeling that I was baby sitting.

We began to talk, and I learned that she was 7 years old. We told each other our names, but for some strange reason, we couldn't remember from minute to minute. So, I named her Baby Ann and she named me Mickey.

We wandered around for a while, with nothing to do. We became acquainted and found each other to be full of fun.

The next thing I knew, these two strange adults came along and led Baby Ann away by the hand. I was left standing there with my hands in my pockets.

I woke up that morning remembering this dream, and shortly forgot all about it, as we all do most of the time, afterwards.

About six months later, I dreamt of Baby Ann again. This second dream triggered the memory of the first dream.

This time, we were at the same bright white location, as we were the first time. The same strange adults walked her over to me, and made me play with her. I didn't mind because I liked Baby Ann. We played games like cops and robbers, etc., and we talked for a little while. She was a cute little thing and we became friends. She asked me why I named her Ann, and I told her that the name reminded me of the color yellow, and it almost matched the color of her hair. She just looked like an Ann.

I remember removing her baseball cap and put it on the right way. But, she kept changing it back to the wrong way.

Shortly, these two emotionless people came by, and took her away once again. Baby Ann waved good-bye and walked away with them.

When I woke up that morning in my bed, it took a little longer for me to forget. I wondered why I was dreaming of the same tiny little girl for the second time. I had never seen her before the last two dreams. But, before I knew it, each night I went to sleep, secretly hoping I would dream of her again.

Two and a half years passed, before another dream came. I was 13 and she was 10 and taller. She still wore her cap the wrong way, and her curled pig tails were longer.

I remember how she let go of the hands of those strange adults and came running to me, when she saw me this time. We were very happy to see each other again and tried to memorize each others address. But, just like our names, 3 years past, we kept forgetting from minute to minute. We wondered why and how were we going to continue this friendship outside of these dreams?

This time, we talked more and played less. We wanted to know everything about each other. We asked each other so many questions. We were anxious to know about each others interests, etc. There was so much to learn about each other.

When those strangers came along to take her away, it became more difficult to say good-bye.

I remember when she pulled herself away from their grip and asked if she could stay longer. They said No, and took her away.

I literally waited 3 years to dream of her again. Three years is a long time for a kid to wait for something. The years dragged on. But, it was worth the wait, because the bonding began.

I was 16 and she was 13. Baby Ann was growing into a lovely young woman. She lost her baseball cap and wore her hair loose. I noticed that there was a change in her body, and I liked it!

We sat on a bright white sandy beach, facing one another. I gave her what she called her very first kiss. Our relationship changed. We constantly held hands, and from time to time, I'd steal a kiss or two.

When it was time for her to leave, it hurt us more and I was getting tired of being left flat, with my hands in my pockets. I protested, but these two fair men didn't give a damn, and took her away just the same.

The older I became, the more I dreamt of Baby Ann. It was fine with me, but it was taking its toll on my "real" social life. It didn't matter who I dated, they just couldn't measure up to Baby Ann. I was old enough to know that I couldn't let this figment of my imagination take over my life! I wasn't handling it very well. What was I to do? By now, I was seeing Baby Ann on a steady basis. About once every six months! The bonding became stronger and stronger. She became more and more beautiful.

I couldn't help myself. What does a boy from the age of 16 to 19 do? These dreams just wouldn't stop! If they did, it would've broken my heart! I've lost control!

By the time I was 25, I was totally beside myself with love. I wanted to get married, and so did Baby Ann. But how? You can't marry a figment of your imagination! What were we going to do? Stay in our dreams, never to return to our bedrooms again? How? I'll tell you Budd, I had a problem. These dreams were torturing me. I wanted them to stop no matter how painful it might have been. I tried therapy and the local Priest too. Nothing helped! The dreams continued.

In the year 1969, when I was 25 and Baby Ann was 22, the bond was completed. We were going to spend the rest of our lives together, no matter what we had to do. I don't think there was ever a greater love than ours.

Until those miserable, creepy bastards came along and attempted to take Baby Ann away from me. We tried to explain our problem. We told them that we never wanted to part. But they didn't care. They took her away from me. I tried to stop them, but they were much stronger than I. She cried so much that she lost her breath, and struggled all the way. I chased them, but it was too late. They were gone.

This meant that we wouldn't see each other again for another 6 months. I knew we would try again to stay together at that time. So, I was left angry and hurt, with my hands in my pockets.

Consequently, these reoccurring dreams vanished, and I never saw her again. Life seemed very sad. The torture I felt went away, but emptiness took its place.

Twenty years later, November 30, 1989. I had a UFO sighting, sitting in a car on Catherine Slip and South Streets. The object hovered over an apartment building about 2 blocks up.

A beam of whitish-blue light flashed on from beneath it. Soon, I saw the figures of 3 strange creatures, and a figure of a little girl, surrounded by light, just after they came out of a window below.

I had to be sure of what I was seeing. It was so very bizarre. So, I went into the glove compartment to get a pair of binoculars.

There I saw "MY BABY ANN" hanging in the light, like a Christmas Tree Bell.

That circle of glass, with the image of her face in it, haunted me for months. I was terrified and confused. I couldn't take it anymore. I had to find her "dead or alive."

I found her alright. Linda "IS" my Baby Ann. She's real and not a figment of my imagination. I came away very angry that night after I left her apartment. How could those two bastards "in my dreams," be so cruel as to let me go on in my life, without her.

It wasn't fair!

Budd, I love her so. But its too late. So, once again, I'm left here, with my hands in my pockets.

I've hinted to Linda, about our bonding "as those bastards named it." But, she doesn't recall. I don't want to interfere with her life anymore, than I already have. She has a life of her own, and she shares it with a family, that could have been mine.

Budd, I don't think she should know about this, if she hasn't remembered on her own. In any case, if she does recall sometime in the future, please tell her that it wasn't all in her mind. Please tell her "I love her" and I've missed her very much over the years.

I've been lucky enough to find out that I've been in love with a real woman, instead of a dream, over a period of a life time. This has made all the heartache worthwhile.

I don't understand what has happened throughout my life. Was I dreaming or not? I don't know and I'm glad I don't know.

In the meantime, this whole situation with the November 1989 incident, and my problem with Linda, has me standing between the fire and the water. If I go in either direction, I'll burn, or I'll drown.

I shouldn't be in her life anymore. It isn't fair to her family. Nor should she be in mine, because it isn't fair to me. It's painful. Too painful and risky.

Budd, I put in for a transfer. It should be coming in at any time.

As for you, kind Sir, I know it hasn't been easy for you. You've been a good friend, and I'll treasure your friendship for the rest of my life.

Whether you know it or not, "you're holding my heart in your hands."

Good Luck in your investigations!!!!! You're the very best in the world and don't let anyone tell you different! Remember, a leader of all Nations holds you in the highest esteem.

Good-bye Budd, and May God Bless.

Respectfully yours,
Richard

Obviously, the major revelation in this moving letter is Richard's claim that the aliens had repeatedly abducted Linda and himself from childhood on, bringing them to the same strange, neutral environment, allowing them to play together and eventually to form a friendship. Then, when he and Linda reached puberty, they fell in love and "bonded," in Richard's sexually suggestive designation. This inevitably long-term operation sounded very like an alien psychological/ anthropological study of human relationships under precisely controlled conditions.

That was the next-to-last time Richard recalled their having been brought together. As I was to learn in a subsequent letter, there was one more, apparently final, "bonding" between them as mature adults. Somewhat circumspectly he described a sexual encounter with Linda that occurred "about ten years ago," which would place it about 1981. Could Linda's son Johnny—born in 1982—possibly be the product of such an artificial process?

Until this letter I had neither heard of nor even imagined such profound alien meddling in individual human lives. Astonishing though it was, I found Richard's account had the ring of truth, the tone of authentic pain and confusion. If it *were* true, it would explain much of his and Linda's subsequent behavior. But could such an outrageous report actually be believed? Or was it an elaborate fantasy? I had to think of ways to test its objective truth.

For the time being I knew I must keep Richard's letter secret in order to objectively explore Linda's recollections of the imaginary playmate she had told him about in the park. Was Mickey the big brother she said she had always wanted, and whose name she had forgotten? I knew that I would need to conduct a hypnosis session to probe her memories more deeply. If Linda *did* remember specific details confirming Richard's account, I would arrange another videotaped meeting with psychologist Gibbs Williams and historian Chuck Strozier. Linda must hear Richard's story of Mickey and Baby Ann for the first time in the presence of objective witnesses, with the camera running in close-up. I would record Linda's spontaneous reactions on tape just as I had with Dan's confirming Lady of the Sands letter. Future investigators must be able to see exactly how she responded to Richard's account.

This would be my initial strategy. But on a broader scale I would begin looking for any replication of this apparent "human relationship study" among the thousands of UFO abduction cases currently under investigation by my colleagues and myself. If Richard's account was true, the aliens' interest in pairing him with Linda had been ongoing for about forty years. And if this situation was not unique, had we for decades been overlooking a significant pattern, a potentially important subset of abduction cases? The answer is yes, we had been neglecting exactly such a cluster of cases. What's more, this discovery of the aliens' interest in studying human relationships and eventual sexual "bonding" from childhood through maturity is one of the most important contributions of the Linda Cortile case. It vastly extends our awareness of alien interest in basic human psychology and behavior.

As I reexamined Richard's letter, I found a number of smaller observations worth noting. It was interesting that even though he knows it infuriates Linda to hear it, he still insists that she is not fully human, that she is "from another place but raised here." Richard expresses amazement at her alleged talent for protecting herself, a reference, I believe, to such incidents as Dan's being frozen and unable to draw his gun against the Lady of the Sands.

Richard also says that the third man ("the third *party*," in Dan's phrase) is currently in poor health, yet overactive and deeply interested in world peace, in art, and in French cuisine. His description provided me with areas for future inquiry into the life and character of this important figure. (Subsequently, I was able to confirm the truth of each of these five observations, the last two of which are unknown to the general public. For example, when I met and talked with the third man many months later I discovered that he had extensive knowledge of the painting and sculpture collections of the Brooklyn Museum.)

Finally, Richard's remarks about Dan were reassuring. For Linda's sake, it was good to know that he had been taken to a hospital for observation (probably after his breakdown at the beach house), and that currently he was in "one of the best rest homes in the country . . . under treatment." For the time being, at least, all of us could breathe easier. But my immediate goal was to arrange a meeting with Linda to explore, without arousing suspicion, her long conversation with Richard and their brief mention of imaginary childhood friends. As I soon discovered, it would be an extraordinary experience.

CHAPTER 17

"A Sunny Place, No Horizon"

Richard's conversations with Linda took place on November 21, and his letter describing their encounter was written the next day. When I received it I was so curious to find out what Linda might remember about "Mickey and Baby Ann" that I set up an appointment for 10:00 A.M. on Monday, November 25, only four days after their meeting. She arrived at my studio in a happy frame of mind, completely unaware that Richard had already reported his view of their complex, decades-long relationship. We sat down at my round dining table, and with the red fabric shade of the lamp above the table giving everything a nice, rosy glow, I turned on my tape recorder. It was important to document everything that Linda remembered consciously about their conversation. Only after we had gone through all of it would we then go downstairs to the lower studio where, on the familiar black couch, Linda could explore the same events in a relaxed hypnotic trance.

We chatted first about baseball and the fact that she had asked Richard about his hobby of collecting baseball cards. I learned once again that she was a baseball fanatic. "I went to my first game when I was around five," she said. "I had a New York Yankees hat that I wore all the time. I treasured it. I even wore it when I went to bed at night. But, you know, I always wore it crooked, with the brim turned off to one side. The reason I did it like that was because I always had to be able to see straight *up*, in case there was something right above me, and I didn't want the brim to be in the way. Now I know why I wore it like that." After all of her UFO experiences, her odd childhood habit now made perfect sense to both of us.

But she was not just a baseball fan. She was a good enough player, she reminded me, to make a neighborhood baseball team when she was eleven years old, winning out over several boys. Trying to keep the conversation as casual as possible, I moved on to more central issues. I asked her about Richard's use of the term "bonding," the meaning of which she didn't quite understand. "Richard told you that you were bonded with him but not with Dan," I said. "Now what does bonding mean to you as a term . . . what do you think about it now?"

"I think it means when something happens that makes you very close," she replied. "Like when a woman gives birth and as soon as the child is born they give the child to her and that's when the bonding begins. Or, a bond is when you solder a metal to another metal. So it's . . . it's something close . . . a mother and a child. When I was in Pennsylvania I had a horse. A relative gave me a horse and I saw it being born. And they all stood away from the horse while the mother and the colt, my Dusty, bonded with one another, so that the mother and child could have the bond."

"What's so interesting to me," I added, "is that Richard said Dan and the third man were *not* bonded with you. . . . Explain that again."

"Okay. He said to me, the third man and Dan were bonded to me but I wasn't bonded to them . . . which I don't understand. . . ."

I was still confused. "Did he explain what he meant by 'they were bonded to you'? Did you ask what that meant?"

"I did and he said maybe we shouldn't talk about it. I said, 'I don't know why we're talking about it, anyway. Apparently you're not giving me any information, so why bother?' He did say that it happened that night [November 30, 1989] on the beach. They were bōnded to me. They felt close to me. But *I* didn't feel that way. *I* didn't feel bonded. But he said between him and me there was a mutual bond. . . ."

"And he didn't explain what that meant? What do you think it meant?"

Linda answered with characteristic honesty. "I don't know what it means because I don't remember anything. See, I told him, 'Why're you telling me all this if you're not going to bother to give me any information?' So he says, 'Well, because you don't remember, I don't want to tell you . . . because if I did tell you, you might have a nervous breakdown.' He wants me to remember on my own. See, he thinks

I'm gonna remember, but I don't know what he's talking about. And when I do remember, he doesn't want me to think that it's just my imagination playing games with me. . . .''

Linda felt that whatever this "bonding" process was, Richard meant that it was not merely an emotional feeling. Instead it was like a specific *event* that happened at a specific time "in the past . . . before '89, which leads me to believe that something [a UFO experience] happened to him . . . even before that incident."

We talked about anything Richard might have said that would suggest earlier UFO experiences, and Linda came up with a new association. It was as if her subconscious mind had suddenly made a connection between our discussion and *her own* gradually resurfacing memories. "He asked me—maybe this will help—if I had any imaginary friends when I was a kid. I said, well, yes I did. But he only came out at night. I think all children . . . not *all* children . . . had some sort of imaginary . . . I mean I had a little girl friend who thought that her dolls came to life at night. She'd go to sleep and their eyes would open and they'd walk around and play and stuff."

I asked if that scared her friend.

"Well, it did scare her. It did, but that's what she thought."

I went back to her original remark. "You said you had an imaginary friend. Tell me about that."

"It was a little boy, but he was older than me. And he was bigger than me. And he would talk to me. See, Budd, I always wished I had a brother. A lot of my friends had brothers, that used to defend them. And I have a sister. She's eight years older than me. Of course, she'd defend me, but she was a girl. The boys didn't find a girl all that threatening. I loved my sister to death—but I always wished I had a brother. I could have, too. It would have been a younger brother but my mother had a miscarriage. So, I guess that's why I had this imaginary brother."

I asked about her imaginary brother. "So what happened? What would he do? Do you remember anything about him?"

"Well, I would go to sleep and I'd say my prayers. Sometimes I'd fall asleep saying my prayers and I didn't think of this imaginary friend—or brother. And, well, we'd play games—in my mind. We'd play . . .''

"So when you had the dream . . .''

"I don't even know if they were dreams. It may be before I fell asleep. Sometimes I used to dream of this imaginary friend. And we'd just play games: hide-and-seek, ring-a-levio, Johnny-on-the-pony. We used to play cops and robbers . . . and army. Cops and robbers and army."

I went on, hoping to narrow down the specifics of her "dreams." "When you'd play these games, where were you? Were you in the house or were you in your apartment?"

"I don't know where we were. I don't remember any environment. I remember . . . yeah, yeah, I do remember . . . I don't know why I'd imagine being in a place like that. It was very, very sunny. It was very bright and sunny."

"Trees?" I asked.

"No. No, none of that. You know, come to think of it there really wasn't anywhere to play."

"How do you play hide-and-seek with no trees?"

She answered with some confusion, as if in retrospect these "fantasies" were more peculiar than she had thought at the time. "Yeah, uh, there were no buildings or cars to hide behind. You know, when you're in the city, we'd hide behind cars or buildings. Doorways."

"Sure," I said. "Of course. How'd you play hide-and-seek?"

"I don't know. It was very bright and sunny—white. Very *white*. Why would I . . . ? You know, I didn't like the sun. Never did. I don't know why I would imagine . . . yeah, it was so, so bright that I'd have to shield my eyes. Gee, that's strange . . ."

"Yeah, that is strange," I agreed. "Did you tell Richard all these things, or not? What'd you tell him?" I had to know if his letter had in any way been influenced by details in their conversation.

"No, no I didn't tell him that. I just told him that I had an imaginary friend."

"So, in these dreams of yours it was very sunny. No cars or buildings or trees."

"You would think," Linda replied, still musing on the unusual quality of her memories, "that we would hide in the courtyard because that's where we played—in the courtyard. No, there was nothing there. In the dream it was all very open, though. Crooked. A slant. I think it was white concrete."

"So the ground slanted real steeply, or . . . ?"

"Well, not too steep, but I always felt like I was on a slant. I don't know why. That's strange. Come to think of it, that's real strange. Why would I think of a place . . . it was like nowhere . . . it was like the sky . . . like there was no horizon. You couldn't see the difference in color."

I tried, once again, to lead Linda into a conventional explanation. "Could you see the blue sky?"

"No. But we were outside. You could smell air."

"Were there any other smells?"

"No. Gee, I don't remember ever seeing the sky. But we were outside because it was so bright . . . it was very sunny."

"Did your imaginary friend have a name?" I asked, feeling a certain quiet excitement about the drift of her apparently spontaneous recollections. Nevertheless, her answer came as a shock.

"I named him Mickey," she said. "I guess maybe because of Mickey Mouse."

I laughed and asked, "Did he have funny ears?"

"No. Mickey. Gee, I haven't remembered that in years. I guess it's always been here [pointing to her forehead] but not in the front of my mind. Yeah, Mickey. I remember that."

"Well, you know how it is with all these memories. Once you begin focusing in on them, they start. Mickey Mouse. Were you a Mickey Mouse person?"

"Yeah, I was a Mickey Mouse fan. I used to watch it every day . . . with Annette Funicello and all of them . . . that's the only time I took my baseball cap off, to put on my Mickey Mouse hat at home. I'd sing [sings] M I C—K E Y . . ."

We both laughed. But I was eager to go on with her recollections of Mickey and the strange white environment. "Were there any other kids who played with you? Any other people, or adults, for that matter? Were there just the two of you in this game? Did you have other little kids running around?"

"Hmm. No, there weren't any other children. No."

"How about anybody's parents, or adults?"

"Yeah, I think so. I think there was an adult—or two. Very tall people. Now why in the world would I put two adults in my fantasy?"

"I don't know," I responded. And, still trying to lead away from Richard's account while remaining logical, I asked, "A man and a woman?"

"No. Two men. Why did I do that? You know how kids are. I don't mean that I didn't really like adults, but they were a sign of authority. Why put them in a fantasy? You don't want that."

"Were these Mickey's parents or something?"

"No. No, they used to bring me to Mickey. You know what it could be? I think maybe I know why I used to put that in my fantasy. Because I wasn't allowed to cross the street by myself. And so I needed someone to bring me to my imaginary friend, or brother. Yeah, that's right."

"That makes sense," I agreed. "But you're sure it wasn't your mother or father?"

"No. No. I remember. They were tall, thin. Didn't say much.

Didn't say much at all. Maybe I preferred it that way because the authority figures, when you're a kid . . . you know, adults, you had to always be respectful and had to be careful of what you said. I'm surprised, though, because I'll bet it was because I was obedient when I was little. Then I grew up and I was a rip. Yeah, they used to bring me over to Mickey."

I had been patiently holding off from the next line of inquiry, but now its time had come: "Do you remember what they looked like? Or what Mickey looked like? Start with the adults. What did they look like?"

"They were tall . . . very strong looking. They wore blue, blue diving suits, like . . . to me it looked like [skin] diving suits or motorcycle suits . . . tight-fitting suits. They were very blond. Might as well make them good-looking, right? In a fantasy. Yeah. They didn't say much. I guess I preferred it that way. They weren't very talkative.

"Mickey . . . He was cute. Let's see, I made him very cute. He was a strawberry blond. He had big blue eyes."

"What was he wearing when you played?"

"He was wearing jeans. If I could remember, did I put jeans on him? Yeah, jeans, polo shirt . . . no baseball cap. I was the only one with a baseball cap."

"So you wore yours?"

"That's right. Sneakers. Yeah, I put sneakers on him. He had those black sneakers with the, you know, baseball on the side? I had those too. Like a real little boy—I had them."

"What were you wearing? You had your baseball cap . . ."

"I had my baseball cap. Jeans, of course. My sneakers . . . those black sneakers. I had another pair too, a white pair. Girls' sneakers. I always wore polo shirts myself. Striped polo shirts, or . . ."

About two years earlier Linda had made a drawing for me of herself as a child, and I referred to it now. "As I remember, in your drawing you have a polo shirt on. You were a little girl wearing your hat with the brim turned to the side and ribbons on your braids. So I know what you looked like."

Linda returned to the subject of the two men in blue skin-divers' suits. "I think they were there [in my fantasy] because I wasn't allowed to go anywhere by myself. See, I went to a school that was only a block away, and my mother used to look for me out the window. We lived on the sixth floor and she'd just look out the window because I would be coming home for lunch. We used to come home for lunch, and I had to have the crossing guard cross me. I wasn't allowed to cross by myself. My mother used to look out the window to make sure . . ."

Again, trying for a conventional explanation, I asked another question. "Was the crossing guard blond and tall?"

"No. Her name was Gloria. . . ."

"Oh, it's a woman. But where, in the fantasy, did these two guys bring you from? Where were you at the beginning? How did it start?"

Once more Linda looked thoughtful, trying to remember. "It just started that I was coming down a sort of a ramp. A slant, and I'd hold on to their hands. Both of them. They're holding both my hands. Because, you see, this crossing guard used to hold my hand crossing the street. Sometimes someone else's mother would hold my hand and I'd have both of them crossing the street. The neighbor or whoever and the crossing guard would be talking and they'd both hold my hands crossing the street. So, I made it that these two people held my hands. Both hands. And we'd walk down a ramp. And I would see like a speck ahead of me. Like a dark speck. Well, in my fantasy that was Mickey. That was Mickey . . . in the distance . . . so he just looked like a speck."

"And he'd be by himself?" I asked.

"All by himself."

"You wouldn't see anything around him?"

"No. No horizon. I don't know why I'd do that. . . . I remember walking downhill, so I would imagine it was like a ramp. I was walking downhill . . . or [musing to herself] did everything look like it was one piece?"

"Was the ramp," I asked, "the same material as everything else?"

"Everything was white. Very sunny. And I never liked the sun."

"When did you start remembering all these things, Linda? Is it just now as we talk?"

"Well, yeah. It's like you're pumping me about all these things and it makes me remember. Because I do remember my imaginary friend."

"What does he call you? 'Linda'?"

"I don't know. I don't remember. Well, maybe at the time I remembered. I guess I was so busy concentrating on him, you know. I don't remember. I guess he called me Linda."

"Okay. Now, when you said you came down the ramp . . . is this the whole landscape?"

"There are walls. Not walls. Almost like the South Ferry terminal [in Manhattan, a curving ramp with waist-high sides]. You have these concrete walls on both sides and you're walking down this ramp and it's all concrete . . . it's like that."

A further conversation ensued about this odd setting in which

Linda made clear that everything—ground, walls, ramp, sky, and so forth are one color and apparently one substance.

I went back to the subject of her imaginary friend. "Now, when you had this friend . . . we'll call him Mickey . . . how often would you have these memories or dreams or whatever?"

"I used to think about him all the time. I mean sometimes I'd think about him during the day, I'd think about him even when I was with my friends. We could be playing skelly. You know what skelly is, don't you? With chalk we used to draw a box on the ground and it would have boxes in it with numbers. And then we would take soda bottle caps . . . and the higher the number the better . . . Coke bottle tops . . ."

"So you might be playing that game and you would be thinking about Mickey?"

"Yeah, I'd think about Mickey and I'd say to myself, yeah, Mickey's gonna help me win this one. Maybe others would say, 'Lady Luck,' if it were dice. And I'd say, well, okay, Mickey, you know, sort of guide my hand and get me to number . . ."

"He was kind of magic? A magic guy?"

"Yeah, I think so. Sure. But at night I would think about him and . . . sometimes I'd get bored with my own fantasy. I wouldn't want to play hide-and-seek, I'd want to play something else for a change. Let's play army."

Again I asked for clarification. "How can you hide when there's no place to hide?"

"I don't know, and see, what I don't understand is, why in the world would I pick a place like that? There's nothing there. Unless I just didn't know where I wanted us to be."

I opened the door of speculation just a crack. "Well, you'd think in a fantasy that you'd almost invent a different location each time."

"Well, sure. I loved the farm. I used to go up to the farm *all* the time—out in Pennsylvania. I loved it there. Why didn't I make it a farm? I don't know, maybe I wanted it to be special and I just didn't know exactly where I would have liked it to be so I just didn't put anything there."

"What did you think of the two big guys in your fantasy?"

"I didn't like them very much. But they had to be there because they were adults. I couldn't go anywhere by myself so I thought maybe I should be obedient in my fantasy. I don't even think they were dreams. I think they were just fantasies because I'd fall asleep thinking about it."

"Was this every single night?"

"I used to think about it almost every night. I'd say more times I fell asleep without thinking about it. Like I'd want to think about it and I'd be ready to think about it but I wouldn't because I probably fell asleep. I'd say that I'd have a good time, oh, every month, every . . . sometimes I'd want to think about it but I'd fall asleep even before I'd finish saying my prayers. So I didn't have time to think about it."

"How old were you when this stopped?"

"That's strange. It didn't stop."

"Hmmm. Usually these things stop, at eight or nine or something like that."

"I was still single. I don't remember. I'm sure it must have stopped when I was a kid, I guess."

"Of course," I explained, delicately fishing for memories of a later period, "one of the things that happens is, as you get older s-e-x comes into the picture in fantasies and so forth."

"I don't really remember when it stopped. I'm sure it must have stopped when I was a kid."

"So you don't have any romantic stuff? Any sense of . . ."

"No. No. Maybe there were. But I don't remember them. He was cute though. I made him very cute. He had a button nose. He was adorable. You don't think I'd pick a brother or imaginary friend and he'd be real ugly? He was cute. He was really cute! Johnny looks a lot like him."

"Who?"

"My Johnny—when I think about it. Yea. Button nose and blue eyes . . ."

"Give me a description of your imaginary friend now—as you think about him; his height, his build, his coloring. Let's start with his height when he was a little boy."

"He was a lot taller than me. Couldn't be a big brother if he weren't."

"Was he kind of plump, like Johnny?"

"Oh, no. I'd say he was average. I made him average. He wasn't too thin. He wasn't too heavy."

"Tell me about his coloring."

"He had rosy cheeks. He had blue eyes. He had strawberry blond hair combed to the side. Sometimes I put it in a pompadour. I think at the beginning of my fantasy I put his hair on the side and then later on I changed his style. . . ."

"When he got older? Well, maybe when you get to be a little older you want to see someone more grown up like that."

"He was strawberry blond. My grandmother was a strawberry

blond on my father's side of the family. She was gorgeous. I was a dirty blond myself. Well, Johnny was a *platinum* blond when he was very little. *Platinum.*"

"Was he really? How long did that last?"

"Till he was about four. Well, no, his hair did get darker. He was a regular blond at the age of four but he was a platinum baby. I was never as fair as John. As I grew older my hair darkened."

I was curious as to whether John's hair coloring was truly unusual in the family, and asked how long he was fair-haired. "He was a platinum blond when he was a baby and now he has ash brown."

Now I decided to take a wild flyer and ask Linda about Richard, since she had already told me about his claim that he might be Johnny's father. I tried to be casual. "For the heck of it, Linda, just make a guess, since I never met him, make a guess about what Richard would have looked like as a little boy."

"Well, I saw a picture. In that beach house—on the wall. It was in black and white. It, uh, it looks a lot like that picture. Isn't that strange?"

I wasn't sure what she meant, but she seemed momentarily puzzled herself. "What looks a lot like the picture?"

"Like Mickey. Like Mickey."

I decided to be direct. "It struck me when you were describing Mickey that you said 'strawberry blond and a button nose.' Those are two features that you've mentioned every time you've mentioned Richard to me. So, I noticed . . ."

"Yeah, it just so happens . . . yeah, the picture. I don't know. I don't remember now if he was with a dog or a bicycle in that picture. But it was in black and white."

"How was his hair fixed in that picture?"

"To the side, I think."

"How old does he look?"

"He looked like he was about twelve. Maybe younger. It's hard to tell the height in a photograph unless he's standing next to someone else. There wasn't another person to compare. I forgot about that picture. But maybe it wasn't him. It could have been anybody's childhood picture. . . . You know, I'll tell you, Johnny, if he were thinner—because Johnny used to be thin at one time—I would imagine Richard looked a lot like him when he was a little guy like that. Yeah." Here Linda paused, seeming to mull over her recollections. "In fact, I remember when Johnny was born, I couldn't understand it, I said, 'Well, what's that on his head? You're going to wash him before you're going to give him to me, aren't you?' They said, 'We did.' I said, 'Well, what's that on his head?' They said, 'Well, that's his hair.' I says 'No.' They said, 'Oh, yes it is. He's a blond.' "

At this point I suggested we go downstairs to the studio and see what Linda might recall under hypnosis. Though I gave her no reason to sense it, I was astounded by what she had remembered consciously, once she focused on Mickey, her imaginary playmate.

She settled down on the couch, I lowered the lights, and began the induction. After ten minutes or so, I set the scene. I told her I wanted her to see herself as a little girl, ten or eleven years old:

B: I want you to feel yourself in those jeans and a polo shirt. Your braids have little ribbons on them. You're wearing your baseball hat with the brim to the side. It makes you seem kind of tough, kind of special. You don't like to wear it in front. You're a pretty strong little tomboy, a good baseball player. You feel yourself small, determined. I want you to see yourself standing on a ramp of some sort. There's a man on either side of you, the men you've been describing to me. They're very tall and blond. Each one's holding a hand. You're in a very brightly lit place, very sunny. Get the feeling of those hands holding yours. When you're ready I want you to tell me what you can see. You can speak whenever you like.

L: I'm not holding their hands. They're not holding my hands. I'm holding on to their thumbs. My hand can't fit around theirs so I'm holding on to their thumbs. And we walk down this hill. It's pretty steep and it has a wall on either side. It's attached to this hill.

B: Is there grass under your feet?

L: No. I think it's concrete. And I'm thinking to myself, this would be a wonderful place to roller-skate . . . down this hill. It's perfect for sledding—very smooth and the, uh, the walls on either side of us . . . it's attached to the ground.

B: I want you to turn and look back over your shoulder, see what's behind you . . . where you're coming from.

L: It's a darker white. Everything was very bright. It hurts my eyes. Too sunny. I don't like the sun at all.

B: Directly behind you, you see darker light? [Linda nods] Do you see the horizon? Hills, or trees?

L: No. Not a horizon. It's a structure.

B: What's the structure like?

L: It has a dome. Round dome on top of it . . . darker white than the sky.

B: Is the sky blue?

L: No. It's the color of the ramp. It's . . . this dome is a darker white, almost a light gray compared to everything else. Silvery . . . maybe silvery. It reminds me of a—a large observation—what they would have in airports.

B: Towers?

L: Yes, but wider, rounder. Round, it's round.

B: What's behind you? Do you have the feeling you came from this . . . ?

L: Yes.

B: Okay. Let's go back in time. Let's move back to your being inside this round place. What's it look like inside? Are there any chairs or couches?

L: Hallways. Narrow hallways. There are doors. Funny doors, rounded doors. Don't see any doorknobs but I can see that they are doorways.

B: So this is something like a building?

L: It might be a building—a round building. There's no corners and I don't see any. That's funny. No corners.

Next, I moved Linda further back in time to where she was immediately before she was taken into this "round building with no corners." With no hesitation, she described how the Cortile family had gone to Raven Hall, a swimming pool in Brooklyn's Coney Island. It was an outing she was very much looking forward to. "My friends are there. The whole neighborhood goes there. And there's that boxing . . . punching bag. I want to play around with that, too. I want to punch it and see if I—if I can do as well as my cousin Michael."

She goes into a small, individual changing room in the women's section and is about to untie her sneakers when the door starts to open. "I said, 'Ma?' I'm calling my mother. 'Would you please tell Cookie to stop that—opening up my door?' Then my sister yells back, 'I'm not anywhere near your room.' And we're all next to one another. They're like, almost stalls, but like pretty stalls. And the door keeps opening and then I called out to my mother again and she didn't answer me this time. And the door is all the way opened. Why is the door opening? I had a latch on it. There's a latch on the door from the inside. How did that happen? Who's out there? So I get up to see who opened the door. And—and I don't see anybody, so I look behind the door . . . and there's somebody standing there. Tsk. I've never seen him before. Why isn't he in a bathing suit? And who is that? I don't know who that is. It's no one from my neighborhood. And he looked at me and behind him was another man just like him . . . tall, this isn't a fantasy . . . no. And they said, 'It's time to go.' And I don't know what they're talking about and I said, 'I'm not allowed to go with strangers. You better go away before I go and get my dad, and my uncle Mike and my uncle Dominic and my uncle Salvatore . . . everybody's here!' And they said, 'No. It's time to go.' And I said, 'Go where?' and they just said, 'It's time to go.' I felt I had to go. I don't know why I felt that way. I never talked to strangers. But I had to go."

B: What are these men wearing? Or do they have bathing suits on?

L: No. They were wearing . . . at the time I didn't know what they were wearing but as I look at it now, they look like tight leather, or rubber suits. Royal blue.

B: Do they allow men in this part of the dressing room?

L: NO! They shouldn't be there. This is the women's side. That isn't right. They shouldn't have been there.

Linda then describes being led out of the dressing area to the street, past a number of people frozen in place, apparently unable to see her or her uniformed companions. Ever the feisty little tomboy, she rebels when she spots the UFO above them: "There's that building [gasps] . . . that's not a building. I look up and there's . . . that's not a building. It's that gray thing! I know what that is, that's a, uh, yeah, it's one of those things, it's a . . . I don't want to go in there. They said, 'Well, it's time to go' and I said, 'Well, I don't want to go in there.' I remember that I said, 'I'd like to see you make me. I'm not going in there.' 'It's time to go.' 'Well, fine, it's time for you to go, I'm not going anywhere . . .' And, uh, well . . . they . . . they . . . How did I get in there? It was way up above the buildings. They took me by the hand—both of them, and we went straight up! Umm! This has nothing to do with my fantasy. Uh, huh. I didn't want to go in there but I did feel that I had to go. You know, I was doing something wrong, I went with these strangers, but it didn't seem all that wrong. I was supposed to go. They said I was supposed to go. I wasn't afraid of them in respect to their being strangers. I don't think they were all that strange to me for some reason."

B: Okay. When they talked to you, what did their voices sound like to you?

L: Monotone. They had no feelings. They had no rhythm in their voices. That's right. No rhythm.

B: When they take you into this place, do they tell you why they're there?

L: No. Because I did ask . . . I said, "Well, why am I here and where are you taking me?" And they said, "Just you wait and see." I thought maybe I was in trouble or something. I've never seen these guys before and . . . but yet they didn't seem strange to me. There are others there that look like them. I saw a woman. She looked just like them—in a feminine way. Wow, she must have, uh, she must be a body builder. They were all built . . . I think that looks silly—when a woman is built like a man. Muscles, smaller muscles . . . I don't think a woman should be built like that. It doesn't look nice at all. All those lumps and bumps. On all of them, even the men. And then we go into a room and there's a table. It looks like a table. I guess . . . there's chairs all around it. I—I expect it's a table. It doesn't look like the kitchen table in our kitchen. It's attached to the floor.

B: Does it have four legs?

L: No. It's one piece. It looks like a block—and there are chairs that are blocks. So all these little blocks around and this one big block and we sat down on smaller blocks, and just sat there and they didn't talk to me. And, and before I knew it, it was time to go. And I don't know where we were. We walked out . . . and like it was a building or something and we walked down. Everything was white. I don't know where we are. It isn't like a place I've ever seen before. It's too sunny. It hurts my eyes. It's all white.

B: Can you see the sun?

L: Oh, no, I wouldn't even begin to look. It was too bright.

B: Do you see big dark shadows from everything?

L: . . . don't remember. Don't remember. I can't even look straight ahead without the sunlight bothering me. But I see a black speck. I don't know what that is but it's the only object I can see—against all that white. And we're walking toward this black speck—and I get there—and it's a little boy. But he's bigger than I am. And I said, "Oh, why are you bringing me to this boy? I don't know who he is." And I look at him and he looks almost like my cousin Bobby. But that isn't Cousin Bobby. And I'm standing there and this little boy is looking down at me. Oh, he has a funny look on his face. Humph. And these two people . . . I let go of their thumbs . . . and I turned around and they were behind me and I went over to this boy and I asked him, "Do you want to play with me?" And he just kept looking at me so strange I felt so strange. I felt annoyed. And he said, "No. No, I don't want to play with you!"

B: How old are you, incidentally?

L: Oh, I think about six or seven. What an insult! And so these two grown-ups walked away. And they left me there with this boy that doesn't want to play with me. Well, I don't want to stay here with that boy if he doesn't want to play with me. What am I going to do with him? He doesn't seem that friendly, you know. So we stood there for a while and he kept looking at me and I kept looking at him, then he said, "Well, why are you wearing your hat that way?" And I said, "What way?" And he said, "Well, you're wearing it wrong." And I said, "I like to wear it wrong. I'm different." So, he said, "Okay," and he said, "How old are 'ya, anyway?" So I said, "I'm seven." So he said, "You sure don't look it." He wasn't nice at all. He said, "Well, you just don't look it. You look like a little baaaby." And I said, "Well, I'm not a baby and don't call me a baby." I really would have liked to kick him in the shins, that's what I really would have liked to do but he could beat me up. He was so much bigger than me and those grown-ups went away, so I wasn't about to do that.

And so he said, "Well, what's your name?" And so I told him, I said, "My name is Linda. And what's your name?" And he told me. And I forgot. And so he said, "What's your name?" And I said, "My name is Linda. And what's your name?" And he told me. And we were going back and forth like that . . . yeah, well what's your name and I said, LINDA! And it was going on and on and on. And then he'd tell me his name, I don't remember. Well, anyway, we started to walk and there was really nothing to do. We couldn't play anything, there wasn't anything to play with and so we started to talk, and . . . and I couldn't remember his name. So I gave him my own name. I said to him, "Your name is MICKEY! I'll remember that." And he called me,

"Annie. Ann." I guess he couldn't remember my name either. So I was Ann.

B: Was there any reason why you called him Mickey? Why did you pick that name?

L: I don't know. He, uh, you know, I began to know him. We started to talk and everything and he seemed to be fun. He was funny—like Mickey Mouse.

B: Uh-huh. Did he explain why he called you Ann?

L: Yes. I remember. I did ask him. I said, "Why did you name me Ann?" And he said, "Because you look like an Ann." And I said, "Well, why do I look like an Ann?" And he says, "Because Ann reminds me of a bright color and you remind me of that bright color and so I'm gonna call you Ann."

B: That was nice. Did he say what bright color?

L: Yes. "Ann, yellow, orange, yellow, YELLOW!" Yeah, yellow. I thought he said I was yellow and I said, "I am not yellow. You put up your dukes and I'll show you I'm not yellow. . . ." And he said, "No. No, Ann, not *that* yellow. Just the color yellow. You remind me of something yellow." Yeah, I remember that. [We laugh] Yeah, I thought that he was saying I was yellow, but he wasn't.

B: Sounds like he likes you.

L: Yeah, I guess he does. And he wasn't bad after all. We started to talk and he wanted to know what sports I liked. Obviously, it was baseball and he wanted to know what team did I root for and he looked on my hat and he saw "New York Yankees" and he liked baseball too and football. . . .

B: Where does he live?

L: I don't know.

B: Is he from New York? Is he a Yankee fan?

L: I don't know. I don't know where he lives or where he's from but he likes baseball.

B: Did he mention any teams?

L: No, I don't remember. We talked about a lot of things. Talked about our schools, our teachers and I told him about the police officer that was on duty across the street from where I lived and what the kids and I used to do. We used to say [sings] "Brass button, blue coat, can't catch a nanny goat . . . !" And we'd ruuun down the block and he'd run after us—holding his bat. Now, we knew he wasn't going to hit us, he was just scaring us away. We'd talk about things like that, and he . . . No, I don't know where he lived. He might have told me—I don't remember, but he didn't understand why he was where he was, just like I didn't understand where I was. We wondered where we were. We talked about it and who those people [the men in blue] were. I remember him saying he didn't like those people. He felt that they had no consideration, they just didn't care and he told me that he didn't want to be a baby-sitter and he thought that that's what he was being. He was surprised that I was seven, he thought that I was younger and said he was sorry, that he didn't think I was a baby after all. I guess I was little for my age—or maybe he was too big for his age. Then again, everybody looked big to me, I was only seven. I think he might have been too tall for his age and that's why I was so little to him. That's what it was. I'm not a baby. He was just too tall.

We just kept talking about our schools, our schoolwork, what subjects we liked, what subjects we didn't like . . . and something about our friends and then, and then these two grown-ups came back and said it was time for me to go. I turned around and I said, "Well, good-bye, Mickey" and he said, "Good-bye." So I walked away with these two grown-ups, only they held my hand this time. I wasn't holding their thumbs. We walked up that ramp, that slant. Yea, it's okay roller-skating down this thing but I sure wouldn't like roller-skating *up* it. And we went back into this . . . looked like a round building . . . but it flies! Yeah, I know what that is.

I didn't have such a bad time. You know, I—I think that Mickey was—was a pretty nice kid. He'd make a good brother. You know, I wish he was my brother. I wish I had a big brother. Oh, my sister's fine, but . . . well, you know, she's a girl and—and it would be nice to have Mickey as a brother. Uh-huh. And we went into this building type . . . round building . . . it flies, though, so I guess it isn't a building. And before I knew it we were inside and we walked through this narrow hallway and we went back into the same room and we sat down on those squares, those blocks, and I don't know what happened after that.

I was outside my dressing room . . . I wasn't inside . . . and I said to myself, well how did I get out here, you know? I was in there sitting down 'bout to take my sneakers off . . . ohhh, I know why I was out here, and I said to myself, it's because someone opened up the dressing-room door and I found myself sitting on my butt outside the door and so I just got up and opened the door and went in and started to do what I was going to do to begin with—get undressed and get my bathing suit on.

My mother was complaining because I wasn't ready and wanted to know what was taking me so long. And we went out after I had my bathing suit on and we went back to our lockers and put our clothes in there. Then we went out to the swimming pool and greeted all of our friends and relatives and I put my toes in the water and the water was cold. Oh, I'd just like to jump in and I forgot to take my baseball cap off. Tsk. So I had a little key around my ankle with an elastic, and I put my cap back in the locker. I didn't want to lose it, you know. It was important to me. Then I just had a nice day. I punched the punching bag and just had a good time.

I asked Linda some questions about time—when they had arrived (about ten in the morning) and what time it was when she rejoined the others at the pool (she wasn't sure). "Dad was already out there talking with all my uncles, my mom's brothers, and they were around the sausage stand. There was a guy named Carmine and he was behind the counter and he was selling sausage and peppers."

After a series of positive posthypnotic suggestions about her ability to remember even more details in the future if she should want to, I ended the session and brought her out of the trance state.

She awoke, stretched, and took a deep breath. "That's strange, Budd, because, uh, that was a UFO, wasn't it? Yeah, that's strange when you think about it. . . . In other words, then, that really happened?"

I replied that we really don't know what happened. "It's hard to know what really happened."

"Why would I fantasize a place like that?" she asked. "There's nothing there. I was in Raven Hall's pool, and of course that had to happen! Oh, no, no, no, that could have been a dream. Now, why would I fall asleep taking my sneakers off? It doesn't make sense."

I asked how long she thought she spent with Mickey, and she answered about forty-five minutes, at the most. I wondered if her mother would have waited that long. "I don't think she would have waited forty-five minutes . . . she would have been frantic if I wasn't there. . . . Unless she'd met some friends and talked to them."

The entire event was, of course, crazy, a mystery, a logical impossibility. An unseen abduction from Coney Island on a sunny weekend morning! Like the entire range of UFO phenomena, Linda and Richard's experience is an enigma that conventional science and everyday common sense demand that we reject. It *can't* have happened, we say to ourselves; therefore it didn't. And yet, despite everything, it is hard not to suspect that it really did happen, in exactly the way Linda and Richard, against *their* better judgment, remembered.

But there is one final detail of her account that goes beyond even these mysteries. It raises the possibility that the UFO occupants are able, somehow, to manipulate time.

"You know what was really strange?" Linda asked at the end of our session. "There were people in the swimming pool already. The kids were in. Everybody was in, swimming. It was crowded and, uh . . . splashes . . . You know when you splash? It was above the pool. It's hard to explain. You splash water and . . . water splashes *up*. But it didn't fall down. It was like a photograph. You know, when you take a photograph of a person splashing in the water, the splashes are up in the photograph. Well, in the pool there were splashes like that, that didn't finish . . . they were still up in the air. Nobody was moving, and the water, the splashes weren't moving either. And we walked right by everybody frozen like that and nobody even looked at us . . . like they didn't even see us. . . ."

C H A P T E R

18

More "Mickeys," Other "Baby Anns"

After hearing Richard's and Linda's descriptions of how the aliens brought them together repeatedly in childhood, I was ready to ask a few new questions. If this type of report was at all common, I would be forced to extend my view of the depth of alien involvement in individual human lives. It was potentially a development of extraordinary importance.

I decided to keep the issue secret in order to ensure that any forthcoming interviews with abductees would remain uncontaminated. But as I thought about it, I recalled that over the years several pairs of abductees had mentioned that when they first met they felt they already knew one another. I had always assumed that such a feeling was either a déjà vu reaction in people who had shared the same type of traumatic experiences, or that perhaps the two of them had actually once been abducted together, perhaps along with others, in the same craft. I never imagined that the aliens might be doing this to some children *systematically*, bringing them together year after year, apparently to observe the way they meet, make friends, and finally "bond." Knowing Richard's general reserve, and sensing his cautious use of the term, I assumed that bonding must involve some kind of sexual connection. The more I thought about it, the more logical it seemed that an alien race, interested in issues of reproduction, might initiate such a program as part of an in-depth psychosocial study of the formation of human sexual relationships.

My next task was to see what I could do to test the authenticity of Richard's and Linda's recollections. Since I had not told her anything about Richard's letter, I knew from experience that when she finally learned of its contents, she would react emotionally. I had two basic options in presenting the letter. One was simply to hand it to her, let her read it, and then make a note or two on her reactions. Future investigators curious about the case would then have to take my word as to how she responded. The second option was to *film* her response with a witness present, just as I had done with Dan's "Lady of the Sands" letter. In this way the videotape recording of her reactions would be part of a visible and permanent record available for historians and researchers to study.

I decided to set up another videotape session in which I would read Richard's "Mickey and Baby Ann" letter to Linda with the camera running and witnesses present. First, Linda would be invited to retell for the witnesses what had happened since the last taping, in order to bring the story up to date. To ensure spontaneity, I would not tell her about Richard's second letter until the filming had begun.

In the beginning of February, Linda and I met with the cameraman and psychotherapist Gibbs Williams (historian Chuck Strozier was unable to attend). We arranged ourselves as we had the first time—Linda seated in the center on the couch, I to her left, and Gibbs to our right in a chair facing us. When the video camera was rolling we began with Linda's account of the traumatic trip with Dan to the Long Island beach house, her description of his bizarre and terrifying behavior, and her ultimate rescue by Richard. Next, I read Richard's long explanatory letter about this sad affair, and we heard from Linda again about her meeting with him when they visited Saint Patrick's together on November 21.

Gibbs asked a few questions, seeking clarification on this or that point, and then we moved on to Linda's hypnosis session about her childhood meeting with Mickey in the strange, white environment. After we listened to the hypnosis tape we talked a bit about it, and Linda answered a few of Gibbs's questions about her recollections. She described how, when she found herself in this virtually featureless bright area, she saw a tiny dark speck in the distance. The two people holding her were "tall, real tall, but they weren't dresssed like we would dress." The distant speck turned out to be her imaginary friend, "and from that day on it was perfect for me. I didn't have an imaginary friend till that happened . . . and from that day on he was with me a lot.

"He was a big kid, a lot bigger than me. He looked as though he was almost as tall as my sister." Linda told Gibbs about the problem they had remembering names and how they came to name each other. "These were good dreams . . . they're happy memories."

Now it was time to present the letter. Frank, the same cameraman as in the Lady of the Sands taping, knew that he was to keep Linda's face in tight close-up during this section of the presentation, and he did a commendable job. When I played the videotape the next day, I noticed many subtle details that had escaped my attention at the time. Viewing it this way, the experience was even more moving.

As this section of the tape begins, I tell Linda that I had received another letter from Richard. She immediately asks its date. "November 22," I tell her. "The day after you saw him and went uptown together." She seems amazed to hear that there is another letter and settles back somewhat uneasily to listen.

The first paragraphs deal with their visit to Saint Patrick's Cathedral and Rockefeller Center. But when Richard writes, again, that he believes "Linda is from another place," she sighs and rolls her eyes upward in weary annoyance. And when he goes on to say that "only Linda knows what [powers] she possesses," she shakes her head "no."

When I arrive at the place where Richard announces that he has something to tell me, "because if I don't, Dan will have my company at the rest home where he's now staying," this remark brings a slight smile and a nod from Linda. When he says that he finds this particular situation harder to accept than the November 1989 incident, she seems surprised and asks, "Has he had another experience?"

I do not answer her question. I simply continue reading the letter. When he writes that from the age of ten to the age of twenty-five he had been dreaming of a girl he didn't know, Linda looks puzzled and a little tense. At his mention of a bright white environment, her eyes widen in sudden shock, but his description of two "tall, fair, emotionless men walking toward me, holding the hand of a tiny little girl" causes her to lift and shift her body and then to turn to Gibbs with a gaze of helpless pleading.

When I come at last to the part of the letter in which Richard uses the names Baby Ann and Mickey, her face assumes an almost horrified grimace. There is a stunned pause, and then she says, "Oh, Budd, that's *weird!* That's *weird!*" Tears well up in her eyes and I ask softly, "Linda, do you want to hear more of this?"

Struggling to control herself, she doesn't attempt a reply. She lifts a glass of water to her lips, but her hand trembles so that it is difficult to drink. She puts the glass down and stares at me. "What's he saying, what's he saying?" she asks, more a helpless wail than a question.

I answer as gently as I can: "That it was real." Then I put the letter away. This is as far as I get in the reading.

Linda is still trembling, her mouth fixed in a kind of stunned rictus. "That's too weird. That's even too weird for me! How does he know? How does he know?"

"It was real, I'm afraid, Linda. This happened." I put my arms around her to give her a comforting hug. "You've been through a lot. . . ."

Her eyes filling with tears, she pulls away from me. I sense that her upper body is stiff and unyielding; she is still too shocked to accept any consolation. "No, that's just too weird . . . it's too weird. I don't understand this whole . . ." and her voice trails off into silence.

"Oh, God, I don't believe this." She turns now to Gibbs. "Could you explain this to me? Are you a doctor? Can you explain it to me? I can't believe this. No!"

As I have often noticed, Linda's need to deny UFO experiences of all kinds can be almost overpowering. She tries desperately to avoid drawing obvious—painful—conclusions because of a process I call "confirmation anxiety." "Is he [Richard] saying that my imaginary friend wasn't imaginary?" she asks, almost to the air, and then answers her own question. "Yes, that's what he's saying. But how would he know? Nobody knew." Her voice drops to an almost inaudible murmur: "Oh, God."

Then I take her hand and hold it while she wrestles with these shocking realizations. Turning to me, her words interrupted by long, painful pauses, she asks again, "Will you explain it to me? This is crazy. It's too terrible. . . . Somebody's screwing around with our minds. . . . There was no such thing as a 'Mickey.' "

I reply, again speaking softly: "It was Richard. Mickey was Richard. And you were Baby Ann."

She lowers her eyes and whispers one word: "God . . ."

It took nearly an hour of further discussion before Linda allowed herself to put her recollections and Richard's together and begin to grasp the enormity of what had happened to the two of them: that for years and years the two had been taken together, had become friends, and even, I suspected, lovers, if that is what Richard meant by bonding. And all this without ever having met in the real world.

Clinical psychotherapist Gibbs Williams was able to give Linda some helpful suggestions in dealing with the profound confusion and anxiety she was feeling. Still, I could see that it would take a long,

long time for her to come to terms with all this. In fact, even now, more than three years later, Linda is still deeply conflicted about the place that Richard—Mickey—holds in her heart.

The videotape offered vivid, tangible evidence of Linda's emotion on hearing Richard's letter. But it was clear that if other, similar cases of simultaneous childhood abductions turned up in subsequent investigations, we could establish a pattern rather than just a single, isolated incident.

So from this time forward, when anyone contacted me about possible UFO abductions and mentioned the feeling of somehow "knowing" another abductee in the past, I began to ask a few follow-up questions. And I discovered that the saga of Mickey and Baby Ann was only the beginning, the first of a new subset of cases. There were, as it turned out, numerous others.

In one case in 1993, I interviewed "Jack" and "Sally," a young New Hampshire couple. After each described somewhat typical abduction recollections, Jack mentioned that they had felt a sense of instant recognition when they met. Sally added that she felt she knew Jack "from somewhere." They fell in love and eventually moved in together, and as they relaxed one Sunday morning, Jack asked her about a birthmark. She said, "You know, we've had this conversation before." He agreed, but neither could remember where or when. Then, a day or so later, as they were loading some boxes of groceries, Sally had a sudden flashback: "Jack, we were in a strange room together once, with boxes all around, all over the floor." He stiffened and said, "I know what you're talking about. Let's forget about it."

After this surprising recollection similar flashbacks continued for both of them. They were sure that when they were sitting together in the strange room they had been teenagers. Sally remembered that there were no chairs, "only these odd-sized boxes all around the floor, in place of chairs." When she described it, Jack immediately recalled this odd setting and, his memory jogged, began to remember bits of conversation they had had there. He recalled that among other things they had discussed the music they liked, comparing favorite groups and albums. They finally decided that the date of this mysterious conversation was 1984. Sally would have been fifteen and Jack, seventeen. They recalled that they were both dressed entirely in tight-fitting black clothes, unlike anything they actually owned.

From that moment on, the young couple began to sense that there had been other days when they had met this way—times when they were even younger—and they were able to describe each other's appearance as children. Eventually I initiated separate hypnotic regressions with both Jack and Sally, and the parallel details each remembered were remarkable. Recalling the issue of nicknames for the first time under hypnosis, Jack, at the time a rebellious and very angry seventeen-year-old, told Sally she was a "preppy brat" and called her "pizza-face," while she named him "Froot Loop." During my session with Sally, held immediately after Jack's with no communication possible between them, she, too, remembered using these mocking nicknames.

Much more could be said about this particular couple and their extensive experiences, but here it is important to point out their parallels with Richard's and Linda's accounts. Like the older couple, Jack and Sally did not seem able to hold on to each other's real names, and so invented nicknames. Linda, in her hypnosis on the Coney Island abduction when she was first taken to see Mickey, had described a room inside the craft as having something that "looks like a block, and there are chairs that are blocks. So there are all these little blocks around, and this one big block, and we sat down." For the child she was at the time, these were blocks; for the teenagers Jack and Sally they were boxes. But in neither account did these objects have legs, arms, or backs. Apparently they were simple, minimal alien furniture, in different sizes for different-sized people.

Most important, however, was the emotional parallel between the two situations. After the hypnosis sessions with Jack and Sally, I told them a little about the similarities between what they had each recalled. Jack was shocked but not surprised. Sally, on the other hand, was deeply disturbed. There were tears in her eyes as she told me the problem. "Jack and I love each other and we're going to get married . . . but is this something the aliens are doing to us? Are we just acting out what *they* want? Did they put these feelings in us? Should we really be getting married?"

In Linda's feelings about Richard, there is also a strong sense of self-doubt. In a few of his more recent letters to me, Richard alluded to Linda's present-day beauty and remarkable youthfulness. In his eyes she looks now almost exactly as young and beautiful as she did when he knew her as an adolescent, a fact he regards as almost magical. In a tone of amazement, he wrote that he can't imagine why she isn't pursued everywhere.

One day, after I showed Linda one of his glowing descriptions, she turned to me sadly and coldly and pointed to the flesh below her eyes. "Do you see these bags?" she asked. "Don't I look like a woman in her forties? How can he see me as a teenager?" She added a thought that reminded me of Sally's concern. "Do you suppose the aliens are making him see me this way?" Though Linda is an attractive woman, she doesn't look like a teenager. I had to assume that either Richard was "blindly, totally in love," or his perceptions might actually have been manipulated by the aliens. Could the natural attraction these "bonded" abductees feel for one another be somehow artificially augmented, as some have come to suspect? The confusion and self-doubt this bizarre situation can engender are profound.

In another such example, "Jennifer" and "William" met at a UFO conference in 1992. Both had experienced lifelong UFO abductions, but their instant sense of connection was so great that they exchanged addresses and planned to meet again. Each knew the other was a probable abductee, but like Sally and Jack, and Linda and Richard, they had never heard of the shared childhood abduction scenario. With their memories jogged by each other's presence, Jennifer and William began to have flashbacks of earlier abductions in which they had been brought together and allowed to interact—even to the point of sexual intercourse. But there was one major problem for both of them. Each was happily married to someone else; William had a son and Jennifer was the mother of two daughters. With tears in her eyes, she told me of her love for William and his for her. And yet, after a decade of marriage she loved her husband deeply and would do nothing disruptive to her family.

"It's not fair," she said, "for the aliens to do this to anyone. Imagine allowing you to fall in love with somebody they bring to you at night and then take away afterwards. And they do that over and over, and yet you aren't allowed to remember much about it. You decide it must be some kind of dream, and that he's a dream partner for you. And then you actually meet him, and you're both married to other people, and yet you're still in love. It's cruel for them to do this to anyone. They don't care what they're doing to people's lives."

Although there are many other elements to the story of Jennifer and William, the central fact is that once again two people, recognizing one another in the real world, recalled abductions in which the aliens brought them together and allowed them to interact, even to form romantic attachments. However, prior to Richard and Linda's jointly remembered account, nothing in the UFO abduction literature even hinted at such a possibility.

Continuing investigations revealed that the UFO occupants' interest is not limited solely to male-female relationships. At the conference of abduction researchers held at MIT in the summer of 1992, I met two heterosexual women, Beth and Anna, who eventually uncovered a similar lifetime of shared abductions, leading to a close friendship when they finally met. [See Appendix III]

There is, however, a basic difference between this account of shared childhood abductions and the others I have investigated since Mickey and Baby Ann. First, it seems to have begun for Anna in infancy when she was barely able to talk, and it also involved two individuals of the same gender, with no later mutual sexual activity. It would seem that here the UFO occupants were only interested in the way human friendships are formed and develop over decades. Whether these individuals are then *deliberately* brought together in the real world or whether their renewed acquaintance is accidental is, for the present at least, unanswerable.

Other unusual examples of the Mickey and Baby Ann phenomenon also vary from the basic pattern. In one case, a young girl from Scotland was regularly paired with a boy from the East Coast of the United States, a long way to be brought for a rendezvous. They finally met when they were in their forties, and each remembered accurately what the other looked like as an adolescent and even younger: whether the other was slim or chubby, how their hair was styled, and so forth. The man recalls having had sexual intercourse with the woman when they were adolescents, an unusual detail, he informed me, since he is gay.

What does this dramatic information say about Richard and Linda and the events of November 30, 1989? First, the subsequent discovery of other examples of the Mickey and Baby Ann phenomenon strongly supports Linda's credibility and the accuracy of her recall. Her testimony, whether consciously given or remembered through hypnosis, has again and again been validated by outside witnesses, in this case by the accounts of many others who have recalled similarly shared childhood experiences. (The reports I have presented here are only a representative sampling of more than a dozen in my files.)

But on the simplest, most human level, the lives of Linda, Richard, and all the rest have been tampered with, altered, shaped by some kind of alien experimentation and interest in human genetics, sexuality, and reproduction. Their basic human emotions and life commitments have been shadowed, even tainted, leaving each of them, at best, confused and, at worst, devastated.

PART FOUR

Dan on the Loose

C H A P T E R

19

"Pack Your Toothbrush"

During the fall and early winter of 1991 when I was preoccupied with the story of Mickey and Baby Ann, I had barely thought of Dan, as I believed him to be safely ensconced in a rest home somewhere. But toward the end of December, this sense of security came to a sudden halt for Linda and, indirectly, for me as well.

She called one day to tell me in a rather agitated voice that she had just received a threatening and irrational letter from Dan, folded inside a seemingly innocent traditional Christmas card. "Dear Pretty Linda," he typed, "Merry Christmas!" With a few minor deletions and corrections, this is what he wrote:

> By the time this Xmas greeting reaches you, I will have managed to get out of this place successfully. If you don't see me then you'll know that I'm still in here thinking my way out. Did you believe that I would let you go so easy?
>
> The staff here usually keeps me pretty much sedated. You see, they like me and give me special favors. This is how I was able to get this letter started.
>
> Friends have been stopping by bringing their Xmas cheer. They brought me a few Xmas cards the last time they were here but forgot the envelopes. So, when they come to visit again, one of

them will have to address an envelope (one that was forgotten), stamp it and put it into the mail for me when he returns to NY. I don't want you to trace my whereabouts, anyway.

In the meantime, I'm trying to get a holiday pass so I can come and see you. This pass may last me a life time (with you).

It seems like yesterday when I wanted you to go back from where you came. I hated you because I needed to live a normal and stress free life again, but the thought of you wouldn't let me. Sometimes the hate still creeps out of me, until I think about looking into those big, deep, brown eyes of yours. Then the hate goes away. In fact, I can't wait to watch you move as you walk by. I'm going to kiss that pretty nose and inscribe our names with my lips on that full, heart shaped mouth that looks unhappy only with me.

I will control the strong unnatural mind you possess. And I will, because I have learned so much about what has to be done here in this place. . . . I enjoy the helplessness you show when you're not in control. You're fragile and lovely, like a blown glass figurine.

But, my little Lady of the Sands, when you are in control—your tears become the swells of the sea. Your breath has the strength of high winds and your eyes become the storm that so faithfully protects you. Yes, you've inherited the unnaturalness of your ancestor through your mother's bloodline. St. Joan of Arc was a powerful woman when needed to be. Her strength came from above, just as yours has. But Joan's came from God. Yours comes from them [the aliens]. You are half of them but very similar to her. You are not a saint, but you are an angel.

Next, Dan goes on to mention certain good deeds of Linda's he has observed while he had her under surveillance: carrying an elderly person's groceries, giving a hot dog to a homeless person, and so on. "I just wanted you to know that I have noticed."

But then he regresses back into thinly veiled kidnapping threats, "half-breed" slurs, and more references to the events of November 30, 1989. He includes a bizarre new accusation about Linda's "alien" cell structure:

Linda, you don't belong here. But I'll find a place for you. When I do, you'll teach me your ways and your special language.

Everyone thinks I'm crazy, you know. It's because they have never seen or heard what I have, coming out of you.

Richard and the other man just let me sit in this place knowing full well that I'm not crazy. They saw the very same things I saw in you.

I want you to know that we have done our homework over all these months. To prove it, I have some information that no one else would have but you and your doctor. I told you that I would prove the difference in you. Linda, it just isn't in your eyes. It's in your cell structure. You didn't think I knew, did you? You can't pretend this isn't true because it's there. We know you were put here on purpose but we don't know exactly when.

You do make good things happen to others, and it's no coincidence. I'll bet something nice has happened to everyone you've been close to or touched. But it hasn't happened to me yet.

If you show this letter to anyone, you know that they won't believe me because I'm supposed to be crazy. That's clever, Linda. But what if they give me the benefit of the doubt? Then they'll find out that you're a halfbreed.

We'll be covering a lot of miles, Linda. Prepare yourself for a happy and comfortable life abroad. Pack your toothbrush in order to travel lightly at any time. You'll make a beautiful bride, dressed all in white just like the morning of November, 1989.

If you see Richard, tell him I said "Go to Hell."

If I don't get out of here I'll be thinking of you. If I do, I'll be looking at you.

Happy Holiday, pretty!

Danny

A final touch has to do with the card that accompanied Dan's letter. Knowing that Linda must dread the idea that he would be able to escape from the "rest home" where he was being held, Dan chose his Yule card accordingly. The illustration depicted a traditional living room with a large Christmas tree, decorations over the mantelpiece, and a roaring fire in the fireplace. A small boy is looking uneasily past the flames and up into the smoke-filled chimney. "How does he do it?" the child asks. The inference I assumed Dan wanted us to draw was simple: If Santa is able to get down a fiery chimney, Dan can manage to escape a mental hospital and return to get Linda in New York City.

Most upsetting, of course, was his promise to take her away for a "life time." "I'll find a place for you," he had written, ". . . abroad." Considering his emotional state at the beach house and his peculiar skills as a security/intelligence agent, I took Dan's kidnapping threat very seriously indeed. His description of Linda as a "beautiful bride, dressed all in white, just like the morning of November, 1989," resurrected the nightmare at the beach when Dan made her wear a white nightgown, sobbed over her image, tried to photograph her, and finally nearly raped her.

When I thought about a worst-case scenario, it seemed clear that if Dan intended to spirit Linda away, he would have a number of options and covert methods at his disposal: drugs, passports, falsified arrest warrants, and God knows what else—the full state-of-the-art intelligence community array. It was a matter of public record that agents from both sides of the cold war had been successfully drugged and quietly maneuvered onto planes before, so there was every reason to believe that a determined, well-trained, and emotionally disturbed security agent like Dan might actually be able to carry off such a crime.

If Linda had been living in a kind of siege state before, Dan's letter made this condition even worse. Joseph, the law-enforcement professional serving intermittently as her bodyguard, was able from time to time to accompany her when she went shopping, but there were still many occasions when she had to make a quick trip to the grocery store and he was unavailable. She began to limit her solo trips out of the apartment and walked warily wherever she went.

Although she looked to Richard for protection and advice, neither of us had a quick and easy way to get in touch with him. Despite the system of drops he had initiated to allow me to send him letters and tapes, he was able to check for messages only infrequently. And if he happened to be out of the country on an assignment, weeks could go by between pickups.

Apart from the literal threats Dan's letter provided, it was also extremely disturbing to Linda to have to endure his references to her half-breed caste, her paranormal powers, and her alleged descent from Saint Joan of Arc. I believe that Linda regretted the day her son innocently tried to rid himself of Richard—the inquisitive "drunk" on the bus—by retelling an impressive family legend. Now, in his fantasies, Dan had blended what he regarded as Linda's near-sainthood to her hybrid alien status, thus making her twice as powerful and, apparently, twice as desirable.

What was to be done? We waited and watched and hoped that Dan would not be able to escape from the rest home. Our hopes were in vain about that, however, and on February 22, 1992, he made his move.

Showdown at the
South Street Seaport

Although I try to hold a monthly support group meeting for abductees from the New York City area, the gathering on Saturday evening, February 22, was weeks overdue, and because of this hiatus the attendees seemed particularly lively and eager.

By contrast, I noticed that when Linda arrived she appeared quite tense and withdrawn. She whispered that she had something to tell me later: Richard had turned up again, there had been a chase and a struggle, but everything was fine now, and fortunately she hadn't had to deal with Dan. She added that she had also done something that I wouldn't approve of.

Naturally I was filled with curiosity, but it wasn't until the gathering was over and people were leaving that I was able to learn more. An incident had taken place that afternoon, only a few hours before our eight o'clock meeting. As Linda described it, she had been on her way to the Seaport to shop, accompanied by Carmela, a girlhood friend, when she saw Richard. He was standing with what she took to be three or four other well-dressed security men scattered about in the usual weekend throng of Seaport visitors. Richard and his men stood out because they appeared to be on the alert, scanning the crowd, searching, she guessed, for her. Fear flooded her. She knew she was going to be seized once again, and this time strangers were involved.

She saw that Richard had spotted her. Whispering to Carmela not to worry, that she would be all right, she ducked down and ran into the crowd, dodging, trying to evade Richard and the men with him. Since Linda had previously told her friend about her misadventures with the two agents, Carmela almost immediately understood what was happening. Richard, being well above six feet tall, towered over many of the passersby. Recognizing him from Linda's description, Carmela walked over and called him by name, asking what he wanted with Linda. Although she said that he did not reply and moved off quickly, I was pleased that I now had a fourth witness to Richard's appearance and made a mental note to ask Carmela for a tape-recorded deposition.

According to Linda's account, Richard soon caught up with her and a struggle ensued. He carried her kicking and yelling to the shelter of the doorway of a nearby office building. Speaking into what she assumed was a small, concealed transmitter, he reported that she had been "secured." He still had his arms around her, holding her in place, when she did what she said I would not approve of.

"Budd, I had a gun. A girlfriend of mine had lent me her little pistol and I had it tucked in the waistband of my jeans. Though Richard was holding me I managed to get it out and I pointed it at him. He tricked me, though. He looked away and said, 'There's Dan!' and I looked in that direction, too, and when I did, he took my gun away."

I was astounded. "What were you going to do, Linda? Were you actually going to shoot him?" She replied that she just wanted to scare him but that she would have shot him if she had to. But then she told me what he had been saying to her just before she aimed the gun at him. "Can you imagine?" she asked. "He asked me to go to his hotel with him. The Vista Hotel. At a time like that he wants me to go to his hotel room with him. I'm not that kind of woman. He's never said anything like that to me before. What could he have been thinking?"

Everything struck me as startling and out of character: Richard's trying to talk "Baby Ann" into a nearby hotel room, Linda's pulling a gun, another wild struggle. I argued with her again about arming herself, about pointing a pistol at a trained security man and running the risk of someone's getting shot. "What if one of the other agents saw your gun and fired at you, or your gun went off accidentally and you killed Richard?"

Linda seemed contrite and rather embarrassed. "How long have you been carrying that gun?" I asked.

"For a few weeks," she replied. "After I got that crazy letter from Dan. I didn't want to tell you I had it. I knew you'd be mad."

I understood all too well how terrified she was of Dan, how much anger she felt toward him, and how truly dangerous he could be. The irony was that when a crisis arrived she pulled the weapon on *Richard,* her friend and ostensible protector.

She told me that Richard had kept the gun, and now she didn't know what she was going to tell the woman who had lent it to her. But there was a great deal more to the day's incident than the business about the pistol. She had somehow—mysteriously—escaped from Richard and run off down South Street. "I just got away from him. He just stood there and didn't move, so I ran off." The thought crossed my mind that she might have eluded Richard the way she had apparently escaped from Dan when they were struggling in the surf: by some kind of alien intervention. Were the aliens actually monitoring such confrontations, using their powers of temporary physical paralysis at critical moments to protect certain abductees? Clearly, both Richard and Dan believed that as a "half-breed," Linda possessed such powers, though she herself vehemently rejected such a disturbing possibility. She told me more than once that she was utterly unable to will any such "magical" intervention, and I believed her. And yet logic eventually forced me to suspend my skepticism that UFO occupants—either invisible or acting from a distance—could actively intervene in certain earthly crises. Although the idea of this kind of selective alien intercession seemed preposterous, I could not flatly reject it as impossible when I considered the other equally preposterous but witnessed paranormal events that had taken place during the past year.

Linda was eager to tell me about yet another extremely odd detail. After she escaped from Richard, she ran down South Street, coming eventually to Battery Park at the southern end of Manhattan. There she rested for a while. Later, feeling someone's eyes on her, she turned around and saw Richard standing nearby, smiling at her. She assumed that he had followed her downtown escape route until he came to Battery Park and found her. The thought crossed my mind that since much of lower Manhattan—the Financial District near Battery Park—is open only on weekdays, Richard could have guessed that with the stores and restaurants closed, a frightened Linda might have decided to seek rest and refuge on a park bench. Still, his being able to find her so quickly struck me as highly unlikely. Though not, of course, impossible.

As she continued telling me what happened, her mood changed entirely. With an expression of warmth and near guilt when she mentioned his name, she repeated to me what she said to Richard when she first noticed him looking at her in Battery Park.

"I asked him, 'Do you want to play?' That's what I asked Mickey when I first saw him years before when we were both so little. And do you know what he answered this afternoon? He said, 'No, you're too little. You're just a baby.' Budd, that's what he said to me when I asked him to play that time when we were both little kids in that strange white place."

As she spoke, the background of crowds and chases and guns with Dan's invisible presence melted away, replaced now by a playful, almost romantic spirit of mutual affection. Richard joined her, she said, and they sat together on a bench near the water. He told her a great deal about the nature of his work, the issue of anonymity, and his concern about becoming part of an "official" rather than an "unofficial" problem. Despite Richard's attempt at an explanation, Linda did not fully comprehend the distinction he was making and so had difficulty explaining it to me. Three days later, when I read his definition of the terms in a letter he sent me, I understood things much better.

But one thing Richard was able to make clear to Linda was his reason for being at the Seaport with some of his fellow security agents. They had discovered that Dan had escaped weeks before from what everyone euphemistically referred to as the "rest home," and had hatched a plan to seize Linda that afternoon. He intended to spirit her away to England later that evening, drugged and compliant. Richard had also learned that Dan had obtained a false passport for her and had purchased two plane tickets on British Airways.

With some embarrassment Linda told me that she was stunned when she realized that though she had kicked and punched and struggled and had even aimed a pistol at Richard, he had come to rescue her. I later learned that this was only one of several half-tragic, half-farcical misunderstandings on that afternoon.

Richard typed his letter to me the next day, February 23, and I received it two days after that. He began by saying that he was writing such a long letter—nineteen pages, single-spaced—so that I could "know and feel the full impact of what has transpired Saturday, February 22, 1992, [and] so you won't think I'm picking on Linda." He had been away on assignment "for a couple of months and had no contact with anyone from the outside world. I knew I had to complete some unfinished business I left behind"—Dan—"but I had no idea that this business had turned into serious problems. When I arrived at the rest home, I learned that Dan had disappeared on December 14th, sometime after 11 PM. I went on to explain to his doctors the full extent of his actions against Linda last October 15, 1991."

Apparently this was the first time the psychiatrists had heard the complete details of Dan's aggressive and irrational behavior at the beach house, because, Richard said, he had to go on assignment immediately after that incident and had no time to talk to them. But now, knowing that Linda was in imminent danger with Dan on the loose, Richard flew immediately from the rest home back to New York.

New York City was the most likely place to find him because most of his friends are there, and so was Linda (hopefully). I kept going over the threats Dan had made to Linda, in my mind. These kidnapping threats made me wonder if Dan had already carried them out. Two months is a long time for a person like Dan, with his problems, to be roaming around freely.

When I arrived in N.Y.C. to speak with a few people to get some leads on Dan, I ran into one of the Security men who was here with us in his car under the FDR Drive the morning of November 30, 1989. Instead of getting a lead on Dan, another problem began to develop. I was aware in the past that these four Security people were tailing Linda. I caught them a couple of times doing so, but that was all there was to it. They found out who she was, they knew her schedule, tailed her once or twice and let it go at that.

Now I was hearing something new. [The four Security people] were planning a round of questioning for Linda that day. I tried to talk one of them out of it but he had his mind set on it. I didn't want to make much of it because I knew I would have to stop them from scaring Linda, and I didn't want this guy to suspect that they were going to have a problem with me, and prepare for it. Something didn't seem right and I couldn't put my finger on it. Why haven't they questioned her over two years ago? They had opportunities to do so. Why not then?

"Although these Security people have seen what I have seen," Richard wrote, "they have only the most minimal open-mindedness to work with." He explained that they haven't had anyone to give them guidance. Unlike Dan and himself with regard to the third man, these other agents refused to involve their "third men," the important senior figures whom they were escorting on November 30, 1989. They probably refrained from reporting the matter and dealing with it through channels, Richard speculates, to keep the incident from escalating to an "Official Problem." They were therefore left with "no one to lean on but themselves, and that isn't saying much."

But these other four men (I guessed that they might be employed by a different security/intelligence agency than Richard's and Dan's) had nevertheless been carrying out their own small-scale investigation of the original incident. Their intermittent surveillance of Linda immediately reminded me of Linda's and Joseph's experience with the men in the unmarked gray surveillance van. Again, something I had just learned explained a seemingly inexplicable incident from the past.

Richard had arrived in New York about 10:30 A.M., which meant that he had "four hours to kill before 2:30 PM rolled around."

> On Saturdays Linda always leaves her apartment between 2:30 and 3:00 PM. She's very vulnerable on a Saturday. I didn't know where Linda was or Dan was. Did he take her long ago? The next logical thing to do was to telephone Linda to find out if she was still here in New York. I called several times but no one answered. This fact began to eat me up inside. So I began phoning buddies of mine, hoping they were at home on this bright and sunny day. My intention was to intervene on Linda's behalf this Saturday afternoon when these Security people pick her up. I also needed leads on Dan and the footwork involved. I was only interested in efficiency and speed and that wasn't going to happen if I went at it alone. . . . I managed to reach five of my good old buddies and told them I needed immediate help to stop four Security people from questioning a good friend of mine. I also mentioned Dan.
>
> I wasn't as worried about these Security people as much as I was worried about Dan. Dan is sick, loaded with money and very capable, maybe even more so because of his sickness. If he can't get what he wants, then he'll take it. Dan wants Linda most of all. I have never seen him want anything more in all the years we were together. . . . This obsessiveness has made him cold and calculating (not that he hasn't been before. But not to this extent) because he hasn't been able to have his own way. He gets what he wants and he keeps it for himself. . . . Linda was going to have a terrible lifelong problem and so was I.

As I read Richard's letter I felt overwhelmed by the complexities of the situation. First, apparently there was a "vigilante" group of four agents, witnesses to the November 1989 incident, who had been independently following Linda around and doing their own unauthorized investigation. For the four of them, as for Richard, Dan, and the third man, the sight of the UFO and Linda and the aliens in the blue light must have been a staggering, incomprehensible event.

Because of the letters and other confidential communications I had received from Richard, Dan, and the third man, I had always assumed that the three of them were also carrying out an unauthorized, informal investigation. Apparently, neither unofficial group was well acquainted with the other. (I was not to learn details of the *official* investigation of the November 1989 incident until 1993.)

With the exception of the third man, all of the people in both unauthorized investigations were professional government security agents, all with training, equipment, and expertise. That made them potentially dangerous to Linda and to anyone else involved with her—her children, her husband, the other civilian witnesses, and even, I suppose, myself. With all the doubts I already had about the stability, morality, and common sense of our "official" covert government operations, from the Bay of Pigs to Iran-contra, the presence of these unsupervised surveillances and rogue interrogations deepened my concern. And Dan was a loose cannon, an emotionally distraught escapee from a "rest home"!

Richard's letter went on to describe the major breakthrough in his search for Dan. Following up on every possible lead, he visited a mutual friend he hoped Dan might have contacted. As it turned out, Dan had been staying in this friend's apartment. The man told Richard that Dan had said with excitement that he was about to get married. He said that he and Linda, his fiancée, were going to fly to England that evening on British Airways.

Frantic, Richard called Linda again to warn her not to leave the apartment.

Someone answered the phone and of course it wasn't Linda. It was John. I told him I was cousin Paul (Linda told me last November she has a cousin Paulie) and asked to speak to his mother. It was already 1:35 PM. John said she wasn't home. I asked if he knew where she had gone and he said she went out to run a couple of errands and then she was going to the Seaport to do her mommy things. I asked, Mommy things? What are those? John said, You know, mommy things, like buying me a surprise and bringing it home for me.

Budd, the shit was going to hit the fan, and fast! Linda was out there feeling safe, doing her lady-like things, with her little painted fingers and toes. We left [my friend's] premises immediately to plan our strategy. Soon all six of us piled into two cars and headed downtown. I had already briefed these guys on Linda's identity, etc. They were going to keep an eye out for Dan and the Security people, too. The problem was finding Linda first, if it wasn't already too late, and the odds didn't look very good. Had she changed her schedule, I thought to myself? I was anxious, nervous and mad. This couldn't all be happening in one day.

We reached our destination, double-parked our cars, and took our positions from Pearl Street to South Street. I quickly walked through the Seaport, Pier 17, and back again. It was already 2:45 PM and no trace of Linda or the others. Which could've meant it was too late. The six of us transmitted to each other the nothingness we saw. I wondered if Linda had been taken by now. Was it Dan or was it one of the Security people? If it had to be, I hoped the Security people found her first. If Dan picked her up he may have drugged her or hurt her in other ways. Not to mention the other problems I'd have if I had to track them down at the airport tonight.

The airport, especially Kennedy, has heavy surveillance and hi-tech security. Their Security people would want to know what was going on, and why. Sure, we could give them some story, but what about Dan and his unstable mouth? The next worry was the thought of this whole situation coming out into the open, exposing our identities. My innocent friends could be implicated, as well as Linda and you, Budd, as a consequence. Dan's sickness was assuring me of the possibility of an "OFFI-CIAL PROBLEM" (which is a National Security excuse to keep a person in government quiet). This leads to the ruination of lives and much worse. Something had to be done about this guy before he brings us all down. I've loved him as a brother over the years. But Dan wasn't dealing with a full deck anymore, and we didn't think he ever would again. Don't forget, I spoke to his doctors. Take my word for it, Dan is 'sixty-cents short.' But if I had to go through these risks to get my Christmas Tree Bell, then so be it. No one was going to take my Baby Ann away from me again, not without her consent, not this time.

It was now 3:15 PM and still no Linda. I walked up through the Seaport to Pearl Street to see if I could see her coming. I turned to walk back to the Seaport area and there ahead of me I thought I spotted her walking through the crowds. I walked forward quickly, and there she was in plain view. She has a special walk and it's very feminine. I called out her name and walked faster. She didn't hear me and kept on walking. I called out her name much louder and began to run towards her from behind, as did my buddies from all directions. Linda turned to see, and when she saw my men and me she turned pale, hesitated to say something to someone, and began to run away. I chased after her as did my friends ahead of her near South Street. Linda must've felt trapped and very frightened because she began to run like a moving target. She weaved in and out of crowds. I called off my friends and told them to concentrate on the surrounding area for Dan or those Security people. She moves fast, Budd. I thought I lost her so I stopped to take a better look ahead of me when I heard a voice say, 'Richard? What's going on? Is there a problem?' I looked down and saw this cute little dark haired girl looking up at me with a scared but angry look on her face. I asked myself, how did she know me? I didn't know her. And I wasn't about to answer her questions, either. I couldn't worry too much about it at the time because I had to find Linda. I continued to run forward, across the street through traffic. I just wanted to quietly but firmly pull her out of the district.

Richard's moment-by-moment account was giving me far more detailed information than I had yet received from Linda. She, of course, knew nothing of the panicky search preceding Richard's sudden appearance. From her point of view, everything began when she first saw him in the crowd at the Seaport.

Richard's letter continues with a disturbing communication from one of his men:

Two of the four Security people were seen in the area, and they were with Dan the Hawk. Yes, Budd, that's what he's called. I haven't reached Linda yet, and once again I received from one of my men that two more Security people were seen in the area. I ran through traffic and pulled Linda across the street while she carried on like there was no tomorrow. She threatened me by saying, 'If you don't leave me alone I'm going to knock you into next week.' I tried to quiet her down to explain as I dragged her away, but she couldn't hear me through her cries. There wasn't any time left and I was losing my patience with her. Yes, she's pretty and delicate, but that doesn't cancel out the fact that she is the most stubborn, mischievous and hot tempered woman I have ever known or had to deal with. I could hardly control her and had a hard time hanging on to her. She's little, she's fast and can hide in small places or corners, and she squirms around a lot.

And what the hell was Dan doing with these Security people? What I thought to be two separate problems actually turned out to be linked together as one. Dan had probably talked these people into questioning Linda about the 1989 incident, offering his help. He must have played on their curiosity to fool them into aiding him with this kidnapping. These guys probably had no idea they were part of a kidnapping or anything illegal. This questioning was perfectly legal because unidentified flying objects (no matter where they are from) are considered a threat to National Security and Linda was involved. . . . So, Dan and these Security people had the right to question her. I know Dan and his calculating mind. Once the questioning was over, he would have taken over and dismissed the others.

Richard describes his simultaneous attempts to hold Linda in place, to communicate by transmitter to his men in order to find out the location of Dan and his cohorts—they were headed in his general direction—and to try to explain to Linda a little of what was going on. "I still couldn't simmer Linda down, but I couldn't blame her. From her point of view there were six large, full grown men coming after her and she was out of her mind with fear." Finally, Richard carried her bodily to a nearby building, "pinning her up against an outside entrance . . . I held her with one hand and pressed my body against her so I could put the other hand over her mouth to tell her she had to listen to me."

What happened next is the most completely outrageous misunderstanding of the entire episode. Richard tells it this way:

As I stood there up against her I felt something. It was little and hard. She was real quiet but breathing heavily. Something was resting up against my groin. It trembled. I stood there with my hand over her mouth and looked into those big, mysterious eyes. I said to myself, "What is she doing? Is she trying to turn me on?" I was surprised because Linda didn't seem like the type. I didn't say a word because I was concentrating on what she was doing. Her hand continued to tremble as it moved up and down my groin. She was trying to turn me on and she was nervous about it, too. I told her not to be nervous and that I

*understood what she was feeling. I went on to tell her that she
was doing the right thing. I was turned on in a matter of about
15 seconds! I had to get her out of the area anyway, so I asked
her to come with me to the Vista Hotel where we could hide
and be safe. I was the happiest man in the world. I would have
given anything to get Linda to behave in this manner. She was
still breathing heavy. I took my hand off her mouth to hear
her answer to my offer. She replied in her soft-spoken voice,
"Shithead Mickey, I'm gonna shoot your face off." I then heard
a very familiar sound, the sound of a firearm getting ready for
firing at close range. This whole situation has turned my beautiful angel into a she-devil. I couldn't believe it. She was going to
shoot my face off, Budd!*

*But she was aiming the pistol in the wrong direction. She held
it unsteady and shook it uncontrollably, and she was angry, too.
I'll tell you, Budd, Viet Nam was beginning to look good to me.
I felt myself going into a cold sweat. I didn't want to hurt her
but I was getting as angry as a hornet. I looked past her but
behind her and shouted out Dan's name. Linda quickly turned
around to see and I removed the pistol from her hand.*

*I held her up against the wall with my body, to lock the gun
and put it away. As I did that I tried to explain as fast as I could
what was going on with Dan. Then I slapped her face. You
would think that she'd had enough, but no. She held off and
with a left curve punched me in the Adam's Apple. I thought it
was going to fly out the back of my neck! She looked at me
defiantly, without fear in her eyes. If looks could talk, I would
say her eyes were saying "I dare you!" I wanted to slap her
face again.*

Despite the real danger of this multileveled encounter, involving
Richard, his five men, Dan, the four security people, and Linda—alone
and pursued by all—a wild moment of black humor had suddenly
emerged. Putting together Linda's and Richard's accounts, this is
what happened: When Linda was pinned between Richard and the
building, her arms were squeezed tightly against the front of his long
body, her hands straight down and slightly in front her. As she struggled to get the pistol out of her jeans' waistband without his noticing,
this delicate maneuver was taking place at the level of Richard's
crotch. But he, of course, felt her fingers fumbling down between his
legs and assumed that a miracle had happened: At long last Linda

had decided to seduce him. Aroused by what he took to be subtle erotic caresses, he leaned back a bit, easing the pressure on her body, and in a transport of passion invited her to his hotel room. In fact, he had eased the pressure just enough to free Linda's arm and allow her to raise and cock her gun. Doubly furious at her capture and Richard's suggestion about the hotel room, she said, "Shithead Mickey, I'm gonna shoot your face off," and pointed her shaking pistol at his head. It was, to say the least, a major misunderstanding.

Immediately after Richard disarmed her, there was a heartfelt exchange of blows—a slap and a punch—which Linda had neglected to tell me about, perhaps out of embarrassment. I was a bit surprised that Richard was willing to tell me he had slapped her, and that after she had punched him, was thinking of doing it again. It seemed inconsistent with his generally enraptured and courtly attitude toward her.

But then, Richard said, the strange power, whatever it was and whoever controlled it, manifested itself again, paralyzing him and leading immediately to Linda's escape.

It happened again, Budd! She did it again. My eyes were forced away from her. She forced me to turn my head away from her. I couldn't move it! When I was able to move my head (after three or four minutes) she was gone. I looked everywhere for her. I knew that either my guys stopped Dan and his men or all hell was breaking loose up at the Seaport. Did she go back there? Was she too upset to listen to me when I tried to explain what Dan had been up to? She was upset. It was too soon for her to be walking around by herself. It was already 4:00 PM and my efforts to keep her safe were all in vain.

As I searched for her I wondered what she was thinking. She called me Mickey! How much had she remembered? What was her state of mind? What was my state of mind? The thought of her remembering put a fear in me. God! She confirmed what I had already known. I never thought about how I would feel. I was always concerned about what she was feeling.

I gave up and stopped looking for Linda. I walked until I reached Battery Park. I strolled along the waterfront of the park and there I spotted Linda. She was sitting at the water's edge. I stood there and watched and didn't want to make any sudden moves. I felt like I was deer hunting. . . . She must have felt my eyes on her because she turned around, saw me, smiled and said to me what she had said about 37 years ago when we met for the first time. She said, "Do you want to play?" I walked through the opening of the gateway fence, sat down beside her, and said, "No. You're a baby." We asked each other our names. She said, "What's your name, my name is Lou Lou." I said, "My name is Ricky, what's yours?" She said, "Lou Lou, what's yours again?" "What's yours?" Budd, we went on and on. I told her, "Your cap looks stupid." She answered, "Hey, don't touch my cap, it's special."

We laughed and laughed and then we held each other in our arms. She thanked me for not letting Dan take her away, as those strange adults did many years ago. I told her I loved her very much and could find her blindfolded in a crowd of 1000 people. She asked me not to say things like that because it frightened her. I asked why it frightened her and she said that it was because she had feelings for me, too. These feelings, together with what I was saying, tempted her to be unfaithful. She said she was feeling frustrated at the moment and needed to simmer down.

As I read these pages of Richard's letter, I was struck by an unusual reversal of a familiar pattern. Previously, as in the "Lady of the Sands" and "Mickey and Baby Ann" situations, I had focused on *Linda's* reactions when she received confirmation of her recollections by way of the letters Richard had sent me. In fact, as the reader will remember, I had videotaped those moments of sudden confirmation. But now Richard was writing to me about *his own* moment of unexpected corroboration when Linda referred to him as "Mickey" and made him aware that she, too, remembered their profound childhood connection.

His feelings were stated with brevity and the kind of touchingly understated emotion that suggested a more powerful reaction than he was willing to admit: "She called me Mickey! How much has she remembered? What was her state of mind? What was my state of mind? The thought of her remembering put a fear in me. God! She confirmed what I had already known. I never thought about how I would feel."

Richard's letter went on to describe in some detail his recollection of one of the later Mickey and Baby Ann encounters, a more directly sexual incident I will return to at another time. But he closed his long communication with an interesting discussion of the government cover-up issue from the perspective of his own security/intelligence position.

Linda is angry because I won't sit down and speak with you. She feels that this whole incident is far too serious for me to be worried about such a trivial matter as keeping my identity unknown. Especially after you've promised me anonymity. I'm not a celebrity, a doctor, lawyer, scientist, blue collar worker or house husband. These people don't have an 'Official Problem' to worry about. I do, because I work for a tough Government Agency that takes pride in their rules, their laws and their unwritten laws as well. We're kept very strict. I do trust you, Budd. I know you would keep your promise. However, as much as I like and trust you, I would always be worried about a slip of the tongue or some accidental leak. I don't think you are aware of what the extent of the consequences are for me, perhaps for Linda and you, if this became an "Official Problem." If you were aware, you wouldn't be asking me to take such a risk. Let me explain in some detail.

Right now this November 1989 incident has to stay "Unofficial" for the following reasons. All Unidentified Flying Objects, no matter where they are from, it could be Russia or from outer space, are considered a threat to our National Security. "Unofficial" means a government person like myself has not released his identity to the public concerning a government cover-up that is Top Secret. Once a Government Official or Government Agency person uncovers a Top Secret event or plan it becomes "Official," and an "Official Problem" for the person who made the exposure. A civilian such as yourself can expose such things without a worry, provided a Government person hasn't come forward to expose his/her identity and Top Secret information.

Keeping this incident "Unofficial" has everything to do with leaving our identities out of it, for the time being. That is, those of us who were in the three cars November 30th, 1989. My superiors (and two of them were present at the time this event occurred) don't care much about how an exposure came about so long as it wasn't exposed through one of us. If it were exposed through one of us (Government people), this would make the whole 1989 incident "Official."

Whether an exposure was made by accident or deliberately, according to the strict rules we abide by the results (damage) are the same and so is the disciplinary action. The disciplinary action goes according to the level of secret information ex-

posed. When a government person such as myself has a UFO experience of this nature, he keeps it quiet and "Unofficial." From word of mouth, talk has been around concerning others in our agency that have had experiences (although not as drastic as ours) and have kept it quiet for fear of an "Official Problem."

As Linda mentioned to me, you need to know I exist. Why would I risk such a problem for myself and others for such a trivial reason? It would be stupidity on my part to take such a risk. Presently, as it stands, I already have three worries. (1) Linda (although I don't believe she will betray a trust). (2) Her husband. (3) Her girlfriend. All three can identify me in a snap. All three have spoken to me. It's worse for the Third Man because he's involved with governments world wide. I don't think you'd want to take part in an "Official Problem." It's for YOUR own good and LINDA'S as well. However, it is perfectly safe for you and Linda to expose the 1989 incident because YOU ARE NOT GOVERNMENT OR OFFICIAL people. There were many (as I'm sure you're aware of) [UFO] incidents in the past that were credible, true, and exposed by civilian people such as yourselves safely, because these incidents were kept "Unofficial." There weren't any Official people involved, Budd, and if there were, you can be sure these Officials managed to cover it up very nicely. As long as our identities remain secret, for the time being, IT IS SAFE FOR ALL OF US, YOURSELVES INCLUDED.

If I took Richard's statement at face value, it explained a great deal about our previous contacts. More than once, he, Dan, and even the third man had stated that they *wanted* the events of November 30, 1989, to be made public. In one letter I was told that the third man had specifically selected me as the conduit through which this could be done. And yet none of the three men was willing to go on record about his "official" participation in such a bizarre string of incidents.

At one point in his long explanation I saw a hint of the hardness, the self-assured toughness, that was usually concealed beneath Richard's polite, gentlemanly exterior. Just as I was a bit surprised when he wrote that he had slapped Linda in the face and was about to do so again, I was irked when he stated his reaction to my quite genuine need to speak with him in order to know that he really existed. "Why would I risk [an "Official Problem"] for such a trivial reason? It would be stupidity on my part," he replied.

But one takes what one is offered. Richard had given me a great deal and had surely run innumerable risks. He had made an audiocassette tape for me on which his voice could easily be identified, he had sent me numerous letters, giving me more and more information, both personal and official, as time went by and his trust in me deepened, and he had certainly put himself at risk to protect Linda. It seemed to me that he was attempting to carry out two irreconcilable roles: his position as a security/intelligence officer, with its myriad official duties, rules, and rigid obligations, and his contradictory role as simple good citizen, wanting to bring the truth about his own UFO experiences to the largest number of people.

Although the strains in his behavior were showing, still there was something about Richard that approached the selflessly daring—even, perhaps, the heroic.

C H A P T E R

21

And Then There Were Two . . .

The year of the February showdown at South Street Seaport, 1992, would be an extraordinarily complex one in my life. It was crowded with events of personal significance to me. In the spring, the film version of my book *Intruders* was shown as a miniseries on CBS. A few months before the airing I underwent major surgery to have a cancerous kidney removed. Despite the success of the operation, my home life remained in a somewhat chaotic state, while in the meantime I helped plan a major conference on the UFO abduction phenomenon. The meeting was held that summer on the campus of MIT in Cambridge, Massachusetts, and there, before a large gathering of scientists, psychologists, investigators, sociologists, and other interested researchers, I first made public some of the events of November 1989. In 1992 there were to be other highly significant developments in this ongoing story, but for Linda, the year's most important event was the disappearance of Dan from her life.

In Richard's February letter, after his long description of the potential danger to a government official who becomes involved in an "official problem," he had added three cryptic sentences: "Dan won't be seen anymore, not by anyone, ever. He met with his own problem within the ranks. Please take my word for it." It would not be until May, when I received yet another letter, that Richard related more details about Dan's capture and subsequent "problem within the ranks" at the end of the South Street Seaport incident.

Now I have no idea whether the terms "official problem" and "unofficial problem" are company jargon—employee slang—or some kind of official classification system. I suspect the former. But I was also unsure which security/intelligence agency Dan and Richard worked for, though the CIA or the NSA (National Security Agency) seemed likely guesses.

Considering the vast alphabet soup of U.S. government security agencies—the Secret Service, the FBI, CIA, DIA, NSA, DEA, and NRO, as well as the military intelligence services and probably a few more highly specialized "black" organizations I have never heard of—it would seem only logical that there are as many different sets of regulations as there are intelligence services. And each service probably has its own company argot. One can surmise that separate usages would be common in different departments and at different levels of seniority. But one thing is certain: Wherever Dan worked, and at whatever level, he had obviously become an "official problem."

Without disclosing its source (and thus compromising his identity), I have a magazine photograph of Dan taken in 1988 in which he is standing within six feet of President Reagan, President-elect Bush, President Gorbachev of the Soviet Union, and a group of other officials. He appears to be acting in a security role, and the importance of the men he is guarding underlines his level of seniority. It seems obvious to me that a high-level agent like Dan, possessing not only extremely sensitive information about the president's security but also covert intelligence skills and a variety of standard-issue weapons and communication gear, would not be permitted to run around loose after suffering a severe emotional breakdown. Especially not after demonstrating that he could easily escape from a so-called rest home and then attempt to kidnap an innocent civilian. When Richard wrote that Dan wouldn't be seen again by anyone, ever, I think he knew what he was talking about.

The first week in May I received another letter from Richard, filling in some of the blanks about Dan's disappearance and the other events of February 22 at the Seaport. On May 4, Richard wrote that immediately after he seized Linda and took her down South Street to the front of an office building, his five associates, Dan, and the other four security people confronted one another. "A verbal understanding was made clear enough for all ten men to leave the Seaport area together, peacefully. I was told that Dan struggled and had to be literally punched out in the car. A sedative couldn't be used on Dan for the sake of a more sensible interrogation intended at a friend's apartment later.

"They had an extremely hard time with Dan when they arrived. It took the energy of nine big men to control him. By the time I arrived at my friend's apartment, Dan was fast asleep in the next room where the interrogation took place. I went into the bedroom to wake him. A struggle began as soon as he realized it was me, but that was soon taken care of."

Evidently the interrogation had been harrowing and in its own way, persuasive. "We came to the realization that Dan's sickness had reached its peak. There wasn't just a danger for Linda. He was a danger for all of us involved in the November, 1989, incident. We considered the rules and unwritten laws Dan had broken. . . . It was safer for all those concerned that Dan meet with his own 'Official Problem.' Take my work for it, Budd. It's safe."

I interpreted Richard's coolly objective words about his long-time partner and former friend to mean one of two things: Either Dan's life or his freedom had been permanently terminated. I don't know if the American intelligence community operates psychiatric hospitals of the old Soviet variety, facilities more like high-security prisons than places of healing, but if such places exist I hope Dan is in one of them. The other, more horrendous alternative is one I do not wish to contemplate.

Nor does Linda. When I told her about Richard's ominous words, she seemed more upset than relieved, even though Dan's menacing presence had created crippling anxiety, making normal sleep almost impossible and causing her to lose so much weight that her health was endangered. Still, to think of herself as having been even marginally responsible for anyone's death was a heavy burden to bear. I tried to reassure her that she bore absolutely no personal responsibility for whatever had happened to Dan, that Richard had acted completely on his own, and that other national security issues were surely factors in his decision. We were walking together on a lovely Sunday afternoon down by the South Street Seaport when we had this discussion, and I well remember the drawn, tense expression on Linda's face and the hopeless sadness in her eyes.

After his chilling words about Dan, Richard went on to write about the four other intelligence/security men who had been present at the Seaport showdown. He told them their attempts to question Linda must cease. "I pulled rank on them. I made it clear that if it was information they wanted on Linda, I was willing to supply them with it. I'm very confident that there will not be an interrogation of Linda at any time. However, there will be an occasional, low-level surveillance for the benefit of their sanity. If I stop them from seeing Linda it will make matters worse. I remember being in their place not too long ago. Seeing Linda proved to me that I wasn't crazy, because she existed. There is absolutely no danger to her. Although I know it's easier said than done, she should be able to let it run its course and fade away."

The remainder of Richard's letter had to do with the issue of flashbacks, those sudden visual recollections of hidden memories and images that are of one of the symptoms of PTSD—posttraumatic stress disorder. The reader will recall that immediately after the incident of November 30, 1989, the three men remembered only what Richard and Dan wrote about in their first letter to me: the UFO above Linda's building, the blue beam of light it emitted, the sudden appearance of the aliens and the woman in the nightgown, and then the craft's plunge into the East River. Everything else emerged later: their own abduction that night, the Lady of the Sands, Richard's experience with Baby Ann, and so on. They explained in subsequent letters that these images came to them through a series of disturbing flashbacks, which Richard now presented in a more specific form.

"The flashbacks still continue, but not as much as they did in the past, thankfully. They are difficult to deal with. They have seriously interfered with my life, 'big time.' The flashbacks we experienced in the past triggered memories for all three of us. Some memories we were better off without."

As I read his letter, I noticed again that certain new details helped me make sense of issues left dangling from the past. For example, although UFO witnesses and abductees often delay reporting their encounters for months or even years, I had wondered casually why these three men had waited from November 1989 until February 1991 to write to me about their experience. Richard explained it in the next paragraph.

Fragmentary flashbacks from the Lady of the Sands experience began "way back in January, 1991. We contacted you and Linda the following month. Each flashback made our situation worse. We didn't know what the hell they were because there wasn't enough in the flashbacks to give us a clue. But we knew they had something to do with the 1989 affair. As these mental images continued, our guilt and curiosity became more agonizing. We had to find this girl, to see if she existed."

And now Richard revealed the reason for the April 29, 1991, seizure and interrogation of Linda. "In the early part of April, 1991, our first memory trigger occurred. This was the main reason for our taking Linda against her will. Our third man followed us not far behind in a car while he listened to the whole discussion of our interrogation. My very first triggered memory was actually a shimmering pair of delicate, bare hands and feet. This is the memory that basically pushed us to the April interrogation we put Linda through. It didn't help us. It only made the situation worse for Linda and us. This [experience in the car] was the first time (as far as we were concerned) that she demonstrated her defensive abilities. We hadn't remembered yet what Linda did to Dan on the beach on November 30, 1989."

Richard is, of course, referring here to the sudden paralysis of Dan's arms that he experienced as he sat on the damp sand and reached for his pistol. But the second bout of temporary paralysis in the car during the April interrogation evidently caused more problems for the three men. It had been consciously observed by both Richard and Dan, and it led, Richard wrote, to further flashbacks in the month of May.

His account of the image of the shimmering pair of hands and feet is particularly interesting, and typical of the kind of sudden, vivid recollection often experienced by UFO abductees. It also helps explain why he and Dan made Linda take off her shoes and socks during that April interrogation: They had to see if her feet in any way conformed to Richard's memory. This flashback, he wrote, occurred while he "sat and ate lunch one afternoon in a dimly lit restaurant."

> The sight of a woman's plastic, transparent, high-heeled shoes caught my eye. Her shoes were studded sparingly with diamond-like rhinestones. They reminded me of something I couldn't quite figure out. The more I looked at them, the more I began to feel uncomfortable. Suddenly I started to—what I assumed was—to hallucinate in a quick frame-by-frame fashion. In each frame I saw small, delicate hands and feet. They sparkled in flashes of bright lights. I remembered rubbing my eyes and holding my head there in the restaurant. But I wasn't aware that I was screaming my ass off and had accumulated a crowd of people around the table I was sitting at. By the time I left the restaurant I had already seen the familiar soft eyes of a girl in the reflection of a pair of enormous, watery black eyes.

I'll tell you, Budd, this started it all. I couldn't work anymore that day. I had to go home. But another flashback occurred on the road as I drove home. I was being sandwiched in on the highway by two tractor-trailer trucks. The sides of the trucks shone in the sunset. The flashbacks began again, along with a panic attack. I had to pull over. The sliding of some kind of contraption made of steel or some kind of metal slid back and forth in my mind. There was a mental image of white silk fabric caught in between the sliding metal. I sat there in my car and lost all control of my emotions. I sat there until nighttime fell.

I half understood what was happening to me, as I'm a Viet Nam vet. However, these weren't flashbacks of anything remotely resembling Viet Nam. I had the feeling Linda had something to do with this. When I arrived home I telephoned the third man and Dan to tell them that I'd been hallucinating. Surprisingly enough, so had they.

Apparently, specific memories of the Lady of the Sands episode began to surface at roughly the same time for all three men.

On May 13, Dan called to tell me his memory was triggered in the worst way. He was extremely upset and vowed that if he could get his hands on Linda he'd find an answer. I didn't like his tone of voice, but I wasn't at all surprised because I'd had a memory trigger the night before, on May 12th. I told him to hold on to his memory until I called the third party. I telephoned, and he, too, had had his memory triggered in a big way the night before, just as I had. I asked him to please call Dan and calm him down. This is when our third man decided it was best for the three of us to write our recollections down and meet to compare notes that evening.

We met, compared notes, and then calmed each other down. . . . One by one I listened to their recollections and at times I thought I was hearing myself.

Again I wondered—were I to accept Richard's account—if this was just a remarkable coincidence or another example of some kind of alien control of human behavior, a time-release memory capsule, as it were. Obviously there was no way to know. Sudden, spontaneous recall of previously forgotten details of UFO encounters is common among abductees, but I couldn't recall an example of similar recollections coming to mind at virtually the same time in three different witnesses.

Yet there were so many other unique aspects of this case that there was no logical reason to reject any one particular anomaly. Its uniqueness began, of course, with the fact that the UFO occupants not only allowed Linda's abduction to be seen by numerous independent witnesses but that the encounter appeared to have been deliberately *performed* for an audience of important political figures, one of whom was also abducted.

But if these and other one-of-a-kind details exceed the usual UFO abduction patterns, many other features recounted by Linda, Richard, Dan, and the third man weld it firmly to the historical model. The abductees' physical paralysis, the aliens' appearance, the bluish white levitating light beam, the telepathic communication, the partial or temporary amnesia, and many other details are typical of most previous accounts.

And on the other hand, certain features that initially seemed unique to this case—details like the "Mickey and Baby Ann" phenomenon and alien co-option of abductees—turned out to be only the first examples of previously undiscovered and highly significant patterns. This factor alone presents a powerful argument for the accuracy of Richard's and Linda's more unusual or even unique recollections.

In his letter Richard goes on to describe more of these unusual recollections, many of them details I was hearing for the first time. It was on May 12, while watching TV, that he had a flashback in which he saw a girl on a beach in a scene so realistic that he could "almost feel the warm wind blowing. I was standing near the sea somewhere. My shoes were wet, and out of the clear dark blue sky this very beautiful woman walked up to me from the nearby beach. It was Linda."

In this extended vision, recollection, flashback—whatever we wish to call it—Richard was handed a shovel of some sort and asked to dig like the others. "I looked to see what the others were doing, expecting to see the third party and Dan. But instead I saw those ugly critters I'd seen earlier in the light of the object that hovered over the building complex. I was frightened enough, I'm sorry to admit, but hell! I didn't know where the fuck I was or how I got there in the first place! When I looked up and saw those creatures digging holes in the sand I became so scared I would've done anything they asked me to, for fear of their killing me.

"Linda was speaking to them in a strange language and she seemed to be directing them in their work." Spacing herself about five feet from the UFO occupants, she had Richard stand five feet away from her. "She started to dig, too. I didn't like the idea, but I started to dig because I would have done anything just so they would leave me alone. I felt like a fool, being afraid of such little critters. . . .

"When I asked Linda where my friends were, she said that I would see them soon and not to be concerned. Before I knew it I found myself sitting on the beach in the sand with the third party and Dan. We sat there watching Linda walk from place to place with the others, digging holes all over the shoreline. She was as busy as a little queen bee. We were completely bewildered and terrified at the bizarre goings-on. I asked the others, where the hell had they been? Why was I left alone with those weirdos? Dan and the third man didn't know where the hell they were, either."

Next, Richard describes the now familiar incident with the fish and Linda's accusation, "Look what you have done." New to me, however, was his recollection that she spoke quietly and privately to each of the three men in turn, apparently delivering conventional messages about the need for "peace and a clean environment." But just before she spoke to Richard, she knelt in front of him, smiled, and looked into his eyes. "She was so close," he writes, "that I thought our noses were going to touch. I was feeling all her emotions. They weren't my feelings, because I knew exactly what I was feeling. I figured she knew what I was feeling, too. I was so scared, I needed a hug and she hugged me without my having to ask (not that I was going to ask). How did she know? She was feeling concerned, but angry. She was feeling sad, and feeling love. She spoke to me like I have never been spoken to before. Budd, I loved her the moment I saw her image in the binoculars, and long before that, too."[1]

I was surprised to hear how completely Linda had apparently been taken over by the aliens and temporarily made to act as one of them. In May, when I first learned about her "alien" conversations with the three men, she was evidently unaware, consciously at least, of the degree of her own co-opted behavior.

In Richard's letter there was another recollection, this time from May 13, that particularly interested me because it explained another mystery from the past. "The flashbacks kept coming," he writes, "and suddenly I was hit in the head with another memory. This particular memory made me lose control of my emotions and I broke down. It was the confirmation of something I'd suspected the night before. If you remember, Budd, [on the morning of November 30] the three of us waited for the object to come up, after seeing it plunge into the river behind us. We waited forty-five minutes for it to come up out of the river with the hope of Linda's return. It didn't come up again because *It Had Just Dropped Us Off.*

"When we saw the UFO plunge into the East River, we didn't know at the time that we had been taken and returned along with Linda. We saw Linda being taken while we sat helplessly *in* the car. The next thing we remembered was the craft plunging into the river while we stood *outside* the car. How did we get outside the car? We took it for granted that Linda was inside the object when it plunged into the water, but in reality she wasn't there at all. What we saw was the craft leaving after we were all returned." [Richard's emphases]

When they met on May 13 to compare notes, these were the main incidents Richard, Dan, and the third man all remembered. "Dan was totally beside himself," Richard added, a reaction I can easily understand.

But there was one final flashback that was eventually to lead to one of the most surprising and valuable recollections of the entire story. It occurred not in May 1991 but months later, in November. "After the Middle East Peace Talks in Spain," Richard writes, "Dan and I went on to Rome for the NATO talks. More memories triggered there in Rome for both of us. It was this particular memory that drove Dan over the edge. We remembered seeing Linda twice aboard the craft. She passed through a corridor as the shiny steel doors of the hospital-like room slid closed. The second time we saw her pass through the sliding doors (which we believe was on the return trip), the doors closed and caught a piece of white silky fabric between them. There we sat on separate tables looking at this white fabric—we believe it was Linda's white nightgown caught inside the sliding doors of the room we were in. The third man has also attested to this. However, no recollections have ever surfaced pertaining to what had happened in the room we were in. That is, except for Dan, but he refused to discuss it and would completely lose control of himself whenever the subject was brought up. He had completely broken down in Rome because of it."

Knowing what is usually reported in UFO abductions, particularly in "hospital-like rooms" when an abductee finds himself sitting on a table, it is my guess that the three men underwent physical examinations and possibly even sperm-sampling procedures. If so, these humiliating and deeply disturbing intrusions might easily have caused Dan—*particularly* Dan—to become enraged whenever he was reminded of what had been done to him. If he felt abased and helpless under such circumstances, with his macho self-image seriously undermined, he might well have felt a profound hunger for revenge afterward. And since in his mind poor Linda was "a half-breed," she was fair game, despite his physical attraction to her.

It seems to me that at least some of the responsibility for Dan's tragic end must be placed upon the UFO occupants. Their typically detached, cold-blooded treatment of abductees—in this case, an emotionally disturbed man—might well have provided the final push that sent him straight over the edge.

PART FIVE

Physical Evidence

Drawings and Sand Samples

On Wednesday, May 20, the postman delivered a bulky padded mailer with a familiar typewritten return address: "Richard, New York City." I was astonished to see what he had sent me. In some respects it was the most important communication I had yet received. Inside were two small, carefully packed and labeled bags of sand and a remarkable set of colored drawings depicting what Richard had seen on the morning of November 30, 1989, while he, Dan, and the third man sat in their car under the FDR Drive. But this was not all. Included was another letter containing a great deal of new information, a paragraph about the drawings, and a detailed account of how he had obtained the sand samples and what he believed their significance to be. The whole thing was staggering.

Over many months subtle changes had been occurring in my relationship with Richard and the third man, changes that apparently had led to this further demonstration of their trust. In his May 4 letter, Richard had asked me to leave yet another audiotaped message in the "drop" he had arranged. This time he specifically requested that I supply whatever advice I could on how to cope with the disturbing flashbacks he and the third man were experiencing. They also required reassurance that I would continue to respect their desire for anonymity. In an unusual kind of quid pro quo, I seemed to have become as necessary to their sense of well-being as they had become to my investigation of this case. The more they trusted me and responded to the counsel I continued to offer, the more information they were willing to share with me.

Shortly after I read Richard's May 4 letter, I fulfilled his request and at the prearranged spot left a fairly long tape on which I discussed various interpretations of some of the things the three men had experienced. I included some reassuring words of advice on coping with their UFO encounters and recollections, and then ended with a series of questions and requests for information.

Richard's response was not long in coming. I received the drawings, the sand samples, and his startling new letter only about two weeks after his earlier communication. He began by thanking me for the tape.

"Your audiotaped message has been more than helpful to us. It has answered most of the nagging questions we've been asking ourselves over the years. We now understand why we have remembered our memories all together and not separately. The 'time-release capsule of information' seems to be a very logical explanation. Your theory on Linda's defensive gifts also makes a lot of sense, and now we're feeling sort of foolish believing that she was entirely responsible for her actions. We also understand that Linda may not be half alien."

With an eye to defusing their persistent distrust of Linda, I had discussed the topic of chronic alien deception and the temporary co-opting of normal humans for alien purposes. Because of his profound affection for her, Richard seemed more than willing to accept any theory I offered that acquitted Linda of possessing alien powers, motivations, or genetic background. "We now know that Linda hasn't picked on us at all. Those creatures picked on her and used us to prove something. I wish we knew what it was. . . ."

He then moved on to other subjects I had spoken about on the tape. "As for me and hypnosis, I'm one of those that isn't a good candidate for it. I believe it's probably due to all the psychological training I've had throughout the years. This training prevents us from being mentally controlled, as a protective measure against enemy brain-washing. The funny thing about it is you have to be brain-washed in order to prevent it. It's too late for me, Budd. Hypnosis will never work."

On my cassette recording I had told Richard about Janet Kimball, "the woman on the bridge," and he offered a pleased response.

We're happy to hear about the other witness. We're certainly thankful we weren't the only ones to see what we saw in 1989.

I'm sure others have seen as well. However, it isn't the sort of thing people are ready to admit they saw. I hope more witnesses come forward for us, but it doesn't seem likely. I wish I could come forward for you, Budd.

Towards the end of your taped message you mentioned that we have a lot to talk about. 'Truer words were never said.' There have been several things I've wanted to tell you, but I've refrained from saying them because I knew I was vulnerable and needed someone other than the third man and Dan to talk to. I knew you wanted me to come forward and speak with you, and it was tempting.

Quite frankly, I've found it difficult to stay away. I've had to stop myself from ringing your doorbell several times. In fact, I've sat near your doorstep in the past, fighting with myself, "should I or shouldn't I?" I'd stand there staring at your gray door, but found the strength to walk away. I needed someone "who knew" to talk to. The only explanation for my logical defense was the fear of an Official Problem for us all. I guess the fear was stronger than the need to speak with you. Staying away has been just about the only productive way of protecting all of us, Linda and you included, of course.

Your cooperation has been equally effective, Budd. It pleases me how your protective concern for Linda and her family has actually protected them. Although I understand your deep concern and worry about Dan in the past, you've refrained from making major moves, in order to protect the third man and I.

Here Richard is referring to something I said on the tape. I had told him that several times I had been about to report them to the police. In fact, I refrained from going to the police for many other reasons, too. Chief among them was the fear that no one would believe a story that could not be told apart from the details of the UFO abduction that set everything in motion.

Linda was opposed to reporting Dan's crimes and threats for the same reason. Had she lodged a formal complaint, she knew that she would be asked how she knew him, what kind of relationship she had with him, and how they met. Being an inept prevaricator, she couldn't imagine what kind of convincing story she could possibly make up and maintain in order to avoid talking about her UFO experiences. Obviously, the moment one of the interviewing policemen suspected her truthfulness, her complaint would be dismissed.

Despite Richard's generous supposition about my motives for not going to the police, concern about protecting him, Dan, and the third man had been way down on the list. The three seemed to me to be virtually invulnerable to any complaint Linda could lodge. Although I had Dan's photograph, I could not identify Richard, and the third man had already assured me he would deny anything I alleged about his involvement. Even if the police could find Richard and Dan, I was afraid that in some informal, off-the-record way they would be able to flash their credentials and assert that this entire matter was a national security issue. As such it would be summarily dismissed. "Lack of evidence" would be a natural excuse for the police to drop any further investigation.

But to at least some extent Richard was correct about my dilemma.

It must have been very difficult for you because you were tossed between Linda's safety and ours. You too, Budd, were standing between the fire and the water. Protecting me and the third man [Richard was aware that I knew his identity] may have interfered with Linda's safety, and protecting Linda by making any major moves against us would most certainly have interfered with our safety. I believe you may have been ready to make a major move only because of Dan. It was hard, wasn't it? We certainly have a friend in you, as you have in us.

The third man has also listened to your audio-taped message. Do you know what he said to me? He said, "Richie, I'm going to sleep well tonight, which is something I haven't been able to do in a long time. Thanks to the Hopkins fellow." He believes that one day we will all discuss together what no one at the present time will let pass through their lips. He asked me to thank you for your message. You have answered a lot of the questions that have been nagging both of us over the years.

But the big news in this letter was not their discussion of the tape; it was the enclosure of the two small bags of sand and the drawings Richard had done at my request. To give the full flavor of this amazing new development, let me quote Richard's first paragraph exactly as it appears:[1]

This letter is in answer to your audio taped message. In your taped message, one of your questions to me was—Was my clothing wet? Or have I found sand in my shoes, etc.? Yes, my clothing was wetter than damp and I've found sand in my clothing. I'll go even further, being that you've asked. But before I go on with this letter, please find enclosed herewith something that may very well be some good tangible evidence. (I hope it will help you). "BE CAREFUL NOT TO INHALE IT." I've enclosed two beach sand samples. One of which I snatched from the hospital like room we were in when we were aboard the craft on November 30, 1989. (I gather, we were on our way back.) The other sample I found in my shoes when I arrived and undressed. I'll always be a G-man whether it be subconsciously or not. It's second nature to me after all these years (I'll suppose). Please let me explain—

My astonishment grew, and I raced through the letter. The two small sand samples, carefully labeled, were sealed inside two plastic Baggie-type sacks. The set of drawings he had also enclosed were amazingly similar to Janet Kimball's sketches, through drawn with more skill and from a much closer location. But first I had to learn more about the sand.

I hadn't realized at the time in November of '89 how or why I found sand in my suit jacket pocket and in my shoes. But later that day when I found it, I placed the sand into the enclosed plastic bags simply because I was aware of what we had seen earlier on that day. The strangeness of the sand matched the strangeness of what we'd seen. The only sufficient explanation I was able to come up with (as to my reaction to what I found in my pocket and shoes) was the simple fact of knowing that what I had seen was potentially important and I wondered if the sand I found in my clothing had anything to do with what I'd seen. So I kept the sand, put both separate findings in two separate plastic bags for future reference, put both samples away in a drawer and forgot all about them.

In November of 1991, while I was in Rome with Dan for the NATO talks, we both had flashbacks which triggered more memories. Dan went over the edge while I remembered the strange sand I managed to save. This is the memory that was triggered out of me:

The three of us sat on three separate tables. The tables were attached to the floor in the rounded hospital-like room we sat in. After Linda passed through the corridor with what looked like her pail and shovel, the sliding doors closed tightly on what we believe to be her nightgown. Then the doors quickly opened and shut, and we watched this white, silk-like fabric quickly pop out of the door it was caught in. It happened so fast that our heads popped to attention as this fabric disappeared to the other side of the door.

I was feeling pretty normal except for the fact that I couldn't move my legs. But that was the only part of my body that I couldn't move. Everything else was fine. Next to the table I was sitting on (about two feet away) was a large, gray, hutch-like table with many drawers. On top of this piece of furniture there was a smooth, desk-like surface. Placed on this surface area was a laboratory-like stand (about 2 × 2 Ft.) also attached to the surface. The stand contained tools I have never seen before. They closely resembled dentists' tools. Also on the hutch's surface was a round glass fish tank (here we go again) contraption also standing about 2 ft. × 2 ft., with metal-like pipes or tubes inside of it. The hutch itself was made from a substance closely resembling plastic.

Below me and in front of me, placed on the floor, was the pail and shovel I used to gather the sand earlier on, along with Linda, at the water's edge. Suddenly the sliding doors opened and seven little ugly critters walked in. The third man and Dan were escorted out of the room by four little creatures. Three stayed behind with me. All three stood in front of me and stared me in the face, just as Linda did on the beach only moments before. One of them took the bucket with the sand samples in it, poured some of its contents through the metal pipes attached to the inside of this round glass-like contraption. (It sort of reminded me of a big bubble-gum vending machine.) He pushed two of about six buttons and waited about three seconds. When the low frequency hum stopped, he placed a metal tray beneath it, a little door automatically opened and let all its contents out onto the tray. I couldn't believe what he put in there and what came out as a result.

He walked away from the hutch and stood in front of me with the other two, as we all joined in a staring contest. That is, until one of them caught me by surprise and pricked my nose, and used a dental pick to do it! It hurt, Budd. That prick gave me a nose bleed, too, and I don't mean the prick of the instrument, either!

The three creatures slid over by the sliding door (which was about 15 feet away from me), and with their backs facing me *examined whatever they found, which took about 5 seconds. During these five seconds I glanced over to the hutch to take another look at what managed to come out of that contraption. I took two fast, big handfuls of the stuff that was in the metal tray and put it into my suit jacket pocket. I then brushed the contents off of my hands, onto my trousers. The contents I've snatched from them is what I've enclosed for you to do with whatever you please. I don't know what they (the creatures) did to it, Budd, but it didn't look like the sand that was dropped into those peculiar metal pipes. I've enclosed a sample of the sand I found in my shoes when I arrived home after the incident occurred. Now you have something to compare the pocket sand with.* PLEASE DO NOT INHALE IT.

I could have had these samples tested myself in November of '91 after I realized what I may have brought back with me from the craft. However, I decided not to because I thought maybe I would never see or hear of it again.[2] So I'm giving the contents to you.

All of this was, of course, completely staggering new information to me. To my knowledge no credible person has ever claimed to have brought objects of any kind out of a UFO. But now, if Richard's account were true, the two sets of sand samples provided a potentially rich new area of research.

However, several aspects of Richard's story raised a particular suspicion in me. Could this be merely another set of incidents deliberately staged by the UFO occupants for official consumption, as Linda's earlier abduction possibly was? There were many reasons for my misgivings. First, of course, is the fact that apparently nothing like this had ever happened before. But second and even more suspicious, the aliens operated their sand machine right in front of Richard, naturally arousing his curiosity and ensuring that the process received his full attention. Third, though he was sitting a mere two feet away from the apparatus, only his legs were paralyzed; he was obviously left with enough mobility to steal some sand if given the opportunity.

Fourth, the aliens turned to him and "joined in a staring contest" both before and after they operated the machine. Can this intense eye contact possibly be connected with Richard's subsequent actions?

But last and most suspicious to me, the UFO occupants simultaneously and conspicuously *turned their backs on Richard and walked away,* apparently busily examining something for just as long as it took him to steal some sand. Alien operations inside UFOs, as they are almost invariably described by abductees, are just not that careless.

If the reader will remember Linda's hypnosis concerning her Lady of the Sands episode, she described the purpose of the sand sampling as an alien search for traces of certain substances "so then they'll know why the sea creatures are dying." She went on to say that "we need . . . to find some traces of basaltic lavas, and the reef limestone, some graywackes and shale. . . . Crustaceans feed on shale. There's something wrong with the minerals. They aren't as pure as they used to be and our sea life are dying and we've got to find out what's polluting the minerals. . . . So, as soon as we get those soil samples [the UFO occupants] are going to test them and they're going to tell everyone why our sea creatures are dying." Needless to say, such an announcement from the aliens has never come.

As we know, Linda can hardly be described as an avid environmentalist, so the question remains: Are the aliens truly interested in our ecosystem or was this sand sampling and analysis a kind of subterfuge, a cover story for a different agenda?

In Richard's account several incidents stood out in my mind as possible attempts to create an illusion of alien environmental concern: his seemingly unnecessary and gratuitous employment as a sand-sample digger out on the beach, the demonstration immediately in front of him of the odd machine, and finally the aliens' near tacit permission for him to steal some of the refined sand. Together, all of these can easily be interpreted as clues in support of a diversionary illusion designed to conceal from Richard the aliens' real purposes. And yet it is possible, of course, to take the UFO occupants' professed concern for our environment as being literally true. I shall return to this very important and controversial issue later.

Richard had one more thing to present to me in response to the requests I had made on my audiotape. "Also enclosed," he wrote, "are three drawings of what we saw as we sat under the FDR Drive in our cars that morning in November of '89. The craft itself was much larger than depicted in the drawing. I didn't have the paper space, and I didn't want to draw Linda and the critters smaller. I wanted you to get a good idea of the actual size I saw through my binoculars. However, true to life, Linda and the critters were visually larger than the drawings. These drawings scratch only the surface of the strangeness of it all."

There were three colored drawings, each carefully placed in a three-ring, looseleaf plastic page, and each bearing a stick-on label captioned with Richard's usual near-military precision:

"#1 Drawn by Richard—A ball of fire before Linda was taken on 11/30/89. Turn over for the next drawing.

#2 Drawn by Richard—Sprung out from her window one by one, each in a fetal position. They straightened out in the next drawing #3. 11/30/89

#3 Drawn by Richard—My Xmas Tree Bell—The lights and shadows were so strong I could actually see the silhouette of Linda's body. We even felt the static cling as the object passed over us. We didn't know we were also taken on—11/30/89"

Richard's drawings, like Janet Kimball's, were done in pencil and then colored in with crayons. Drawing #1 of the UFO itself shows the craft in perspective, its leading edge tilted *down* slightly toward the viewer. This would probably not have been Richard's point of view when he first saw the craft above Linda's building. Then he would most likely have been looking up at the ship from below at about a forty-five-degree angle, the view he correctly represents in his other two drawings. I don't know if this first drawing is just a more conceptualized, more conventional rendering, or whether he is unconsciously remembering the way the craft looked when it swooped down a few moments later toward his car. If, as seems likely, the leading edge of the UFO tipped down toward the ground as it approached him—aiming itself at the car rather than flying parallel to the ground—then he would have drawn it correctly.

He depicts the craft as having a relatively flat bottom, a convex but shallow red body, and a small domelike structure on top that he shows as being more orange than red. Kimball's drawing does not show this domelike structure—she was, of course, much farther away and without the benefit of binoculars. Yet in all other respects—color, proportion, and general shape—her version matches his remarkably.

In his second drawing Richard shows the underside of the craft and beneath it, seen almost from the side, the three compacted aliens and Linda, stacked vertically in a streaming blue-white light. In the dramatic final drawing all four figures have unrolled to their full height and are now depicted frontally. This raised a small but interesting question. From where the car was parked, Richard essentially had a *side view* of Linda's apartment wall, not a front view. The rolled-up figures would therefore have necessarily popped out of the window from right to left, straight *across* his field of vision. One would assume, then, that when they unrolled they would still be facing in that same leftward direction and that Richard should have depicted them in profile rather than frontally.

Without stating why I was inquiring, on a later audiotape I asked him to describe as precisely as he could the four figures' actions after they came out the window. He subsequently wrote to answer that and a number of other questions I had raised on other subjects. "Even before Linda and the creatures unrolled," he wrote, "they turned to their left and faced us directly. . . . Then they unfolded right before our eyes in one second flat." The point of view of his drawing, therefore, is correct. But there is something even more important here than the accuracy of Richard's renderings. If all four figures somehow turned to face the important individuals in the cars stalled below the FDR Drive, then there is further reason to accept the theory that Linda's abduction was a deliberately orchestrated performance.

Many more things can be said about these remarkable drawings, and I will return to them later. But after I examined them that May afternoon, I realized that the more immediate task was to have the sand samples analyzed. I had no idea what kinds of information might be derived from their study, but the process must be begun.

Richard Answers More Questions

After sending the bulk of the sand samples off for a preliminary study at the University of Nevada, I left another audiocassette for Richard, thanking him for the sand, the drawings, and the new information he had included.[1] Naturally, I had more questions to ask him, and to my surprise I received a response to my tape within the week. It was as if in Richard's mind I had passed some kind of test of trust, and now he felt willing to discuss almost everything I inquired about.

I had asked more questions about the appearance of Linda and the three aliens as they levitated within the bluish white beam of light. His answer, dated May 23, 1992, contained some telling new images. Before they unrolled, he said, they were very still. "There was absolutely no movement. It was almost as though time had stopped for them. No gravity, either. . . . They just remained suspended up there in midair, defying nature's gravity. It was so bizarre, I couldn't help but think of how Linda reminded me of a still photograph resembling a Christmas tree ornament hanging from a Christmas tree. You know, a Christmas tree bell or angel.

"Before they were pulled up into the craft, there were two more movements. First, they simultaneously straightened up at attention with their arms down at their sides, and turned their heads upwards as if to look at the underside of the object. Secondly, they were all pulled up into the craft." This detail nicely corroborates Linda's recollection of the incident during her 1989 hypnosis session about her abduction. Then she had vividly recalled staring up at the underside of a large, circular craft—the only part of it she had seen—and rising toward it through no effort of her own.

In his previous letter Richard wrote that he now realized he and his companions had also been abducted only moments after Linda, and that what they believed to be the very next incident—the UFO's plunge into the East River—actually occurred much later, after they had been returned to their car. He now had some important new details to relate.

After Linda and the three small creatures disappeared inside the UFO, it began to move. "It was in motion and shooting straight towards the FDR Drive. We thought it was going to crash into the Drive as we sat beneath it! It was flying too fast and too low, Budd. But as it came towards us, we felt a strange and very strong pulling sensation in front of us. We screamed our butts off because we thought we were going to be pulled forward and out through the windshield of the car, shattering its glass. After the object began to look much bigger to us, things started to get a little fuzzy."

Based on my knowledge of similar cases, I assumed that the three men probably *did* pass through the windshield, however such an "impossible" thing is managed, and that this was the moment they were taken into the UFO.[2] After these sensations of "fuzziness" and of being pulled, their next conscious and sequential memory was actually some time later, after they had been returned:

> *We felt a static cling on our bodies, as we watched the object plunge into the river behind us. After that we helped our third man off the roof of the car. I hope we never experience anything even remotely resembling this experience, Budd.*
>
> *You wanted me to ask our third man if his clothing was wet and sandy. His clothing was damp and sandy. In fact, after he arrived home and undressed, he telephoned me to ask me about my clothing. He also went on to tell me that his trousers lost their crease. We came up with a good explanation for the dampness of our clothes. We thought we probably wet our pants from fear. However, we couldn't find a logical explanation for finding sand in our shoes, etc. I saved the sand for that particular reason. I didn't know where it came from and kept it as a reminder of the strange, but potentially important sighting. Finding sand in my clothing was almost as strange as experiencing the incident. Our third man has not saved a sand sample.*

In his orderly way of writing, Richard moved on to what he designated as "Question number 4."

You asked me if I thought I may have been allowed to see Linda's abduction, the sand being refined, and my being able to take a couple of handfuls of the changed sand. About a year and a half after it happened, we began to realize it was too coincidental for people such as ourselves to just happen to stumble upon such a sight. Remember, there were five important figures with us at the time. (Two US Government officials, two foreign Statesmen, one World Leader).[3] Six more of us included as US Government enforcers. If the occupants of the craft wanted to get a message out to the world, they've chosen the right group of people to do it for them. However, these Alien characters, I'm sure, didn't count on the difficulties of avoiding an Official Problem.

We have the feeling that there was a reason why we saw what we saw November 30, 1989. We've come away with the impression that they were trying to fool us somehow. It's possible that you are right, Budd. Maybe these creatures did stage the whole event. We aren't sure, but these are some of what our thoughts were these past years:

It was almost as though we were forced to watch them abduct Linda. From there, we were brought to a beach somehow, somewhere in the world. Linda made me work alongside of her and then we had to sit on the beach and watch Linda and those creatures work together as friends. However, we don't believe they were talking through Linda. It was Linda talking, all right. Linda has said some pretty strange things to me when we were together in Central Park and Battery Park last February. I don't know if she remembers this, but she asked me if I've taken care of our third man during his difficult work. That's what she said to me on the beach in 1989! Yeah, it was she that did the talking on the beach, all right. She has a sweet mouth at all times and can talk our third man and I into anything. Yeah, it was her talking on the beach, all right!

However, we do feel that what we saw at the beach in 1989 was their trying to tell us something. They might as well have said: "Look and see how nicely we can work together. Look at us! Linda isn't afraid! Your people work very nicely with us.

EVERYBODY SHOULD LOVE US! WE'RE ALL DOING YOU A FAVOR! TELL THE WORLD HOW WONDERFUL WE ARE!"

In the meanwhile, those rat bastards are probably stealing our eyes out of our heads, and want us to help them do it. They most likely have stolen the very essence of us. You know, the stuff that makes us what we are—human beings. We know they toyed with Linda, etc. How do we know they aren't taking our food and water and want it pollution-free? We believe they want to clean up our pollution so they can plant and harvest their own food here, without impurities. These sons-of-bitches are probably even dredging for oil and taking that, too! World Peace would certainly make it easier for them, wouldn't it?

My surprise at Richard's virulence was mitigated a bit when I realized that in addition to his suffering at the hands of the aliens he was also a professional agent of the cold war. He was truly a warrior—an active fighter in the Vietnam War and a covert one in the undercover world in which he currently operated. His strange notion that the UFO occupants might be interested in our food and water and might even be "dredging for oil" has a distinctly geopolitical cold-war flavor. (Among all the various theories that have been put forward about the aliens' motives—both benign and malign, both sensible and crazy—this one was new to me!) But the simple truth is that for anyone who has been through what Richard has been through and received the kind of relentless ideological training he has probably received, a degree of paranoia is unavoidable. His letter contained a few more speculations:

I don't know if I was allowed to take the sand samples or not. I'd like to believe I'm a good sneak. However, it's possible they let me. Anything is possible, especially after what we saw. I'll guess the results of the sand sample studies will give me the answer. I believe they let me see the sand processed because they watched me watch it happen. Yes, it's possible that Linda was used as a tool. We all were, Budd, for whatever selfish reasons they had at the time. We believe that these creatures have always wanted the world to know they've been around. Why else would they be lighting up the night sky with their obvious flying objects? They haven't been discreet, have they?

There was one more very important question that I had asked on my audiotape, and it had to do with any of Richard's or the third man's childhood memories that might suggest imperfectly remembered abduction experiences. In Richard's case, because of his Mickey and Baby Ann recollections, I assumed that he would recall at least some suggestive circumstances.

> *You asked if I remembered what I was wearing when I found myself in that strange, bright, white place. Yes, I remember. I was wearing pajamas most of the time. Other times but not too many I was wearing my street clothes. Linda, too. I remember her most of the time wearing pajamas or nightgowns. Early on in our lives I saw many different pairs of her pajamas. One pair in particular stands out in my mind. She was about 8 years old and very little. These pajamas were white with little pink bunny rabbits on them. Ha Ha. They went very well with her little tiny pig tails. The first time I met her she was tiny, about 7 years old. She wore her street clothes. However, I remember that no matter what she wore, that baseball cap was placed wrong on her head, even in her night clothes. When we grew older I saw her in some of the most fantastic nightgowns, although they weren't revealing, they were gorgeous.*

But Richard had other evocative memories from his childhood.

> *I remember feeling numb on several occasions in my sleep as a small boy, into adulthood. I remember thinking that perhaps I had a health problem. But I didn't. I've had several medical examinations to keep my job.*

> *Do I remember being moved or taken? Yes, both, as a young boy. One night (and I know I wasn't dreaming) a bunch of little sickly-looking midgets came in through my bedroom window. Although they were taller than me, somehow I knew they were adults and not older children. They behaved with authority (adult-like). We owned our own home in California before we made the big move to New York. The little people coaxed me out of the window with them. They used a piece of something that looked like candy to do it. When they got me outside there was no candy and no friendliness. I began to scream holy terror as I stood outside my parents' bedroom window. Their window was open, too! I couldn't believe they didn't hear me.*

> *They forced me to walk a long way through a nearby forest in the neighborhood. I didn't want to go (because my parents warned me not to ever go) there alone or with strangers. I was about 9 years old. The little people dragged me through the*

forest and in the distance I saw the lights of many big Mack trucks there in the forest. I can't remember what happened after that, but I woke up and found myself on someone else's lawn at the beginning of the forest.

Apparently that particular neighbor saw me and called my parents and came out on her lawn with a blanket to wrap around me. She wanted to know why I was there. So I told her about the midgets. My parents came running down the road. My dad was upset and my mother was crying. They wanted to know where I was because when they woke up they didn't see me and thought I was still asleep, which was unusual for me because I was always an early riser. When my mother checked on me in my room and I wasn't there she became nervous, as did my dad. The wide open window is what put the fear into them. I remember dad complaining in these exact words—'I hope this boy doesn't have a sleepwalking problem. I don't want to have to put a bell around his ankle.' I told them what happened to me the night before, but they said I was dreaming and sleepwalking. I was angry because I remembered what happened, yes, but it wasn't a dream.

But whatever dad said, went. I loved him but I could've used a little more understanding that particular morning. Once in a while, and presently, I feel numb and heavy. I still have the fear of the little people (midgets). I'll try not to feel fear when I see these harmless people because I'm sure my fear stems from this experience which may be UFO related.

You asked if the third man has had childhood memories. No. He doesn't remember being abducted from his room as I have. He remembers being in the strange white environment several times. Sometimes I think he doesn't want to remember.

Through many months and many letters, one of the strongest impressions I had received from Richard's remarks about his UFO experiences has to do with the wide, internally contradictory range of theories and emotions he'd expressed over time. He had once written that he believed the aliens were here to help us clean up the environment—that, indeed, was the manifest message of the Lady of the Sands tableau—and to create world peace by ending national boundaries. Now he says that they are here to deceive us and steal our very essence. Our one-time selfless helpers are now "rat bastards," mining our resources, our oil and water—stealing from us again. Even the notion that they favored world peace he also sees as a selfish act, a deception.

From Richard's point of view, I could see that he would believe the UFO occupants had reunited him with his beloved Baby Ann. But they had also ended, perhaps tragically, his years-long relationship with his best friend. The aliens had terrified him, paralyzed him, abducted him, and yet made his childhood dream a reality by bringing him together with Linda. Were the aliens good? Were they bad?

Over all the years I had worked with abductees I had come to recognize this kind of perplexed frustration and ambivalence as a virtually universal reaction to the UFO abduction experience. On one side, most abductees do not believe they are dealing with implacable and insidious enemies, and on the other, most do not feel they are being helped by kindly extraterrestrial visitors, either. The vast majority recognize the existence of a distinct alien agenda or modus operandi, similar in case after case, the ultimate purpose of which remains a mystery.

So, if Richard's present fury at the way he had been treated was very real, so had been his earlier hope that the aliens might actually bring peace and a safer environment to the world. For someone unfamiliar with the basic patterns of the abduction phenomenon, this seemingly contradictory series of reactions might appear as a reason to doubt Richard's credibility. But for me, after a decade and a half of careful observation of abductees' emotional and ideological behavior patterns, this mix of ambivalent yet strong feeling weighed in on the other side of the scale: as but one more factor supporting the inherent truthfulness of Richard's account.

I once remarked on the fact that the UFO abduction phenomenon, its investigators, and the abductees themselves had been labeled a cult by a particular debunker. I pointed out that it is quite the reverse. A true cult, such a that of Reverend Moon or the Branch Davidians, is all beliefs and no miracles. The UFO phenomenon is all miracles and no beliefs.

Blood and Mystery

Memorial Day in 1992 was celebrated on Monday, May 25, and for the Cortile family the three-day holiday was a welcome respite from school and work. Steven, Linda's sixteen-year-old son, invited his friend "Brian" to spend the weekend with him at their apartment. The boys had known one another since the sixth grade, and as so often happens when children are close, their respective parents had become casual friends.

Normally, in the rather small Cortile apartment, Steven and his brother Johnny shared twin beds in one of the two bedrooms. But now, to make room for Steven's guest, Johnny had been moved to the master bedroom to sleep with his father while Linda took the convertible bed in the living room. Everything went pleasantly that weekend and the boys got along well—until early Sunday morning, May 24.

Linda was the first to awaken. She was choking and gagging on an unpleasant, sharp-tasting liquid at the back of her throat. She climbed out of bed and ran the fifteen feet or so from her convertible couch to the kitchen to grab some paper towels. When she switched on the light, she saw that the liquid was blood and that it was running from her right nostril. When she was lying in bed the blood had run back and down her throat, causing her to gag. Glancing at the kitchen clock, she saw that it was nearly 2:30 A.M. As she pressed dampened towels against her nose to stop the bleeding she heard stirring in her sons' room. In a moment or so, Steven and Brian both appeared in the living room, bleeding from their right nostrils. She provided them with damp paper towels, and in their sleepy, somewhat dazed state they all sat down to concentrate on creating enough pressure on the bridge of the nose to stop the flow.

Moments later they were joined by Johnny and his father—also suffering from nosebleeds, again from the right nostril. For the next half hour or so, all five adults and children sat around the living room in their nightclothes, pressing the bridges of their noses and dabbing at the blood. Despite their rather disoriented state they tried to fathom what had happened. All five instinctively knew that this was a coincidence so remarkable as to be almost unimaginable. Whatever her husband, her sons, and the weekend guest might have thought, for Linda this simultaneous set of right-nostril nosebleeds could have but one explanation, an explanation she did not want to face.

The next day, when she called to tell me what had happened, her account was underlined by a massive sense of guilt. "Budd, what am I going to say to Brian's mother? This happened in my house. If he hadn't been here, this would never have happened. I feel terrible about it." I tried to calm her and assure her that this was no one's fault, that if it was UFO-related it was outside her control. She shouldn't blame herself in any way. I don't know if I was able to help her or not, but the reassurances I offered were not new to me; I have had to say the same things to quite a few other abductees in similar circumstances, when a friend or relative has an apparent abduction experience in their company.

Throughout the unpredictable twists and turns of this case, I had put the well-being of the Cortile family ahead of my investigation. Knowing how protective Linda was of her boys and how uneasy her husband was about the subject of UFOs, I approached Steve and his sons cautiously. (As I subsequently learned, Johnny's recollections of what happened that night were the clearest and by far the most important.) With regard to Brian and his parents, I had no option but to completely respect their privacy and therefore made no attempt to contact them on my own. Whenever Linda felt ready to raise the issue with this family she could do so, but until then there was nothing I could do.

I had seen the toll these incidents were taking on Linda and her family. From October 15, the day Dan seized Linda and took her to the house on Long Island, to the time just before Christmas when she received his crazy, threatening letter, she had lived under a constant state of siege. In January 1992 she had gone to visit a friend on Cape

Cod for a few days, just to escape New York and Dan's ever threatening presence. Linda's husband, Steve, drove her to the New York Port Authority bus station and I went along to stay with her until she was safely on the bus. Both Linda and Steve looked haggard and drawn. "He's lost so much weight," she told me, "that his waist size has gone from a forty-two to a thirty-six. It's driving him crazy that he can't really protect his family, and for a proud Italian man, that is the worst." On the drive home, Steve told me that Linda "hardly ever sleeps very long and is so jumpy at home that we're all getting on each other's nerves. It's a terrible situation."

About six weeks after the Memorial Day weekend incident, I received the inevitable phone call from Linda. "I just heard from Sue," she reported, "Brian's mother. She said she wanted to talk about the night that we all woke up with nosebleeds. I told her I'd been meaning to call her. I didn't say it, but actually I've been afraid to call her because I really didn't know what to say.

"Sue told me that when Brian came home after the weekend and unpacked, she'd found a bloodstained T-shirt in his laundry. She asked him about it, and he told her about the five us waking up at the same time with the same kind of nosebleed. She asked me if I didn't think that was strange, and I had to say that yes, I thought it was very strange.

"I really didn't know what to say to her. I surely wasn't going to tell her about our UFO experiences. But you know what she said to me? I was amazed. She said, 'Linda, did you happen to see that movie on TV a while back, *Intruders*, that had to do with UFO abductions?' I told her I'd seen it, and she asked me if I remembered a part in the movie where a little boy had a nosebleed after an abduction. I told her yes, I remembered it, and then she asked if I thought that the night that we all had nosebleeds might have had anything to do with UFOs. I said, well, maybe so—I didn't know what else to say—and then do you know what she told me? She said that she thought maybe something had happened to all of us because Brian had had some strange things happen to him when he was a little boy."

For weeks Linda had been afraid that she and her family had "infected" their house guest with alien contact, whereas ironically it was possible that Brian's mother had been afraid that her son had infected them!

"Sue said that when Brian was very young, before he'd gone to school, he told her that little people would come into his room at night and talk to him. He called these little people the 'emergents.' She has no idea where he got that word or what it meant as a name of anything, but he insisted the emergents were real."

On the assumption that as a small child Brian might have picked up the term somewhere, I've tried to find "emergents" used as a noun in children's literature or TV or popular films, but have not been successful. Parenthetically, my dictionary defines the adjectival form of *emergent* as "rising from a liquid or other surrounding medium, coming into view or notice, issuing." All in all, a decent description of the sudden appearance of UFO occupants.

But Sue had more to say about her son. "She also told me that when Brian went away to summer camp he was always afraid to go into the woods because there were strange lights back there that frightened him. She asked me if I thought maybe we had all five had UFO experiences that night when we had those nosebleeds and I told her that maybe we had."

Linda's new information about Brian's family was only the beginning. I subsequently talked to Sue and her husband and found out a few things about their own experiences. "A couple of years ago we drove down to Atlantic City to spend time with some friends of ours," Sue told me. "We'd done it before, and the trip usually takes us about six hours. This time we got into a sudden rainstorm and had to go slow, so we stopped and called our friends to tell them we'd be late. They said we were already late, which we couldn't understand. The rain suddenly stopped and we started off again, and when we got there the trip had taken just about twelve hours! Twice as long as it should have. There was no way the rain delayed us that long. Maybe a half hour, an hour. But not an extra six hours. It just didn't make any sense."

Since Brian's father is in poor health and generally restricted to his home, I've only spoken to him a few times on the telephone. He, too, made very clear to me his concern over the period of missing time on the drive to Atlantic City. He also described a few more events in his life that his wife had not mentioned, so I resolved to interview her in person.

When I met Sue, I found a slim, attractive woman who exhibited a great deal of tension when the UFO subject was broached. She told me that she suspected her entire family was involved with these phenomena. One of the most dramatic episodes she recounted involved her elderly parents, who live in an apartment in Manhattan. Recently, she said, her mother got up in the middle of the night to walk down the hall to the bathroom. As she stepped out of her bedroom she saw a strange, small, white figure dart out of the bathroom and move very quickly down the hall. Terrified, she cried out for her husband, who could find no trace of the interloper.

For days after, Sue told me, her mother refused to go into the bathroom until her husband first checked it out, and then she would ask him to remain outside to guard the door until she was finished. Sue explained that this was entirely unlike her mother, who had never before seemed unduly imaginative or afraid.

Later investigation of what actually happened on the night of that Memorial Day would reveal yet another incident in the case of Richard and Linda, but the presence of Brian in the Cortile apartment on the Memorial Day weekend and the information I received from his parents about themselves, their son, and his grandmother added four new secondary participants to the story of Linda Cortile.

On June 13, 1992, not quite three weeks after the night of the five nosebleeds, I took the train to Boston to attend the MIT conference on the UFO abduction phenomenon, where I was to make the Cortile case public for the first time. Although I had no reason to suspect it then, Linda's nine-year-old son Johnny was soon to be a major factor in the Cortile family's ongoing UFO saga. His recollection of that strange night would underscore the fact that the UFO occupants were systematically carrying out their agenda across generations of the same family.

PART SIX

Johnny

Another Generation

By the summer of 1992, Johnny, Linda's younger son, was nine years old. He had been only six when I first met him at his mother's apartment, but even at that early age he seemed to possess unusual intelligence and articulateness. I was aware that he had told his mother about an experience in December 1989 that had frightened him badly and that had all the earmarks of an abduction. His drawings of that incident were both meticulous and revealing. He had said that the "little men" who were "in the round room" had "funny hands with just four long fingers and no thumbs," and he carefully drew their hands as quite different from his own. He also told me that when they talked "their mouths didn't move," and in his sketch he indicated the aliens' slit mouths with a simple line, while he showed his own as not only open but also possessing teeth and a tongue. He explained to his mother why he had depicted his mouth this way: "My teeth were chattering 'cause I was so scared."

This 1989 abduction memory was only one of several apparent UFO encounters Johnny was to report over the next few years. But now I was to hear about an experience that bound Johnny ever more firmly into his mother's strange adventures. I was, of course, aware of Richard's apparently unshakable belief that he was Johnny's actual father, that the boy was the product of a remembered "bonding" with Linda that she was presently unwilling to explore. Knowing the UFO occupants' penchant for both deception and experimentation, I did not know what to think about Johnny's connection to Richard.

A day or so after I heard about the five simultaneous nosebleeds in Linda's apartment, I called back to talk to her in more detail about her recollections. Since she said she still remembered virtually nothing but waking up with a bloody nose, I asked about Steve and her sons. Neither her husband nor young Steven was home during my call, but Johnny was. She handed him the telephone and went back into the kitchen where she was preparing dinner. I was routinely recording calls such as this as part of my investigation, and the following is a transcript of our conversation. I began by asking Johnny what he remembered about that night.

J: We all woke up, including Brian, and we all had nosebleeds in the same nostril. In the right nostril.

B: Did you have your head on the pillow at the time?

J: I don't remember.

B: Well, I was wondering if there was blood on the pillow . . .

J: I don't know. It was running down my throat. I woke up 'cause I almost choked. I was sleeping in my parents' bed with my father because Brian was in my bed.

B: Do you remember anything at all about that night? Let me put it this way. Whether you remember anything clearly or not, you can sometimes have dreams. When you're choking and stuff is running down your throat you can have funny dreams that can wake you up. Did you have any dreams at all?

J: Well, yeah, just the usual dreams.

B: Tell me about the usual dreams? What were they about . . .? Fooling around in school and causing trouble?

J: No, I dreamt about my imaginary sister.

B: Your imaginary sister? Well, tell me about her. That sounds like a nice dream. What did she look like?

J: She had long blond hair . . . she had white pajamas.

B: White pajamas? You mean, like two-piece pajamas?

J: Yeah.

B: Like a kid would wear? Pajamas and not street clothes?

J: Yeah.

B: Well, that's a nice dream to have about an imaginary sister. Was she your age [nine] or was she older? Was she, like, fifteen?

J: No. She's seven, about. Seven or eight.

B: How do you know? Does it just seem that way?

J: Yeah, it seems that way.

B: Does she have a name in your dream?

J: Yes [responding quickly]. Her name's "Melody."

B: Melody. What a pretty name.

J: And you know, Budd, "Melody" kind of reminds me of lemon, you know.

B: Why does it remind you of a lemon?

J: Because "Melody" reminds me of yellow, and yellow reminds me of lemon.

B: You said she had blond hair. Were you thinking of that when you thought of yellow, was it connected with that?

J: Well, not really. It's just a name that kind of gets me on it.

B: What's she look like?

J: Well, she's very pretty. And she's . . . very nice.

B: Do you kind of like her?

J: Yes [said quickly and assertively].

B: Well, it's nice to have a dream like that. Now, in the dream, where was she? Was she in your room with you, or in your house, or where was she?

J: No, she was in a room . . . a place . . . it was all white, lots of sunlight, all white. . . .

B: Well, lots of sunlight, that's pretty. Were there lots of trees? Palm trees?

J: There were no trees, it was just all white with sunshine. And there was this building in it. It kinda looked like . . . you know, airports have these little . . . like little . . . flying saucers . . . little dishes. . . .

B: Wait a second. What . . . dishes?

J: You know, those little dishes that you put coffee on?

B: Saucers?

J: Yeah. It looked like that.

B: The building did?

J: Yeah. It looked like, at airports, you know where planes come in and out? It looked like that.

I assumed at this point that Johnny was trying to describe something that resembled a round airplane hangar, although I didn't pursue it. I have learned not to unduly interrupt someone's initial account—particularly a child's—lest the spontaneity be compromised. One can always go back later and ask for clarification. Anyway, I was too interested in hearing more about Johnny's "imaginary sister."

B: Well, in this dream was anyone else there? For example, was Steven there?

J: No. It was just me and the little girl and a man.

B: A man?

J: Yeah. A man and my mom.

B: Tell me about the man.

J: The man was really tall. He had dark blue pajamas. No pajama top. He had kind of a light, light sandy hair with gray going through it.

B: Yeah. Was this a bad guy?

J: No, he was very nice.

B: Did you and the guy talk in the dream?

J: Yeah. He hugged me when they took her away.

B: Who took her away?

J: Two really tall blond men.

B: Uh-huh. Were these two nice guys, bad guys, or what?

J: They were very mean. They didn't even give me a chance to say good-bye to her.

B: They didn't?

J: They were very mean. They didn't listen to me. They didn't answer me. They just kept walking her away, and we both felt very sad.

B: Yeah, I can imagine. Have you ever seen this girl before?

J: Yes, in several other dreams.

B: Melody. Does she know your name? Does she call you "John"?

J: [Tentatively] . . . Yeah.

B: In the dream, does she call you John?

J: Yes, she does [more affirmatively]. And we always make believe that we're brother and sister, 'cause we like each other a lot.

B: I see. Well, you had a nice dream. That's terrific. Was Steven there, talking?

J: No. Nobody was there except for me, the little girl, the tall man, and my mom.

B: Uh-huh. And you said he was wearing blue pajamas?

J: Blue pajama bottoms—dark blue—with no pajama top. I was in my underwear. I don't know why. Every time I go to sleep in my underwear I always dream I'm in my underwear.

B: Do you sleep in your underwear or do you wear pajamas?

J: I sleep in my underwear, and I don't want to, you know, be in my underwear in front of a nice girl.

B: Well, of course not. Do you mean like a T-shirt and Jockey shorts?

J: No, briefs.

B: What was your mom wearing?

J: She was wearing a white nightgown. No sleeves.

B: Does she have one like that in the real world?

J: Yes. Of course she does. She sleeps in it almost every night. She has a robe, too, that matches.

B: Was she wearing it that night?

J: Yes. And it was half on.

B: How did this dream start? You go to bed, you go to sleep. How does it start? Are you suddenly with her, or do you get in a car, or get in a bus or taxi?

J: I really don't remember. I'm just there.

B: And there's nobody there but your mom and this other man?

J: Nobody's there but me, my mom, the tall man, and the little girl.

B: This tall man . . . is he a stranger to you in the dream or is he a friend or is he scary, or what?

J: Is he a stranger to me in the dream? Yes, but he's very nice.

B: Does he have a name in the dream?

J: I don't know.

B: Well, Melody had a name.

J: I don't know his name. I just call him "the tall man."

B: So he's in the dream and he's a nice guy, not a bad guy.

J: No.

B: The bad guys, you said, are the people who came and took Melody away from you?

J: And [the tall man] was very nice, he started comforting me when they took her away.

B: How did he comfort you?

J: He started to hug me and stuff, and I was crying.

B: Do you think that Melody is, in the dream, is she somebody who goes to school with you, or. . . ?

J: I don't know. There's nobody like her in my school.

B: After they take her away, how does the dream end?

J: The dream ends . . . I just wave good-bye, crying.

B: And that's the last thing?

J: Yes.

B: And the next thing is you wake up and you've got the nosebleed?

J: No. I'm left alone with my mom and the tall man. . . .

B: Dreams are always kind of crazy and they do funny things. . . . When they take her away, where do they go? Do they get in a car and drive away?

J: No. They go into the building.

B: Does she seem sad to say good-bye?

J: Oh, yes, we're both very sad.

B: Isn't it nice to have a dream girl like that? [J: Yes.] You know, we all talk about dream girls. When I was a kid I had a dream girl. Maybe you'll meet her someday. Did this seem like a dream?

J: Did it seem like a dream? Uh, not really, it kinda felt really, really real, you know.

B: What were some of the things about it that seemed more real than other things?

J: Well, what seemed very real was . . . the tall man, and the tall men, too. Everybody was very real. But the place, it seemed make-believe because it had no trees, it had no flowers . . .

B: It must have had some grass and some roads. I'm sure it had them.

J: No, it didn't even have that. It didn't even have a pebble.

B: Well, it must have had a building in the background, apart from what you've described.

J: Yes, that's all, and all that was there was that building, and the sunshine and everything was white. And me and Melody and Mom and the tall man and the tall men.

B: These tall men, did they seem like anybody you've ever seen or met before?

J: Yes, they were, but they were very tall, and had blond hair, and they just took her away. They didn't even turn around to say "shut up" to me, or anything like that.

B: Have you ever seen these men before? Or dreamed about them?

J: Yes. I've had dreams about them before. . . .

B: Have you ever dreamed about Melody before?

J: Oh, yes.

B: How many times?

J: Oh, about four.

B: In the past year, the past two years, three years, or what? How long has it been since you dreamed about her?

J: I don't know how long it's been.

B: But you feel like she's a sister.

J: Yeah, she treats me like a brother, and I treat her like a sister.

B: When you were with her, John, what did you talk about in the dream? Silly stuff, or what?

J: We wouldn't talk, we'd just laugh and play and run around. We didn't talk about anything, I don't think. I can't remember. The only thing that came out of our mouths was laugh.

B: You laughed. It was fun, then. A nice dream. Now I'd like to get this absolutely straight. You went to bed and you're sleeping, you said, with your father. [J: Yes.] And you were wearing your underwear. [J: Uh-huh.] And you had this dream. And then you wake up and you're having a nosebleed.

J: And, Budd, I went into the bathroom and I felt like I was going to completely throw up. And when I saw blood, I mean I was scared. I didn't know what was happening. And then I ran into the living room, and my mom and my brother and Brian were sitting on the couch, and they all had nosebleeds in the same nostril as everybody. And my father was there, too, and he was bleeding and he never has nosebleeds.

B: It's odd that you would all have them at once.

J: I wasn't surprised when I saw I had a nosebleed. I always have nose-bleeds, it's not new to me, but with everybody else . . .

B: Anything else you can think of that you want to tell me?

J: I don't remember anything else.

B: You've been very helpful. You know, John, what I try to do is to put pieces together and try to figure out what's going on. And I don't know what's going on here.

J: Yeah, and I'm scared about it.

B: You're scared? [J: Uh-huh.] Tell me what you're scared about.

J: I'm scared that I'm going to keep having these dreams, and I don't want Melody to be taken away, I like her. And there may be some-thing wrong with me because I keep having nosebleeds.

B: Well, I know you, and you're a very healthy little boy, and I don't think that there's anything the matter with you at all. So I wouldn't worry about that at all. The thing about Melody being taken away from you in dreams, that's sad. I understand that, and I sympathize with you. But you think she's only in your dreams? She's not in school with you or something?

J: No, but I hope I really meet her in school someday where I can actually be with her.

I was stunned by what I had just heard. A second generation of the Mickey and Baby Ann relationship, including the setting, the two blond men, the "UFO hangar" or whatever it was, and the intense sunlight. The only point at which I didn't exactly trust Johnny's account was his answer when I asked him if Melody called him "John." "Yes," he said, but at first there was a great deal of hesitancy in his voice. Naturally, he would have wanted her to call him by his real name, and in retrospect there was no logical reason for her not to have done so. For these reasons I feel his affirmative reply was more a product of hope than recollection. My guess is that, like Richard and Linda, neither child could consciously remember the other's name, as if those details had somehow been selectively blocked out. Johnny seemed to imply that he invented the name "Melody" just as Richard explained how he had come up with the name "Baby Ann": because in both cases, the names suggested "yellow" to their inventors!

I was extremely impressed by the way Johnny had resisted my various attempts to lead him. Some of these were so forceful that they can more truthfully be characterized as pushes than leads. For example, when he said that the peculiar white place "seemed make-believe because it had no trees, it had no flowers," I pushed hard by saying, "It must have had some grass and roads. I'm sure it had them." Now, I was the adult in that relationship, the authority figure, and I had even claimed to know a bit about dreams. Johnny was a nine-year-old, trying to describe a strange experience, imperfectly remembered, and if he were fantasizing, he probably would have gone along with my insistence on such marginal details. But he didn't yield an inch. Instead, he contradicted me with the kind of firmness one usually hears only when a child is telling the truth: "No, it didn't even have that. It didn't even have a pebble."

I tried to add his brother Steven to the group in the bright, white place, assuming that since Johnny was fond of his brother (who had also wakened with a nosebleed) he might be subtly persuaded to amend his story enough to include him. But he was adamant here, too.

A number of months later, with another researcher present, Johnny reiterated his view that the experience was definitely real and not a dream. "Do you know how I can tell it was real?" he asked us. "I can tell because I was standing right next to Melody and I could smell her hair, and it smelled like Johnson's baby shampoo. That's the kind of shampoo I use, and I know what it smells like. And you know, you don't smell things in dreams."

So now I was forced to add another layer of complexity to the aliens' manipulation of human affairs. Their interest in bringing together selected pairs of children again and again and allowing them to form relationships could be seen as a precisely repeated intergenerational experiment.

Sometime after the memorable "night of the nosebleeds," I made another audiocassette tape for Richard, including some queries about his recollections, offering suggestions, such as renting a post office box so that I could communicate with him more directly, and presenting one piece of news as bait: I told him that the four members of the Cortile family and their house guest had all awakened with nosebleeds at the same moment on the same night during the Memorial Day weekend. I deliberately withheld the additional information I had received from Johnny about the scene with Melody and the man in the blue pajama bottoms.

After finishing my part of the recording I turned the microphone over to Linda so that she could add some thoughts of her own. Then I used our prearranged drop to leave my tape, and I waited for Richard's reply.

I didn't have to wait very long. In a letter dated May 28, 1992, he responded to my questions methodically, point by point, but it was the information he added about the Memorial Day weekend that I found most interesting. He first asked about the progress of the sand sample testing, adding one suggestive remark: "I do believe that if I had anything to do with the studies of these sand samples, they would've disappeared somehow."

Next he rather curtly declined my suggestion that he rent a post office box to make our communications easier: it "doesn't seem feasible." He also stated with the kind of professional understatement so typical of his letters that he dreaded the idea of having any more spontaneous abduction flashbacks: "They're too hard to handle on the job."

I had asked him if the third man had ever mentioned recurring childhood dreams or particular fears or phobias. He answered that his friend "does not remember offhand if he has had other childhood recurring dreams outside of the bright, white area he has dreamed of as a child. He knows they were not dreams." And even though he said the third man claims to be free of any "strange, nagging fears," it was obvious from his letter that Richard doesn't believe him.

Earlier in May, before this exchange of communications, Linda had found outside their apartment door a package containing a stuffed bumblebee toy. She assumed it was intended for Johnny, and felt that Richard must have left it as a present. I asked about it on my tape, and he responded affirmatively. "Did I leave a stuffed Bumble Bee toy for John behind his door? Yes, I did. Also, in the event of my death (if it should happen, sooner or later) John will be taken care of, as well as his older brother. John loves his brother, so his brother will not have less than him." Richard's generosity and his obvious affection for John, whom he clearly regarded as his son, were touching to me, as was his somewhat inappropriate choice of a gift—a stuffed-animal toy for an active nine-year-old boy.

In her comments to Richard at the end of the tape, Linda thanked him for having made her feel safe once again. She did not directly allude to what may have happened to Dan. She made a few rather neutral, low-key remarks expressing her affection for Richard, words that brought a disappointed reply:

She wished I was her brother. She said I protected her from Dan last February as if I were her brother after all. She's wrong. First off, I protected her the way a husband would've protected his wife. I cannot be a brother image for her. She will have to look elsewhere for her brother image. I realize she is married, but if she wasn't married I understand there would not be a chance for me anyway. Linda loves me as a sibling. I'll guess I'm left with my hands in my pockets again, only this time I know my hands will have to stay there. I'm feeling heartsick, but what can I do? Linda is another man's wife. I'll never forget her. From time to time, I will be checking on the safety of her family, her and you.

At the end of my audiotape, Linda reiterated that she, her family, and their house guest had all awakened with simultaneous nosebleeds. Naturally, neither she nor I provided any more details. But since I had come to feel virtually certain that Johnny's "man in the blue pajama bottoms" was Richard, I was curious to know if he had remembered anything about that particular night. In his letter, immediately after describing his feelings for Linda and admitting that he was "feeling heartsick," he provided the following answer:

Now I'd like very much to get on with what happened Memorial Day weekend. I was shocked to hear Linda talk about the nosebleeds, because Saturday night, or into early Sunday morning about 4:00 AM or so, I dreamed of Linda and John. I woke up with a nosebleed too at that hour. I don't believe I was dreaming.

Linda, John and I were in that white environment. We clung to each other as a threesome. There was a lot of love felt there. We were a family. It breaks my heart, Budd, because John has a little friend. Her hair is long and golden. She's about 7 years old and lovely, too. Up there, they look at each other with stars in their eyes.

Two strange adults came along and took her away. John was left standing alone. I cried out to them to let the children say a proper good-bye, but they didn't listen. I took John by the hand, bent down on one knee and hugged his sad little face against mine, as his mother (Linda) watched on tearfully.

I wasn't dreaming, Budd. I don't know what has happened to the rest of Linda's family and their guest, but they weren't up there with us. I believe our being together as a family up there was the first and the last time. We said good-bye, and it was sad. I've begged God in heaven. Please, not our little John! Will this little boy endure the agonizing effects I have felt my whole life through?

With that and a few closing lines, Richard signed off. I would not hear from him again until a year later, in the summer of 1993. For the time being he disappeared from our lives.

From the beginning, the recurring patterns in thousands of credible UFO abduction accounts have raised as many questions as they have seemed to answer. In light of the Mickey and Baby Ann phenomenon, why did the aliens feel the need to bring Linda and Richard together for Johnny's meeting with Melody? We must consider the possibility that Richard may have been the individual selected by the UFO occupants to sire little Johnny, but there are several alternatives to this idea that must be considered. Was Richard's "fatherhood" merely an illusion instilled by the aliens for what might be called research purposes? If, as seems certain to me, they are interested in issues of parenting, bonding, and so on, might they be curious about how humans treat children that they falsely think are their own flesh and blood? Or can it be that some kind of genetic manipulation has occurred, a mix of some sort, and Johnny is carrying characteristics of both Richard and Steve, his putative father? Facially at least, Johnny resembles Steve, but in stature and perhaps in other subtle ways it might be said that he resembles Richard. Though Steve is of medium height, Johnny is the tallest boy in his class—taller than Linda in her high heels; he is solidly built and, currently, at the age of thirteen, wears a size twelve shoe. His older brother Steven is of only medium height.

So what are we to make of all this? I am not interested in putting the issue of Johnny's parentage to a scientific test for the obvious reason of its potentially destructive effect upon the Cortile family. Here again, simple human concerns must override our need to know. Johnny resembles his father, Steve, in terms of coloring and facial structure. For him, Steve is his father, and for Steve, Johnny is his son. To run the risk of disrupting this years-long, deeply felt family relationship is something I feel no one has the right to do. It is probably to be expected that Linda still wavers occasionally on this issue, an emotional problem for her that will probably remain unresolved.

On Johnny's thirteenth birthday, the Cortile's answering machine recorded a message from Richard. In his authoritative voice, with its strong New York accent, he sang to Johnny: "Happy Birthday to You." For Richard, at least, it would seem that the issue of Johnny's parentage was never in doubt.

The Helmet

A short time after my conversation with Johnny about his "Melody dream," I asked him to make some drawings of the events in the strange white place. A week or so later he presented me with two sketches in pencil with additions in crayon to indicate color. The first depicts at the left a large circular structure—the hangarlike space he had described—with what looks like a wide ramp leading downward. Otherwise the space is featureless. At the lower right, lined up from left to right, are: Melody, wearing her two-piece pajamas; Johnny in his Jockey briefs and undershirt; Linda in her sleeveless nightgown with her robe draped over her right shoulder; and finally the very tall man in the dark blue pajama bottoms, which Johnny has carefully colored in.

Behind this smiling group stand the two tall blond men, scowling fiercely. They are wearing one-piece garments—like jumpsuits or coveralls—which are colored with a lighter blue crayon than the one used for the tall man's pajamas. The only detail is a dark pencil line from chin to groin indicating, perhaps, some kind of seam. These two cruel-looking men are shown as having human features, distinctly different from the bald, gray-faced, noseless aliens Johnny depicted in his drawing of an earlier abduction experience.

In several cases of what I have described as alien co-option, when the co-opted abductees find themselves aiding the aliens in moving terrified human abductees about, they discover that they are wearing skin-tight blue jumpsuits made of some kind of thin material they describe as feeling "slick" and "plasticky." Although there is no reason to assume that the tall blond men Johnny recalls were co-opted humans—for one thing they looked very much alike and were quite blond—the color and style of their outfits is interesting. Johnny carefully colors in their costumes to indicate that they have turtleneck tops, another detail frequently reported in descriptions of alien garb.

One final detail about his rendering of Melody should be pointed out. Johnny presents himself, his mother, and the tall man in the blue pajama bottoms as each having a single, curving, upturned line as a mouth, while Melody is given a full pair of smiling lips. A Freudian observer might argue that, along with Johnny's suggestive rendering of the seams of his briefs, his drawing of Melody's mouth offers an insight into his more-than-childlike feelings about her.

The second sketch depicts the group's general sadness after Melody has been taken away. Linda's mouth is now downturned, she is frowning, and for some reason her robe has slipped off her shoulder and is lying on the ground. The man in the blue pajama bottoms has the same mournful, downturned mouth as Linda, but he is now holding Johnny up off the ground, hugging the sad little boy who sheds a few carefully delineated tears.

In the background at the upper left, Melody is shown ascending the ramp between the two blond men, each of whom holds one of her hands. Resting on top of the large, circular structure they are about to enter is a shallow-domed UFO with a ring of rectangular shapes around its lower perimeter. This same craft is also delineated in Johnny's first sketch, but there it is hovering (taking off? landing?) above the hangarlike building. The narrative shift of these two drawings is from happiness to sadness, just as Johnny had described, and the resemblance of this setting to that of the Mickey and Baby Ann encounters is extraordinary.

In all of my work on this case I had sought, so far as possible, to confirm each new detail by querying other potential witnesses. But with regard to Johnny's Melody experience, both of the other two potential witnesses presented problems. First, before he sent the two sketches to me, Johnny had shown them to his mother and had obviously explained their meaning. Therefore, since she already knew about the incident, whatever might surface from a hypnotic session would have little or no evidential weight. (After all, it was Linda's credibility that was at stake, not Johnny's.) And as for Richard, I had no way to contact him on short notice, even by using our system of drops.

Although I had a very good idea of the importance of Johnny in Richard's life, I pondered the role he was playing in the thoughts of the third man. In a (previously unquoted) passage from one of his letters, Richard wrote that he had told the third man all about his belief that Johnny was his son, the product of an alien-controlled "bonding" procedure with Linda. Even before that letter, Richard informed me that the third man had secretly observed Linda on several occasions, apparently when she was escorting Johnny to or from the school bus. Of all those involved in this complex affair, Johnny was the youngest and most vulnerable, a fact I felt might weigh heavily on the third man, the oldest and, I assumed, probably the most stoic of the group.

Linda was another concern. I knew all too well about her "confirmation anxiety," the fear and shock she felt each time she heard a piece of news (like Johnny's "Melody dream") that seemed to confirm the physical reality of her own UFO experiences.

As I've described earlier, one of the mundane ways she fought against this confirmation anxiety was to go shopping, and when the fear was strongest it was not unusual for her to buy several similar items at once: the same blouse, say, in two different colors. When she returned home from these infrequent sprees, she would often be overcome by remorse: I've spent too much money, I don't really need these blouses, what will Steve say when he finds out, and so on. At times like these she sometimes hid her new purchases for weeks at a time, like a chocoholic guiltily stashing away the M&M's.

In October 1992, about five months after the night of the five nosebleeds, I received an intriguing phone call from a woman friend of mine, "Elizabeth," an abductee who lives on Cape Cod. A year before, during her visit to New York, I had introduced Elizabeth to Linda, and since then they had become good friends. Both women were roughly the same age, are of Italian American parentage, and freely shared their personal problems with the UFO abduction phenomenon.

In her phone call to me, Elizabeth said that she had just spoken to Linda and had found her very agitated. On the floor at the back of her closet, concealed under a pile of shoe boxes and towels, she had recently found a full-size antique diving helmet made of copper and brass. She had no idea where it had come from. Since she had also found two new blouses, still tagged and unworn, that she had forgotten buying, she was concerned.

"Am I losing my mind?" she asked. "Did I somehow buy that thing and forget all about it? Is that possible? Why would I ever buy a thing like that, anyway?" Elizabeth suggested that she call and tell me what she'd found, but Linda replied that she didn't feel she should. "What if I am going crazy? What if I did buy that thing and can't remember? What will Budd think?"

Elizabeth suggested I call Linda, so shortly after I hung up I phoned her. I brought up the subject of the helmet and asked for a description. It sounded like a genuine antique, making it potentially valuable and even more mysterious. Where had it come from? It was easy enough to imagine Linda spending money on a couple of blouses on sale at Century 21, but not thousands of dollars for a big, heavy, mechanical object as useless as this.

It was November before I was able to visit the Cortile apartment to see the helmet for myself. It was beautiful, roughly spherical and equipped with attachments for, I assumed, an air hose, a rope, and perhaps a communication wire. It also contained three small, round windows protected by metal grills, enabling the diver to see ahead and to the sides. It was quite heavy to lift, and, in the confines of the Cortile's small apartment, an obvious white elephant.

The entire family—Linda, Steve, Johnny, and young Steven— were present as we puzzled over what they should do with this strange new addition to their household. "Why don't you try to sell it?" I asked Linda. "I'm sure a thing like that is worth quite a lot of money to antique collectors." We chatted a bit more about the mystery, and I left with the understanding that Linda would try to place the helmet with a dealer.

The next day, I received a message on my answering machine— the voice of a breathless little boy speaking in an urgent whisper. "Budd, this is Johnny. I can't talk because my mom is just outside in the hall talking to somebody, and she might come in anytime. You said she should sell that helmet, but she can't, because it's mine! It's a present to me, and I had to hide it 'cause I'm not allowed to get presents from strangers. But it's mine, and she can't sell it!" And then he hung up.

I suppose that I should have been immune by now to further surprises from Linda and the many other people involved in this case, but I wasn't. Johnny's message made me see what I should have guessed before: Linda hadn't bought this expensive, clumsy object and then simply forgotten about it.

Late that afternoon, when I knew he would be home from school, I called Johnny and in a whispery voice he confided the story of how he came to be given the helmet.

A few months earlier, on a Friday evening in September, he was, as he put it, "working" for his father and "the other guys" (his dad's fellow employees at the nearby *New York Post* building). His "job," buying coffee and hamburgers for the men in exchange for tips, involved running back and forth from the area where his father worked to a luncheonette at the front of the building, a route that took him briefly outside.

During one of these expeditions on the street he was approached by a man and offered the helmet. The story was extraordinary. He told me that if his parents were to find out he would be in serious trouble. "Mom will ground me," he said, his voice fearful. "I'm not allowed to take presents from strangers." I assured him that I would speak to his mother, but I asked that in the meantime he not talk to his parents about the helmet. The request was unnecessary; Johnny was too afraid of being punished to risk telling anybody anything.

After our conversation I decided to make another videotape, this one recording Johnny's retelling the story of the helmet. Again, my concern was for the historical record: to record Johnny's story and his credibility as revealed in his voice, manner, words, and behavior. His account was of major importance.

In the morning, when I assumed he would be in school, I called Linda and told her that I knew where the helmet had come from. I promised to tell her everything Johnny had told me, but I asked her not to punish him. I also asked her not to tell him that I had called, and not to bring up the helmet until I could get there to document his story.

Before I went to the Cortile apartment I made some preparations. First, I went through a pile of recent issues of the *New York Times*, and from the business sections, the obituaries, and the international news pages I clipped out nineteen photographs of distinguished-looking older men—businessmen, politicians, an architect, a doctor, and so on—none of whom nine-year-old Johnny would be likely to know. My files already contained the crucial twentieth picture, one I had also clipped from the *Times*. It was a good, current photo of the third man.

I took all twenty photographs and had them xeroxed, scaling them all to approximately the same size. Then I stacked them in a sequence that placed the photo of the third man near the end. I did not tell Linda that I had prepared these twenty Xeroxes, or what I intended to do with them.

About five o'clock I arrived at the Cortile apartment. Johnny answered the door and seemed genuinely surprised to see me. As I expected, Steve was also at home—he wasn't due at work until later that night—and he had his video camera ready. I explained to Johnny that his mother knew what he had told me about the helmet, but that he would not be punished for it. He seemed both anxious and relieved that the cat was finally out of the bag.

Without explaining why, I told him that I wanted to videotape his account, and asked him to sit on the living-room couch between me and the gleaming helmet. His father stood on a straight-backed chair and aimed his camera. There was no tripod, no special lighting, nothing but a somewhat nervous little nine-year-old boy telling his story while his father tried to keep the camera steady.

Johnny spoke naturally, even casually, but with the clarity and precision that I had come to expect from him. Again, there were a few moments when I tried to lead him, but again he wouldn't be led. And there were other questions I asked that he simply said he couldn't answer; he didn't know or hadn't seen. In my view, his responses were demonstrably straightforward and truthful.

B: This is what this is about, Johnny. I've talked to your mom about the helmet and she knows all about it. I want you to tell your dad what you told me. Look at him [at the camera] as if you're speaking to him.

J: As you know, Dad, I went to work with you and, you know, I go out and get burgers and coffee for the guys, and I was walking out into the diner and I was walking minding my own business and I hear this voice saying, "Hey, John." So I stop, I look, I turn around, and I see this guy [in a car] in the front seat on the passenger side with the window open. And I think to myself, Well, I don't know this guy, so he probably isn't calling me, so I—I just kept walking, took a couple more steps and I heard it again, so I turned around and I said, "Are you talking to me?" And he said, "Yes, somebody wants to see you."

So at the back on the passenger's side, the door opened and I saw this old man, and he had tinted glasses, and he said, "Hi, John." And I said, "Do I know you?" and he said, "No, but you're gonna get to know me." So I thought to myself, like, weird . . . So . . .

B: And your parents had told you to be careful. . . .

J: So he said, "Do you like this?" and he turned around and went into the back, you know, where he was, to the other seat, and he got this [Pointing to the helmet] . . . and he put it in front of him and said, "Do you like it?" I thought to myself, "Cool!" So he said, "Do you want to take it home?" So I said, "But I'm not supposed to take things from strangers," and he said, "Oh, I'm not a stranger, I'm your poppy." Umm, what's a "poppy"?

B: I don't know what he means . . . "I'm your poppy." I didn't know about that before . . . you didn't mention it yesterday.

J: So I said, "Still my parents would get mad, 'cause look at it. It's big and heavy and everything," and he just said, "Is there any time we can deliver it to you?" And I said, "Well, you could, but my parents are gonna see it and my parents are always here. And he asked me if there was any time when my parents weren't here and I told him the only time my parents weren't were on the days when my father works and my mom's in the shower and I'm eating breakfast. So he says like, "Would you like us to deliver it to you then?" and I said, "Cool, yeah!"

B: Did you give him a time, or how did you . . . ?

J: Well, I told him that Mom's always in the shower about 6:00. So he said, "We'll deliver it to you then." But I thought to myself, Where am I gonna put this, 'cause it's so big and, if Mom finds out, she's gonna really kill me. So, he put the helmet back and then he closed the door and asked for a hug. And I said, "No," because, I mean, I thought he was just gonna grab me and pull me back into the car and you know, kidnap me, so I said no and . . .

B: It was very wise to do that. . . .

J: And when I said no, he looked very sad . . . he put his head down, had a sad look on his face and then I just walked into the diner. And then, a couple days later . . .

B: Okay. Let's go back to this. What kind of car did it look like?

J: Umm, well, it looked kinda like a limousine but, it was like a mix of a regular car and a limousine. It was black and . . .

B: What did he look like? You say he looked old. . . .

J: Yes, he looked old. He had white hair. He had glasses that were just a little tinted.

B: How close were you to him where you were standing?

J: Well, like I was standing almost . . . like, here's the diner [Gesturing with his arms]. I was standing over here getting ready to go in, and the sidewalk is over here, so I'd say I was about a couple feet away.

B: As far as from the cabinet right there?

J: Maybe up . . . like from over here to the fridge . . .

B: I see. That's about six feet. That's pretty close—five to six feet.

J: Yeah.

B: Okay, now, anything else about him? You said he had white hair, looked old. . . .

J: Yes, he looked very old. He looked about in his eighties and he was wearing a very fine suit . . . and that's really all. . . .

B: Anything about his voice?

J: Well, yes, he had a [foreign] accent.

B: Did you watch him drive off?

J: No. I didn't see him drive off. I walked into the diner and when I went back out . . . I wanted to say thank you but he just drove away. I didn't see the car. So I thought maybe he just disappeared, or . . .

B: Now, you were going to go back to your father. Did you tell him about any of this?

J: No, I kept it a secret. When they came I was eating my breakfast. It was about 6:10—6:05, and I was eating my breakfast and I heard a knock on the door. And I went to the door and as usual, I say, "Who is it?" The same guy who was in the front seat came to the door and he gave me the helmet—out the door—real fast—it was real exciting! [Johnny moves quickly, demonstrating the speed of the transaction with enthusiasm.]

B: What did he say to you when he knocked on the door?

J: He said, "John, I have your helmet!" He gave me the helmet and it was real, real heavy. So I sort of dragged it into my mom's room and hid it behind the curtain. [He told me later that he eventualy moved it into the back of Linda's closet.]

B: Now at this point, where was your brother?

J: He was sleeping.

B: And your mom was in the shower? [J: Yeah.] Your dad was at work? [J: Yeah.] Right. So you were the only one there. And what did you think would happen if your mom and dad knew about this?

J: I thought that maybe I'd get grounded or something.

B: Yes. So he gave you this. And what did this man look like, the man who delivered it at the door?

J: Well, he had sunglasses. He had, like, a hearing aid that—it went into his ear and a wire went all the way down into his pocket, and he was wearing dark sunglasses and a black coat.

B: Was he tall, short? Thick, thin?

J: He was kinda tall. He was kinda tall. He was in the middle between thin and chubby. He looked like he was very bulky. He was tall, pretty tall. I'd say he was about maybe six feet.

B: [Here I tried to lead Johnny] Was there anything about his voice, or . . .

J: No, he just had a regular man's voice.

B: Did he sound like he was Spanish?

J: No.

B: Sure he wasn't Spanish?

J: No. I'm sure.

B: Okay. Did he have black hair?

J: I really didn't get a look at his hair because I think he was wearing some sort of a hat but I really didn't get a look at his hair.

B: I'll bet you were busy looking at your helmet. [Johnny smiles and rubs his hands together] Okay. Now. Your parents aren't going to beat up on you . . . because you've been very good. Even though they're going to tell you, stay more than six feet away from anybody who says anything like this in the future, right?

I choose this moment to present the twenty xeroxed *Times* photographs. Linda leans over, curious about them, as I explain what Johnny is to do.

B: Now, Johnny, I've got some pictures of men. What I'm trying to find out is what the person who gave you the helmet looked like. I've got a bunch of pictures and this is what I want you to do. I want you to look at them and I want you to say, "He didn't look so much like this one," or "He kind of looked like that one . . . he looked more like this . . . he didn't look at all like that." Do you know what I mean? You know when the police try to get somebody to identify someone, the witness will say, "Well, he was kind of like that but he was a little more . . . he was thinner, he was fatter." You know what I mean? [Johnny nods enthusiastically, obviously eager to proceed.]

　　We're going to make two piles. Put the ones—the discards over here—the ones that don't look like him. The ones over here are the ones that kind of look like him. We'll take the ones that kind of look like him and try to figure out what's the closest we can come. See? It's like a narrowing down. Okay, now let's take this one [Handing Johnny the first of the twenty photos].

J:　All right, he doesn't look like him . . . [Going through the pictures one by one] He . . . no. He . . . no, he's a little thinner . . . No.

B:　Incidentally, some of these men don't have glasses on. Most of all of them have white hair. But you know, people sometimes take their glasses off when their pictures are taken, so you have to not let that mislead you. . . . You have to kind of think past it.

J:　Okay. Okay. This looks a little . . . just a little . . . A little . . . No . . . A little . . . [Finally we come to the photograph of the third man.] Wait a minute . . . now, that looks more like him. . . . [Studying the photo carefully] Maybe that's him . . . yeah, maybe that's him.

B:　You think that looks like him?

J:　Yes.

B:　Uh-huh. You think you've ever seen that man before?

J:　Yes.

B:　You think you've seen him other times?

J:　No, when the incident happened.

B:　So would you give it a 50 percent chance, 80 percent chance, 100 percent chance?

J:　[Studying the photo carefully] Well, I'd give it a 70–75 percent chance.

B:　70 percent chance. [To Steve] If we could get a close-up? We'll put that one over to one side. [I move on to the next photo.] How about him? [Continuing through the pictures, all of which Johnny rejected.]

B:　Now, okay, let's go through these again. You've got twenty pictures. Let's look at them together. [Picking up the photo of the third man] This is the one you thought looked most like him, right? Now, let's look at these two. Which do you think is more like him? [I systematically lift photos from the pile Johnny felt bore some similarity in order to compare them one by one.]

J: Him, still. [Pointing to his original choice—the photo of the third man]

B: We're narrowing it down. Which of these two?

J: Him still.

B: Okay, and how about him? [Showing another of the similar photographs]

J: Still him.

B: Okay, so this is the one. You said he had sort of tinted glasses, he had sort of white hair. Let's try to think. Anything else we can think of? Let me ask . . . you say that could be him?

J: That *could* be him. That could be him.

B: When he wanted a hug, did he have the door shut on the car?

J: Yes.

B: Tell me how he looked when you wouldn't go over to get a hug.

J: Oh, he looked very, very sad. He looked like . . . like, "I can't believe it."

B: And what did *you* think about this, John?

J: Oh, I think the man was a very nice guy and . . . if I would have known he wasn't gonna like kidnap me, I would have gave him a thank-you hug. I mean I was kinda scared, 'cause it was kind of late at night and, you know, that neighborhood is kind of bad . . . and people can disguise themselves as [good] people. . . .

B: Now, he was in the backseat of a fancy car. . . . Make a little guess for me about the kind of person he was.

J: Well, he looked like he was rich, 'cause he had a very fine suit. He had an expensive car. . . . Maybe he could have borrowed it from a friend or something. . . .

B: What about the way he spoke? Sometimes people speak in a little more elegant way, sometimes it's a little more coarse or direct or something. How about his speech?

J: Well, he sounded like he's been in America for about . . . like . . . I really don't know but . . . he knew English very well.

My next few questions had to do with the approximate date and time of the incident. Naturally, Johnny didn't remember either exactly, other than feeling that it had most probably occurred on a Friday night. He said that he usually goes to bed at 8:30, but that on Friday nights, when he works with his father, it might have been as late as midnight. He later told me that he thought the incident happened toward the first half of September, in the early days of the school year.

B: What I want you to do now is tell me about what went through your head. You really wanted to get that helmet. You knew you were doing something wrong, because your parents said not to pay attention to strangers. But what was going through your mind when he called you, what did you think?

J: The first thing that came to my mind is to run. But I thought to myself, I'm standing, you know, as far away as possible and if he gets out of the car, all I have to do is run into the diner and get Eddie, 'cause cops are always hanging out there getting coffee and donuts. . . .

B: Yeah, you're close to the diner . . .

J: . . . and I'm really close to the diner so I can just run as fast as I can into the diner. . . .

B: Did you think he was kidding you at the time that he wanted to give you the helmet?

J: Well, I thought he was trying to lure me into his car, but . . .

B: Uh-huh. Do you think that when he was sad at the end he was really sad or just faking it?

J: Well, the first thing I thought was like, ah, you're kidding me, but he just kept doing it and I was, like, "I'm sorry," you know.

B: That you couldn't give him a hug . . .

J: That I couldn't, but I still thought maybe just a little bit he was faking, so I just went in the diner. I was a little concerned.

B: [Turning now to Johnny's mother for her reactions] Linda, do you have any things you want to ask Johnny?

L: Well, the first thing I want to say is, what you did was right, and in a way it was wrong, because your mother thought that she was crazy. I thought maybe I'd purchased this thing—I'd asked everybody if they knew where it came from. And because no one knew where it came from I thought I was maybe losing my mind and that I'd gone out and bought it and didn't remember. That meant something was wrong with me and that I'm crazy. So, I really feel angry that you didn't have enough confidence in me to tell me what had happened.

B: This is what you have to do, Johnny. You have to be absolutely honest, and direct, whatever it is. If something funny comes up, you've got to tell your dad, your mom, immediately. Even me sometimes, if something strange like this occurs. Will you do it? Promise? [He nodded with enthusiasm and relief that his confession was over.]

Throughout this long taped discussion, Johnny's demeanor had been that of a highly intelligent nine-year-old child trying very hard to tell the truth without embroidering, exaggerating, or evading my questions. When I tried to lead him into saying that the person who actually delivered the helmet might have had a Spanish accent, he demurred, even when I pressed the matter. Trying yet another lead, and still acting as if I might know something about the deliverer, I asked Johnny if the man had black hair. He replied that the man was wearing a hat so he couldn't be sure what color hair he had. Apart from its resonant clarity and tone of credibility, Johnny's testimony was extraordinarily important to the overall case. In addition to the documentary evidence I had amassed from the third man's letters (I would ultimately have three of them), plus Richard and Dan's oblique but informative references to his identity in their letters (and still more confidential evidence from another high-ranking European political leader), Johnny provided a second eyewitness identification. (Linda, of course, had known for many months.)

The only way the committed "debunkers" could deny the obvious implications of Johnny's testimony would be to insist that he had been lying from beginning to end, acting, reciting a memorized script. The little boy would have to have been trained—bribed or threatened or possibly both—by his mother, who would now have to be seen as a virtual sociopath. By any standard of behavior, to force one's nine-year-old child to memorize a series of falsehoods, and then coach him in the techniques of successful lying, is literally to commit child abuse.

It was in order to counter the skeptics that I decided to present Johnny with the twenty photographs *on camera*. If Johnny were merely a frightened child following an abusive mother's orders, my presentation of the photos would have come as a shock to him and to his mother as well. Such an unforeseen turn of events could be certain to thoroughly derail any well-rehearsed scenario.

Unscripted and thus completely at sea, Johnny would not have known what to do about this new development, and therefore might be expected to glance anxiously at his mother for guidance. At the very least, his facial expressions and body language would express his growing concern and quite possibly a degree of panic as well. In creating this trial for him I realized that the way Johnny reacted at the outset would be as significant as the picture he would ultimately select.

To say he passed the test perfectly is not an exaggeration. He never once glanced in his mother's direction, nor did he betray even a trace of anxiety as we went through the photos. He entered into the identification process eagerly, with the excitement of a little boy at a police station being asked to help the detectives identify a perpetrator. It was clearly *fun* for Johnny to go through the twenty pictures.

The day before our videotaped inquiry, when I first spoke to him about the person who gave him the helmet, I was virtually certain that it must have been the third man. Not only did he fit Johnny's description, but other than Richard, no one else I could think of would be motivated to offer such a strange and valuable antique to a little boy on a New York street corner. Johnny's description of the man with the "hearing aid" who actually delivered the helmet appeared to me to be of a security agent equipped with a communication earphone.

Johnny provided another crucial piece of information in his first phone call. I asked him if either the driver or the white-haired man in the back seat had asked for his home address so they would know where to deliver the helmet, and he replied that they hadn't. It seemed to me that Johnny had never before given the matter any thought. "I guess they already know where I lived," he said with the insouciance of a little boy whose usual common sense had just been overwhelmed by the magnificence of the proferred gift.

One of the odder details of this incident was that the third man said to John, "I'm your poppy." I assumed that the word was a term of endearment that an elderly man might like to be called by a child with whom he felt a special connection, even though they were not literally related. It was clear by now that the third man felt a connection with Richard, and with Linda as well—especially, perhaps, after learning what Dan had subjected her to. It was easy to speculate that, like Richard, the third man must be feeling guilty at not having come forward to tell what he saw on November 30, 1989. He must know that had he done so, adding his prestige and credibility to that of ordinary folk like Linda and Johnny, it would have eased the burden of abductees around the world who are subject to ridicule and insults at the hands of benighted "debunkers." It is plausible to think that his gift to Johnny was an attempt to atone for his ultimately damaging refusal.

Still, knowing the third man's desire to remain anonymous, I marveled at his having dared to meet Johnny face-to-face. What if someone—Johnny's father, for example—had suddenly appeared on the street and recognized him sitting with the door open in his distinctive long black car? What if—as actually happened—Johnny himself were able to identify him later? Speculating again, it seemed to me that his desire for anonymity was balanced by a profound need to contact Linda and her family, to demonstrate his support, his connection with them as a fellow victim of the UFO occupants. Contacting her nine-year-old son would be less risky, of course, than meeting Linda or Steve face-to-face. And the odd but valuable gift he was offering them would be especially appreciated by a little boy. The third man might have been surprised and perhaps a bit disappointed if he had known that his gift had been successfully hidden from the rest of the Cortile family for nearly three months.

One final puzzle has to do with the nature of the gift itself, a puzzle to which only one man, the donor, has the answer. Why an antique diving helmet? Was it meant to have a symbolic meaning? Was it supposed to relate to the Lady of the Sands in some way? To the head of an alien? To the idea of the ocean and its teeming undersea life? As a gift to Johnny, at least, it was dazzlingly right: big, glamorous, scary-looking, and something no little friend of his would ever own.

Or perhaps it was meant to be sold, a disguised cash contribution to the Cortile family. Its value, I have been able to estimate, is between three and five thousand dollars. But for whatever reason it was given, it remains today in a place of honor in the Cortile apartment.

C H A P T E R

27

Around the Conference Table

In the months immediately preceding the November 1992 discovery of Johnny's gift of the helmet, a potentially important development in the case came to light during a support group meeting for UFO abductees in the New York area: a "dream" simultaneously recalled by Linda and another abductee who, as far as we knew, was uninvolved in the case. Toward the end of this meeting, one of the participants, a young woman I shall call "Marilyn Kilmer," told the group that a few weeks earlier she had had a very strange and vivid dream involving a woman she took to be Linda's mother. Though she knew Linda from the support group, she had never met her mother, who had been dead for a number of years. Marilyn thought that Linda had appeared in her dream, too, and she recounted a struggle with two rather frightening "black men." The dream had seemed very real.

Linda was immediately interested. "A few weeks ago I had a very vivid dream a little bit like that, too," she said. "I dreamed that my mother and I were in a room and we were trying to hold the door and keep out these two black guys." I asked the two women not to talk anymore about their dream to each other or to anyone else. There was something about the serious tone of voice each had used and the similarity of images that made me wonder if this were just a bizarre coincidence or if it had been a shared, UFO-related encounter.

Over the years, many abductees have recounted experiences such as these that they have described as "dreams" or "dreamlike." Many of these recollections seemed specific enough, disturbing enough, and close enough to specific abduction patterns with which I'm familiar to bear further investigation. Several times such similar recollections have been presented by *two* or even *three* individuals. Often—although not always—further investigation has revealed a legitimate UFO abduction experience.

And so the shared "dream" that Marilyn and Linda brought up at our September 30 support group meeting seemed to be worth looking into. I decided to begin the investigation with Marilyn, who on November 7, 1992, arrived at my studio for an interview and possible hypnosis session on the "shared dream." Also present that day was a colleague of mine, Don Donderi, a Canadian psychologist and professor of psychology at McGill University in Montreal. We had first met at a UFO abduction conference and had both attended the recent symposium at MIT.

I had begun working with Marilyn almost two years before, in January 1991. She is an attractive, intelligent young woman whom I found to be gifted with a remarkably good visual memory. Like Linda Cortile, she is interested in fashion and is also naturally observant, so much so, in fact, that I can usually rely on her the next day to recall what each of the attendees at a support group meeting had been wearing. In November 1992, Marilyn was single and holding a responsible job in Manhattan where she lived.

We began our inquiry by reviewing her rather spotty conscious recollections of the dream, and after some further discussion, we ultimately decided to proceed with hypnosis. I settled Marilyn down comfortably on the couch, lowered the lights, and began my usual induction. After I was satisfied that she was deeply relaxed, I took her back to the night in August when she had her strange dream:

In it, she is sleeping in her Midtown apartment when she awakens and is moved involuntarily into her now unnaturally illuminated bathroom. As she floats upward toward the skylight she sees two small figures levitating behind her, creatures she describes as "white cats." I ask if they are long-haired or short-haired cats. "They don't have any hair," she replies, and adds that they are very big.

The next part of this "dream" involves a change of scene to her parents' apartment in Brooklyn where she sees her father in the presence of the aliens. (I had been aware from Marilyn's earlier interviews and conscious recollections that she had good reason to believe her father was also an abductee, a suspicion he did not reject out of hand.) Now, when she first describes seeing him, I ask what he is wearing.

She replies, "A T-shirt and his pajama bottoms. And white socks . . . He's not moving," she says. "He's stiff . . ."

Next, she and her father are somehow being transported through a hallway. "Does it have a wooden floor?" I ask, assuming they are still in the apartment, and she answers in idiosyncratic shorthand style: "White floor. Everything's white. Very bright. No light. No light fixtures. Just bright." I ask if they are alone. "No. There are others. They're behind us. There are three of them. These things aren't walking on the ground. They're gliding. The two little creatures [the cats] . . . they're on my right. The door opens up . . . the door in front of us. My father's pulled back. I'm pulled [forward] . . ."

Now, apparently, Marilyn is in a different room, no longer accompanied by her father. "I'm standing at the edge of the table. It's steel. Very uncomfortable. No legs . . ." I ask the whereabouts of the little beings. "They're opposite us."

"When you say, 'us,' " I ask, "do you mean you and your father?"

"No," she replies. "Linda."

B: You didn't tell me . . . Is Linda there?

M: Yeah.

B: Tell me what she's wearing.

M: She's wearing a silky peach nightgown . . . two-piece. Buttons up the front. [After a pause in which she seems to be studying Linda] She has thin arms. [Long pause] There's another being standing next to her . . . the one that's giving instruction.

B: Does Linda say "Hi" to you?

M: Doesn't know I'm there.

B: Even though you're right next to her?

M: Won't look at me. [Perplexed] Why doesn't Linda look at me? [Long pause] There's something on the table. Just at the edge of the table . . . It's a narrow table.

Here Marilyn goes into a somewhat lengthy and confused description of the white objects along the opposite edge of the table, as if she is trying to bring them into focus and understand what they are. Ultimately she realizes they are pairs of crossed white hands—bony-fingered nonhuman hands. Having settled that matter she moves on to the next incident:

M: Linda picks something up off the table. It's red and silver. I don't know what it is. She's looking at it.

B: Do you communicate with Linda?

M: She doesn't know I'm there. She won't recognize me. She's being instructed.

B: Can you hear what they're saying to her?

M: No. Conversation's one-way and I can't hear it. These beings . . . I can't see all those beings. Now [the figures across the table] are in shadow.

B: How does your body feel at this point?

M: I'm stiff. I'm also uncomfortable. I'm standing. My body's pressed toward the table. . . . Table is low. There are people all around us, just walking back and forth. They're staring at us . . . it's very, very misty . . . smoky. [Long pause] I hear something. They ask Linda how she is. . . . Linda knows this woman. She's standing next to Linda . . . with black hair. She has beautiful long hair . . . thick hair.

B: Is she Linda's age? Older?

M: She's younger. She's got high eyebrows . . . no hair at the eyebrows. Her eyes are black.

B: Let's look at her beautiful, long black hair again. Is it perfect, freshly combed? How does it look?

M: It looks like a wig. Thick hair. *So* thick. Wavy hair, curly, wavy hair.

B: Let's look at her black eyes. Are they small, medium, large?

M: They're large.

B: How is the woman dressed?

M: [Pause] She's wearing a long garment. She's very narrow. She has narrow shoulders. She's like a counselor. . . . She's related.

B: She's related to you? [M: No.] Related to Linda?

M: Linda knows her very well.

B: Does Linda talk to her? [M: Yes.] But Linda still hasn't noticed you? [M: No.] Okay. Linda speaks to her. What sort of language does Linda use? Do you understand what they say?

M: [Long pause] No . . . I . . . wait. [Pause] Squeaks.

B: Squeaks? Is Linda making the squeaks, too?

M: No. She understands it.

B: Is Linda making any sounds?

M: Linda's head is turned away from me. She's not looking at me. . . . It sounds like guinea pigs. I feel like a sentry.

B: Is your father still there? [M: No.] Where do you think he's gone?

M: [Inaudible] . . . I hope he's okay. . . . Our posture is we stand straight. We have to pay attention.

What follows is Marilyn's recollection of some statements (thoughts?) that she picks up from the woman and the other nonhuman figures in the room. They ask, "How are you getting on?" and then, as if they feel that something is wrong, "It was premature." Marilyn has no idea what this means, but thinks that it somehow concerns Linda and herself. Then comes a major surprise, spoken quietly, with little inflection:

M: I see Johnny.

B: You see Johnny? [I was aware that she had met Johnny only a few months earlier through his mother.]

M: He's lying on the table.

She describes him as lying on his back along the table with his head near her and his feet close to the strange woman with the thick black hair. His eyes are open and Marilyn describes his expression as "glassy." She senses that the strange woman is saying that "decisions have to be made," but she doesn't understand what these might be. Linda is "concerned, but she's not nervous or anything. I think she was holding [Johnny's] hand. . . . We're pressed up against the table."

I ask if Johnny is on the same table she is pressed against or if it is a different table. "He's on the table we're standing over. There's a lot of walking around outside . . . a lot of commotion . . . walking fast. Some are standing and just staring . . . I see a lot of red outfits . . . jumpsuits . . ."

Marilyn recalls more having to do with her feeling that some kind of communication is taking place between Linda and the woman with the thick black hair although she has little sense of what it all might mean. At the very end the two "black men" make a threatening appearance but are otherwise not major players in this incident. Whatever is going on, this is most definitely not a typical UFO abduction experience. After more details about how Marilyn is returned to her apartment, I bring her out of the trance state and end the session.

Afterward, I asked if she had any idea what this strange scene was all about, and she replied that she had no idea. To both Don and me she seemed genuinely perplexed. I was curious to find out if she knew whether Linda in fact did own a two-piece peach-colored nightgown with buttons on the front, and again she said she did not know. In fact, at the time she had never been in Linda's apartment and their friendship was still fairly casual. "Marilyn, you're not going to say anything to her about this, are you?" I asked, reiterating an admonition I had given before we started. "Because I'm going to see her tomorrow." She gave me her word that she would not tell Linda anything.

"I don't want this to be true," she said with a tone of weary sadness. "I really don't want this to be true."

Before Linda arrived for her appointment the next day, I phoned to ask if she had any objection to Don Donderi's joining us, and, like Marilyn, she was entirely agreeable to his sitting in. When she arrived and we settled down to talk about her conscious memories, Linda said that this "shared dream" had taken place around the end of August. It actually unfolded on three successive nights. As she described her lengthy but fragmented recollections it began to sound to me like a mix of normally confusing dream material with what might well turn out to be recollections of an actual abduction. In order to make any sense of it, all of these discontinuous memories would have to be recovered, sorted out, and compared with Marilyn's recollections.

Since the mother figure represented a definite link between Marilyn's and her own memories, I asked Linda about the person that she took to be her mother. "She was taller [than my mother]," she said, "the woman in my dream. But for some reason I felt she was my mother. . . . My mother was only four feet eleven. This woman was taller than me. . . . Her hair was dark, though my mother was a redhead. In the dream she had dark hair. I don't understand. [The woman's] hair was long and wavy. . . ." With such glaring contradictions I wondered why Linda thought of this woman as her mother.

There were other details I was curious about. Earlier, Linda said that in her dream she thought she "must have been wearing a light color. I had my hair pushed back. . . . They could have been white jeans or a baggy white top, depending on what time of the day the dream took place. Of course, it was evening when I fell asleep . . . they could have been lounging pajamas." I inquired about these pajamas. "They are white, a little collar, long sleeves about to here [indicating the elbow]." I asked if they pulled over the top of the head. "No, I have buttons going down. But in real life I'll just unbutton a few because I'm lazy, and just pull it over. . . ."

"And those lounging pajamas are white you say?"

"Yeah, they are white and I have a pair also in pink. It could have been either one of those."

Further questioning about the dream brought out more intriguing details. "We were sitting at this table," she recalled, "and it was dark, dingy, shadowy, and Marilyn was sitting to the left of me. To the right of me was my mother."

"What does Marilyn look like in this?" I asked. "What was she wearing?"

"She was wearing something dark. It was a top that had a dark background but there were bright colors. They say you're crazy if you dream in color, I'm sorry but I do—but it was patterns, I don't know if it was flowers or swirls or squares, but it had patterns. I'm gonna guess that the background was dark blue with bright color patterns on it."

Linda remembered other people being there, too. "I don't know who they were . . . they were sitting—it was a long rectangular table— and they were sitting across. I didn't see them, I just knew that they were there. I just saw their arms, their hands . . . but I didn't see . . . the faces. And I don't know if they were males or females, either. But their hands were all crossed."

Linda had more conscious recollections, including what she thought was the final scene involving the two black men, and then, she said, she suddenly woke up in bed. "And when I woke I was sitting up. I was really scared."

"You were already sitting up when you woke up?" I asked.

"I think I must have been . . . because I was so afraid I must have sat up."[1]

Now it was time to try a hypnotic regression in the hope that a core series of incidents could be disentangled from the jumbled dream material.

"Let's just try to get a sequence of events," I told her. "We're going to start in your bedroom and we're going to assume that it's a normal late night. Since you said you woke up with this memory, let's go back to the night it took place. Where were you sleeping: in the living room, in the bedroom?"

"In the bedroom," Linda replied, as I made her comfortable on the couch and began the by-now familiar induction. I set the scene, and we began the inquiry, not knowing what we might discover.

L: I slipped my shoes off and got into bed. Rocky is on my nightstand, night table, and I just gave him a pat. Rocky is my 150,000-volt stun gun. He's better than Gloria. She was only 50,000 volts. And so I gave him a pat.

B: Do you do this every night when you get into bed?

L: Every night. As long as I'm by myself . . . And I just shut the lamp off. And I just slid down into the bed and went to my side. I sleep on my left side to begin with.

B: Uh-huh. What are you wearing?

L: I'm wearing lounging pajamas. And . . . then I realized I forgot to look behind the drapes. I always look under the bed and behind the drapes and in the closets. . . . I looked under the bed and in the closet and I forget to look behind the drapes in the bedroom. And I don't know if I should put the lamp back on and get up out of bed and . . . I was so comfortable, and I figured, no, I'd better do that. Because I'm not going to be able to sleep. I'm going to feel funny. I'll have to get up and I'll have to look behind the drapes. So I did get out of bed and . . .

B: Do you turn the lights on? Before you look?

L: No. And I just get up from the bed and I walk to the window . . . OOOHHHHH!!! [Bloodcurdling scream]

B: It's all right, Linda. It's all right.

Linda's fear is so intense that it takes a while to calm her down. I reassured her that she was only remembering something from the past, and that whatever it was, she survived.

B: Everything's okay now. Relaxing . . . just looking very slowly back into the past now from the present, slowly you're going to look back. What did you see behind the curtain when you got up?

L: I put my hand behind the curtain and there was something behind the curtain. There's nothing behind the curtain but then there was something behind the curtain.

B: Uh-huh. So you felt something but didn't see anything?

L: Yes I did. [Starts to cry]

B: Okay, what do you feel? What are you feeling? Tell me the sensations in your hand.

L: I saw something that was dark, and very like a—a dark khaki color illuminated just a little bit—just a little bit but enough to see.

B: What was the sensation of touch? Did you touch this?

L: Oh, my, yeah.

B: What did you feel? Was it fabric or was it . . . ?

L: Oh, no. No. It was something. It was something of substance. It was alive.

Next, after another period of calming and reassurance, Linda described her attempt to use her stun gun.

L: I'm standing there and I got my stun gun but [starting to cry a little]—there are two buttons on my stun gun and I don't remember . . . if I switched it on. You know, you have the on and off button and the safety switch and the button that you push that zaps. . . . Damn, I should have checked that out before I went to sleep. I want to put the light on. I really want to put the light on. But I'm, I'm afraid to turn around and look at the lamp because [voice trembles, almost crying] . . . I don't know . . . is he going to do something to me while I'm not looking? I don't want to waste a split second. I don't want to turn around and turn on the lamp 'cause I'm afraid that he'll do something to me behind my back. So how am I going to put a lamp on? I'm just standing by the nightstand. And I'm just waiting and I'm holding Rocky.

It's there! It came out from behind the drapes and it started to walk toward me.

B: Uh-huh. What does it look like?

L: Oh, it's the usual—I've seen him before—I've seen him before. And I don't like this one. I don't like him. Well, none of them are really friendly but this one is particularly mean. He's holding a . . . rod. And he's walking toward me and I know what he's going to do.

So, I try the button that zaps him but it didn't go on. So I kind of figured that I didn't put it on. It's on a safety latch and so I turned the safety latch off and I tried Rocky again and he wouldn't work. He just wouldn't work. I'm telling this, this creature [voice trembling with fear] "I'm gonna zap you. You better get away from me—you better stay away from me because I'm gonna zap you," [begins crying again] and he's coming closer and he has this rod and Rocky doesn't want to go on. I keep pushing the button and he doesn't want to go on. So I ran across the bed to the other side. . . . And I was going back and forth from one side of the bed to the other and I kept saying, "I'm gonna zap you. I'm gonna get you." And I kept pushing the button, I kept pushing the button and he just wouldn't work, Rocky, he wouldn't work so I just threw him on the floor, and [the intruder] came over to me and he hit me, he hit me with the rod.

B: Where does he hit you, Linda?

L: He hit me between the neck and the shoulder.

B: Did it hurt?

L: Yes, it did. It probably felt what Rocky would have felt like. I felt electric . . . Oh, nooo . . .

B: What's the matter?

L: There's more of them. I'm not going to get out of this. I go in the living room and I don't want to go—but I'm going. And that damn window. And now, I don't know. I can't feel anything. I can't see anything either. But the odor, the odor is different. That's not the way my home . . . my home has a different odor. And then I can see . . . I can see where I am now. I'm not home now.

B: What do you see—around here?

L: Where am I? I don't know. I'm in a room. I'm in a room and it's dingy . . . there isn't enough light.

And now Linda begins to describe this dark place. Its main feature is a long table. I ask if it's in the center of the room, and she answers that she doesn't know because she can't see what is behind her. Then:

L: Oh! Marilyn is there. Oh, no! What's she doing there?

B: What's she wearing?

L: She's wearing this dark blue top. I can't see the bottom. She's right next to me. I don't believe this!

B: [In a deliberate attempt to mislead] Is she at your right?

L: She's on my left. There's someone next to me on my right. I don't know who that is.

B: Let's get a description. Let's get a look at the face . . . his face. Is it a he or a she?

L: A she. I think it's a she. You know, it must be tall because it's taller than me. And she has long dark hair. Very pale. She has a cute little nose like my mother. Little lips. Thin. Very pale.

B: How about her eyes?

L: She has beautiful eyes. Big eyes. She's very quiet.

B: What's she wearing?

L: Something white. Maybe that's why she looks so pale. She's pale enough and she's wearing white, I don't know what it is . . . it's like a medical . . . I don't know . . .

B: You mean like a lab coat?

L: Yes, something like that.

B: Let's look closely at her hair again.

L: It's wavy and it comes down to about between the neck and the shoulder. Just about touching the shoulder. She must be tall, because, you know, I'm looking up at her. Marilyn's on the other side of me. What the hell's she doing there? I looked at her and I said, "What are you doing here?" But secretly I was glad she was there. I felt more comfortable. I'm really surprised about this.

   Someone over near to me, or was it next to me, handed me this thing.

B: Someone hands you something?

L: Yeah. It looks like a tube. Reddish silver. And . . . hey, you know what it looks like? A Coca-Cola can. [Laughs] And told me to look at it. So I took it and looked at it and I don't have my glasses, my reading glasses on, so I don't know if it says anything on it.

B: How do you have to hold it when you don't have your reading glasses on? Close to your eyes?

L: No. I'm farsighted so I have to hold it away from me. And I still can't see it so I still can't see if there's any writing on it. I know it's not a Coca-Cola can. It just makes me think of one. And all those other people [on the other side of the table], I can see from their elbows down. It seems to be lighter down there and their hands are . . . their hands! Oh, their hands are different! LOOK! "See, Marilyn! Look at that!" I keep telling her, "Look! Look at their hands!" I think Marilyn's telling me to stay and keep quiet because it was important. It was like a meeting. A conference. And I said, "No! No! No! No! No! I don't want to look! I don't want to look!" And she says, "You ought to be quiet . . ." because this is like a meeting. I don't know if she was telling me . . . I don't know if she was telling me with her mouth!

B: What makes you think this is coming from Marilyn?

L: Because it was coming from the person that was on the left side of me and that is Marilyn. [Whispers] Is it coming from her? I think it comes from her.

B: And she's telling you to keep quiet?

L: Yeah, she's telling me to stay quiet because it's important. It could have, could have been the other woman that was next to me.

B: Might be. Let's look out at the hands again. I'm kind of curious where they are in relation to the table. Are they leaning forward so their arms were out toward the middle of the table?

L: No. They were very . . . they were long thin fingers . . . only four of them! And I said, "Marilyn, Marilyn, look at that!" And they were folded over each other. And I'm holding up this tube and I'm holding it far away and they're telling me to look at this tube and I keep looking at the tube.

   And then I put it down and I said, "Why am I here? I don't want to be here. I have to get out of here." I remember I looked at Marilyn and . . . I don't know if I was moving my lips, either . . . but I remember I said to her, no matter how it was said, "Marilyn, I'm going. I got to get out of here. You're coming, aren't you?" And I can't feel or remember what she said to me.

B: Did you watch her facial expressions change?

L: Yeah, she wasn't too happy either. Not at all. She was pretty nervous and upset. And I get the feeling that she didn't want me to know, and to tell you the truth I didn't want to scare her myself, you know, and maybe . . . maybe it's not so good having her there because I want to yell. I'm really scared but if I do I'll scare her and I don't want to scare her! So I said, "Come on, Marilyn. Let's go. Let's go." And she was afraid. She was really scared.

   There was a man there. No, it's not my Steve. It isn't Steve. It's someone else, another man there and he's holding this little, little baby. A cute little baby, but I don't know who it is. The whole thing was just strange and I really don't want to be there. I said, "Come on, Marilyn. Let's go." And she isn't saying anything to me. I think she was really scared.

B: Okay. This is what I want you to do now. Take a look at the table. Now see if there's anything else on the table. It may be a completely blank table. We know there are some hands folded across each other on the table and we know there's this tubelike thing. Let's see if there's anything else on the table or whether it's completely blank.

A few moments earlier Linda had stated, "It's like a meeting, a conference." And then, with sudden emotion, she said, "No! No! No! No! No! I don't want to look!" I hadn't inquired about what she was afraid of, but it occurred to me that she might be referring to the as yet unreported sight of little Johnny lying on the table in front of her. So now I was attempting to find out if, when she was directed to look down on the table, she would recognize her son stretched out "glassy-eyed," as Marilyn had earlier described. I was prepared to use a false lead or two to test Linda's perceptions—and, indirectly, Marilyn's recollections, which until this moment Linda had been corroborating very closely.

L: I didn't look down at the table. I only saw across the table where these hands—and . . . it was dark—a dark table. And I don't know if it was because there isn't enough light . . . their hands are lit. I can see their hands. I think there are some buttons.

B: Buttons on the table? Are there any . . . sometimes in a conference somebody puts writing things on the table, pads and pencils.

L: I see books here. Books. The size of a telephone book.

B: That's pretty big.

L: No, a telephone book for the house, you know, you write numbers in it. There are some almost as big as an album. Picture album. And there's writing in them. I don't know what that writing is.

B: Can you see it? The writing?

L: [Linda's reply is somewhat evasive.] Can I see it? The writing? I was looking at their hands. And I want to go. I don't want to stay there. I want Marilyn to come along but she isn't saying anything to me. And then I whisper to her, but I don't know if she can hear me because she just acts as if she's not paying attention. She just looks so frightened but like she's not paying attention. And I said, "Marilyn, I'm going to count to three. When I get to three, we're both going to get up real quick and we're going to run." And I said, "One. Two. Three." Pushed back from the table, ran down the stairs and . . . it's a ramp! A big, wide ramp—with a divider! Oh, here comes Marilyn! She's coming! She's coming and we get—we get to the door . . . and then [voice trembling] there's two of them! There's two! These two big . . . they look like bigger aliens, they seem bigger but a little darker. And they're standing by the door and I say, Aaoohhh, you know, they're not gonna let us out. We got to get out. We got to get out. So I say, "Let's just push them away. We'll just push them away." And we pushed them away and we kept pushing them away and then we got the door open and we got outside, I'm holding someone's hand—and when we got outside it's like the door kept opening and we kept closing it and the door kept opening and we kept closing it. And the next thing I know, I'm sitting in my bed. Really scared. Really scared. I don't know what that was all about. It was a meeting. But I'm sitting in my bed now and I'm really scared.

B: Now let's go back inside before you got away. You're at the table again. There's a man that you said is holding a baby. When we talked before the session you said something about thinking it's Johnny at an earlier age. Let's go back to the idea of Johnny. Do you see Johnny?

L: No. I don't see Johnny—unless I don't want to see Johnny—I don't know. I just see the man holding this baby. And I think maybe it's Johnny. He looks like Johnny did when Johnny was little.

B: Do you think it's Steve when he's younger?

L: No. It isn't Steve.

B: Is it anybody else you've ever seen?

L: You know, I would think Steve would be holding Johnny. No, it's another man.

B: What kind of hair does he have?

L: He has thin hair. Very thin hair. And he doesn't look young. And it looks like he's holding Johnny when Johnny was a baby.

B: You know, sometimes people have identifying features—they wear glasses, they have facial hair, beards, mustaches . . . some people don't. Is there anything like this?

L: I don't remember seeing glasses.

B: A mustache or beard?

L: No, I don't remember seeing that, either.

B: How old a man would you say he is?

L: I'd say maybe he's in his late sixties.

B: Is he thin, medium-sized, heavy?

L: Looks kind of thin to me. Not . . . not . . . You know, nice thin. He's not overweight.

By now, Linda had corroborated virtually every detail that Marilyn had described—from the strange woman's thick, black hair and Linda's button-down-the-front lounging pajamas to the red-and-silver "Coca-Cola can." She had omitted only one crucial detail from her friend's account: Johnny's presence on the table. I realized that Linda *might* be deliberately refusing to look at the table because to do so would simply be too harrowing. I remembered the strength of her earlier denial when she had said, "No! No! No! No! No! I don't want to look! I don't want to look!"

Trying to get her to glance down by leading her in a false direction, I had earlier suggested that there might be writing materials or books on the table. I was astonished when she took my lead and went on to describe "phone books and albums" on the table. It was the first time I had ever been able to lead her in a direction that I had deliberately invented, and something about the ease with which she followed didn't seem right.

Therefore I decided to try a simple dissociative technique. I asked her to imagine the strange room as a kind of movie set, with a long, two-person camera boom set up alongside it. I explained that Linda and I would sit in the seats on this camera boom and that we would rise up so that we could see the entire room below us, including actresses playing Marilyn, the strange woman, and herself. And, of course, we would be able to see the table very clearly.

I started the camera boom and then asked her to look down and describe the scene, including herself. Apart from the fact that she said she was wearing pale *pink* lounging pajamas (Marilyn had said they were peach, a close enough call), almost nothing new emerged. Still somewhat perplexed, I decided to end the session, and in my usual way, counting back from five, I brought Linda out of the trance state.

Our posthypnosis debriefing yielded a few new details, such as the fact that Marilyn's shirt or pajama top had no buttons and that the man with the thin white hair, standing near the table, was wearing pajamas as well. I again swore Linda to secrecy, insisting she not discuss the session with Marilyn and she immediately agreed. She was as eager as Marilyn to explore the situation in order to discover, finally, whether or not it was all an amazing coincidence or—worse—a real experience. For me, it had been a remarkable session because of the many exact correlations between the two women's accounts, though I did not know what it all meant.

But there was to be a kind of coda to the day's proceedings. About an hour after Linda left, she telephoned me. "I have to tell you, Budd, something about the table. When you asked me if there were books on it, I said yes, there were books. But I really don't think I saw any books. I think I *wanted* to see books there, so when you asked me, I said yes. I don't think I wanted to look at what was on the table."

I asked her if she now thought she knew what was there, and she said, "No. I don't know. But I think I don't want to know." We left it at that. However, considering everything else that she had recalled, I sensed that she would allow herself, sooner or later, to experience the shock of seeing her son. As it happened, that sad moment came quite soon.

C H A P T E R

28

The Man in the Striped Pajamas

After Marilyn's Saturday session, psychologist Don Donderi and I had a chance to talk about what we had seen and heard. He felt, as did I, that there was no evidence that Marilyn was deliberately inventing or trying to deceive, and nothing about her demeanor suggested mental illness. We were both struck by her emotional affect, which seemed appropriate to the incidents she was reporting, although the meaning of these incidents was obviously elusive.

For the time being I was unable to discuss the results of Linda's hypnosis with Donderi because he had to start back to Montreal immediately after the session ended. But a day or so later, when I finally reached him by telephone, he seemed as astonished as I at the corroborative nature of Linda's recollections and equally mystified as to what it all might mean. In addition to the two women's almost palpable honesty and lack of sophistication, he was struck by the fact that neither of them claimed to know what the "meeting around the conference table" was all about either.

So far as I know, almost every confessed or suspected hoaxer in the field of UFO "contact" phenomena has invented a story making him/herself privy to "cosmic truths"—often nothing more than New Age bromides—which are later peddled in lectures, books, and seminars as teachings of great profundity.[1] The hoaxer invariably casts himself in a priestlike role; one must come to him for "the truth" because he is a true conduit to the Space Brothers. In one infamous case, a European hoaxer claimed to have traveled back in time—with the help of a beautiful blond female alien—to a cosmic "place" where he held a philosophical conversation with Jesus, Moses, Buddha, and the rest of the world's religious leaders.

By contrast, Marilyn and Linda were baffled by their shared experience. It had no discernible meaning for them. Instead of claiming any special wisdom, they admitted to ignorance and confusion. Instead of hearing cosmic truths, Linda was asked to pick up a red-and-silver tube that to her resembled a Coca-Cola can, and simply to look at it. There were no long, flowing, priestly robes; essentially everyone was wearing pajamas. Although Linda was being "instructed," she was unable to remember any of it—just the kind of confused UFO experience that the skeptics love to ridicule.

In reviewing the two sessions I noticed a few apparent discrepancies that required further examination. For example, Marilyn said that when she saw Linda standing to her right, she wasn't speaking and didn't seem to realize she was there. Linda, however, remembered speaking to Marilyn, at one point urging her to flee. The problem seems to abate, however, when one considers the chronology: Linda's testimony suggests that she spoke to Marilyn *later* in this experience, and nowhere suggests that they conversed at the outset.

While Marilyn's account did not include the precipitous flight down the ramp at the end of their encounter, nothing she said precluded it. The central discrepancy, of course, involves Johnny. Linda felt that she saw the thin-haired man holding Johnny *as a baby*, yet Marilyn nowhere confirms this detail. For her part, she saw Johnny as he looked at the time—a nine-year-old lying glassy-eyed on the table in front of them, an image missing in Linda's account. Interestingly, neither woman dealt in detail with the image of the two ominous "black men" who figured so sharply in their prehypnotic recall. Clearly, another pair of hypnotic sessions was called for to help resolve the Johnny issue, as well as to clarify as far as possible the meaning of the experience itself.

On Sunday, December 6, Marilyn arrives at my studio for her final session about this event. I begin the induction and shortly thereafter take her back to "that odd place" we have been talking about. Marilyn again describes the man who seems like her father, but who, at the same time, seems like an older man with thinning hair. I ask for a description, and she complies in her idiosyncratic shorthand.

M: He has a slender face. He has a bald head . . . big head . . . forehead. Big nose. [Pause] He has an egg-shaped head. . . . His hair is combed back. He's my height. My father's not my height. My father's taller. [This man] is a thin man. My father's not thin.

He's narrow. He's got a thin waist. My father doesn't have a thin waist.

B: So he doesn't seem to be your father, exactly.

M: No. But I feel it's my father. . . .

After giving me more details of this early part of the experience, Marilyn finds herself alone in the "conference room," where she sees Linda and the black-haired woman. "We're crammed in there. It's very tight. I don't feel like I should be there. I don't know what's going on, I'm just there."

Again she describes the red-and-silver object that Linda picks up from the table. It has a "little silver streak" and Linda holds it away from her, tilting it up somewhat. The room, Marilyn says, is like a hospital waiting room where "you're going to see a doctor and then people come in and out."

M: Johnny's on the table. Linda's not looking at Johnny, she's looking across. . . . They're not doing anything to Johnny. . . . He's not wearing anything. . . . He's pudgy, but he's got fat little feet. He doesn't have any ankles.

B: Does he have any body hair?

M: On his legs . . . faint. I don't want to look at this. I'm looking at the other people around the table.

I ask her to describe what Linda is wearing, and once more she says, "She's wearing silk pajamas. Peach. Very pastelish. Her hair is tied back. She has her hair in a rubber band, and it's loose."

Next, I inquire about the woman to Linda's right, and again, in answer to my various questions, I hear Marilyn's new and fuller descriptions. Her account is punctuated by many pauses as she apparently takes her time to study her subject:

"She's beautiful. . . . She's got a long neck. . . . She motions with her hands. . . . She has beautiful hands . . . she's got four fingers [and no thumb]. Three of her fingers are long, one is shorter. Very narrow wrists. Elegant . . . There's a little palm. . . . She doesn't have any fingernails. No fingernails, no claws . . . [Her fingers are] not as long as the ones opposite [on the edge of the table]. She also has softer skin. The others are very hard looking. . . .

"She's wearing a robe. No buttons. I don't know how she gets into it. She's flat-chested. Her hair is, like, black. She looks like Batgirl. Marlo Thomas. No bangs."

I ask if she is wearing lipstick. "She's not wearing lipstick, but there's pigment to her lips. She's soft, white, but where her bones are you can see shade. She doesn't need makeup. . . . Her nose is tightly pulled around her bones. . . . It's very plasticlike. She looks like a doll, a porcelain doll. . . .

"She has no eyelids, no eyelashes. She does have an underlid. She's very beautiful. . . . Her eyes are like shark eyes. They're black, but they're not as harsh as the grays. They're softer. . . . She has no flaws."

I ask if she moves her mouth or lips. "No. No, she expresses herself with her hands and she communicates in the mind. She could move her lips, but she doesn't speak. She has expression. She's trying to comfort Linda. She's accommodating her."

Again Marilyn mentions the woman's statement about something being "premature," a reference, she thinks, to Marilyn's having met Linda. "We're being scolded in a way. Linda's not happy. She wants to get out of there. I want to hear what this woman has to say. There's too much interference. Linda's not paying attention. She's jabbering. . . . I can't hear what the woman has to say. Linda's talking. There's too much confusion in my head. I can't break it down."

I now try to move Marilyn's attention from the strange woman to the shadowed figures whose hands rest on the table. ". . . They're listening. They're waiting for us to finish talking to this woman. She knows Linda very well. She's been following Linda. I thought she was Linda's mother. She's Linda's older sister."

Again I try to get Marilyn to describe the four figures, asking if she can perhaps see any outlines within the shadows. *"They won't show themselves!* We are only supposed to pay attention to the woman. They're going to do something to Johnny after. They're waiting. Linda's being scolded." I ask if she knows what Linda's being scolded for. After a pause, she answers, "Johnny. He musn't know. It has to go along its natural course. She shouldn't tell Johnny." But again, Marilyn said she didn't know *what* Linda wasn't supposed to tell him.

Now I tell Marilyn to continue around the table, moving counterclockwise, from the four shadowed figures to the man at their right. She describes, again, his white hair and shiny forehead. "He's watching . . . he's like a grandfather, in a way." I ask if he's familiar, and Marilyn answers no. "He's got nice teeth. He's pleasant looking. . . .

"He's just wearing pajamas. Blue stripes down it, or something

. . . I don't understand why he's there. I don't know who he is. He's well groomed." I ask if he seems to have a function or if he just stands there with his arms at his sides. "He had his head tilted . . . his arms dangling . . . and he doesn't believe what he's looking at . . . he's in total denial . . . he doesn't know what he's looking at. [Pause] This is embarrassing. It's like, all of us together here . . . something went wrong here."

Again I direct Marilyn's gaze back to the man in the striped pajamas. "He's my height . . . a little shorter. He's got high cheekbones . . . not too high. He's got beautiful eyes. I think they're brown."

I ask Marilyn to imagine, if he spoke, what kind of voice he would have. "He's soft-spoken. He's a kind man. He's worried about Johnny. . . . He's in his sixties . . . sixty-five, early seventies . . . sixty-fiveish."

In another very subjective foray, I ask Marilyn if she thinks the man knows any of the people in the room. "He's concerned about Johnny because he's focused on him, he's looking at his head. [Pause] He's got nice eyelashes. Well-groomed man."

Again I ask her to describe his demeanor, his emotional state. "He knew it was right . . . he just knows it's true . . . he knows . . . a confirmation. He's happy." I remember that a moment before, Marilyn described him as seeming worried about Johnny. I wonder if these aren't contradictory emotions arising from the same situation: his sudden awareness of Johnny's presence.

"And Linda's agitated," I add. "She's going into a panic," Marilyn says. "I don't know what to do. There's commotion all around. She wants to get out of there."

Now I try another tack, another deliberate attempt to lead Marilyn. I remind her that during the past few weeks she has met Linda's father, so I ask if the man in the striped pajamas could be he. "No," she replies firmly. "Please, no. This man is not old-old. He's like a grandfather, but not as old as Linda's father."

"Now if he seems to be concerned about Johnny," I say, "does he seem concerned at all about Linda, or does he know who Linda is? You don't know who he is, but do you think he knows who you are?"

"No. [Firmly] It's embarrassing, because I don't know who this man is, and I feel I'm not supposed to be here . . . this is a family thing. . . . He knows who Linda is. . . . I'm just there.

"[Pause] The man is wearing jewelry. Rings. College ring? On his right hand. It's flat on the top, and it's got a little thing on there . . . it's not a wedding band. [Pause] He's a wealthy man. [Pause] He has hair on his hands."

Pleased by the highly specific quality of Marilyn's powers of observation, I try yet another avenue of inquiry. "You know how there are different types of people, people who have WASP kinds of faces, faces that look English, faces that look somewhat Negroid, Jewish faces, Arabic faces . . ."

"He doesn't look American. [Long pause, as if studying his physiognomy] He's a combination between an Italian old man and someone from Spain . . . the way their skin is. Shiny. He's not a little old man. He's not. He looks like a very handsome older man to me."

I now move the scene forward, and Marilyn describes being back where the ramp is. "I think I'm being dragged. . . . She's getting upset, she's getting really out of it, Linda. I think I'm gonna trip. I have to go down the stairs to the ramp. I'm being pulled and I remember going fast. . . . We're running away. I open a door . . . the only door in the whole place . . . and we're trying to get out . . . Linda . . . [breathing heavily] they're trying to prevent us. . . ."

(Her account of their escape will be described later, but she and Linda once more find themselves under alien control and are brought into yet another strange room.)

"The walls are white . . . and it's like there's a fog machine in there . . . smoke machine. Linda's standing by me . . . we're not communicating . . . I can't talk, I can't speak and I can't think. I know she's right there. We're waiting. . . . Johnny walks in first . . . he's in his pajamas. . . . It's foggy . . . I can't see his pajamas. . . . I don't know what they look like. . . . He was dressed, though. I know Johnny walks in first.

"And then the old man comes after . . . he's in blue striped pajamas. He looks very . . . he looks *rich,* I can't explain. He's got that rich look. Johnny's wearing a T-shirt. And I think boxer shorts or something like that. He walks in, he looks okay, he has no expression on his face. Linda doesn't do anything. She doesn't go to help him. . . .

"It's very awkward being here. . . . I'm nervous, embarrassed. It's a family thing . . . Linda, Johnny, and the man. I have to control myself. My emotions are shut down."

To help Marilyn express any feelings that she might be repressing, I suggest that she imagine she is back in the original room with the woman and the figures around the table. "If you could move and speak then, what would you say to the woman with the dark hair at the end of table? Say it now, whatever you would have liked to have said."

Marilyn spoke with firmness: "How could she have allowed this to happen? How could she go along with this? Doesn't she know what she's putting Linda through with this? [Sighs] It's not fair. . . . They're manipulating the whole situation. They're too smart, and we're catching on. . . . It was premature to have grandfather see all this."

"If you had something to say to the grandfather, whatever we want to call him, the older man, what would you say?"

"Help out," she replied, "help . . . [sighs] . . . I don't know who this man is. I'm not being told who he is. [In an exasperated voice] He is in shock, this man. He's in shock. He's surprised, he's not surprised, there's just so much confusion, and Linda's causing such confusion, there's so much in my head, I can't take it. It's a fight. It's all in the head. I don't want to be here."

I ask Marilyn to move the scene ahead to its next stage. "They're preparing us," she says. "We're being separated. The man stays behind. Johnny and Linda walk out first. Then I'm being led out. Linda . . . blank on her face. She's not even holding him, she's not touching him. Johnny's just walking in front of her. . . . [Sighs] We're not saying anything to each other. It's embarrassing. What happened? Linda wouldn't treat me like that. It's awkward, like if you have a fight with someone and they won't talk to you."

Finally Marilyn describes the process of being brought back to her apartment, two gray beings taking her through the skylight and down into the bathroom. "I'm worried because I have things on top of the toilet. I have a lamp and I have potpourri and I'm afraid I'll break it. I don't know if they know that, and I don't want a mess."

As she goes in, the aliens lift her feet up so that she is in a sitting position. "One of them is in the bathroom, and I feel I'm being helped. I remember going through the door of my bathroom, and I remember being escorted back to the bed. They put my legs down first and then they bring my back down to rest on the bed. No covers. I didn't have covers. It's hot [late August or early September]. When they do it they support my back, and they let me go, and it kind of felt uncomfortable, like a thump on my bed. They didn't put my head on a pillow until my head hits the mattress. They don't go back out through the [bathroom] door, they go into the corner of my room, and they disappear. [Sighs]"

After a series of calming and empowering posthypnotic suggestions, I bring Marilyn out of the trance state. The session had been remarkable in many ways, but, for me, surely the most important information was her highly detailed description of the man in the striped pajamas. As a result of this hypnosis, I had come to a disturbing but stunning conclusion. It was something I had originally never even *suspected*: that this handsome older person was most probably the third man.

But dramatic as this new possibility was, I still had no idea of what it meant. Why was the third man there rather than Richard, Johnny's putative father? What was *Marilyn's* involvement in all of this, a question she had several times asked herself? What did it all mean?

Immediately after the session ended I decided to hand Marilyn the set of twenty xeroxed photographs I had shown Johnny, with the same basic instruction. She was to sort through the pictures with the goal of finding the one or two that most closely resembled the man in the striped pajamas. After a careful study she came up with two that she could not decide between: One was the photo of the third man and the other was of a somewhat younger man with darker hair and a thinner face. In the third man's photo, he was wearing lightly tinted glasses, while the thinner gentleman in the second photo had none. Obviously, during their experience at the table, the man in the striped pajamas was not wearing glasses, a factor that I realized might cause Marilyn a bit of confusion. Johnny had no such problem, since he saw the third man wearing tinted glasses like those in the photo.

Marilyn thought that if the two photos were superimposed she would have a much better approximation of the face of the man in the striped pajamas. But she finally ascribed a numerical probability to each photo on a scale of one to ten: The third man's picture rated an eight, the other photo a seven.

At 10:30 on Tuesday morning, December 8, two days after Marilyn's hypnosis, Linda arrived for her second hypnosis session. I began the induction and set the scene. She describes entering the strange room through a hallway after walking up a ramp. I ask if the ramp has a railing, and she replies that it does have a railing on one side: the left side of the wall. (I make a mental note that Linda has scored one out of two; Marilyn had also said that the ramp had only one railing, but she put it on the *right* side.)

Linda walks over to the table and describes the shadowed figures across from her: "Their hands are wrong. Their hands are wrong and their fingers are wrong. Some [fingers] look like they're the same size—and there aren't enough fingers. It's like there's one missing. They're a white-gray, almost white."

But Linda's next observation comes as a surprise, which, for the moment, I let pass. "And I look and I see a human hand this way. There's [a pair of alien] hands here and I see a human hand the opposite way. . . . It doesn't belong there."

Next I ask about Marilyn, and her simple reply echoes Marilyn's own confusion: "Why is she there? . . . She's staring across. She's looking . . . Oh, she's looking at a man at the other end of the table." Linda has trouble observing the man because her gaze is drawn in the opposite direction, to the woman at the head of the table. "I can't stop looking at her. I'm so confused. . . . I thought she was my mother."

"Why did you think she was your mother?" I ask.

"I don't know. I've seen her before. She interrupted . . . it was her! She interrupted one of my favorite TV commercials in 1985! I was sitting and watching TV and knitting and I put down my knitting and this Michael Jackson Pepsi-Cola commercial went on. . . . The colors were so pretty. I was halfway looking up and looking down at my work when this black-and-white figure on the TV said to me, 'Where were you?' And that's something my mother always said to me when I was late: 'Where were you?' So I see this woman [now, at the table] and I remembered watching TV and thinking that was my mother. It can't be my mother, my mother passed away—long ago."

I ask again if the woman says anything to her. "No, she's watching me watch her. I think she's annoyed with me. She's very authoritative. She's an authority figure to me. I don't want her to be annoyed at me. I'm afraid of her . . . but I think I like her."

I now direct Linda's attention to the place opposite this woman, down at the other end of the table.

"There's a man. Pretty tall man. Maybe six feet, six one." [Moans] He's still . . . very still and he's wearing a white top. Ohhh . . . it looks like pajamas. There's stripes—vertical stripes! They are pajamas. [The stripes] sort of looked purple but I think it's blue because the light . . . it's like a yellowish white light. He's wearing pajamas and the stripes are vertical and blue."

I ask if his pajamas are rumpled. "People sleep in the same pajamas night after night," I say, "and they can get awfully rumpled looking."

"No," Linda replies, "they look pretty elegant, but he does look a little disheveled. He has double-breasted pajamas.

"I see hands, I see his hands. Oh, look at that! He has long fingers and he's wearing jewelry. I think he's wearing a ring on each hand. One ring like . . . oval? It's oval and it's flat and, well, they could be make-believe . . . but it looks like . . . diamonds. And on the other hand is, I think, a wedding band. In fact, I'm sure it's a wedding band.

"[Whispers] I recognize this man. You know who this is? Poppy! It's Poppy. He looks different though. Yeah, what's he doing there? He looks different. . . . He's not wearing his glasses. His hair is a little messy. And he looks like he's . . . comatose—with his eyes open. I don't like the way he looks. He's just standing there like a zombie. He's looking down at the table."

"Let's see what he's looking at at the table. Let him look down, and you follow his eyes—see what he's looking at. The surface could be blank or it could have something on it."

"Every time I look at those [alien] hands," Linda replies, "I see a human hand facing the opposite way between two [pairs of] theirs. . . . It's pudgy. It's pudgy. It's smaller, much smaller than theirs . . ."

B: . . . Allow yourself to look up the hand . . .

L: . . . Aaahhh, I see books . . .

B: . . . No. Let's just allow yourself to look up the hand. I want you to know one thing: This all ended, didn't it? [Reassuring her] Look at the table, Linda.

L: Ohhh, there are telephone books there on the table. . . .

B: We're talking about that arm and the hand. You said the hand was small, it was pudgy. Let's just move our eyes along the hand and the arm.

L: I see the palm of the hand—open. I see leading from the palm of the hand the underside of an arm. . . . There's somebody on the table! And laying out there are books. I see books, telephone books. Every time I look through the books I see an arm—a hand. It keeps getting in the way. It's wrong. It doesn't belong there with the other hands and arms. . . .

B: Linda, whatever was going on here ended, didn't it? Is everybody safe right now here in December in the real world? You're here with me. We're here in the studio. Everything that night ended. Everything is okay. We're just looking back at an event that happened in the past. I want you to tell me what you're afraid of.

L: I'm afraid of that table.

B: Tell me why you're afraid of the table. Say what your fear is. It's much better to say it.

L: I'm afraid I'm going to see somebody on the table. . . .

B: What's your worst fear about who you could see on the table?

L: Somebody was being operated on. It's supposed to be a conference.

B: What would be the worst you could imagine on the table? Your worst fear?

L: Somebody I knew—a friend. Maybe a friend? . . . I'm afraid of seeing anybody on the table.

B: Let's just take a peep at who you're *most* afraid of seeing on the table.

L: Family members. Friends.

B: You mentioned family members. Let's just start with that. What family members are you most afraid of seeing on the table?

L: Any one of them.

B: How did you describe the hand as looking?

L: Smaller, but maybe it just looks smaller because their fingers are so long. . . .

B: . . . Uh-huh. Describe the hands some other way. . . .

L: . . . Pudgy. Pudgy.

B: What does that mean to you?

L: Someone's on the table. Someone pudgy. It's those hands.

B: Look at your fear. Who are you afraid that might be? It's okay to talk about it, Linda. Fears lose their power when they are stated, when you say them. When the fears are kept locked up they have much more power than when you let them out. Tell me what you're most afraid of seeing on the table.

L: A family member or friends. If someone I think is on the table—and if I look I'm going to get upset.

B: Can I tell you who *I* think *you're* thinking of?

L: I know. . . . It might be John. But I don't know that unless I look on the table. . . . If I look at the table I'll see . . .

B: Okay. Let's move this back to this morning. Did you get up early and get John's breakfast for him?

I proceed to use the image of John at breakfast to reassure Linda as concretely as possible that her little boy has survived whatever may have befallen him in the past. It takes a few minutes, but finally she is able to move past her fear.

B: Would you say that if he was ever on that table, that he survived it? [L: Yes.] Good. Of course, he would. You saw him this morning. . . . He's alive and well, isn't he, and healthy? [L: Yes.] Okay. Let's look back at that table.

L: [Nervously] I'm going to look. [Pause, then speaking very softly] Yes, it's him on the table.

I spend a few moments reassuring Linda about Johnny's having survived this experience, and then, after we've crossed this powerfully emotional hurdle, a few more potentially significant bits of information come to light. Linda turns her attention back to the woman who is communicating with her.

L: I don't know if this woman is talking to me with her mouth or with her mind. She tells me it's my fault if Johnny is the size he is [a bit overweight], and that he isn't ready yet, either, for whatever purpose, because he's still young. And I keep telling her, get him off the table because he doesn't belong here, [crying] and she won't listen. I think she's angry at me . . . and so I'm talking back to her.

B: Do you think, Linda, in your heart of hearts, that she has any legitimate reason to criticize you about Johnny?

L: Yes . . . she told me [crying] that they were gonna . . . and I said no you're not gonna, and she said yes we are, and I said Noooo. [Sobbing] He's *mine!* She wanted to *keep* him!

As I tried to reassure Linda that Johnny was hers and that no one could take him, she said, "Johnny was asleep, he didn't know what was going on . . . he's crying in his sleep . . . I can see he's whimpering." I ask how he's dressed. "He's wearing a white undershirt and cut-off sweatpants. They look like shorts now, and he's like whimpering in his sleep, and the man, Poppy, it's the only time I hear him say something. [Sobbing softly] He says, 'Johnny, don't cry, don't cry, I'll give you something nice. Please don't cry.' And I turn around and I said to him, 'If you really love him, you'll get him off the table.' "

Linda was so upset at this point that she developed one final, desperate line of defense. She decided that maybe the woman was trying to trick her and that that wasn't really *her* son on the table. "Maybe she just wants me to *think* it's Johnny on the table. I don't like being tricked. I don't like being fooled. I said to Marilyn, I'm going to count to three . . . that isn't Johnny on the table . . . and so I can leave. [Whispering] I'm going to count to three, and we're gonna *run*. So I said, One, [whispering again] two, three—let's go! But she doesn't go anywhere! She's just standing there, looking at that man!"

Linda pulls on Marilyn's arm, counts to three again, and finally they run out the door and down the ramp. Here, since her account merges almost exactly with Marilyn's, I will point out only one new detail: When they are recaptured and returned to a strange white room, she sees Johnny and suddenly recognizes him: "That *is* my Johnny! That *was* my Johnny . . . ooh, that was my Johnny and I left him there! Oh, ooh. [Moaning] What kind of a mother am I? I didn't believe that was my son and I left him there. . . .

"Poppy doesn't look very happy. I see that he has his hand on John's shoulder . . . and John walks away, and I can see the man's hand drop to his side, away from John's shoulder. John walks over to Marilyn and me, and he smiles, but he doesn't look right, he . . . he looks strange, like he's sleeping with his eyes open. And I looked at that man and he didn't say a word. He just kept staring at the three of us. Marilyn is staring at John, and she looks like she's sleeping with her eyes open. And I yell to the man, Are you coming with us? and he had tears in his eyes . . . and he turned around and just walked away. [Long pause] And then . . . and then . . . I'm back in my room.

"Oh, I think I fell into my bed again. A terrible feeling . . . it feels like going in a down elevator in the World Trade Center from Windows on the World [the top floor]. That feeling you get in your stomach."

Once more I calm Linda about Johnny, reminding her of how safe and healthy he is, and after a few positive posthypnotic suggestions, I bring her out of the trance.

Musing on this remarkable session I was left with many thoughts, but above everything there were two linked pictures in my mind: the image of the third man looking down and saying, "Don't cry, Johnny, don't cry. I'll give you something nice . . ."; and then Johnny receiving a beautiful antique diving helmet in September from a man in a long black car who asked the boy to give him a hug.

C H A P T E R

29

"That's My Little Boy on the Table"

The four sessions we had just completed on the "conference" had raised many staggering new issues, all of which required investigation, analysis, and speculation. But my most immediate concerns were with Marilyn and Linda; they were anxious to find out if their recollections of the event were in any way similar. Each was nervously trying to chart a day-by-day course between two disheartening possibilities: the fear that the remembered images were the result of some kind of mental illness, of imagination out of control, and the dread that the bizarre recollections of one might actually be corroborated by those of the other. Neither woman wanted this encounter to be real, yet neither was eager to feel as if she were teetering on the edge of psychosis.

Apart from the obviously therapeutic function of letting Marilyn and Linda finally know what each remembered, my role as investigator and historian obligated me to record as fully as possible each woman's reactions as she first listened to the other's testimony. A videotape of this three-way meeting was a necessity.

On December 8, after my final hypnosis session with Linda, I called both women to set up an appointment for the morning of December 10. I explained that I wanted the three of us to discuss the results of the investigation so far and compare their individual recollections. To handle the crucial forty-eight-hour period before the meeting, I had come up with an interim strategy designed to calm them down and ease their curiosity. I told them that I was puzzled by the results of the hypnosis sessions, and though I had noticed some similarities in their accounts, there were also a number of contradictions. I said that I thought the meeting I proposed might help to clarify some of these remaining problems. The truth, of course, was that there were almost no contradictions, and that the corroborations were virtually across the board.

I felt uneasy about misleading Marilyn and Linda in this way, but I also knew that debunkers would eventually launch fierce assaults on their integrity. Logically, they would have to claim that Linda had hired Marilyn as yet another member of an ever expanding conspiracy, and that the consonance of their recollections only meant that the two of them had cooked up their stories as part of a hoax. As I had done three times before—twice with Linda and once with Johnny—I intended to create a videotaped record so that any future investigator could see for himself/herself exactly how the principals reacted. Were these people lying, acting, or working to trick me and any other observers? With videotapes of these confrontations, skeptics could see for themselves.

During phone conversations in which I arranged our three-way meeting, I asked Marilyn and Linda if they had any objection to my videotaping the discussion for the record; neither did. Elizabeth, the Cape Cod woman who had alerted me to Linda's discovery of the diving helmet, happened to be visiting New York during this time. Since she and Linda were good friends and she was familiar with Marilyn from our support group meetings, I invited her to attend this get-together, knowing both women would feel comfortable with her. I wanted her there for two reasons: as a witness to the proceedings, and as a camerawoman, since someone had to run the camcorder.

The meeting was scheduled for 10:00 A.M. Marilyn, who happens to be a talented graphic artist, was the first to arrive, bringing with her a remarkable trio of colored drawings she had made about this encounter. The first depicted the pairs of crossed alien hands along the edge of the table, and the second was a startling frontal view of the face of the woman with the thick, black hair. The third showed the "conference space" in perspective, with the woman at the head of the table, the alien hands at one side, Linda and Marilyn standing at the other side, and Johnny lying on the table in the center. In order to clearly depict these three sides of the table, Marilyn explained that she had omitted the man in pajamas at the table's foot. I put the drawings away before Linda arrived, with the intention of showing them to her only when the camera was running and her reactions could be recorded.

The third drawing presented an immediate problem. From our hypnotic sessions I knew how strongly Linda resisted seeing her son stretched out on the table, and how profoundly upsetting it had been for her when she gathered her courage and actually saw him there. I was also aware that only a few moments after she had admitted to me and to herself that Johnny was actually in that room lying on the table, she persuaded herself that the child she was seeing was not really Johnny and that the aliens must have somehow tricked her into thinking so.

In the face of all this resistance and denial, I wondered how Linda would react to Marilyn's testimony that she had also seen Johnny on the table, and even worse, had produced a sketch depicting him lying there. I dreaded the moment when I would finally have to show Linda the drawing.

We arranged our chairs in front of a large three-paneled painting, and put the video camera on a tripod about ten feet away. With Elizabeth at the camcorder, we sat down, Linda in the center and Marilyn to her right, and began our discussion. Again I informed the two women that some details from their accounts were similar and some were not, and that our goal was to try to reconcile these differences. I asked each in turn to explain briefly how she first discovered the apparently very similar dreams, and then tell the content of her dream. After establishing this baseline, we moved into the material that had emerged under hypnosis.

I ask Linda, first, what she remembers about the strange hands and to describe them as best she can. She begins, speaking carefully and repeating what she had recalled under hypnosis about the eerie, nonhuman-looking fingers. When she finishes, I tell her that we have several sketches to examine.

"The first thing we're going to look at is this drawing of the hands that Marilyn made as *she* remembered them. We're looking for differences and similarities between your two accounts." Linda puts on her reading glasses and studies the sheet somberly. "Do they look like what you saw?" I ask. She nods "Yes," and looks warily at Marilyn, who shakes her head, surprised that Linda's recollections so clearly corroborated her own. It should be remembered that until this moment, neither woman had the slightest idea that the other had recalled so many of the same details.

Then I ask Linda, "What's the next thing you notice as you look around to your right?"

"I see that woman," she replies, pointing up at a slight angle, as if to indicate that the woman is taller than she. As had just occurred with the issue of the hands, Linda goes on to describe the strange woman in much the same way as she had during the hypnosis sessions. When she says this person "wasn't bad looking," Marilyn smiles and nods in agreement.

After she describes her thick, shoulder-length hair, I mention that there are many descriptions of reputed hybrids whose hair doesn't really cover their scalps. Linda breaks in before I finish, saying, "Oh, no, this woman had nice thick hair with bangs. It reminded me of a sixties hairdo . . . it went up at the ends. But somehow it didn't go with her—it didn't *belong* on her. You could almost look at it and say 'a cheap wig.'" Smiling, Marilyn nods in agreement, having made exactly the same observation during her first hypnosis session.

It is now time to show Linda Marilyn's drawing of the woman's face. When I hand it to her, she gasps and looks at her friend, shaking her head in amazement. Marilyn says, "I know."

Turning back to the drawing, Linda points to the woman's hairdo with its upturned ends, and whispers, "Ohh, she's got a flip!" After studying the image for a few moments, she continues, speaking thoughtfully: "You know, I didn't dislike her. I felt I needed to be obedient. I don't like that word. It's the only way I can say it. I had to be obedient."

Now I ask Marilyn to tell us her view of the woman's relation to Linda. "I thought when I first saw the woman that it was Linda's mother, and later on, when I realized it wasn't . . . I felt it was Linda's sister. It felt like when you have an older sister, you have to obey an older sister. I have an older sister and she treats me like a baby. This woman—she *knew* Linda and she knew that there was a connection between them: that she was the oldest and Linda was the youngest." Linda agrees that Marilyn's sense of their relationship seems right.

Next I ask Marilyn to describe how Linda was dressed.

"Linda was standing next to me. She was wearing pajamas with sleeves up to here [pointing to her elbow]. They were peach pink with buttons down the front. [Linda looks at Marilyn with a shocked expression.] Long pants. Her hair was tied up in a little ponytail . . . it was loose fitting, with a rubber band."

Here Linda closes her eyes and shakes her head slowly in apparent disbelief at the accuracy of Marilyn's account. It occurs to me that perhaps no one but her immediate family had ever seen Linda, usually so perfectly groomed, with her hair so casually fixed; so, on top of everything else, the very idea of appearing this way "in public" might be adding to Linda's embarrassment.

Marilyn continues with her description. "There was something on the table like a can . . . [Linda's eyes widen in stunned surprise] and she put it in her hand, and she went like that [gesturing as if she is holding it at arm's length; Linda lifts her body off the chair and reseats herself in an automatic nervous reaction]. It was like a Coke can. . . . This thing was so real. . . . She bumped me when she reached over to move the can."

I ask Linda why she picked it up and held it as she did. She answers softly, seemingly devastated by this new confirmation: "Because I needed my reading glasses, 'cause I'm farsighted. Who sleeps with their reading glasses on? I thought there might be some writing in it, but I still couldn't see. My arms don't stretch out far enough to see."

Next, I want Linda to describe to me how *Marilyn* appeared during this experience: "Marilyn was standing next to me, but her eyes were fixed on the man . . . over here [pointing to the left] at the foot of the table. And I couldn't understand what Marilyn was doing there. She was unresponsive."

Now, recounting how Marilyn had been dressed, Linda interrupts her description with a sad aside: "Marilyn was wearing . . . I realize this wasn't a dream. I have to get out of the habit of saying it was a dream. . . ."

After a moment she resumes, going into detail once more about the flowered or abstract patterns on Marilyn's long, dark shirt. I ask if it has buttons on the front, knowing that it doesn't, and she says, "I don't remember seeing buttons." At this point Marilyn dips down into a shopping bag at her feet and takes out the actual shirt she had worn that night, a long batik T-shirt that perfectly matches Linda's just completed description. As she holds it up for the camera, both women seem equally shaken.

When, for Marilyn's benefit, I ask Linda to describe what she was wearing that night, she speaks very softly, looking at her friend, while virtually repeating Marilyn's earlier description of her peach pink pajamas with the buttons on the front. When she has finished she sighs deeply, while Marilyn, looking toward the floor, again shakes her head in denial.

Next, Marilyn describes the older man to her left, her details precisely echoing those Linda related during her hypnosis on December 8. By now, both women seem almost dazed by the situation. Each revelation, each confirming detail, has served to more firmly cement the reality of an experience they cannot rationally accept.

"Did you see the man, too, Linda?" I ask.

She nods, and, beginning to cry, speaks slowly and with difficulty. "He was . . . wearing pajamas, blue stripes, going up and down. The pajamas were double-breasted. Gray-haired. No glasses . . ." Marilyn reaches over and takes Linda's hand in a warm, reassuring gesture of solidarity.

And now comes the moment I have been dreading—the moment when I show Linda Marilyn's third drawing, the one that includes Johnny lying stretched out on the table. I pass it over to her, and, with her hands shaking, she once more puts on her reading glasses. "Oh, Jesus," she whispers, beginning to cry. "You know who this is? You know? That's . . . that's my Johnny. Can you see what they do?"

She turns to me, to Marilyn, and to Elizabeth, holding this last drawing so that it faces the camera like the earlier ones. Though I try to comfort her, reminding her that Johnny is home now and fine, my words have no effect. She speaks urgently, with tears streaming down her face.

"I know he's fine now but what I want to know is why doesn't anybody help? Why doesn't anybody care? . . . Why doesn't anybody believe us? Do you know how many children . . . and parents . . . are being taken, and all we do is go through ridicule and nobody believes us? Can't you see, look—that's my boy—that's my boy on the table! That's my Johnny! See, *my John!*

"I don't know what they've been doing to him, and they're not just doing it to him. They're doing it to millions of people that are going through this. . . . Now I want to know why! There's money for cancer, there's money for AIDS, there's money for all these diseases— now I want to know why nobody is helping these millions of people around the world. . . .

"That's my boy on the table, and my boy is not the only little boy or little girl. . . ." She turns now to Marilyn, and once more dissolves into tears. "We were little girls once! And we were on the table just like John. I want to know why nobody's helping and why is it expected of Budd . . . why is it left up to Budd. . . .

". . . That's my little boy on the table, and now [indicating Marilyn] one of my friends—she's a young woman. She shouldn't be treated that way. Nobody should be treated that way. . . . You too, Elizabeth [pointing toward the camera], you used to be a little girl, too. . . ."

As Linda cries softly, Marilyn sits with her face buried in her hands. I can see that Elizabeth has tears in her eyes, as do I. The camera is switched off, and there is silence. I feel nothing but helpless despair.

PART SEVEN

Closing the Circle

"It Looked like a Giant Christmas Tree Ball"

As 1993 began, I realized with some bewilderment that I was facing more questions now than I had had to deal with at the beginning of 1992. If the case had inched forward in time, it had also spread out in every direction. For example, two new major participants had been uncovered—Johnny and Marilyn. And there were new issues involving Linda, such as her relationship to the bewigged woman she had mistaken for her mother and felt she should obey. In truth, it had been a long, long time since I had had the luxury of thinking of Linda as "only" an abductee who floated out of a twelfth-story window in front of witnesses.

There was the deepening mystery of the third man, whose complex role I had obviously underestimated. What was his relationship to Johnny? Why did he risk being identified in order to give the boy an expensive but puzzling gift? Why was he present in the mysterious "conference scene"? And finally there were the aliens themselves, literally floating above this ever expanding cast of humans like enigmatic puppet masters.

The next person to play an important role in the case was Cathy Turner, an ailing, middle-aged bookkeeper, a resident of Brooklyn, New York, and as unlikely a participant as any of the others. Cathy came to my attention in a very roundabout way. A friend of mine, a biology professor at a major university, had for some time been conducting a CompuServe dialogue about UFOs with Cathy's nephew, a man named Frank Turner. Although Turner had an abiding interest in UFO literature and consequently had come across a few brief articles about the Linda Cortile case, he had had little experience as an active investigator.[1]

As a resident of the New York City area, Turner was naturally curious about the Brooklyn Bridge case and had thought seriously about looking into it. Since one of his CompuServe regulars happened to belong to a trio of virulent debunkers, Turner wasn't sure whether Linda and the others were telling the truth or were merely scam artists. But in the summer of 1993, he sent the following on-line message to my professor friend; obviously this conversation with his aunt Cathy made him question his earlier suspicions:

> I was on the phone with my aunt just now and we were discussing books when she said that she read *Billy* by Whitley Strieber. . . . She says she doesn't like his books because they're too scary. I said, "Yeah, he claims to have been taken by a UFO." She said, "I saw a UFO once." "Where?" I said. "Near the Brooklyn Bridge!" Now of course my ears lit up [sic]. I was cautious not to lead her on and didn't tell her any information without first eliciting her response. Firstly, she's not at all sure of the year. She said it was years ago but had to be at least after 1988 because she remembers the car she was in and didn't have it prior to 1988. Next, she says it was early in the morning, 1–2 A.M., maybe later. She's also not sure of what bridge she was on. She at first said the Brooklyn Bridge, but when questioned further she said it could've been the Manhattan [another East River bridge, a few blocks north of the Brooklyn Bridge] or even one of the bridges going into Queens [located further north on the East River]. She's sure of the general area and the general time and year, all without a word of disclosure about the Hopkins case from me.
>
> Now for the "UFO." She says she had the "UFO" in sight for almost the entire length of the bridge. It was bright fire-engine red and spinning like a top. When I tried to get an apparent size from her she says it was smaller than the moon but much bigger than stars. Another impression was that of looking at the bottom of a top, swirling, fire, red, spinning, etc. It didn't move like a plane but hovered. It was higher than the buildings in the area and the apparent position was over the East River. She noticed the object out of her right passenger window on

her way back to Brooklyn. She never told anyone and never thought much of the incident. At first she thought "UFO" but then thought that was "crazy" and decided it was some kind of "government test."

After fielding questions from his immediately interested on-line correspondents, Turner decided to take time out to phone his aunt once more. A moment later he returned to the keyboard with a few clarifications.

. . . She's pretty adamant about seeing this thing. She changed the description from spinning to "pulsating." She said it was violently red almost like the sun. She says she looked in the papers for a few days but saw nothing, and so decided it was something more prosaic. . . . She says there may have been other colors but bright red was predominant.

Certain intriguing details immediately stood out. Her description of its unusual color—a pulsating, fiery red, but possibly having other colors—was right on the money, as was its movement—hovering, and its altitude—higher than the surrounding buildings. The time of night she reported—1:00 to 2:00 A.M. and possibly later—was close enough, as was the vicinity of the sighting—the area around the Brooklyn Bridge. In the summer of 1993, Cathy's feeling that the sighting took place after 1988 but "years ago" was also suggestive.

If all of these details were consistent with the November 1989 event, there were two other details that were not so corroborative. First, there was her assertion that she saw the UFO "out of the passenger window on the way back to Brooklyn." Had their car been on the bridge at the time, Cathy's view would have been in the wrong direction—south, toward the harbor and *away* from Linda's building and the New York skyline. Second, she described the craft's "apparent" position as over the East River. This issue became moot when Frank said later that this wording was the result of a misunderstanding in discussing the general area of the sighting. In fact, his aunt always maintained she saw the object close to a building.

Logic and topography combined to suggest a solution to the first issue. Cathy said she was on a bridge at the time, heading home to Brooklyn, but wasn't sure if it was the Brooklyn or the nearby Manhattan Bridge. But the FDR Drive in that area is an *elevated, bridgelike* structure with a ramp connecting it to the Brooklyn Bridge. If, in fact, Cathy's car was headed south down the FDR Drive, a timesaving way to get to the Brooklyn Bridge, her window view would then have faced Linda's building. If her car had been on the FDR Drive, Cathy would have passed *directly over* the part of South Street where Richard, Dan, and the third man sat in their stalled automobile.

After getting Frank's permission, my professor friend sent me his address and telephone number, so we were able to have several phone conversations before we actually met. He appeared to be a serious, cautious man who was genuinely wary of believing his aunt might actually have witnessed the November 1989 UFO. He explained that he was hesitant not because he doubted his aunt's credibility—he did not—but because it was just too disturbingly coincidental that he, an interested UFO researcher, would discover a witness to the Linda case within his own family.

I told Frank that he might very well find himself in an extremely odd situation. If the evidence were to persuade him that his aunt probably did see the November 1989 craft and her account were to be made public, the debunker with whom he had been communicating would be forced to add Frank and his aunt Cathy to the list of "conspirators" working for Linda. The Turners' plight would be amusing if it weren't so unfair and potentially damaging.

With Frank's permission I had several phone conversations with his aunt. In answer to one of my queries, she told me why she had left Brooklyn to drive to Manhattan the night she saw the object: She and a friend—"Robert"—wanted to drive around to see the Christmas decorations. She emphasized that whenever she and Robert drove to Manhattan—frequently to Chinatown—they always came very late to avoid the traffic. She was certain that the date of this particular drive was sometime after Thanksgiving, and the year, she felt, was 1988 or 1989. I noted the fact that she admitted the sighting had been *upsetting* to her—not "interesting" or "intriguing."

Since Frank and I were both very curious to see what Cathy might remember when we revisited the Brooklyn Bridge area after dark, we arranged for him to bring her to my home for a conversation and then a drive down along the East River. But ever the cautious investigator worrying about possible contamination, Frank telephoned Cathy for one last tape-recorded interview before he introduced her to me.

The transcript of this conversation begins with the following exchange:

F: I wanted to go over this thing before we go [to Hopkins's place] tonight.

C: Yeah, but you know, thinking about it makes me very nervous. Why should it make me nervous?

F: It makes me nervous, too.

Cathy then describes the object as looking "like a big Christmas ball. I know it wasn't a Christmas ball—that thing was alive! It was all glowy and shiny. What kind of tree would you have to have to have a ball that big?" She says that when she first saw it, it was right next to the windows of an apartment, like a giant Christmas-tree ornament suspended somehow at the top of the building: "Well, that's what I first looked for . . . a flagpole or anything holding it up. Nothing. Nothing. I looked all around it. Then, once I studied it, that was it. I was transfixed. I couldn't see anything else. Couldn't talk."

Cathy is a little clearer about where their car was during the sighting: "It was on some kind of highway. That's all I can say. Could've been the FDR . . . it could've been . . . I noticed the end of the bridge [where she was driving] has no poles. . . ." The FDR Drive, being a continuous elevated highway at that point, has no major structures—towers, "poles," cables, trestles, or otherwise—rising above the shallow guard walls at its sides.

She describes the red object's odd but subtle bobbing movement as resembling "a ball on water, sort of like a light airball on water." She can see it clearly " 'cause this thing illuminated everything around it." But then comes a detail of crucial importance. Cathy states that the object was *very* close to the top of an apartment building, which "looked like it had three windows. Okay. Now, the end of each window, there wasn't much wall left. So it either had to be a narrow part of a building or a narrow building."

This detail provides crucial support for the idea that Cathy witnessed at least the initial stage of Linda's November 1989 abduction. As will be remembered, the Cortile apartment is on the twelfth floor. Immediately above it is a smaller penthouse apartment, but above that, crowning the building and enclosing the water tank, is an open brick structure with *three very large vertical openings*—"windows"—that are clearly visible from the FDR Drive. If, as the other witnesses all claimed, the UFO was hovering not too far above the windows of Linda's apartment, it would inevitably have been very close to the three-windowed tower. And in the intense, radiant light that Cathy and the others described, this square, windowed tower would have been dramatically illuminated.

"When I first looked at [the object] it looked like it could be a flagpole away," she tells her nephew, "you know, those flagpoles that hang out? . . . I looked for anything hanging out of the building, holding it. Nothing. It wasn't holding on to anything. . . . It was there under its own steam. . . . It was just weird. I have no idea what it could have been [doing there]. . . . It almost looked like it was looking into the building."

Cathy also remarks that she did not see the big red object arrive at the building. "It was just there," she tells Frank. "It wasn't there, and then it was just suddenly there." This description agrees exactly with the other witnesses' accounts. Apparently no one saw it arrive. Its red glow, like an attention-getting beacon, appeared instantly; Janet Kimball, from her position on the Brooklyn Bridge, thought of a sudden explosion or fire.

At 2:00 or 3:00 A.M. on a weeknight, there is almost no traffic on the FDR Drive, so people tend to drive at or above the forty-mile-per-hour speed limit. Thirty miles an hour would seem dangerously slow at such an hour on such a stretch of elevated highway. But if one were traveling at a more normal forty or fifty miles per hour, the buildings intervening between the Drive and Linda's building would permit a good view of her apartment for only a few *seconds*. Yet Cathy claimed that she had the building and the red object in sight for enough time to roll down her window, gaze at it carefully, and even call Robert's attention to it. At fifty miles an hour that would have been impossible.

In her telephone interview with Frank she says something that suggests a solution: ". . . I do know we were going slower than usual. I'm beginning to think that maybe other cars stopped to look at it. I don't know. I don't know what was on the highway, 'cause I was only paying attention to this thing. I opened the window all the way down. I know it was cold. . . . I think it made me very nervous. Thinking about it gets me very nervous."

These words suggest to me the possibility that, like Janet Kimball's car on the Brooklyn Bridge and Richard's car down below on South Street, Cathy's car was also stopped by some kind of electromagnetic effect, and that she and her companion might have been "switched off" during the next stage of the encounter. In this context I remembered another provocative remark about the sighting early in Cathy's interview with Frank: "Once I studied it, that was it. I was transfixed. I couldn't see anything else. Couldn't talk."

Cathy's companion, Robert, has for some time been suffering from acute emotional problems dating back to traumas suffered in the Vietnam War. His testimony about that night is obviously less clear than one would wish. He will admit now only that he saw something over a building that reminded him of the rising sun. This, of course, is the same image Dan used many months earlier, and important for another reason: Far fewer than half of those who report close night-time UFO sightings describe this kind of burning red color.

Apparently Robert does not remember slowing down or stopping, nor, in fact, anything else much about that night. Cathy, a feisty, funny lady, describes their exchange to her nephew: ". . . We were going slower than usual, you got to understand, when I saw this thing. Then I said to Robert, 'LOOK!' and he said, 'Don't bother me while I'm driving!' So I said, 'Fuck you!' I looked up at the thing and that was it . . . that was the end, I didn't notice anything around it no more. . . ."

One can speculate that as the UFO suddenly turned on its lights and some kind of electromagnetic force took effect, automobiles within its range began to stop. As a corollary effect some of the nearer drivers and passengers—such as Robert and Cathy—might have been placed in a state of suspended animation.[2] Then, moments—perhaps seconds—later, *after* Linda and the aliens popped out of the building, were floated up, and the craft departed, automobile engines would spontaneously start up and consciousness would suddenly return, leaving the witnesses feeling nervous and confused every time they thought about the strange, fragmentary images they remembered.

Cathy is determined, however, to accept some kind of conventional explanation for the strange red object. She tells Frank that though she doesn't believe in "flying saucers," she does believe in "UFOs." In explaining this distinction, she says that "a UFO could be a missile from Cuba. It could be somebody shooting balls up in the sky. It's an unidentified object. I really think that the navy and, uh, the air force do tests that they don't tell us about . . . tests that go into outer space . . . NASA." When Frank tries to counter her argument by asking a question: "Why would they test something like that over [New York]?" Cathy replies that "maybe they shot off something and a piece fell off, and they don't want us to know about it . . . you know, secret tests and stuff. . . . Maybe Russia's sending something in. It definitely was a live-looking thing, full of pep inside.

"How many people saw this?" she asks, and Frank has an answer that is sad but true. "There was supposedly a lot of other people, but you know how New Yorkers are . . . they'll see somebody getting stabbed and won't say anything. You know." Cathy agrees. "Me, as big a mouth as I am, I never mentioned it to anyone. Nobody. People would say you were drunk."

Although Cathy and I had talked on the phone several times, it wasn't until early December that she, Frank, and I were able to arrange a visit. Leaning heavily on her nephew's arm, Cathy arrived shortly after dark, a big, jovial woman who moved slowly with a cane because of acute circulatory problems resulting from diabetes. Despite her obvious discomfort and rapidly failing vision—she had recently suffered what she called "a hemorrhage in the eyes"—she was alert, smiling, and very curious about our interest in her sighting. When she answered my questions she was forthright about what she had seen, and in no way did she embroider her earlier statements, nor try to exaggerate her role. She "saw what she saw" without knowing what to make of it, and that was that.

Explaining that she had already started wrapping some Christmas presents, she produced a piece of red-orange metallic gift wrap. "I brought you this," she said, "because it's as close as I can get to the color of the thing I saw." (Later, when I placed the paper next to the colored drawings of the UFO that Richard and Janet Kimball had sent me, the match was extremely close. It was yet another reason to believe that Cathy had seen the 1989 craft.)

After an initial interview in which we reviewed her recollections, the three of us got into Frank's car for the main event, a drive down to the Brooklyn Bridge area to see what she might recognize. Almost as soon as we pulled out of the parking place near my house, Cathy lit up the first of many cigarettes. I soon realized that she was not the kind of person who would easily follow doctor's orders, and despite her very precarious health, she was hopelessly addicted to nicotine. We drove east toward the FDR Drive with Cathy seated regally up front, gazing through the window and chatting amiably in a blue haze of tobacco smoke.

As we headed south on the FDR, she gestured to her right, saying that it was "over this way" that she had seen the object, not, as we had at first thought, to the right, over the East River. As we passed under the Manhattan Bridge and approached the area where the November 1989 incident occurred, Cathy pointed to a building to our immediate right. "It wasn't this close to the road," she said. "It was more like those buildings back there," waving casually toward the very block of buildings in which the Cortile family lives.

Frank slowed down as we passed their building off to our right, but I had time to notice that the rooftop tower Cathy described is completely unlit. The *only* way she could have seen it clearly enough to make out the three large "windows" would have been by artificial illumination: temporarily installed klieg lights, for example, or a helicopter's searchlight—or a fiercely glowing UFO.

I was aware that Cathy's eyesight was currently very poor and that instead of clearly seeing architectural details as we drove along, she could only generalize as to the location and building type she remembered. I was naturally concerned because in an eyewitness, visual acuity is a central issue. The matter was ultimately resolved to my satisfaction by an exchange Frank recorded in a phone conversation with his aunt regarding her eyesight at the time of the sighting.

"Sure, it was good," she responded. "I don't drive when my eyesight's bad, and I was driving [that year]."

"But your eyes started to get bad . . . when . . . the last two or three years?"

"No!" she answered with some vehemence. "My eye trouble was a sudden thing. I had a hemorrhage. It's not like they were slowly going bad. They went two years ago." Recent laser treatments administered after her hemorrhage, she said, had further damaged her sight.

We drove around the area for a while, hoping on the one hand to jog Cathy's memory, and on the other to see if she might change her story in any way. She did not, but she did add one suggestive detail. She said she had the feeling that night that there "must have been traffic stopped on the Brooklyn Bridge, or something. Maybe they were doing repair work. I sort of remember being stopped in traffic." I was well aware that at 3:00 A.M. there is virtually no traffic on the FDR, and Janet Kimball, who was actually driving on the Brooklyn Bridge, reported nothing about roadwork. Again, the evidence suggests that the reason Cathy's car stopped had something to do with the presence of the UFO. But beyond that, her reference to "traffic stopped" conjures up an image, perhaps only dimly remembered, of *other* stalled vehicles nearby.

Frank was curious to meet Linda and see her apartment from the inside, so within a few weeks of our downtown drive, I brought him to the Cortile residence. When I had first asked Linda if she wanted to meet Frank, she was hesitant. The problems she'd had with Dan, followed by what were by now a series of debunkers' attacks on her family, made her suspicious whenever she met anyone new connected with the case. But a short time after they met, Linda and her husband were quite relaxed with Frank, a casual, easygoing man, and they have been friends ever since.

Unfortunately, Frank's aunt's condition continued to deteriorate. Cathy was not a woman who would easily change her diet or follow a doctor's orders. A few months after our meeting her circulatory problems worsened and she was admitted to the hospital, and shortly thereafter it became necessary to amputate some of her toes.

I'd had only that one evening with Cathy Turner as we drove around lower Manhattan in her nephew's car. Though she'd been a valuable and highly credible witness in this complex case, she died in July 1994. I found that her death touched me in ways that had nothing to do with November 1989. She was colorful and vital, a sharp, no-nonsense woman, and her passing left me saddened.

By then I'd heard from six eyewitnesses to the red UFO on the night of November 30, 1989, six credible people in four different locations. First, and farthest away, was Erica near the FDR Drive at about Thirty-sixth Street, who saw the red UFO sometime after 3:00 A.M. Then there was Janet Kimball, who observed the UFO, Linda, and the aliens from her stalled car on the Brooklyn Bridge. And of course there were Richard, Dan, and the third man under the FDR Drive on South Street. Finally, there was Cathy *on* the FDR Drive. Though we cannot *prove* that her sighting occurred on November 30, 1989, I feel comfortable in claiming her as an eyewitness. I have no reason to doubt that she was telling the truth, and as we have seen, all of the details she recalled corroborated the testimony of the other witnesses. Therefore, she either saw the beginning of the November 1989 event—or she witnessed an entirely *different* event on a *different* date that was almost exactly like the 1989 abduction, an idea that strains credulity.

If there were six witnesses at four different locations, could there be more? After all, the sight was, in Dan's words, "like the greatest light show I'd ever seen." Even though the operation took place quickly—particularly Linda's levitation from her apartment into the ship—all the witnesses said that many people should have seen at least some aspect of it.

To violate for the moment the general chronology of my investigation, I will move ahead to a phone call I received from Linda in April 1995, dealing with yet another possible witness. Linda, who was quite distressed, told me that her son Johnny plays with two other boys who live in the same large apartment complex as the Cortile family, and she is somewhat friendly with the boys' mothers. While their sons were playing together on the afternoon of Easter Sunday, Linda invited the other women to her apartment for a drink. They chatted about this and that, and then one of the women, "Julia," mentioned that she had had some strange things happen in her apartment, things that she just couldn't explain. She said she thought perhaps they were ghosts, but whatever they were, they were very frightening. Julia said she had once seen a tall, pale figure "with cheekbones like Abraham Lincoln" standing in the doorway to her bedroom. Another time she had seen a "weird-looking thing like a deformed baby" go through her living room. As they talked, Linda realized that neither of her guests knew anything about her own experiences, which made Julia's account even more disturbing. Linda told me that she thought to herself, "What's going on in my building?"

But the worst was yet to come. After discussing Julia's ghosts, the third woman, "Francesca," added her story. The apartment where she lived with her husband and son was located in the same south end of the complex as the Cortiles' apartment. There was a major difference, however. Linda's view, as we have seen, was south, toward the Brooklyn Bridge and downtown New York; Francesca's apartment (on a lower floor) was on the other side of the hall, so her view was north, toward the inner court with its shrubbery and walkways.

She told Linda and Julia that a number of years before, she had wakened in the middle of the night, feeling terrified and afraid to look out the bedroom window. "All of a sudden," she said, "everything lit up outside like daylight. I could see every leaf." She was still so frightened the next day that she made her husband move their bed away from the window.

Linda said she tried hard to sound casual as she asked her friend when this flash of light happened. Francesca was pretty certain of the date: 1989, late November, just a few days after her husband's birthday, which was November 27.

As Linda told me about this conversation she was obviously upset. It was the same confirmation anxiety she suffered from whenever she learned of new evidence that supported the reality of her own bizarre encounters. I told Linda I wanted to speak to Francesca and Julia, but without raising the suspicion that she might have had her own UFO involvement. We talked things over and soon worked out a plan. Linda would speak to them first, saying that she had described their conversation to an old acquaintance, a man who investigated odd events like those they had described.

I called the two women and set up appointments for Tuesday, April 25. Julia was first, and though the dates of her encounters with the hollow-cheeked "Lincoln" and the strange "baby ghost" had nothing to do with Linda's November 1989 experience, the accounts were compelling and she seemed credible. After asking her a few deliberately misleading questions, I was satisfied that she knew very little about the UFO literature and that she had so far made no connection whatsoever between her ghosts and any abduction phenomenon. I strongly suspected, however, that Julia's ghosts might well turn out to be the familiar hollow-cheeked, fetuslike UFO occupants of so many other accounts.

Francesca's story was another matter. A round-faced, pretty woman in her late thirties, she seemed both innocent and vulnerable. From our preliminary conversation, I learned that she had been struggling with major domestic problems, including a rather insecure marriage. As with Julia, when I asked if I could tape-record our interview, she immediately agreed. Francesca began by giving me some background information:

I know Linda for about—well, ever since I moved here—ever since 1981. . . . She was on twelve and I was on eleven and I really know her more to talk to because our children are only a year apart and now they're attending the same school. Our building's pretty friendly. Everybody has open house on New Year's Eve, so the last few New Year's Eves—now it's a tradition that we go to Linda's house . . . so we became friends. . . . I moved [to this apartment] in June of '89.

Francesca was determined to tell me first about something she regarded as more compelling than her 1989 experience—a UFO sighting she had had in either 1981 or 1982:

Well, it's not so much what happened. It was the feeling *about* what happened? Okay, but I can only explain it in my own words. You know how they say sometimes you just see something and it gives you an odd feeling? Or you get what they call the heebie-jeebies? . . . I'm pretty open-minded, but you think you're open-minded until you see something and then you doubt yourself.

My husband was working for a meat company and he had to be at work by a quarter to six in the morning, so it was a routine that every morning I'd get up at five and make coffee. The window I had there faced the Chinatown area—it faced this big building that they called Confucius Plaza. I'd get up every morning and put coffee on and smoke a cigarette and look out the window. But that one morning something startled me because I saw what I thought was a zeppelin. But what piqued my interest was . . . whenever I see those things I always look at them . . . when I looked, it didn't have a tail—and it didn't look like anything weird like you'd see in a science fiction movie. It was just like a cigar-shaped silver object, no lights, nothing unusual. But it was obvious because it was about five in the morning and the sun was just beyond it and it wasn't moving. It was just still. This thing looked like it was about forty stories up. Here was the building—and here was this thing! And I was watching it, expecting it to pass because zeppelins can go really slow. It didn't move. It was just still. I was in awe and I must have looked at it for what seemed to me like a good full minute. And then I called my husband in the bathroom and I said, "Al, you have to see this. There's something out there. . . ." And he gave me the usual answer, you know, "You're nuts." Now I'm insisting, "You HAVE to . . . there's something there. . . ." And it just disappeared! It didn't—SHOOT—disappear. It didn't TAKE OFF—it just DISAPPEARED! Now that gave me the heebie-jeebies for, like, three days! Not that I'm expecting somebody to walk out of this, but it was just ODD and I think I would have just felt better if it just would have took off. It just DISAPPEARED. . . .

Her account made me wonder if there wasn't more to her sighting that she was not consciously remembering, since a number of other things she mentioned that day are familiar symptoms that abductees frequently report. Without commenting on her sighting, however, I moved on to her 1989 experience and asked her to tell me her conversation with Julia and Linda about the light out her window.

F: . . . Julia and I have become very close friends—I think I'm one of three people she told about her ghost, and we were talking about it at Linda's. . . . "Abe Lincoln" didn't bother me. The "baby thing" she saw did bother me and when I'm in her house . . .

B: Why? Why do you think the one did and the other didn't?

F: Because . . . the creature that she said she saw—to me it was just eerie because it seemed like a hybrid of some sort 'cause she said it reminded her of a deformed baby. It reminded me of, like when you read about babies born with [deformed faces and heads]. It just gave me an eerie feeling . . . because it was something that wasn't right. And when I sit in her house I sit against this wall: I don't want to see it. I don't want to see Abe Lincoln either. Because sometimes when you're in her house, and I don't think it's because it preys on your mind, you feel like you're not alone. And it's not anything eerie or something you're gonna see in the movies, you just feel . . . But she's very sensible. We felt comfortable talking about it. . . . What we were talking about were eerie feelings and I had remembered when I was sleeping at night and my head was facing the window . . . I'll show you the bedroom—how it's situated.

B: Okay.

F: . . . and I woke up one night and I didn't know if it was a flash of light that woke me up but it was LIGHT that woke me up. When I glanced to look out the window, the courtyard was lit—not the floodlight—

not like a flashlight; it was LIGHT—like I thought maybe it was morning? It was bright—IT WAS BRIGHT!

B: I take it you looked at a clock to see what time it was?

F: No, I didn't. I have to show you how everything was situated, but when I saw the light, I didn't know if the noise woke me up first or it was the light, but I woke up with a very bad feeling. I just—I'm nosy but a little voice was going "Don't look out the window." I did not want to look out the window.

　. . . There was something saying to me, "Don't look out the window. . . ." And I woke up my husband and I told him, "Get up. I see something out the window."

B: . . . And it's still bright?

F: It's still bright. Now, at that point I had to turn him this way to wake him up. When I had gotten him awake, I said, "Al, there's something out the window. I saw something." And by the time he turned and got me calm, this is all like in two or three minutes, it's dark outside. And he said to me, "It's dark outside." And I said, "No, no, no. It was LIGHT outside! It was LIGHT . . . !"

B: What kind of noise did you hear?

F: It's an airplane noise, like a jet plane, it has like a higher-pitched noise, and it lasts longer. That gives me very bad heebie-jeebies. I literally will get palpitations from that if I'm up or alone. And I know it sounds crazy but for the longest of time I couldn't take that noise. I'd say at least since I'm twenty years old. That noise drives me insane and it will give me an anxiety attack. . . . I don't know why. I've never been on a plane. . . .

B: Back to when Al looks up and doesn't see anything . . .

F: Nothing, it was dark.

B: Did you look at the clock? It could have been dawn.

F: No. When I saw the light, I had a very bad feeling. . . . It was a very bad feeling and I don't want to look out the window. I knew that if I looked, I would have seen something I didn't want to see.

B: What do you think you would have seen?

F: I really think I would have seen some type of an aircraft or something that I didn't want to see. Nothing in a supernatural, ghost-type thing—that wasn't even entering my mind. I really thought I was going to see—when you use the term "UFO" so lightly, but that's what I anticipated if I looked out.

B: Where would it have been?

F: Oh, I had no idea. I had the impression that if I would have looked out the window and strained to look up I would have seen something . . . because of how the courtyard was light. But I wasn't even attempting to do that.

B: All right. Now, let's try and figure out when this was.

F: Well, I put it toward November of '89 . . . because my husband and I were separated . . . and he had come home October 22 of '89 and we were so busy rendezvousing at that point—so we didn't move the room around till then, but he had gotten used to sleeping near a window and that's why we had this argument, because I don't like to have my headboard near a window. And we have a radiator there and I kept telling him, when the steam comes up, one of us is going to sweat and then we're going to get a draft, but he pushed the bed toward the window. Now I'm sure it wasn't there for a long time— especially after this I wanted the bed back. His birthday is November 27, so my house was in order for his birthday, so I know it [the bed] was still moved. So this had to happen, like, around the end of November, somewhere between the middle to the end of November. . . . It might have been right after his birthday. [In other words, on November 28, 29, or 30, 1989]

Next, I was interested in finding out just exactly how long Francesca thought the bright light stayed on, illuminating the courtyard.

F: I think it had to be at least a whole minute, because, whatever woke me up, woke me up . . . and then I saw the light, and then I got that bad feeling . . . so I really thought about it for—it would seem to me a while—'cause I was thinking why don't I want to look out the window? What is this? And then I got scared.

B: Why do you think you didn't want to look out the window?

F: I don't know. I really think I didn't want to see whatever was there. It was just something in me saying, "You don't want to know what's out there." And I don't get spooked easily. . . .

B: Francesca, I'm curious what you might have read about, ghosts, UFOs . . .

F: Nothing. The closest I've come to UFOs was I saw *Close Encounters.* I've seen *E.T.* Ummm—ghosts, I don't really know.

. . . I think like it's very presumptuous to think we're the only ones here. But I never really thought I would see anything scary, because I believe in the premise like it says in the Bible: God made man in his own image. So I always assumed that if I would see anything it would basically look something like us, you know—a head, two arms, two legs—or maybe look exactly like us. Maybe it's silly, but I figure God made everything and if he made everything in his image, then we must all basically have the same stuff!

And we keep sending stuff up there and I figure, in a way, they should send something down here. You know, I would like to see like an E.T. that I could pat on the head or something. But that's the movies. That's why I couldn't understand why I had that feeling like, "You don't want to know." Everybody has a fear of the unknown, but I don't have a horrific fear, like a twilight zone . . . like, oh, my God, you're gonna see a man with an eyeball in the middle of his head! I don't have *that.* It's just, I don't know, like a little voice telling me, "Don't look out the window. You don't want to see what's over there." And that's what made me feel funny. . . . I think the *feeling* was more overwhelming than the seeing. It's not *usual* for me to feel that way.

I asked Francesca if she had ever talked to anyone besides Julia and Linda about her experience with the light in the courtyard, and she said there was only one woman friend she had mentioned it to. "You wouldn't talk to anybody around here about something like that," she added. "They would think that you're nuts. . . ."

In probing the possibility that Francesca may have had abduction experiences, I asked her about any recurring childhood dreams or phobias, other than her reaction to the high-pitched airplane sound that drivers her "crazy."

"I have my little idiosyncracies. . . . I have to have the closet doors closed," she replied. "Other than that, no. As a matter of fact, the only thing that used to scare me as a child, that I didn't like, is clowns. I just never liked any kind of clowns. I think I didn't like anything staring at me. And I just don't like clown faces. Till today, I don't like clowns. Julia has clowns all over and I don't like them. I just never liked them."[3]

When I asked about her reactions to medical procedures, Francesca mentioned another almost crippling phobia. "I had a big fear of anaesthesia, almost to the point where it cost me my son Patrick. Because with him I needed a C-section, and I refused to let them put me under! It really got to the point where they had to say, you're going to lose the baby, and I said, I don't care. I would not let them do it . . . and they had given me a spinal at the time."

I made no further arrangements to meet with Francesca, but before I left I gave her my card and asked her to call if she wanted to talk again about her experiences. To date I have not heard from her, although I strongly suspect that her particular set of phobias, fears, and odd experiences is symptomatic of buried abduction recollections. Admittedly, this is only a guess. One must always bear in mind that each of these symptoms, taken alone, may well have other, more prosaic causes.

And so what was I to make of Francesca's testimony? First, there was absolutely no reason to doubt her sincerity or truthfulness. She seemed genuinely disturbed by her various experiences and unaware of the subtleties of the UFO case material. Surely, anyone wanting to invent a UFO encounter could come up with something more compelling than Francesca's fragmentary accounts.

With regard to the events of November 30, 1989, she was definitely in the right place at the right time. If she was awakened—how? why?—at the time the UFO shined its bluish white beam downward, she might have recognized the levitating light as something familiar she did not want to see. She described it as "hazy," just as Linda had many months before. Again, if we accept the truthfulness of Francesca's basic account, we have to assume that the date she has given— one of the three last days in November—points to the night of Linda's abduction. To my knowledge, no one else in or around the neighborhood reported such a sight at any other time.

It might be helpful to try to construct a hypothetical time line to make sense of the various witnesses' testimony. First, the UFO arrives dark and unseen at around 3:00 A.M., the aliens enter Linda's apartment unperceived, and begin the abduction. Meanwhile an electromagnetic effect slows and finally stops Richard's car on South Street, Janet's car on the Brooklyn Bridge, and, perhaps a moment later, Cathy's car on the FDR Drive. Other vehicles in the vicinity are also affected. Richard, Dan, and the third man, sitting in their car, and Janet Kimball, sitting in her car on the bridge, suddenly and simultaneously see the UFO brighten into a burning red. Cathy and Robert also coast into sight of it, but here their memory ends as they are "switched off," as are other occupants of other cars nearby. This is all they will see this night.

Perhaps while it has been hovering above the building, the UFO has been making a soft but high-pitched engine sound. Although this hum is too quiet for the other witnesses to hear inside their automobiles, it might be just loud enough—and familiar enough—to disturb Francesca, sleeping a few floors below. As she begins to stir, the UFO's fiery red color fades and the enormously bright, bluish white beam suddenly illuminates the ground below. This change in the light is observed by Janet and the men on South Street. Within seconds, Linda and the aliens roll out of the apartment window, straighten out, and are levitated up into the craft in full view of the stunned witnesses. Meanwhile Francesca has awakened and sees the intensely bright light illuminating the courtyard, but she is too frightened to look up to discover its source.

In a moment the bluish white light blinks off, and for Francesca, all is dark again. The fiery glow in the UFO's superstructure immediately reappears as the craft dives toward the three men under the FDR Drive. They are scooped up in seconds and the UFO gains altitude, flying over the Brooklyn Bridge, where it is observed as a small, distant red disk by Erica from her vantage point at the East River near Thirty-sixth Street.

Although the distance was great, Erica alone in her location uptown near the East River was in a position to watch its continuous path as it flew away. Janet Kimball's view of it was stopped by a feature of the Brooklyn Bridge—a wide pedestrian walkway above the roadbed. Cathy and Robert were still in their car on the FDR Drive in a state of suspended animation, and saw nothing. Francesca lay trembling in her bed, afraid to look out the window from which she would not have been able to see the UFO anyway, since it flew southeast and her apartment windows faced north. And neither Richard, Dan, nor the third man could see it depart for the best of reasons: They were inside it, along with Linda.

Did things really happen this way? Does this chronology present a reasonable accounting of the various witnesses' testimony? The answer to the first question is "not necessarily," but I believe we can answer "yes" to the second. We will never know *exactly* how things unfolded in the minute or so that the encounter lasted. But one thing is clear: When the personal recollections of all of these credible witnesses are put together, they form a consistent, interlocking, and harmonious account of an unthinkable event. In a court of law, if this many credible men and women presented such intricately corroborative eyewitness testimony against earthly criminals caught in the act, the defense attorneys might well suggest a guilty plea.

C | H | A | P | T | E | R

31

Expressways and Blind Alleys

Like many other UFO investigations, the Brooklyn Bridge case has had its share of serendipitous discoveries, disappointing dead ends, and sudden breakthroughs. At the same time, there are enormous differences between this complex story and any other UFO abduction case I have ever heard of. In reviewing my findings, it may be helpful to consider it from two perspectives: Quantitatively, no other abduction investigation I know of has had the sheer *number* of important revelations. None since the original Betty and Barney Hill case has disclosed new patterns as crucially significant as the Mickey–Baby Ann phenomenon and the alien co-option of humans.[1] And from the point of view of evidence supporting the physical reality of UFO abductions, none had ever involved such a large number of credible witness-participants.

Looking at the Brooklyn Bridge abduction case qualitatively, it is uniquely important, first, because of its *eyewitness* accounts of three aliens and an abductee floating twelve stories above the ground in a blazing blue-white light. Almost as important is the inference that the aliens intended this spectacle to be seen, apparently for the benefit of an important political figure. If so, this would mark the first time in the history of the UFO phenomenon that the crafts' occupants appeared to be trying to affect earthly politics by a selective demonstration of both their power and their presumed interest in our ecosystems.

But along with the surprising breakthroughs, there have also been a number of disappointments and blind alleys. For example, I originally hoped that some of the workers employed by the *New York Post* might have witnessed at least part of the November 1989 incident. Since the *Post's* South Street home office is very close to the Cortile apartment, this was not an idle hope. In my rosiest view, I imagined lines of trucks and busy newspaper loaders stopping in their tracks to view the fiery red UFO. I learned, however, that the newspapers are loaded in a roofed-over garage. The doorway to this closed loading dock faces *south*, so no one casually glancing out would have been able to see Linda's building. And as I also discovered, the area is hardly a sea of activity at 3:00 A.M. Although the *Post* then owned about forty-five trucks operating more or less around the clock, I was told that at any given time most of them were either on the road or in a West Side garage. This was just one lead among many others that didn't pan out.

Somewhere between success and failure, there is the complex issue of the sand samples Richard sent me. I hoped, first of all, to find out where the sand might have come from, and thus to understand where Linda and the three men had been taken. Was it a tropical beach? Florida, perhaps? Richard and Linda both described the temperature as comfortable enough—Richard thought it might have been in the seventies. However, Matthew Moniz, a researcher at a distinguished New England laboratory, informed me that the sand's relatively low percentage of calcium carbonate meant that it had not come from a tropical, shell-strewn beach, yet no precise location has ever been posited.

So far, the two sets of sand samples have been studied at three institutions: by Roger J. Smid, a laboratory assistant to Dr. Vernon Hodge in the Department of Chemistry at the University of Nevada; by "Samuel," a biologist friend of mine who for professional reasons wishes to remain anonymous, at a midwestern university; and by a team of researchers working on their own time at a large, very well equipped Massachusetts laboratory. To no one's surprise, the sand is mostly made up of silicon, with trace metals such as silver, iron, and aluminum. However, one of the more interesting findings in the Nevada report has to do with a feature found only in the processed sample—the sand that Richard took from the machine inside the UFO. Roger Smid reports, "The [refined] sample appeared to have a 'milky coating' on all the crystals. . . . Luster was a dull milky finish. . . . The

Biotites appeared to be enhanced (greenish to black)." Smid went on to say that "trace analysis has shown a presence of Rare Earths . . . which would indicate an overall structure of Monazite sands. . . . The Gallium present is interesting from the standpoint that Gallium residue or globules containing Zinc, Indium and Lead are found in smelting furnace residue. Higher traces than normal were found."

Since I presented these sand samples to the University of Nevada "blind"—giving almost no information about their origin or presumed significance—Roger Smid had been unable to offer much specific guidance outside the bare facts in his report. I have no idea what to make of these findings, beyond the fact that there are subtle differences between the sand Richard found in his shoes and the "refined sand" he took out of the machine. What caused these changes? Did the refinement process add or remove something? What were the aliens looking for? Did they use some arcane kind of smelting technique that produced the milky coating?

As part of his investigation, my friend Samuel took a series of electron microscope photographs of the two sets of samples that showed the contrasting size of the sand grains in each. "No major differences could be seen looking at the 'bulk,' " he wrote, " 'A' [the refined sample] would appear to be a 'cracked' version of 'B' [the raw sample]." The differences in percentages of the various elements present in the two samples were negligible; for example, the refined sand contained less barium and silver but *more* lead and tin than the raw sample. It would seem that something affected the raw sand when it passed through the aliens' machine beyond the mere pulverizing of the grains.

But what? And why? The investigation is still very much alive, as scientists try to imagine what sort of experiments might yield further information. As one researcher put it, "Now we're trying to figure out what we should be testing the samples *for*."

And as if there were some kind of evenhanded justice being meted out to investigators such as myself, frustration in one area was often met by a flood of new information in another. In early August 1993, shortly after the death of Cathy Turner, I received what to this point stands as a final letter from Richard. In it he provided a great deal of new information about two areas I had carefully avoided: the destination of their official motorcade on November 30, 1989, and the subsequent reaction in government and intelligence/security circles to the UFO sighting. The central reason I have steered clear of these sensitive intelligence/security issues is to spare Richard the worry that I may somehow cause him to become, in his phrase, "an official problem." He always passed information on to me gradually, in small increments. From the beginning he seemed to be testing my willingness to respect his confidentiality. The more he felt he could trust me, the more information he would share, and in this latest packet he enclosed copies of some highly confidential letters and documents. Though he had blacked out most of the names and addresses, he asked me to not make this material public. I'm honoring his request in exchange for what I take to be his implicit promise to step forward one day as soon as feasible—perhaps after his retirement—to describe publicly what happened to him, to Dan, and to the third man on November 30, 1989.

But there is a second reason I have hesitated to relate certain details about the security/intelligence side of this saga. When Richard and Dan (in his earliest letters) wrote about their *personal* experiences with the UFO phenomenon, I trusted them because I had many ways to check their veracity: through the testimony of other witnesses, such as Janet Kimball or Linda or Cathy Turner; through my knowledge of obscure abduction patterns known only to a few researchers; through detailed personal information I was privy to about the third man; and so forth.

But whenever the two agents chose to inform me about intelligence/security issues, I remained cautious. Over the years I had read a bit about the rules of their craft, so I was aware that disinformation, cover stories, and outright dissimulation are considered legitimate tactical methods. I also remember that in their first letter to me they presented themselves as undercover police officers—a natural cover story of temporary usefulness. It was not until they decided to tell me about the presence of the third man that they admitted this earlier deception.

Since Richard clearly specified in this last letter which issues were confidential and which were not, I feel free to discuss some of the material he sent me. However, I will stay well within the limits he has set for a reason of my own: I still cannot automatically assume that he is acting with total independence and truthfulness to me *on high-level, internal-security matters*. It is at least plausible that, as a good soldier in his intelligence agency, Richard might be required to plant a red herring or two in the interest—mistaken or not—of national security.

The first new piece of information Richard sent me—and one I see every reason to believe—has to do with the destination of their small motorcade on November 30, 1989. In Dan's second letter to me, dated April 10, 1991, he wrote that "our orders were to bring this third party safely to the meeting and then safely to the heliport, way downtown afterwards. From there the three of us were to board a helicopter. . . ."

One detail about the motorcade's route had already been explained to me. I had been curious as to why the official cars were traveling on the lower road—South Street, with all its traffic lights—rather than on the FDR Drive, a virtual expressway by comparison. Dan wrote that their cars had been on the FDR Drive, but they exited onto South Street. In talking to Secret Service personnel I learned the reason. Wherever possible, for security reasons motorcades avoid using *elevated* expressways, especially those with a limited number of exits. The FDR Drive becomes a freestanding elevated highway at the point where Richard's car and the others turned onto the lower road.

As to their final destination, my initial guess was that Dan must be referring to the Wall Street Heliport, located just off South Street a number of blocks below the Brooklyn Bridge area. Subsequent investigation revealed a few contradictory pieces of information about this Wall Street facility. I learned that it doesn't operate late at night, but I also learned that the president and other VIPs occasionally use this heliport. Presumably it could have been used at 3:00 A.M. under special circumstances.

Richard's newest letter resolved the matter. He wrote that their motorcade was headed south to the tip of Manhattan, from whence they would take the ferry to *Governors Island,* a secure, authorized-personnel-only complex currently operated by the U.S. Coast Guard.

Governors Island lies a very short distance from the southernmost part of Manhattan in New York Harbor. It is a former army base and has its own heliport; significantly, it was the site of the 1988 summit meeting between Presidents Reagan and Gorbachev, and President-elect Bush. If the third man and other political-diplomatic VIPs had been meeting uptown, perhaps at the UN, and then had to fly to another location by helicopter, Governors Island would have been the natural venue.

Richard had said in earlier letters, and he reiterated it here, that in the motorcade that night there were several important American government officials, the third man, representatives of one or two foreign governments, and an appropriate security detail. I wondered what the gathering might have been about and who could have been present. My perusal, via library microfilm, of the *New York Times* for the days immediately preceding November 30 revealed an international mood of near crisis as a result of the approaching breakdown of the once monolithic Communist bloc. In a banner headline in its November 11 edition, the *Times* says, JOYOUS EAST GERMANS POUR

THROUGH [Berlin] WALL; PARTY PLEDGES FREEDOMS AND WEST EXULTS. On November 14, President Gorbachev appealed to the United States for restraint "in response to the tumultuous changes in Eastern Europe," and on November 28, millions of Czechs demanding their freedom and independence from the Soviet Union brought the country to a standstill by means of a general strike.

On November 30, 1989, the day of Linda's abduction, President Bush left Washington for Malta and his first summit meeting with President Gorbachev, while Gorbachev, en route, met Pope John Paul II for another historic first. Truly, international politics was aboil.

The only important foreign official whom the *Times* reported as being in New York City during the last few days of November was Lech Walesa, who, as leader of Poland's Solidarity movement, was a prime force for Polish independence and the country's future president. It is common knowledge that in times of crisis there are many secret diplomatic meetings of which not even the press is aware, as well as other not-so-secret but still off-the-record high-level conclaves. So it is not too daring to speculate that such a late-night meeting took place in New York with an important group of participants— including, perhaps, Lech Walesa—an event dramatically upstaged in the early hours of that morning near the Brooklyn Bridge. One wonders how these leaders would have reacted, and to whom would they report what they saw?

What, exactly, *did* the passengers in cars other than Richard's see when their engines died as they drove along South Street? If, as he hinted in his recent letter, there were as many as five cars in the procession, any vehicles *north* of Richard's car might have had their view of Linda's apartment blocked by the *New York Post* building. We must also consider the possibility that some or all of the occupants of the other official vehicles might have been "switched off" during the minute or so of the abduction, and therefore might have remembered nothing, as had been my suspicion in the case of Cathy Turner.

There is evidence suggesting that some of the people in the official procession were, in fact, placed into this strange state of suspended animation. Without breaking my vow of confidentiality to Richard regarding official matters, I will quote very briefly from two of the letters he sent me—*personal*, unofficial letters he received from other security agents who were present that night.

In the first letter, stamped with the date December 18, 1989, the writer says, "I keep hearing about what happened to us the morning of 30 November 1989 after our vehicles went dead, but for the life of me I can't remember anything after that. All I know is that the vehicle

I was in simply died, and so did everyone else's. I must have blanked out for some odd reason. . . . But I can tell you one thing, at about an hour later, around 0400–0420, when I came to, [deleted in original] was giving me mouth-to-mouth because he thought I'd stopped breathing."

Another friend of Richard's writes, in a letter dated December 21, 1989, ". . . I honestly don't know what else to say. At least I know we haven't lost our minds, have we? I've always known about stuff like this, but I never thought it could happen to me. . . .

"Thinking about it now and looking back, I'm not sure if I can handle the agency's sly remarks and the flashbacks (if that's what they are), all at the same time. . . ." This writer raises questions about the whereabouts of their backup team, an issue I had wondered about myself and that Richard alludes to in his accompanying letter. (His interesting but cryptic comments about the backup team naturally fall under his proscription against revealing security matters.)

Unlike the first writer, this second correspondent glimpsed Linda, the aliens, and the UFO, at least for a moment, and in his letter to Richard, he wondered how "the young woman could have survived that powerful magnetic hold. We felt it ourselves from two to three city blocks away."

One of the debunkers' basic attacks on the validity of this case and the credibility of its many witnesses has to do with a *theory* that such a thing couldn't happen without everyone knowing about it, that the press would have published the story, and that everyone would be talking about it.

History shows that cover-ups *can* be maintained and official secrets *can* be kept for years or even decades, most famously in the case of the Manhattan Project to build an atomic bomb. The case of the "Ultra Secret" is possibly even more remarkable. Early in World War II, the British developed a sophisticated decoding machine that enabled them to read virtually all messages sent by Hitler and his high command to German troops in the field. On the Allied side, literally thousands of civilian and military personnel, from privates to publicity-hungry generals, knew about Ultra and handled these top-secret messages daily, from Eisenhower's headquarters all the way down to scores of headquarters at corps and division levels. Because the Allied governments were afraid that after the war ended a resurgent German military would claim that they had been defeated solely by this "unfair" means, a directive went out that ordered the secret to be kept for a period of twenty years. Until the chief of Ultra, F. W. Winterbotham, revealed the truth in 1974, apparently none of these thousands of men and women revealed what *Time* called "the best-kept military secret of all time."

Outside the parameters of the kind of military discipline that Richard and most of the others were subject to, civilian witnesses can also be kept quiet. The fear of ridicule combined with the threat of social ostracism and job loss is an almost foolproof way to keep witnesses from talking. For example, in at least three cases I am aware of, police officers have been fired for taking UFO reports seriously, and I have worked with one highly experienced pilot for a major airline who lost his job in similar circumstances. Without suggesting that there are any exceptions, one well-known debunker has publicly libeled the often traumatized people who report abduction experiences as nothing more than "little nobodies trying to get on TV." A widely watched 1996 PBS science program dealing with the UFO abduction phenomenon presented an array of ill-informed "experts" who implied that *anyone* reporting such an experience is either mentally ill or unable to tell fantasy from reality. Sadly, in our easily frightened culture this kind of intimidation and character-assassination-in-advance really works.

In my twenty years of research in this field, I have been approached by a number of military people, a NASA scientist, psychiatrists, psychologists, doctors, well-known people in the entertainment industry, professionals of all kinds, and just plain folk from at least fifteen countries, all of whom related their personal abduction accounts to me with varying degrees of anguish. All of them demanded confidentiality. Of the more than five hundred men and women I have personally worked with, fewer than fifteen have been willing to come forward publicly, using their names and discussing their cases with representatives of the media.

So it is not surprising to me that of the many participants I have dealt with in this case, none of them—*none*—ever reported what they had seen to the news media, to the police, or to any government or military agency. And even now, years later, most will not allow me to include their full names on these pages. Under the circumstances, who can blame them?

C H A P T E R

32

The Meeting at O'Hare

Richard's packet of papers contained one personal letter that I found especially moving. In addition to its tone of real but subdued emotion, it helped to fill in one of the blanks in this case. It was a letter Richard had received almost a year before from the third man.

It is typed on a sheet of eight-by-ten-inch typewriter paper without a letterhead and dated "18 September 1992" in the official military or European style.

> *Dear Richie,*
>
> *I've confronted the precious little boy named John. His small round face reminded me of when I was a boy. . . . He's a bright and strong-willed child. John had a special gleam in his blue eyes, after all, because he was carrying out an important mission (as young boys do) to the diner on the corner street.*
>
> *I took a foolish risk and presented him with a gift I had promised him in a presumed dream weeks ago. I saw admiration in his face as he was so eager to take it. But he couldn't. With John's help we found a way to enable him to keep the gift. Richie, he didn't know me. The boy most likely thought I was a dangerous child snatcher, but at that moment I would have liked to snatch him up to embrace him. Of course, under the circumstances I held myself because that embrace wasn't*

possible. Consequently our little meeting was extremely amus-
ing but heartbreaking at the same time.

Richie, I don't know if I am having dreams relating to this
phenomenon or if I'm experiencing flashbacks again, but in my
sleep. I'm feeling so alone and I've grown tired. . . . I want so
much to get away from it. Therefore, I have come to a decision.
I shall not seek out help regarding this phenomenon, nor shall I
ever speak of it ever again, not even with you.

Please accept, Richie, my fond regards. Keep in touch with
me and remain in good health.

The first thing I did with this letter was to try to check its validity by comparing it with the other two letters I had in my possession from the third man. Everything was the same—the format of the date, the spacing between paragraphs, the indentations at the beginning of each paragraph, and even the familiar presence of Briticisms, such as "I shall" and the strained, stiff-upper-lip use of the adjective "amusing."

I was aware that for the past year or so the third man had been living in Europe. It now became crucially important to find out if he had visited the United States during the month of September 1992, when Johnny remembered seeing the "old man with tinted glasses" who had given him the beautiful diving helmet.

In November 1993 I received a phone call out of the blue from a reporter friend of mine with a strong interest in the UFO phenomenon. (Because of my desire to keep the name of the third man confidential, I cannot identify certain newsmen and media sources in the following paragraphs since doing so would lead to his identification.) The reporter knew about the Linda case from my presentation at the MUFON Symposium in Albuquerque the previous summer and from articles that I'd published about it as well as from attacks launched by the handful of determined debunkers. He had formed an opinion as to the identity of the third man and, as an accredited reporter with a national news agency, he'd set up an appointment with him at Chicago's O'Hare Airport on November 12. Arriving in Chicago from Europe on his way to a southern destination, the third man would have a layover at O'Hare for several hours. The reporter had scheduled the interview ostensibly to discuss international questions, particularly problems in the former Yugoslavia. But he told me that he intended at some point to ask the third man outright if he had been in that car near the Brooklyn Bridge on November 30, 1989. He was determined to force him into either an admission or a denial.

My immediate reaction was to ask that he not lead off with such a baldly confrontational question. Based upon what the third man had written to me, I had no doubt that he would immediately deny any knowledge of the November 1989 event and we would have learned nothing. I suggested, instead, that the reporter ease into the subject gradually with more general questions. How did the third man think government should deal with UFO reports—should they be taken seriously? Did *he* take such accounts seriously? Only after he had exhausted these more theoretical issues should he turn to the more confrontational questions about the events of November 1989. After a discussion, I decided that the most efficacious plan was to fly to O'Hare myself to join the reporter for the interview.

Under these circumstances, I realized that I was running the risk of incurring the third man's anger because, in arriving with a *reporter*, I could be seen as deliberately creating a situation of entrapment. Also, I thought it unlikely, in the context of an interview, that I would be able to speak to him privately. But at any rate I would be able to meet him, to observe him under questioning, and at the least to present him with a package of material on the case. I knew that what he *didn't* say during the later, more confrontational part of the interview, could prove as important as what he *did* say.

Ever since my 1992 presentations at the MIT Conference and the MUFON Symposium, rumors had been passed back and forth about the third man's identity, and various names had been proposed. As a matter of policy I had neither confirmed nor denied any of the rumors (beyond admitting, tongue in cheek, that the third man was *not* Margaret Thatcher). It has always been my hope that he would come forward voluntarily and describe what happened, even though his letter to me said that, for the present, he could not do so. For moral *and* practical reasons I had no desire to try to "out" someone who had told me he would automatically deny his role if he were named publicly. Also, I had no way to gauge what kind of pressure he might be under from government or intelligence community sources. No one, I believe, had the right to make such a portentous decision *for* him, certainly not I. The issue of his telling the truth was between him and his conscience.

Since speculation as to the identity of the third man had been published several times, I knew that he was aware he had been named publicly in some places, mainly by debunkers seeking his denial in order to discredit all of the other witnesses in the case. I also knew that a journalist had recently sent him a fax asking for an admission or a denial and that his request had gone unanswered. A month later he was sent a second fax with the warning that if he declined to answer with a denial, it would be assumed that he was admitting he had been present on November 30, 1989. He declined to reply to this fax, too. A tabloid newspaper had even printed the third man's photograph in a garbled, speculative article about the case. Consequently, I believed that he must surely be aware of the speculation surrounding him.

There was, of course, the major problem I have alluded to: I would be meeting the third man in the company of a news-service reporter, the kind of person I assumed he would least want to know about his connection with the UFO phenomenon. But since this was the only way I had to approach him, I would simply hope for the best.

The evening before my flight to Chicago I decided to prepare a package for the third man. I thought about the powerful emotional force of Linda's and Marilyn's taped discussion of the "conference scene" in which they both described the third man in his double-breasted blue-and-white-striped pajamas looking down at Johnny as he lay helpless on the table. I remembered Linda's bitter, angry tears when she cried out, "That's my little boy on that table! Do you see what they do?" A copy of that videotape would go into my package.

I also decided to include a copy of the tape in which Johnny describes receiving the gift of the helmet, although I was a little nervous about his describing the man in the black car as "very old . . . he looked like he was in his eighties." Outweighing that were the sequences in which Johnny identifies the third man from my collection of photographs, and another in which he says that if he hadn't been afraid of being kidnapped he would have given the man a "thank-you hug."

At my request, Johnny penned a thank-you note for his gift:

"Dear Poppi," he wrote, "Thank you very much for the diver's helmet. When I look at it I think of you." Below was a little drawing of himself looking at the diving helmet and thinking, via a balloon, "Poppi." Below, he wrote, "Did you know my grandfather in Italy died before I was born. This means there has been room in my life for a grandfather. Someone like you!! I hope you feel the same way. I would like to give you a hug, but I can't because you are not here with me. I hope I can see you again." The note is signed, "Love, John," with a row of Xs underneath. That, too, went into the package, along with a personal letter from Linda imploring him to make a public statement about his UFO experience, an explanatory letter from me about my reason for coming to Chicago to meet him, and copies of my previous articles about the case.[1] Sealing everything in a bulky nine-by-twelve-inch padded envelope, I left for O'Hare Airport, wondering just how the coming scene would play out.

In Chicago, I met my reporter friend at the appointed place and after asking directions, we set off for the VIP lounge where he had arranged to meet the third man. I wondered about the problem of a possible security detail, and since I was coming in completely unannounced and without credentials, I was concerned that I might be barred at the last minute. In these terrorist times airport security is tight. As I carried the parcel I had brought for the third man, I heard an unsettling announcement that was being broadcast at regular intervals: "For security reasons passengers should never accept packages or gifts from unknown persons."

Walking slightly behind my reporter friend so as not to be immediately seen by the third man, I entered an airline's VIP lounge, a quiet place with deep, luxurious seating and a discreet bar. A dozen or so people waited for their connecting flights, and I immediately spotted the third man sitting with his wife, reading. My nervousness abated somewhat when I saw no sign of a security detail.

Walking over, the reporter introduced himself and then said, "This is my friend, Budd Hopkins, a colleague from New York." I looked at the third man whose passive, phlegmatic expression registered no change. He asked no questions about me—who I was or why I was there—and turned to the reporter, who began talking about finding a more private place for the proposed interview. Nervously, I handed the third man my bulging package. "Sir, this is some material I think you'll find interesting," I told him. With the warnings about not taking packages from strangers fresh in my memory, and with the awareness that the third man must have been thoroughly briefed by previous security details about the danger of hidden explosives and letter bombs, I watched to see what he did with my suspicious-looking parcel. Without a break, he continued speaking with the reporter while unobtrusively unzipping a small carry-on suitcase. He quickly tucked the package inside and closed the case.

Not a word was directed to me, not a question about the package, what might be in it or why I gave it to him—the kinds of questions anyone would raise at an airport when a total stranger hands one a package. It crossed my mind that I would never accept something like this from a stranger at an airport, or at any other place for that matter, without asking at least a few questions. And unlike the third man, I have never been the target of terrorist threats. His behavior allowed only one sensible interpretation: that I was *not* a stranger, that he knew who I was, trusted me, and was curious as to what I had given him, though he was not about to say anything in the reporter's presence.

He excused himself to his wife, and the three of us settled down in a nearby alcove for the interview. The reporter turned on his tape recorder and, microphone in hand, began asking about Bosnia and related international problems. I was sitting no more than three feet from the third man and watched him carefully. He answered each of the reporter's questions at interminable length and in something of a soporific drone. Speaking precisely and with a light accent, he spun out very long, complex sentences that tended to run into one another. I began to think that he was stalling for time.

At last the reporter managed to break in and change the subject. He started by saying that "over the years many people around the world have reported UFO sightings. . . ." The third man's gaze was steady as he listened; his hands were lying still in his lap, his fingers intertwined, but when he heard the term "UFO," his hands involuntarily lifted a few inches, his wrists pressed forward, and his knuckles cracked resoundingly. This nervous movement was the only thing that suggested a reaction to the reporter's question about whether the governments of the world or the UN should take notice of sighting reports and do something about them. The third man answered by subtly changing the subject to issues of radar and the problem of Iraq's invasion of Kuwait. He continued on this tack, his face expressionless, his voice a slow, steady murmur.

The reporter broke in again and tried to return to the subject of UFOs. Again, and with amazing skill at avoidance, the third man managed to segue into general talk about internal problems and abstract issues of governmental authority, all with no mention of UFOs. Desperate, his voice rising a bit, the reporter asked, "Have you thought about the so-called UFO phenomena? Spaceships from other planets? The phrase *unidentified flying objects?* Sir, what does that mean to you?"

Again the third man launched into a theoretical discussion about the United States having embassies in 180 countries and about nations sharing information, and, incredibly, brought the subject back once more to Iraq and Saddam Hussein. Finally the reporter switched off the tape recorder and brought out a copy of a magazine with a debunking article about the November 1989 event. He showed the third man the piece and pointed out his name as having been allegedly involved. Reading the paragraph carefully, the third man muttered something to the effect that he didn't "remember anything like that . . . let's see . . . the Brooklyn Bridge . . ." And now, instead of Kuwait and Saddam Hussein, he was off on another tangent. "My wife and I used to go to that nice restaurant on the Brooklyn side, down near the water. . . ." He turned to me, asking, "What's the name of that restaurant? We used to go there often . . . it's an excellent restaurant." I supplied the name, and he continued musing. "The Brooklyn Bridge is a very beautiful bridge. I used to cross it whenever I went to the Brooklyn Museum. You know, the Brooklyn Museum has an excellent pre-Columbian collection. . . ."

The frustrated reporter continued to press the issue, asking if he ever remembered seeing anything strange late at night in that area. And again the third man paused and thought for a moment, saying softly that maybe one of his bodyguards "might have seen something . . . a light . . . years ago. . . ." But he didn't remember anything now. "I'm sorry I can't help you," he said. "You could try to contact some of my bodyguards. Let's see, I believe one of them had a Russian name. What was his name?"

Throughout, his responses had been gentle, extremely unruffled, and very low-key. What was missing was any sense of surprise or anger when he saw that his name had appeared in print in such a context. He did not say, "How did my name get mixed up in this?" or "This is ridiculous," or "Who wrote this piece, anyway?"—the responses one would logically expect a well-known person, protective of his reputation, to make.

The reporter and I thanked him for the interview, bade him good-bye, and headed for the airport bar. "I've seen evasiveness in my time," the reporter grumbled over his Scotch and soda, "but this is extreme. I just couldn't get him to respond to my questions. He kept answering questions I hadn't asked!" As we discussed the third man's masklike demeanor, I remembered a quip from a *New York Times* crossword puzzle: "The wise diplomat thinks twice before saying nothing." After a short time the reporter said good-bye and left to return to his office in downtown Chicago.

What did I have to lose, I thought, by bearding the lion in his den once more? Why not go back to the lounge and hope for a more personal conversation with the third man? I still had to find out an important piece of peripheral information that would not compromise him in any way. I had to know if he had been in New York during the previous September when Johnny received the helmet.

When I entered the room, I saw that he was again sitting with his wife, who was reading a magazine. But I was surprised to see that he had opened my package and was quietly reading Linda's letter. Clearly, he hadn't been concerned that the parcel might contain a letter bomb, or any other type of explosive for that matter. I walked over to him and he asked me to sit down, introducing me to his wife as he did so. I was aware, from one of Richard's letters, that he has apparently never told her about his strange experiences, so, taking my cue, I continued speaking very discreetly.

"Mr. Hopkins," he said softly as he held Linda's letter, "I don't believe I've ever met this woman."

Since his wife was listening attentively, I said, "Perhaps it's just a case of mistaken identity." I could see that he had already opened the envelope that held Johnny's little thank-you note, and that he had my letter in his hand along with Linda's. Wanting to include the third man's wife in our conversation, I mentioned a prominent mutual friend, a gentleman who had recently attended a dinner party with the third man and his wife. She remarked about how charming and nice our friend was, and our conversation rambled on politely.

By now I was feeling depressed and hopeless about learning anything more. The third man seemed willing to talk, but only on a noncontroversial social level, with his wife as a participant. There was one crucial thing I had yet to determine, however, something that did not require mentioning the November 1989 incident in front of her. I asked him if by any chance he had visited the United States at any time the previous September. He paused, looking a bit uncomfortable, and replied, "Well, I don't know . . . I don't think . . .," when his wife broke in. "Don't you remember?" she asked. "We were here for the whole month of September, and went back to Paris in early October."

"Oh, yes, I guess we were," he said, again speaking with an edge of uneasiness.

We chatted a bit longer, until I said I must take my leave; my plane back to New York was due to take off within the hour. When I stood up, the third man shook my hand cordially, though his expression remained inscrutable. I wondered if his absolutely neutral demeanor was something he had learned to put on automatically after years of politics, diplomacy, and high-level, high-stakes conferences: "The wise diplomat says nothing . . ." As I left, he was still firmly holding both my note and Linda's letter—the letter he had said was from a woman he didn't think he had ever met.

What he *did not* say during our conversation was crucial. He did not say, "Mr. Hopkins, this is all a mistake. Obviously I'm not the man you want, so I think you should take these letters back with you." He did not say, "I'm angry that somebody has used my name and involved me in this bizarre business. I want you to see that my name is removed from any connection with UFO sightings." He did not say, "Since I don't know what these letters are referring to, you should tell this lady and her little boy that they've mistaken me for someone else." He did not say, "I haven't much room in my luggage so you should take these videotapes with you now. I have no use for them and have no idea what they are about." And he did not say, "Mr. Hopkins, my wife and I were in Paris for the whole month of September." Had that been so, he could not possibly have given Johnny the diving helmet. But he *was* in New York in September!

I walked away from the third man with a sense of sadness for his almost impossible position. He could not—would not—admit his involvement in the events of November 1989 in the presence of the reporter or his wife, and I gathered he was not eager to admit it directly to me, either. In fact I sensed an undertone of irritation in his dealings with me. After all, my sudden arrival must have caused him at least an inward shock, especially when he realized I was accompanying a reporter.

But neither did he appear comfortable denying the truth, which he had done softly, diffidently, and with virtually no emotion. He had hemmed and hawed and qualified his responses to the reporter, yet he clung silently to all the material I had given him. It should come as no surprise that I have not heard from him since our Chicago meeting, nor has he returned any of the very personal material I gave him. I'm sure that his present emotional state cannot be a very happy one, and I feel a great deal of pity for him. It seems to me that until he decides to go public with what he remembers from the night of November 30, 1989, he cannot have much inner peace.

C | H | A | P | T | E | R

33

Final Thoughts

So what does all this finally mean? Why did the events of November 30, 1989, unfold as they did? After all that has happened, what can we say about the aliens' ultimate intentions?

In considering the implications of the things we have learned, it seems obvious that the UFO occupants—whoever or whatever they are—are deeply and intimately involved in the lives of certain human beings. Apparently they can manipulate the behavior of these people, at least temporarily, with nearly absolute precision. Consider this: Richard, Linda, and the third man—abductees all—grew up in different cities. Linda and Richard were connected virtually from the beginning, having been systematically abducted together again and again from childhood on, no matter where they lived. "Poppy," the third man, behaving as if he, too, had had an intimate pre-1989 connection with Linda and Johnny, was somehow brought together with Richard in a professional context. Despite various family and professional moves and different lifestyles, all three distantly connected individuals were reunited one night in lower Manhattan. In what would appear as a dramatic illustration of cosmic micromanagement, the two men, along with other important political leaders, were brought together in front of Linda's apartment building at what seems like a prearranged time: a little after 3:00 A.M. on November 30, 1989.

In this perfectly orchestrated operation, the unseen UFO would necessarily have had to be in position above the Cortile's apartment building with several of its occupants already in Linda's bedroom when the motorcade swung off the FDR Drive onto South Street. The timing and control had to be exact. The aliens would have had to immediately block all radio communication from the stalled vehicles—Richard confirmed the fact that their radios and car phones ceased to function when their engines died—and to understand and meet the potential problem of a backup team. Everything had to move with absolute precision.

On top of all of this, there are the issues of the third man's prominent political position and the fact that he was apparently traveling with other important political leaders at a time of international crisis and change. Had the aliens arranged any of this, deliberately bringing these people together so that they could be given a demonstration of the UFO's awesome technological power? We often hear the hoary anthropocentric complaint, "If UFOs are really here, why don't they ever land on the White House lawn?" Was the November 30, 1989, event meant to be just such a public declaration?

Next, there is the issue of the aliens' proclaimed concern with earthly ecological problems, as indicated by the Lady of the Sands incident. It is obvious to me that the third man had been brought to the beach for one purpose only: *to observe,* and presumably to report what he saw to other world leaders. He was there as part of a three-man audience to watch the UFO occupants and Linda, in her co-opted, mind-of-an-alien state, digging together for sand samples and scolding members of the power elite for wrecking the environment. "See what *you've* done," she said, blaming the three men but excluding herself from responsibility, as she held up the dead fish.

Many abductees recall having been shown visions of a dying planet, harrowing 3-D images of earthquakes and fires and nuclear destruction.[1] Their usual reaction is to believe they are being warned to take better care of our environment. Perhaps, but I have seen no sign that abductees as a group are more ecologically concerned than the population as a whole. If cigarette smoke is seen as creating an environmental hazard, I would estimate that there is at least as high a percentage of smokers and other substance abusers among the abductee population as there is within the general population. (Since UFO abduction experiences almost always include frightening moments, this should not come as a surprise; substance abuse is a common reaction to repeated trauma. Ironically, the aliens may unwittingly be *adding* to the world's health problems rather than helping us solve them.)

Linda Cortile, an ecological scourge in her co-opted state, is in her regular life not only a meat-eating heavy smoker but a woman who wears a politically incorrect fur coat. If, as some people would like to think, the aliens have come here to teach us to respect our environment and have been delivering that message again and again over many decades to thousands upon thousands of abductees, then their mission to earth would have to be reckoned a colossal failure. There are probably more active, devoted ecologists among the UFO-skeptical workers in scientific laboratories and research institutions than there are among the abductees who have actually been in contact with the aliens.

In light of all of this, how should we interpret what took place that morning on the beach—the sand-sample gathering, the talk of ecological problems, and Linda's fierce imprecations? Could it not all have been merely a performance designed to mislead an important political leader? Could Linda have been waving not a dead bluefish but the ultimate red herring?

Everything I have learned in twenty years of research into the UFO abduction phenomenon leads me to conclude that the aliens' central purpose is not to teach us about taking better care of the environment. Instead, all of the evidence points to their being here to carry out a complex breeding experiment in which they seem to be working to create a hybrid species, a mix of human and alien characteristics.[2] A careful reading of the various witnesses' accounts suggests that here, as in many earlier cases, reproductive issues appear far more frequently than alien ecological concerns. Indeed, apart from the suspicious Lady of the Sands scenario, references to the environment are virtually nonexistent in the Linda Cortile case. The possibility Richard raised—that the aliens may need a safer environment on earth in order to carry out their own central agenda—is not to be dismissed. Crudely put, one wants the hotel one stays in to be clean.

With regard to suggestions of genetic manipulation and reproductive experiments, Linda and Richard separately recalled the circumstances in which their "bonding" took place under alien control and direction. They each described a unique "bonding arena" in which they were placed, and in which they believe they had sexual intercourse. Linda, as might be expected, remembers the experience with anger and shame and a sense of helplessness, while Richard thinks of it as the moment in which Johnny was conceived.

I have deliberately withheld the highly specific details Linda and Richard have recalled about the appearance of this special "bonding environment." Yet almost exactly the same details have later been reported in another "Mickey and Baby Ann" case, in which another young man and woman met and recognized each other as having been friends since childhood without being able to remember where or how. After they had become reacquainted in what I choose to think of as the real world, they were abducted again. After being floated into a UFO, their clothes were removed and they were placed in the same kind of highly specific environment that Linda and Richard described. They apparently were made to participate in their own "bonding" experiment, and to be brutally frank, I think of their use of the term "bonding" as a euphemism for alien-enforced copulation.

There are two reasons I am withholding these individual descriptions of the "bonding arena." The first is because I have researched only these two similar cases so far, and two cases do not yet establish a pattern. Caution demands restraint in what one can claim about alien technology and behavior. The second reason is practical. In all of my research I have consistently withheld certain details from publication as a means of testing the veracity of new people reporting the same kinds of experiences. The highly precise descriptions I have been given of the bonding arena provide exactly the kinds of details I have found useful in the past, and so for the present I choose not to reveal them.

In his various letters to me, Richard expressed his profound anger with what he saw as the UFO occupants' cold and brazen experiments with various combinations of human and alien genetic material. Why, he asked like so many others, do they feel they have the right to use us as laboratory specimens without either asking our permission or explaining their purposes? "Who are those creatures up there?" he wrote, "or should I ask, who do they *think* they are? God? It can't be. My God is good. Although they look human, they are below human standards. They have been bringing people together, making them lovers, and taking a lifetime to do so. Then we're torn away from each other. To make things worse, if we find one another again, whether it be by mistake or on purpose, one is made to remember and the other has little or no recall and is completely turned off.[3] After all of the above, those bastards gave us the impression they thought they were better than us! To us, they are the lower form of life and they know it, too. Why else would they be cross-breeding themselves with us? Yes, they're advanced all right. But what good are brains if there is no heart? How many of us have been left holding our hearts in our hands? The third man, Linda, Dan, and myself are good examples of the results of being tampered around with. . . ."

He went on to speak in even more personal terms, his confusion and his passion hopelessly intertwined. "Budd, I'm left with the loss of the wife and child I have always dreamed of, only to learn I haven't been dreaming after all. I feel as though this is my second divorce. The difference between these divorces is that I didn't want to stay married to my first wife, but I love Linda enough to stay with her and her children until I die. Linda is left feeling scared, disloyal, guilty, resentful toward me, angry and unaccepting of the facts revealed by this whole mess. The third man is left feeling heartbroken, confused, worried about his self-worth, concerned about Linda's state of mind, and Johnny's as well. Dan, well it's obvious what has happened to him. He fell in love with a girl he saw in the light of an object, and on a beach. He tried to suppress his feelings about her and the whole incident over a long period of time. It destroyed him."

To show the degree of emotional complexity these experiences can cause, Richard continues to maintain that Linda is, in some way, one of "them." He feels that she has at least some alien characteristics, presumably as a result of genetic manipulation at her conception. Despite the anger his belief causes her and the love he proclaims for her, he will not yield in this impression.

Linda's actual connection with the aliens remains a tantalizing mystery. Beyond any doubt she has been taken by them often enough to have learned something of their language (much to her own surprise). She, herself, felt some kind of unusual connection with the mysterious, black-haired woman who presided over the "meeting" with Marilyn, the third man, and herself. It's important to remember that when Linda first recalled the dream in which she appeared, she thought the woman was her mother—a person she "should obey." Marilyn described the tall, black-eyed alien or hybrid woman as acting and looking as if she were Linda's older sister. Is there, in fact, some kind of tenuous genetic relationship between them? Or is this potentially subversive question one which none of us has the right to explore?

In every moment of her day-to-day behavior I have found Linda to be a completely normal person, a good friend, and a loving, nurturing mother. She has the typical strengths and weaknesses of the rest of humankind, and despite Richard's and Dan's claims to the contrary, she has never demonstrated to me or to her many friends any extraordinary or even unusual powers. Put simply, Linda is just Linda.

However, for her part, she has suffered deeply from many different quarters, first, and most abidingly, at the hands of the aliens. Yet many humans also added to her misery. The terror Dan inflicted on her was nearly unbearable, and even Richard's behavior at times was ominous and disturbing. And then there were the other security agents who subjected her and her family to occasional but unnerving surveillance.

For sheer, unwarranted cruelty, perhaps the worst has been the tiny band of debunkers who portrayed her as a lying scam artist, and then violated the confidentiality to which every UFO witness has a right by publicizing her real name. As they well knew, this violation subjected her family to the threat of personal abuse and her husband to possible loss of employment.

On a domestic level, all of these experiences have increased the strains on her marriage and have been extremely hurtful to her husband, Steve. Johnny and Steven, her two boys, have also been caught up in these wide-ranging problems, although both have shown remarkable resiliency. Johnny has recently won a major children's literary prize and a scholarship to an excellent private high school. Both boys are currently doing well.

Linda's health has suffered and for many months her usual insomnia worsened. Yet she has slowly pulled herself out of what had been a downward spiral and is feeling stronger day by day. She has kept both her courage and her sense of humor. "If I was only having a hallucination that night in 1989," Linda said to me recently, "why not ask a psychiatrist how so many people could have seen my hallucination?"

She thinks often about Richard, wondering where he is and how he is handling the strain of isolation and continued government service in light of his UFO experiences. She misses him. He calls her from time to time, leaving short, often cryptic messages on her answering machine, which she copies for me to hear. On one, his voice sounded thick and emotionally distraught, and I had the impression that he might even have been drunk. On yet another message, which she received on a special day in June 1995, he sang "Happy Birthday" to her, and though his singing voice is not all that it should be, his affection came through in his familiar rough but tender way.

One can ponder forever the meaning of the incidents that I have presented in these pages, and I will be gratified if productive, wide-ranging speculation is stimulated by my long account. On the most practical plane, I hope that other witnesses will be moved to come forth with their eyewitness accounts of the events of November 30, 1989. (I have deliberately withheld a few details as an aid to checking the veracity of such reports.) If credible people should come forward in the future, and if the third man should publicly add his great prestige to the accounts I've included in these pages, then science, the governments of the world, and the international news media would finally be forced to admit the truth: that powerful, nonhuman intelligences have long been at work on a covert agenda involving thousands upon thousands of traumatized men, women, and children. That it is happening is certain, but what it portends, no one can say.

I can offer only two absolutes: my faith in the veracity of the witnesses whose testimony I have presented here, and the certainty that sooner or later, all of humankind will have to deal with the fact of an alien presence on our planet.

Despite the fears of many, nothing in my twenty years of research into this phenomenon suggests that the UFO occupants are inherently malevolent. I have seen absolutely no evidence that they are bent upon invasion and the enslavement of the human race. But despite the hopes of many others, there is not a shred of evidence supporting the idea that the aliens are benign and that their central goal is the healing of our endangered planet. It seems to me that these powerful hopes and fears are nothing more than badges of the human condition, signs that many of us still live in dread of demonic conquest or in expectation of angelic rescue from our problems. For the truth is much more complex: The UFO occupants are here for their reasons, not ours.

On November 30, 1989, the aliens made an overt attempt to affect the thinking of governments worldwide by portraying themselves as benevolent environmentalists. Based upon the later comments of the third man and his companions, this attempt seems to have failed. However, November 30, 1989, is likely to be seen in retrospect as a watershed event in our strange, one-sided relationship with the UFO occupants. What ultimately comes from it, no one can tell, but one major side effect appears inescapable. From that November night onward, the reality of the alien presence will be increasingly difficult to wish away. The skeptics will nevertheless mount a determined effort to assure us that such things are impossible and that all of the witnesses in this case are liars joined in a vast, subversive conspiracy. The general public, for its part, will try to avoid thinking about the unsettling implications of November 1989. And yet the UFO phenomenon will remain ever more vividly present. On some level, all of humankind will one day have to deal with it.

How will we bear up against what is likely to be history's most profound moral and intellectual challenge? Can earthly culture continue to flourish alongside an intelligence that possesses an awesome technology but lacks our emotions—an intelligence that is able to read our every thought? Can we exist without the safety and privacy of our once inviolate minds? Although my faith in the human spirit is boundless, we have never been tried as we shall be tried. One day the UFO phenomenon and the alien presence on our planet will become inescapable even to the most die-hard skeptic and the most determined survivalist. Each of us, then, will become aware of the aliens' goals, for better or for worse.

How will our priests and our philosophers, our political leaders and our generals, our children and the wise people of earth react to this awareness of human limitation and alien power?

Will we rise to the challenge?

Will we survive?

Budd Hopkins, New York, May 1996

APPENDIX I

Addressing the Attacks on the Credibility of the Linda Cortile Case

An "Alien Study Conference" was held at the Massachusetts Institute of Technology on June 13, 1992, and because of its importance, I chose this venue for my first public presentation of the Cortile case. The MIT gathering was the third such conference I'd helped to plan, but of the three, its list of invitees was the longest and perhaps the most prestigious.[1] Though it was not officially sponsored by MIT, the fact that Dr. David Pritchard, a distinguished professor of physics at MIT, had arranged for the conference to be held there added to its significance. The attendees—from Europe, the United States, Canada, Australia, and South America—were scientists, psychologists, sociologists, medical practitioners, researchers, and investigators, some new to this area of study and some, like Dr. David Jacobs of Temple University, among the most experienced in the field. In fact, one of the two conference chairmen was psychiatrist John Mack, a Harvard Medical School professor and a Pulitzer Prize–winning author who, months before, had met and interviewed Linda Cortile. Dr. Mack later wrote an article defending her credibility and mental stability.[2]

I realized that after my lecture the event on November 30, 1989—the witnessed UFO abduction—would be known to almost all of the leading researchers in the field and to at least some press representatives. And since the list of those invited to the conference included at least one person known to to be unalterably opposed to even the possibility that such a thing could happen, I knew I could expect the beginning of a systematic attack on the case's credibility. I was not to be disappointed.

Like most speakers at the conference, I presented several papers on different aspects of the abduction phenomenon, but the most significant, surely, was my discussion of the events of November 30, 1989. In the short time allotted, I began with Linda's first phone call and my subsequent hypnosis of her abduction. I then covered Richard's and Dan's first letters to me, and ended with Janet Kimball's independent eyewitness "woman on the bridge" account. I had no time, nor, for the moment at least, any inclination to present more of the complex sequence of events involved in this case. It seemed obvious that without the extensive documents, interviews, transcripts, letters, and categories of physical evidence that I have been able to present here in these pages, to attempt a fuller outline would be not only hopelessly confusing but almost impossible to carry out.

For the conference attendees, the case presented a kind of evidential watershed. Logically, if the independent eyewitness testimony was to be believed and the various kinds of evidence accepted, it would no longer be possible for anyone to think of the UFO abduction phenomenon as merely some sort of psychological delusion. If unrelated witnesses at different locations could see three aliens and a human abductee floating twelve stories above the street, then the phenomenon had a physical existence as real as any earthly kidnapping.

I was not surprised that many UFO researchers, despite their acceptance of the evidence, found my report personally unsettling. I sensed both enthusiastic support and a strong undercurrent of the confirmation anxiety I've alluded to before. One man confided to me that the evident prominence of the third man and the positions of Dan and Richard in the intelligence/security hierarchy made him so uneasy that he felt concerned for my personal safety. I did what I could to reassure him that, based upon our continuing communications, my relations with Richard and the third man were quite cordial and that I did not feel threatened in any way.

During the five days of the conference, I was able to brief a few of my closest colleagues privately about additional incidents in this ongoing saga that I hadn't presented in my talk, but there was simply not enough time to lay out anything approaching a full chronology of events. I left the meeting pleased with the response I'd received and curious to see what would happen next, now that the central fact of a witnessed abduction had been formally presented.

The number of people aware of the core event of November 30, 1989, would increase drastically in only a few weeks. I was scheduled to present a lecture on the subject at the 1992 MUFON gathering in Albuquerque, New Mexico, on July 11, in a setting that would provide both more time for my talk and a larger audience. "MUFON" is an acronym for Mutual UFO Network, the largest UFO research and investigatory organization in the United States, and this annual open-to-the-public symposium is traditionally a three-day affair. Linda flew to Albuquerque to attend, along with some other abductees from our New York support group and a group of researchers who had just heard my shorter presentation at MIT. I was aware that under these conditions interest in the case was bound to be high, yet I was determined to honor Linda's desire to keep her name and address confidential.

As it turned out, she agreed to join me on the podium for a few minutes after I ended my lecture, though without revealing her real name. She spoke quietly and eloquently about what she'd been put through by the UFO occupants and by Richard and Dan as well, and expressed great sympathy and understanding for all those who were also experiencing the fear, confusion, and ridicule that inevitably result from UFO abduction. At the end she received a standing ovation.

A few self-appointed "debunkers" in the audience were outraged that such an "impossible" event could be accepted by anyone as real. Among this group was Philip Klass, a writer and editor in the field of aviation journalism who has made a reputation as a fanatic believer that *all* UFO abduction accounts are false and that nearly all of the people reporting such experiences are merely liars seeking publicity—"little nobodies trying to get on TV" is one of his more charitable descriptions.

A belief system as rigid as his leads to the the following syllogism with regard to the Linda Cortile case: Since UFOs don't exist, abductions can't occur, and since abductions can't occur, the events of November 30, 1989, never occurred, either. Therefore this report has to be a fraud and all of the witnesses liars.

At Albuquerque, as one might guess, I presented only a preliminary account of this many-leveled saga, a fact that I stated at the time. I explained that the full story of the events of November 30, 1989, and their extraordinarily complex aftermath would eventually be made public and documented in book form. Only now, for the first time, is the full range of evidence, incident, and number of participants being publicly presented.

Though the debunkers were aware that they knew only a very small part of this case, their ignorance did not deter them for a moment. People who operate under such a rigid belief system are certain that, whatever the evidence, they already know the truth and so do not hesitate to denounce as liars a large number of people they have never seen, met, or interviewed. In their view, everyone involved in this case would necessarily have to be an active conspirator, operating in lockstep as part of a massive scam.

Linda would undoubtedly be seen as the creative and controlling force, the central plotter. The list of lying coconspirators would include her older son, Steven; her younger son, John, a key figure in this saga, whose identification of the third man is of major significance; Linda's husband, Steve, who testified to meeting Richard and described his physical appearance; Erica, the uptown witness who reported the orange-red UFO over the East River at three A.M. on November 30; Janet Kimball, the eyewitness who saw it all from the Brooklyn Bridge; Lisa Bayer, the doctor who took the X ray of Linda's nasal implant; Joseph, the law-enforcement agent who observed the gray surveillance van and its occupants watching Linda; her friend Carmela, who spoke to Richard and described his cohort of agents during the showdown at the South Street Seaport; Cathy Turner, an eyewitness to the UFO; Francesca, the tenant in Linda's building who awoke to see the courtyard flooded with light in November of 1989; and Marilyn, a central witness who had contact with the third man, among other participants. In the eyes of the debunkers, all of these witnesses and still others involved in this years-long series of events were participants in an unbelievably complex plot. But against whom, and to what end?

What common goal could possibly have united all of these individuals in so complicated and risky a scam? Most of them are members of families with jobs or professions that would immediately be put at risk if their testimony were revealed to be a pack of lies. One witness is in law enforcement, for example, and another is a physician.

The possibility of any financial gain for so many individuals is so remote as to be laughable. To the best of my recollection, only three books on the subject of UFO abductions have ever made the *New York Times* best-seller lists, and in any case, it is the author, not the witnesses, who receives the royalties.

A friend once suggested that, as a test of its feasibility, I should hire an experienced accountant to estimate what Linda's yearly expenses would be if this were, indeed, a scam. Costs would include payment for two male actors hired to impersonate Richard and Dan on the two audiotapes of their voices; payment for the testimony of all of the other individuals on the long roster of participants in this case, including people not named in the list above, such as Brian and his parents. And since any one of these many people could confess at any time and bring the entire edifice crashing down, they would have to be paid off again and again, year after year, to assure their continued cooperation—a truly nightmarish prospect and a potentially unending expense.

And then there would be the initial three-to-five-thousand-dollar expense of purchasing the antique diver's helmet and the more modest cost of the engraved diamond friendship ring that Richard gave to me.

Hunger for publicity is also an implausible incentive because almost all of the witnesses—including the Cortile family—want their real names kept secret. Again, one must ask, if all of this is a hoax, what is the motive?

By any account, carrying out such a scam would have taken years of meticulous planning and flawless acting on everyone's part, as well as a nearly perfect ability to memorize and retain complex narratives and descriptions. In this respect I am reminded of a marvelous observation that "always telling the truth means never having to remember anything."

As the central conspirator, Linda would have had to possess the skill to successfully forge many letters in different emotional, literary, and typographical styles while maintaining their individual consistency of tone and format over the years. She would have had to invent many different kinds of physical evidence, such as the (staged) beach photographs, mysteriously affected sand samples, and a fraudulent X ray. But perhaps most difficult of all, she would have had to keep in frequent contact with her many accomplices (ranging in age from nine to sixty) to make certain, year after year, that none of them, child or adult, suffered remorse or backslid or changed their stories, even for a moment.

That Linda was virtually a criminal genius ruthless enough to accomplish all of this was to be the official "debunking" line against all the eyewitness accounts and the various kinds of physical evidence in the case (or against, at least, the limited evidence and shortened list of witnesses I presented at the Albuquerque conference).[3] When I raised this conspiratorial possibility to various professional law-enforcement people, they were unanimous in their view that it was preposterous to think that a plot so complicated would ever be undertaken. They reiterated the adage that for a hoax to be successful it must have as few participants as possible and a minimum of details that could later on lead to slipups and inconsistencies. Certainly it needs to have a clearcut objective.

For them as for me, it was easier to believe that the unanimity of eyewitness testimony and the existence of many kinds of supporting physical evidence attested to the reality of the event, rather than to believe in the existence of a vastly complex plot, dazzlingly conceived and orchestrated by a middle-aged housewife of modest means, a mother of two young boys, who would forever be dependent upon (and hostage to) a small army of accomplices.

Soon after the MIT conference and the Albuquerque MUFON symposium, the expected attacks came.[4] To no one's surprise, a tiny but highly vocal coterie of debunkers—epitomized by Philip Klass—weighed in with diatribes based on what I had publicly presented, which was roughly ten percent of the data presented in these pages. The self-styled "skeptical investigators" circulated a great deal of erroneous information because none of them ever bothered to call me for clarification of any issue about which they were uncertain.

Beyond that, they simply warped the facts for maximum effect. For example, as a teenager Linda had sung briefly in a pop girls' trio. The debunkers twisted this innocent bit of biography into the claim that she was "a former actress." (Obviously they felt her moving appearance before the MUFON audience in Albuquerque had to be denigrated in some way.) Typically, these "skeptical investigators" also claimed that on November 30, 1989, Linda remembered being taken underwater; that a Yemeni automobile was somehow involved; that Linda's husband, Steve, was not home as she had said; and that the window through which she was abducted is not visible from the Brooklyn Bridge! All of these assertions are false, and a simple phone call to me—or a wave out of Linda's window—could have resolved all of them.

APPENDIX II

A Comparative Study of the Third Man's December 23, 1991, Letter

In order to check the authenticity of the December letter, I obtained a photostat of a letter he had written to a European political leader. The spacing and paragraphing in this letter are identical to those in the third man's letter to me. In both cases the beginning sentence of each paragraph is indented exactly six spaces. The lengths of the paragraphs are also similar. The longest paragraph in the rather brief "official" letter is eleven lines, and only one paragraph in my letter is longer. Though my copy of the note is a slightly blurred photostat, the typeface of both letters appears to be the same.

The third man's official communication, obviously typed by a stenographer, is neat and perfectly positioned on the page. Many typical business letters consist of lines containing sixty to seventy characters (that is, the total number of typed characters *plus* the spaces between them). In the third man's letter, the longest lines contain only fifty-three characters. His letter to me, probably typed by him personally for reasons of confidentiality, also contains fifty-three characters in most of its longest lines. Toward the bottom of page one, however, several successive lines are longer by two or three characters, making that part of the letter somewhat cramped at its right edge. One can surmise that the third man, not a professional typist obsessed with neatness and regularity, became impatient at that point and used the margin-release button to slightly lengthen several consecutive sentences.

The evidence suggests that the typewriter that produced both communications was the same, and according to their dates, the two letters were written only three months apart. (And, as one might expect, both use the commaless date format.) If both were typed on the same machine, one can also surmise that the margins on the office typewriter the third man used had been preset at a standard line length for short official communications. Under these circumstances the two letters were bound to resemble one another. All of the internal evidence supports the authenticity of the third man's letter to me, and none contradicts it.

APPENDIX III

Beth and Anna

When I first heard Beth and Anna speak on a panel of abductees at the MIT conference, I was struck by their obvious intelligence and credibility. Months later, Richard Hall, a veteran Washington, D.C., investigator, phoned and asked me if I could come to Washington and meet with them. Arrangements were made for the trip, and when Richard introduced us, I learned that Beth had had both partial and extensive conscious recollections of several different abductions through hypnosis, including incidents involving three generations of her family. At one point in our meeting she hesitantly brought up another strange situation. "Anna and I think we've somehow known each other before, but we don't exactly understand how." I have heard this kind of statement several times, though I did not tell Beth.

For her, there was a central, triggering memory of a childhood friendship. After both women had remarked on the unusual sense of familiarity they felt with each other, Beth had described to Anna a vivid memory from her early adolescence. She had been "about twelve or so at the time. I was on a picnic with my family, and I walked off into the woods by myself. When I came back, I told my parents that I'd met this nice little blond girl, and that she talked funny and she told me all about living in England in this quaint little village with cobblestone streets and little shops and everything. When I met Anna years later, I realized that she reminded me of that little girl; so one day I asked her if she'd ever lived in England. Well, she had. For about three years, starting when she was nine, she lived in England, in a place called Gravesend, where her father was stationed. She said that she'd picked up a strong Cockney accent. Everything I'd remembered about this little blond girl who looked like Anna seemed to be true. And if I had been twelve or thirteen or so when I went on that picnic, our ages would have been right, too."

At the time, Anna did not recall this meeting, but she was astonished at the details Beth remembered about her years in England. Subsequent hypnotic sessions with both women have led to this and several other identically recalled incidents, one of which involved a nickname.

Throughout her early childhood, Beth had a succession of stuffed toy animals, all of which she named "D.J." without knowing why. For some reason the name "D.J." was extremely important to her. Anna was astounded to hear this because her "private" nickname as a toddler was "D.J.," something Beth could not have known. One wonders if the initials "D.J." came into existence in the same way as "Mickey and Baby Ann" and "Froot Loop and Pizza Face"—childish inventions to cover the (alien-controlled) inability of young abductees to remember one another's real names.

The fact that in this case enforced pairing began for Anna virtually in infancy suggests an alien role in the manipulation of human relationships more fundamental even than that in the case of Linda and Richard. I fully expect that abduction researchers will eventually turn up other examples of this extremely early pairing.

Under the names of Anna Jamerson and Beth Collings these two women have jointly written an eloquent book about their UFO experiences, *Connections—Unravelling An Alien Abduction Mystery*, (Wild Flower Press, Newberg, Oregon).

ENDNOTES

CHAPTER 4

1. The Trent photographs were extensively analyzed thirty years ago by a skeptical Condon Committee investigator (Hartman) who concluded, "This is one of the few UFO reports in which all factors investigated, geometric, psychological, and physical appear to be consistent with the assertion that an extraordinary flying object, silvery, metallic, disk-shaped, tens of meters in diameter, and evidently artificial, flew within the sight of two witnesses."

The 1981 Trans-en-Provence case is the best-documented and most carefully investigated UFO landing case in history. An official French government scientific body (GEPAN) found extensive physical changes in the immediate vicinity of the landed object. For an account of the case, see Jerome Clark, *UFOs in the 1980s*, The UFO Encyclopedia, Vol. 1 (Detroit, MI: Apogee, 1990), pp. 205–207. For an account of the Trent photographs, see Clark, ibid., Vol. 2, pp. 238–240. Jerome Clark's three-volume encyclopedia is an invaluable reference work and is available through Omnigraphics, Inc., Penobscot Building, Detroit, MI 48226.

CHAPTER 5

1. In what was, for her, a deeply disturbing 1989 abduction experience, Linda's younger son Johnny reported being taken from his bed and into the living room by small, black-eyed figures while his mother stood by, apparently in a switched-off state. The next morning, Johnny was extraordinarily upset when he thought about what had happened. "Why don't you love me anymore?" he asked Linda. She assured him that of course she loved him. "No you don't," Johnny said. "When those little people were holding me and I was crying to you for help, you didn't do anything. You didn't even look at me." It took hours for Linda to convince her son that she had been unable to help him. She, herself, remembered nothing of this incident in which the little boy was apparently taken through the same living-room window as she on the morning of November 30, 1989.

CHAPTER 6

1. Out of concern that the identity of the third man not be revealed I can't be more specific about the unusual color of what is a rare, and thus easily identifiable, automobile.

2. The identification of the Rolls-Royce was absolute, since Linda's recollection of the license-plate number matched the known color and make of the car. The black Mercedes posed a more complex problem, since these cars are more common among missions to the UN, and Linda had not recalled all of the numbers. Based upon her partial recollection, my informant felt that the car was probably owned by one of four missions.

CHAPTER 8

1. This extraordinarily complex case cannot be easily outlined. It involved the kind of "imaging" procedure that David Jacobs discusses at length in his book *Secret Life* (New York: Simon and Schuster, 1992), in which abductees are shown images or situations as, we believe, a kind of projective emotional test. I hope, one day, to publish Erica's experience at some length.

CHAPTER 9

1. Budd Hopkins, *Missing Time* (New York: Marek/Putnam, 1981), pp. 34–50 and 51–88.

2. In one of these cases from the Hartford, Connecticut, area, a young woman who had recalled many abduction experiences found herself one night aboard a UFO and wearing a skintight blue uniform. Somehow she knew what she was to do. She left the landed craft and walked to a car that had been pulled off the road. The driver was a tall African-American man who appeared to be terrified and unable to move. The woman opened the door and helped him out, and then led him easily up a ramp and into the UFO. There she turned him over to the small gray aliens. She seemed to have no will of her own at the time, and only later viewed her actions with guilt and confusion.

CHAPTER 13

1. In one such case, the five-year-old daughter of a soldier and his wife stationed in Germany reported "little men with big black eyes" coming into her room and various other symptoms suggesting possible abduction experiences. On a family vacation trip to Italy, the child had an accident of some sort and was taken to a hospital with a possible skull fracture. The three X rays that were taken showed no skull fracture, but instead revealed a somewhat square metallic object deep in her brain. The radiologist reported the anomaly, and when the family returned to their base in Germany, another set of X rays was taken by the military radiologist. The object had vanished some time between the taking of the two sets of pictures. Dr. Paul Cooper, a distinguished neurosurgeon at New York Hospital, examined the original Italian X rays and said that they clearly reveal a metallic object. He had no idea how the object was installed or how it disappeared.

CHAPTER 14

1. Richard's original letter was printed or typed with a rather unusual typeface. Dan's and Richard's later letters used a second typeface, and Dan's note on his Christmas card to Linda was the result of a third. The third man employed a fourth type-style, and Linda's recollections, which she typed at my request, used yet another face. Janet Kimball's letter was typed on a sixth. (I am also taking into account here subtle differences in type size and spacing.)

CHAPTER 15

1. The third man seems to be alluding to a dubious theory espoused by writer Whitley Strieber that there is a connection between sounds and symbols associated with the UFO phenomenon and the Celtic language. I was eventually to learn that the third man did some research as to which UFO investigator to contact about the events of November 30, 1989; presumably he read one or two of Strieber's books before instructing Richard and Dan to write to me.

2. The letter from the third man that I obtained came from a high official in a European government with whom he was well acquainted. Unfortunately, issues of confidentiality preclude me from discussing the matter any further.

CHAPTER 21

1. Richard seems to be basing this remark upon his *later* realization that Linda was, in fact, Baby Ann. We have no way of knowing how certain he was of this on November 30, 1989. Perhaps this sense of earlier feelings of love is due to subconscious memories bleeding through to the present.

CHAPTER 22

1. I have edited Richard's and Dan's previous letters very lightly to correct egregious spelling and grammatical errors of various sorts. Also, I have occasionally melded together two very short sentences for more comfortable reading, but here I present one of Richard's letters verbatim in every respect.

2. This remark suggests that Richard himself might have been under some kind of surveillance by others in the intelligence community.

CHAPTER 23

1. These cassette tape recordings were addressed to "Richard" and to the third man by his full name; I had long since given up the pretense of declining to use his name and title. For reasons of space and confidentiality, I am neither presenting a transcript of these twenty- or thirty-minute monologues here nor describing the drop that Richard had suggested I use to get the messages to him.

2. Central to the "impossible" aspects of the abduction phenomenon is this one, in which individuals are moved through glass, metal grates (in Linda's case), and even solid walls. I first learned of this alien technique in the late 1970s but declined to include it in my book *Missing Time* as too radical to contemplate. It is now a frequently reported procedure, with glass apparently being the UFO occupants' material of choice.

3. By this count, Richard has expanded the list of people involved in the events of November 30, 1989, to eleven, traveling in three automobiles. Whether those figures are exact is uncertain, since the entire purpose, destination, and makeup of the group was clearly a security matter. There are indications (which I am not at liberty to discuss) that there were perhaps a few more people and perhaps two more cars traveling downtown that night in an informal motorcade.

CHAPTER 27

1. Research into many nighttime abduction cases has produced a very common pattern: when an individual—or in several instances, *two* individuals—

awake *already sitting up* in bed remembering a disturbing UFO-like dream but *not* recalling a startle reaction in which they suddenly sat up, the possibility of an abduction must be considered. Linda's recollection is therefore quite typical.

CHAPTER 28

1. In the 1950s and early 1960s a number of so-called contactees claimed to have ridden in flying saucers to Venus or Mars or elsewhere in our solar system, and there to have received from beautiful Space Brothers and Sisters antiwar messages and warnings about the environment. Some contactees were such outright charlatans that one individual was busily selling little packets of hair from the tail of a Venutian dog. Though some of these individuals seem not to have been crooked so much as self-deluded, virtually all of their accounts were designed to make them seem special—honored Earthlings, proud recipients of the Space Brothers' flattering attentions and intergalactic wisdom.

CHAPTER 30

1. Budd Hopkins, "The Linda Cortile Abduction Case," *MUFON UFO Journal*, No. 293 (September 1992), pp. 12–16.

Budd Hopkins, "The Linda Cortile Abduction Case Part II, 'The Woman on the Bridge,' " *MUFON UFO Journal*, No. 296 (December 1992), pp. 5–9.

Various authors, "The Linda Case—Hoax or Breakthrough?" *IUR*, International UFO Reporter (March/April 1993), pp. 4–17.

2. As has been pointed out, the UFO occupants are apparently able to handle the problem of "inconvenient" potential witnesses to an abduction by placing them in a state resembling a coma and thus rendering them unable to see or remember the targeted abduction. And yet the process does not seem to be an exact one. Various potential witnesses lose consciousness at different moments and thus are often able to recall different segments of the abduction. As I was to learn later from Richard, several of the participants in the third man's motorcade remembered seeing the UFO; others also recalled seeing Linda and the aliens in midair; while still others remembered only having their cars stall.

3. I have encountered at least five abductees with this same dread fear of clowns, in every case dating from childhood. Most cite clowns' scary, exaggerated eyes and the masklike painted faces. It would seem that for some abductees, seeing the natural human physical body and/or face stylized or distorted triggers memories of the aliens' nonhuman appearance. Richard himself admitted to a continuing fear of very small human beings.

CHAPTER 31

1. The 1961 abduction of Betty and Barney Hill was the first UFO abduction case to be studied carefully and to be the subject of a book, John Fuller's *The Interrupted Journey* (New York: Berkley, 1961). It established the following aspects of the phenomenon, later replicated again and again by other researchers: Alien-induced amnesia and paralysis of the abductees; physical examination, including some reproductively focused procedures; the usefulness of hypnosis in recovering blocked memories; and the presence of posttraumatic stress syndrome.

CHAPTER 32

1. See Chapter 30, Note 1, for the three journals I gave the third man.

CHAPTER 33

1. As part of the process that Dr. David Jacobs has called "imaging," UFO occupants have, as part of the abduction process, frequently shown abductees horrifying pictures of both man-made and natural disasters. These visions are often reported to be very realistic, even three-dimensional. Many abductees assume that they are intended to be predictive—warnings of future catastrophes—though some researchers believe they may be a kind of projective test of human emotionality, since aliens usually stare intently at the abductees while they observe these scenes, presumably reading their thoughts and feelings.

2. This theme is covered exhaustively in *Intruders* and in David Jacobs's *Secret Life* (New York: Simon and Schuster, 1992).

3. Richard is here alluding to the fact that he had, over the years, remembered a great deal more about Baby Ann than Linda had remembered about Mickey. He had grieved at the gnawing loss and assumed that she barely thought of him. This pattern has turned up in other similar cases.

APPENDIX I

1. The first such abduction conference was held in 1989, at Fairfield University in Connecticut, and the second in 1991, at Temple University, Philadelphia, Pennsylvania.

2. John E. Mack, "Stirring Our Deepest Fears," *IUR,* International UFO Reporter (March/April 1993), Chicago, Center for UFO Studies.

3. Those participants I discussed at Albuquerque were as follows: Linda, her husband, Steve, and son Johnny; Richard, Dan, and the third man; Janet Kimball; Erica.

4. Over the next several months a broadside entitled *A Critique of Budd Hopkins' Case of the UFO Abduction of Linda [Cortile]* was circulated widely, with George Hansen, Joe Stefula, and Rich Butler listed as the authors. As part of their assault on Linda, these three gentlemen published her real last name in the *title* of their tract, thus violating a basic rule of UFO research. This error-strewn and occasionally incoherent ad hominem attack included the following charge: "Hopkins discerns the skeptical investigators as agents of a secular satan." The March/April 1993 issue of *IUR,* the International UFO Reporter, the official publication of the Center for UFO Studies, contained a number of articles on the case, including my reply to the debunkers' attacks entitled "House of Cards: The Butler/Hansen Stefula Critique of the Cortile Case."

How to Report a Suspected
UFO Experience

If you believe you may have had the kind of experience dealt
with in this book, or have additional information concerning
the events of November 30, 1989, please write your recollections
in detail to:

> Budd Hopkins
> P.O. Box 30233
> New York, N.Y. 10011

As time permits, an investigator will be in touch with you. All
communications will be kept strictly confidential.